The Grey Goose Wing

BY THE SAME AUTHOR:

In Pursuit of Archery
(with C. B. Edwards)

Archery, the Modern Approach

Frontispiece:

The Prince of Wales, later to become George IV, in the elegant uniform of the Royal Kentish Bowmen. Besides being patron of several exclusive archery societies, he formulated many of the rules and conditions for English archery which remain in force to this day. This portrait, by John Russell, ARA (1744–1806), hangs in Buckingham Palace and is reproduced by gracious permission of Her Majesty the Queen.

Saint Sebastian, Roman martyr, patron of archers.

E.G.Heath

THE GREY
GOOSE WING

NEW YORK GRAPHIC SOCIETY LTD.
GREENWICH, CONNECTICUT

First published in Great Britain in 1971
by Osprey Publishing Ltd.
Reading, Berkshire, England

First published in the United States of America 1972
by New York Graphic Society Ltd.
Greenwich, Connecticut

SBN 8212 0449 1

Library of Congress Catalog Card No. 75–183970

Printed in England
by The Berkshire Printing Co. Ltd.
Monochrome illustrations
by Cotswold Collotype Co. Ltd.

Design by David Scurfield

Author's Acknowledgments

THE conception of this book was the result of a close collaboration with Barry Daniels, whose artistic enthusiasm and sincere affection for a subject which was entirely new to him, provided a special influence for its ultimate production. I am happy to record my warmest gratitude to him for his part in making the whole thing possible. The preparation of this book involved a great number of people who have been most generous in their encouragement and constructive advice; I am indebted especially to the following for their invaluable help and example: Mrs Erna Simon, President of the Society of Archer-Antiquaries; C. Bertram Edwards, President of the Royal Toxophilite Society; Frederick W. Isles, President of the National Crossbowmen of the United States; Lieut-Cdr. William F. Paterson, RN; Dr Charles E. Grayson; Dr David J. Finnemore Hill; Charles Miles, Gil Glover and Robert Hardy.

Graham L. Anderson, Willard E. Bishop, James Goodspeed and David Skinner are among those who readily provided personal photographs and allowed their publication. Peter Hambrook, David Newman Manners and Jack Farley expertly took numerous photographs, Vilma Chiara Schultz kindly allowed access to a mine of unpublished ethnographic material, Jill Bevilacqua helped to trace special photographs, Edward Telesford of the Photographic Department of the British Museum gave invaluable assistance in providing illustrations, Kazuo Kaneko initiated me into the mysteries of Japanese ceremonial archery, Reginald Doe drew the maps and plans and Brenda Chancellor patiently typed and re-typed the manuscript. To all these I owe a special debt of gratitude for their unstinting help.

Her Majesty the Queen gave her gracious permission for the special photography and reproduction of the portrait of HRH George Prince of Wales. The Royal Toxophilite Society; The Queen's Bodyguard for Scotland, The

Royal Company of Archers; N. H. MacMichael, FSA, Keeper of the Muniments at Westminster Abbey; the Reverend H. W. Moore, B.Com., and C. B. Edwards Esq., all gave permission for special photography and in some cases allowed access to private material which is very much appreciated. The reproduction of other valuable illustrations is by permission and due to the kindness of the Marquis of Salisbury; the Hon. Mrs Mervyn Herbert; Christopher Hussey Esq.; M. F. M. O. Jodrell Esq; Dr George I. Scanlon; the Dean and Chapter of Christ Church, Canterbury; the Trustees of the British Museum; the Trustees of the Victoria and Albert Museum; the Trustees of the London Museum; the Trustees of the National Gallery; the Trustees of the Wallace Collection; the Master and Fellows of Trinity College, Cambridge; the Lowie Museum of Anthropology, University of California; Bureau of Ethnology, Smithsonian Institute; the Society of Archer-Antiquaries; the National Geographic Society; the Wellcome Historical Medical Museum; the Powell-Cotton Museum; the Imperial War Museum; the Metropolitan Museum of Art; the Louvre; Musée de Cluny; Musée Guimet; Dorset Natural History and Archaeological Society; the Frick Collection; National Museum, Copenhagen; Burgerbibliothek Bern; the U.S. Signal Corps; the American Numismatic Society and others. A full index of the sources of illustrations, which includes the commercial credits, appears at the end of this book.

Finally my very special thanks to my wife who, in addition to coping with some secretarial tasks, patiently and uncomplainingly suffered an interminable period of household disorganisation and upset schedules. Her ready co-operation and ever-present inspiration has made my authorship of this work a delightful and easy task.

Swalecliffe, Kent, 1970   E.G.H.

Contents

Introduction

"YET well fare the gentle goose which bringeth to a man, even to his door, so many exceeding commodities," said Roger Ascham the father of English archery, in his panegyric upon this humble bird. Apart from the obvious benefits of an excellent dinner and, in the sixteenth century at any rate, a down-filled mattress and a ready supply of quills for writing, possibly the most important commodity supplied by this bird was its strong and supple wing-feathers, which were used in vast quantities for fletching arrows. This fact alone would be a sufficient reason for naming a history of archery *The Grey Goose Wing*. Feathers from the grey goose's wing were used more than from any other variety of bird to provide vanes for arrows used both for war and for activities of a more peaceful nature, so our title embraces an enquiry into the character and influence, both warlike and peaceful, of that extraordinary and universal weapon: the bow and arrow.

The bow is a weapon of great antiquity. It has occupied an honoured and ineffaceable place amongst the armaments of the nations of the world, in addition to being much favoured as a weapon of the chase and an "implement of polite amusement". Its universality and versatility commend it to us as being worthy of study in a general history showing its use and development from the earliest times. Such a history is attempted in the pages that follow. We have tried to support this general historical account of the bow and arrow with sufficient geographical, environmental and sociological background to clothe the bare technical detail with the warmth of human endeavour, ambition and accomplishment.

The history of archery has many facets. We have endeavoured to present the widest possible range of ways in which mankind gained and applied his vital knowledge of missile projection. Much of this story is astounding, little is widely known, and it is all fascinating. Having been superseded by the gun in some civilized nations only as recently as 100 years ago, the bow is still in general use by a number of primitive groups in quite accessible parts of the world. The continuity of the use of this weapon is one of its extraordinary features. "Shrill and low, do the grey shafts sing, the Song of the Bow, the sound of the string." There is a special kind of primitive magic in any form of archery and its appeal is immediate and strangely familiar. The sophisticated target archer practising on a country house lawn has something in common with the savage bowman of jungle or plain, using his skill with a bow to defend and preserve his very existence. Whether or not prehistoric man used the grey goose feather to fletch his shafts we shall never know, but we do know that he was a bowman of some competence, and the evidence of his activities with the bow and arrow is included in our first chapter, which is devoted to some 50,000 years of man's existence.

"Our Englishmen in fight did use, the gallant grey goose wing", said one old ballad, and another recalled, "with the grey goose wing such sport show as you would do in the presence of the king". This reminds us of the dual rôle of the bow, on the one hand providing king and commoner with a gentle pastime and on the other arming the soldier with an incomparable weapon of war. The English were famed as users of the bow in battle for possibly a longer period than any other nation, and to them also goes the credit of having promoted one of the greatest sporting revivals ever known. "England were but a fling but for the crooked stick and the grey goose wing" probably exaggerates the situation a little, but we have accordingly recognised the pre-eminence of the English influence by devoting three chapters to the development of the art of archery in Europe. In these chapters the development of the longbow is traced from the period of prehistory, through the Middle Ages—the time of its greatest prominence as a weapon of war—and, after examining its not uneventful decline, we finally unfold the history of the amazing revival of archery, a sporting renaissance which grew in popularity on a scale quite unprecedented.

The heyday of the use of the longbow as a weapon of war called for special measures to provide for a constant supply of fletchings in vast quantities, apart from other requirements, and it would almost seem that it was "for this the wild geese spread the grey wing upon every tide". Perhaps we ought to explain that we continue to speak in this context of the grey goose, and not just of any goose, because the bird grazing on the village green, from which most of our feathers used to come, is probably a descendant of the much darker, wild, grey lag goose, which is now only an occasional winter visitor in England, but has a fast straight flight, and, in flocks, forms great arrow-heads in the sky. However, in different parts of the world feathers from birds other than the goose provided the flights of arrows. The eagle, hawk, heron, buzzard, turkey and numerous other species gave up their plumage to the fletcher. The multifarious arrangements for fletching arrows were no less bewildering than the wide variety of equipment and the diverse techniques of shooting in a bow, differing from nation to nation and even from tribe to tribe, as widely as did their habits and languages. These individual variations in the design and manufacture of bows and arrows and the particular methods of their use developed according to the requirements of environment, fashion and custom. These, and the many other contributory factors involving the use of the bow, are described in the several chapters dealing with archers from many different parts of the world.

Some thousands of years before Christ the most revolutionary development in bowyery emerged, which was to become known as the composite bow. In two chapters we fully examine the history and importance of what must be one of the greatest technical advances in the history of warfare. How this powerful secret weapon was evolved and how it was used with devastating effect over most of Europe and Asia is studied in detail in these pages. This is a story of extraordinary achievement almost without parallel, and as such it stands by itself as a tribute to man's ingenuity and invention.

The history of the bow among the American Indians, from the earliest occupation of the American continent by tribes from Asia to the final replacement of the bow by the gun in the nineteenth century, is thoroughly discussed. The account of primitive archery in America is rounded off by graphic personal anecdotes of encounters with the Indians by explorers and soldiers, and by the stirring story of the last "wild" Indian discovered in the early part of the present century. In complete contrast, the use of the bow as an adjunct to training in Zen Buddhism caused it to become regarded as a sacred weapon, and this curious aspect of its history is explained in the chapter which deals with Japanese archery. From an early period the bow featured prominently in Japan as a weapon of the Samurai and many of the notable incidents included in the legendary history of that nation are here retold. These excerpts from the annals of the past emphasise the special importance placed on this weapon, for whereas in England the bow was the weapon of the yeoman, in Japan it became the exclusive weapon of the knightly class. The bow itself was evolved in a peculiar and unusual form and the techniques of its use were developed in an individual fashion peculiar to Japan.

The history of archery would be incomplete without some account of the crossbow. Long before the Christian era the ingenuity of the Chinese produced the first hand-held and mechanised device for projecting missiles. The historic progress of this contrivance across Asia to take its place in the forefront of battle in Europe, finally ending its career as a fancy sporting weapon, is set out in considerable detail in the penultimate chapter.

Every nation in the world used the bow at one time or another, with but one exception, and proficiency in battle became a vital requirement.

Practice for war took up much of the leisure time of peoples in many lands; but eventually, as the needs of war became more easily served by the use of other and more murderous inventions, this practice became solely a pastime. Hunting with the bow also called for specialised training, and alternative forms of shooting were devised with this application in mind. It is not surprising, therefore, that over many centuries a special regard grew, not only for the bow itself, but also for those who became especially skilful in its use. Before long a series of legends, myths and marvellous tales about archery and archers flourished and became part of the folk-lore of peoples accustomed to using the bow and arrow. Some of the most important of these tales are told again in the pages that follow, together with numerous examples of the extraordinary symbolism which has grown up around the bow and arrow.

He who has scoffed at the fabulous tales of Robin Hood and the prowess of William Tell, or who has rejected other bowmen of folk-lore and would even deny the existence of the most expert marksman of all, Cupid, has yet, if our aim is successful, to experience wonderment, the most human of contemplative emotions. The ancient heritage of archery has indissoluble ties with the present day and its essential vitality remains as part of our daily lives in colloquialisms, folk-lore and superstition. If some inspiration had been necessary for the writing of this history, the *Prayer of the Grey Goose Wing* would have sufficed:

I will retain the honour to emblaze
Of the grey goose, that on the green doth graze.
Throughout the world the trump of fame loud rings,
To spread the glory of the goose's wings.
The Huns, the Goths, the Vandals, and the Gauls,
With arrows made great Rome their several thralls;
Yea all the nations the whole world around
The grey goose wing hath honoured and renown'd.

1 Bowmen of the Stone Age

He that grasps
The skilful-aiming bow, hath in his hand
One thing that much avails him.

EURIPIDES

UP to about a hundred years ago it was believed, in accordance with the chronology propounded by Bishop James Ussher in 1650, that the first man was created in 4004 B.C., and it is only in comparatively recent times that the prehistory of man has been studied seriously or that scholars have shown a marked interest in the emergence of *Homo sapiens*. It is not so many years ago that any discussion of early man was confined to generalisations about "the Stone Age"; and within living memory a series of sensations were created by the introduction of Darwin's "Missing Link" and the remains of Java, Clactonian Man or the spurious Piltdown Man, increasing the conception of man's time on earth to span as much as fifty thousand, a million, two and even five million years. Possibly the most sensational announcement of all, made quite recently by Dr L. S. B. Leakey and occasioned by his find of the skull fragments of *Kenyapithecus Africanus*, is that man emerged from the primeval mist 26,000,000 years ago. This adds a new perspective to earlier reasoning and those more cautious arguments which suggested that the family of man was of considerably more recent development. During the ages-long early period of man's existence he must have lived by his bare hands alone, his complete transition from animal to human finally being marked by his emergence as a maker of tools. According to archaeologists the first implements made by man were crudely formed hand-axes. This was a distinct

A reconstruction of a cliff-dweller of central America using an *atl-atl* or throwing stick. (From *The Arrow* by Frank Hamilton Cushing.)

improvement on the casually collected stones of convenient size which he had used to supplement the crushing power of his own bare hands. The club became an effective extension of the hunter's own arm, and in fixing the stone and the crude haft together the primitive toolmaker performed the first manufacturing process.

INVENTION OF THE BOW AND ARROW

How prehistoric man first devised the bow and arrow we can only conjecture; it would be reasonable to assume that the hand-held club presently became a throwing weapon, and that thereafter a means to project it was devised, the eventual outcome of which was the bow. Numerous ingenious suggestions have been made to account for the transition of stick and stone from a hand-held weapon to a missile-projecting device, and one thought-provoking theory is that it was a purely accidental process. A prehistoric experimenter may have been testing his prototype fishing rod or game-trap and suddenly found that although it did not catch fish or trap game it projected a twig to an amazing distance; his contrivance, like so many other revolutionary discoveries, failing in its original objective but producing a secondary and more important result. Another theory, supported by a certain amount of related evidence, is that the arrow itself was the first component to be developed and that initially it was projected with a form of throwing device similar to the primitive spear-throwers of the aborigines of Australia and elsewhere. This throwing device developed into a more complex instrument provided with a string of gut, somewhat akin to the pocket-catapult of modern times, but large enough to propel an arrow rather than a stone. The final stage in the evolution of the bow, according to this theorist, would be the replacement of the inflexible arms of the catapult with springy and supple limbs which could be bent back, operating on the principle of momentarily storing energy ready to be used when the held-back string was released, taking with it the arrow.

The bow is the earliest instrument we know in which mechanical power is used; the advance it represents and the superiority it gives its user over the wielder of the more archaic spear are comparable to the superiority of the gun over a medieval crossbow. Whereas only a single spear, or at best a small number, could be carried by a skilled hunter or warrior, large numbers of arrows presented no great burden. They were lighter and easier to handle, and had a tremendous effective range compared with that of the heavy hand-thrown spear. The earliest bow and its string were made of organic materials, and traces of them will probably never be found, but prehistoric sites yield large numbers of small, carefully shaped, stone points which are identified as being the arrow-heads used with these weapons.

When prehistoric man invented the world's first missile weapon he could never have dreamed what epoch-making events would be shaped by its use, how his personal well-being and social economy would be improved due to the advantages it held over previous hunting methods, or what simple and exhilarating enjoyment it would give to countless generations of archers. The simplicity of its mechanical arrangement, little changed since it emerged many thousands of years ago, makes the bow easy to understand but, at the same time, because of its inherent unpredictability of performance, perhaps the most difficult to master of all sporting weapons. The bow was without doubt the principal implement used in the struggle for existence. Its discovery may be regarded as of equal importance to that of fire and the wheel. It is not difficult to imagine its impact on the primitive world, and from the outset it was a weapon with untold possibilities; a new method of killing game, far less dangerous and much more certain than the close-quarter methods of club and spear. It became a very positive insurance against enemies with territorial

Children the world over handle bows and arrows instinctively and with very little training soon become adept in their use. These young Umutina Indians from the mouth of the Bugres river in Brazil are shooting fish at close quarters.

ambitions or possessive inclinations and, in addition, it released some of the wonderful handicraft potential in *Homo sapiens.*

The literature of archery includes a number of profound works which deal entirely with the theory of the mechanical functioning of the bow and arrow and, if these serious expositions are studied carefully, the use of the bow is found to be less simple than it at first appears. The conflicting forces of mechanics, ballistics, physics and psychophysics, and variables such as moving targets, environment and climatic conditions, with the consequent deviations of the flight of the arrow from the horizontal and direct course to the target, would seem to present insurmountable problems to the practical archer of the present day who studied these matters, let alone the primitive relying on instinct alone. The ethnographer throws some light on the subject, however, in stating that "practice and heredity have evolved a peculiar aptitude for archery"; and when one considers the entirely natural way in which small boys the world over use a bow and arrow of their own making, revealing the instinctive methods of technique inherited through hundreds of generations, there is reasonable support for this assertion. Primitive man lived by hunting and was solely concerned with continuing to live. With a bow a man of average physique found that he could keep up with his more muscular cousins, and the survival of the fittest gave way to the emergence of the bowman. The bow served as a leveller, and we can trace the gradual develop-ment of a new social pattern embodying warrior skills, hunting techniques and a new-found craftsmanship, together with a mystique handed on from father to son which over the centuries became almost a religion.

The technological advance experienced by man which accompanied his use of the bow and arrow can be assessed in terms no less than revolutionary. The working of stone artifacts, for instance, although not entirely devoted to the manufacture of arrow-heads, represents a remarkable development in man's aptitude for using his hands to create objects of special utilitarian value. The application of his new knowledge, by the use of the tools and weapons he made, had a profound effect on his domestic and social environment. For reasons hard to explain the bow never superseded the spear in Australia but, apart from this exception, it has been found in every part of the inhabited world. It is likely that this contrivance was "invented" many times during the history of man at widely separated locations and in many different periods. Fresh evidence of the antiquity of this weapon is constantly being unearthed, and much that has hitherto been a matter of conjecture has now been con-firmed by modern scientific methods. The study of the history of the bow can be an absorbing pastime and, because of the unique position it occupies in the development of man from very early times, it is worthy of the deepest research by antiquarians, ethnographers, archaeologists and social historians.

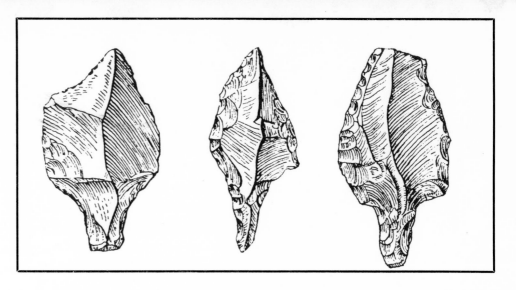

The earliest man-made artefacts which can be associated with bows and arrows are these stone points known as Aterian. First discovered in archaeological sites at Bir-el-Atir, Tunisia, other examples were discovered in Morocco, Algeria and Sahara, and they date from the Middle Palaeolithic period.

THE FIRST STONE ARROW-HEADS

In tracing the development of archery among the earliest primitive peoples we must commence somewhere in North Africa, possibly fifty thousand years ago, in the period contemporaneous with the Würm Glaciation, or the last Ice Age in Europe. It is fitting that Africa, considered the cradle of the human race, should have given us the first evidence of archery, when a remote village in Tunisia, Bir-el-Atir, gave its name to archaeological finds of special importance to the archer-antiquarian. These finds were named Aterian, and disclosed an industry which produced the oldest known tanged points of stone, examples of which have also been found in Morocco, Algeria and the Sahara. The earliest of these points were rather larger and heavier than the type usually associated with archery, but it is suggested that these could well represent the artefacts used during a transitional period, when the earlier stone-headed club had been converted and reduced in size and weight to conform with the requirements of a missile projected from a bow. Be this as it may, Aterian points from a somewhat later period, and dating from the Upper Palaeolithic of Europe, are certainly true arrow-heads.

Prior to the addition of stone points to arrows the ends of the wooden shafts themselves were probably sharpened; alternatively, readily available natural objects may have served as arrow tips, such as the sharp tooth of some animal, the claw of a large bird, the thorn from a bush or a piece of bone splintered to a sharply pointed bodkin—all of which articles, being organic, perished long ago. The Aterian point, as we have noted, appeared in the Sahara as well as in other parts of North Africa, and the neolithic culture of this region is characterised by the abundance and variety of the arrow-heads found there. It was hunting rather than food-gathering which supplied man with sustenance and these finds point to the existence of communities favourably disposed towards hunting with the bow and arrow. The stone principally used for these arrow-heads was flint, chalcedony, jasper, or occasionally obsidian, and a bewildering variety of shapes are found in this general area. Most of the points were provided with tangs, but the most ancient types are those without tangs, being of triangular form and having a

A beautifully fashioned 'swallow-tail' arrow-head made by flaking a chip of jasper. From the Faiyum, Egypt, and dating from the pre-pharaonic period.

A Mesolithic archer carrying his bow ready-strung and a supply of arrows in preparation for the hunt. Copy of a rock painting from Santolea, Teruel, Spain.

slightly hollowed base. Other shapes include one picturesquely termed "*en Tour Eiffel*"; others are said to be "shield-shaped", "lozenge-shaped", or "spindle-shaped", and still others "pistillate". All these forms are found in the western French Sahara; in the Spanish Sahara the arrow-heads are not tanged and they range from slim leaf-shapes to lozenge-shapes with rudimentary barbs and serrated edges. In addition to those spread along the North African coast, various inland sites have given up large quantities of arrow-heads which have included various selections of the designs already mentioned, indicating the singular importance of the bow and its extensive use in this vast region.

EARLY CULTURES

Human remains of great antiquity have been found on many sites in Africa, including such centres of culture as Abyssinia, where man existed 32,000 years ago; Kenya, possibly his earliest home, where we find the prehistoric Bushmen, a group of people who have remained at a mesolithic level of culture until today; the Orange Free State and Lesotho, where, some eight thousand years ago in the Late Stone Age, hunters with the bow stalked and killed their game; together with numerous other locations which have been excavated and have given up their evidence of many prehistoric cultures. Without exception all these widely separated locations have revealed the presence of early archery, primarily through the finds of arrow-heads. The traditional use of the bow and arrow which has survived in some of these areas serves as additional proof of the much earlier usage of this weapon. One area which is particularly important in the study of the progress of the bow is Egypt. We shall see in later chapters how, in this centre of ancient civilization, the bow reached a very special stage in its development; and it was here, in prehistoric times, that archery became more advanced in many ways than in other parts of the continent of Africa. Arrow-heads of a great variety of form have been found in large numbers in Egypt, ranging in date over many thousands of years. The early Seblian industry of the mid-palaeolithic period, for instance, produced crude leaf-shaped points of flint ten thousand years ago, and it is from this time that we discover the transverse arrow-head; made with a flat, chisel-like cutting edge. This became a standard type of point among the archers of Eygpt over a long period. In neolithic times, five or six thousand years ago, the output of arrow-heads from Egypt mainly comprised those of ogival shape and having a concave base. The points provided with tangs came later. Barbs appear in the pre-Dynastic period and by the Amratian culture of Middle and Upper Egypt, possibly four thousand years ago, arrow-heads of "fish-tail" design began to appear. This latter point was one of the marvels of the stone-chipper's art; it consisted of an arrow-

Neolithic archer, holding a bow of advanced design, from Ti-n-Tazarift, one of the sites of the Tassili-n-Ajjer, in the Sahara.

head of oval form tapering to a point, and provided with two gracefully backward-curving barbs, having the appearance of the tail of a fish or a swallow, beautifully worked from a solid piece of jasper or flint.

PREHISTORIC CAVE-ART

Without actual evidence of an archaeological nature it is impossible to describe in detail the bows of the earliest periods; but an inspired guess, based

Mesolithic hunting scene from a rock painting at Los Caballos, Valltorta, Spain. The line of deer is presumably being driven towards the waiting ambush of archers. The majority of arrows have struck the game at precisely the most vulnerable area on their bodies.

Neolithic leaf-shaped arrow-head of flint. The earliest regular form of point, it is found in a wide variety of proportions and materials.

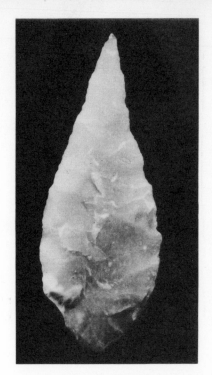

Barbed and tanged flint arrow-head of the Bronze Age. The most refined form of the stone arrow-head, this continued to be used contemporaneously with bronze weapons.

on inherent toxophilitic probability and supported by very early graphic representations of archers in action, would be that they were simple wooden bows with staves about five to six feet long, fitted with bowstrings of animal gut and drawing an arrow of between 26 and 30 inches. Much of this sort of conjecture is based on the evidence of prehistoric cave paintings uncovered in recent years in parts of Africa and on sites in Spain and France, which show the earliest representations of bows dating from the mesolithic period. The first discoveries of "prehistoric" cave art in Europe were met with polite scepticism or incredulity; indeed, in the case of Altamira in Spain, with downright charges of forgery. It was not until the Abbé Breuil proved their authenticity that a serious interest was taken in this new subject. Exciting details of bows are depicted in these paintings, together with many clues as to the type and power of these weapons, the methods of shooting and the techniques of hunting; all are graphically displayed for the serious student of prehistoric archery. To find depicted on the walls of the subterranean home of primitive man evidence of the use of bows and arrows, and action scenes of archers themselves, was a unique experience. These pictures, full of vitality and freshness, immediately convey the importance placed on the bow by these long-forgotten hunters, together with a clear indication that by the time the pictures were painted the practical lessons of archery had been thoroughly absorbed by the descendants of a much more ancient race of bow

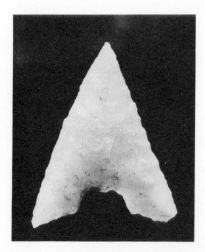

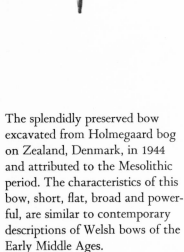

The splendidly preserved bow excavated from Holmegaard bog on Zealand, Denmark, in 1944 and attributed to the Mesolithic period. The characteristics of this bow, short, flat, broad and powerful, are similar to contemporary descriptions of Welsh bows of the Early Middle Ages.

Hollow-based arrow-head of flint from the Mesolithic period; a well-developed form which continued into the Bronze Age.

Neolithic leaf-shaped flint arrow-head, common over most of Europe.

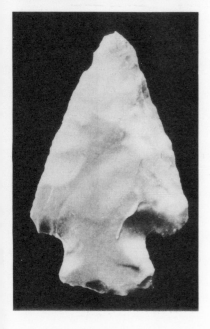

Mesolithic tanged arrow-head of flint. This was an improvement on the leaf-shaped point and it is represented in most areas where stone missile points are found.

users. One of the richest and most active areas of prehistoric art, although not the oldest, is the central Sahara, and exploration of the Tassili massif has revealed hundreds of rock paintings of extraordinary richness and variety of styles and subject matter. Other paintings from the caves of France and Spain, reaching back twenty millennia into the past, tell the same story with only slight modifications of detail.

POINTS OF STONE

Primitive craftsmen fashioned countless quantities of arrow-heads chipped from many types of stone, and much can be learned from the many surviving examples in collections in almost every museum throughout the world. It is soon apparent that the prehistoric artificer in stone possessed a delicacy of touch which would be hard to match in modern times. The improvement in penetrating power given to the simple arrow by the addition of one of these points must have been most impressive, and the general practice of adding a stone point to man's first missile weapon continued for a very long period, even overlapping the years during which bronze and iron were in regular use for tools and weapons. This practice survives today among Stone Age peoples in various remote parts of the world who have not yet received the advantages of metal. Persistence in the use of stone when a more up-to-date material becomes readily available seems at first sight inexplicable, but in recent years Dr Hans-Günter Bucholtz has conducted some researches into the comparative penetrating power of various substances. These have proved that a stone point, chipped to give sharp cutting edges, produces a deeper wound, causing greater haemorrhage and thus quicker death than does a steel point of the same design. This, then, was a revolutionary advance in primitive toxophily which would be difficult to equal throughout the whole history of the bow and arrow.

Although we have rightly given special attention to North Africa as a region rich in archaeological evidence of prehistoric archery, there are other regions, particularly in Europe, Asia and America, which have made important contributions to our knowledge of the earliest bowmen and their equipment. The primary evidence in each case, as in the North African example, has been provided by the finds of arrow-heads. To correlate each type and classify it according to form, workmanship and distribution is a task for the archaeologist; the mineralogist would undertake to determine its geological origin, and the toxologist would concentrate on a study of its practical archery applications. Our review can only include a brief note of the archaeologist's work and merely indicate that there is research work awaiting the mineralogist. It is the utilitarian aspect of these artefacts that demands our particular notice. Some comment having already been made regarding the penetrative

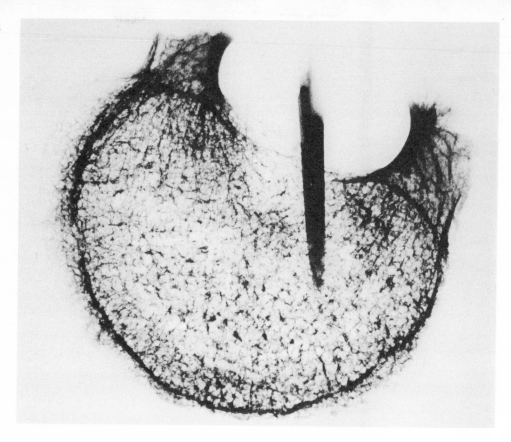

This X-ray photograph of an arrow-head of bone embedded in a human vertebra demonstrates the penetrative power of such a missile. Bone arrow-heads, as an alternative to stone, were often used by primitive peoples but, being organic, traces of early examples are rare.

power of stone arrow-points, let us now consider their several basic shapes, and the relative performance of each together with some reference to the manner in which they were fastened to the arrow. There are six main forms, of which some are known by their shape—leaf-shaped, lozenge-shaped and triangular; a few by their most pronounced feature—the tanged and barbed types; and one by its general characteristic—"*petit-tranchet*" or transverse type sometimes called the chisel-ended arrow-head.

A BASIC CLASSIFICATION OF ARROW-HEADS

An accurate dating of arrow-heads is only possible when individual finds can be associated with other items of definite age and, as Sir John Evans* has commented, "it would be unwarrantable to attempt any chronological arrangement founded on mere form, as there is little doubt of the whole of these varieties having been in use in one and the same district at the same time, the shape being to some extent adapted to the flake of flint from which the arrow-heads were made, and to some extent to the purpose which the arrows were made to serve". The triangular form of arrow-head is often considered to be the primary form from which the other types in the series developed, but whereas this type represents the simplest of all, it was not necessarily the prototype for the rest and its appearance extends over a wide range of time and place. The only notable variation to this type was an occasional concavity at its base, and generally, because of its form, its lower

Late Neolithic lozenge-shaped arrow-head of flint, which was a more carefully designed version of the commoner leaf-shape.

*EVANS, SIR JOHN, *The Ancient Stone Implements, Weapons and Ornaments of Great Britain (1897).*

23

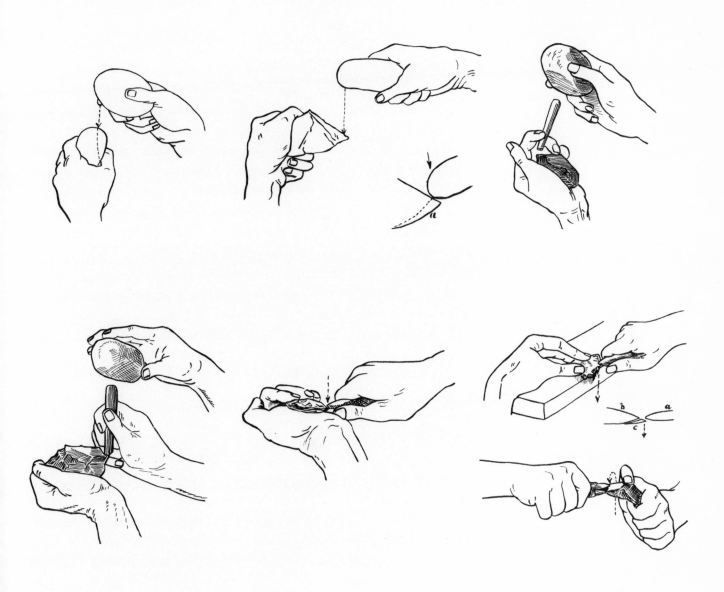

Some of the stages in the making of a stone arrow-point.

angles formed simple barbs. It was probably the simplest to make of all the completely worked points.

The most curious way of tipping an arrow with stone was by using the *petit-tranchet* arrow-head. This was widely dispersed and persisted for a long period. When a flake of flint was knocked from a "core", a straight knife-edge was invariably created on one or other of its sides. This razor-sharp edge was utilised, unworked, as the business end of an arrow-head, the remainder being chipped and worked to form a convenient shape for attachment at right angles to the shaft; the typical outline of a true *petit-tranchet*, which formed a chisel end to the arrow, was roughly wedge-shaped. It is difficult to see why the wedge should have been adopted so universally as a proper form for arrow-heads, and the matter is more curious when we consider that this shape is by no means the simplest and most natural form. It was common in the latter half of Mesolithic times and in standard use among early farmers of Europe, being popular in Spain, Brittany, northern France, Scandinavia and Britain. Examples of these points have been found mounted on their original shafts set in resin, probably birch-pitch. Slots were cut in the end of the shaft into which the points were inserted, and occasionally secured by binding with thin strips of leather or sinew. The advantage of such a point is obscure; possibly it was used in hunting small game so that the animal was not too badly mutilated, yet stunned enough to fall victim to the *coup-de-grâce* of the hunter. In some of the rare burials of the Mesolithic period, transverse arrow-heads have been found deeply embedded in vertebrae, showing that sometimes man himself was not only hunter, but hunted. Several forms which are derived from the *petit-tranchet* arrow-head include those sometimes called "halberd" or "lop-sided", plus other kindred types; the former gives the appearance of having only one barb and may be identified by the inevitable unworked flake edge.

One of the most common forms of arrow-head, which made a very early appearance, was the leaf-shaped point. These are to be found in a great variety of shapes ranging from the wide birch-leaf to the narrow willow-leaf patterns, all of which are distinguished by the absence of tang, barb or notch of any sort. These were true hunting points designed to make the deepest and widest cut, and made without any projections so that they could be withdrawn easily from the slain beast and used again. In almost every region where arrow-heads are found the leaf shape is in evidence, generally of Neolithic origin, although used as a standard form by some cultures over a much longer period. The lozenge shape differs only slightly in form, having a tapered point at its base in addition to the normal sharp tip for penetration. It also often has well-defined angles on its two edges, giving a definite lozenge silhouette. A simple development from the two similar shapes, the leaf and the lozenge, was the tanged point. The base of this type of arrow-head was elongated to form a stem or tang which was inserted into a slot at the end of the shaft, and this refinement produced a neater and more streamlined finish at the joint between shaft and point. With more care and greater patience a lozenge or leaf arrow-head could be transformed into a point with both tang and barbs.

A barbed arrow-head can be defined as having projections, like a divided tail or wings, extending sideways and backwards and being exposed when the head is fixed in position on the shaft. This development, introduced principally during late Mesolithic times and often associated with the Bronze Age, was intended to provide a rankling arrow-head which could not be knocked out by the animal, or withdrawn by the human victim. It also provided the maximum possible cutting edge, necessary if extreme haemor-

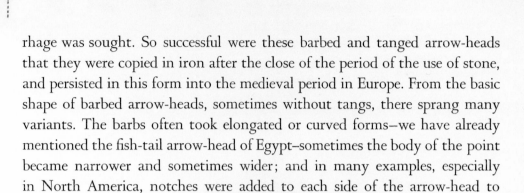

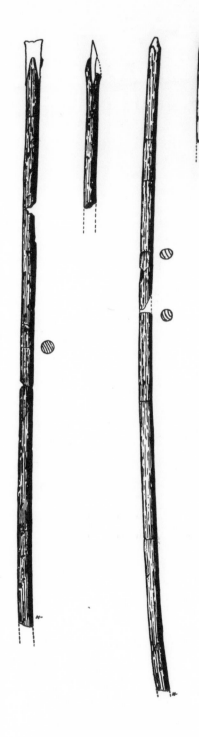

Arrow shafts and a transverse
arrow-head of the late Ertebølle
culture from the Muldbjerg settlement, Aamosen, West Zealand.
The shafts are carved of ash and
the transverse, or *petit-tranchet*
head, fitted to the lower shaft, is
shown from four sides. (From
*Aarbøger for Nordisk
Oldkyndighed og Historie.*)

rhage was sought. So successful were these barbed and tanged arrow-heads
that they were copied in iron after the close of the period of the use of stone,
and persisted in this form into the medieval period in Europe. From the basic
shape of barbed arrow-heads, sometimes without tangs, there sprang many
variants. The barbs often took elongated or curved forms—we have already
mentioned the fish-tail arrow-head of Egypt—sometimes the body of the point
became narrower and sometimes wider; and in many examples, especially
in North America, notches were added to each side of the arrow-head to
accommodate the sinew thongs binding it to the shaft.

WORKING IN STONE

The techniques of stone-flaking have been carefully studied by a number
of experts, particularly during the last fifty or sixty years, and fortunately
much of the information gained, principally from observations of surviving
Stone Age peoples, has been carefully recorded. The methods demonstrated
by groups of people still living in the tradition of Stone Age cultures can
safely be assumed to be similar to those used by their prehistoric ancestors.
The technique of stone working has passed through many stages in the
course of man's intellectual and technological development, and each of
these stages is characterised by certain tools and methods. In Europe they
correspond with certain time-periods in the prehistoric chronology of this
part of the world. In some outlying areas there has been a considerable time-
lag, and numerous native peoples have lived, until recently, at the same
technical level as our most distant ancestors. To discuss the time-scales which
illustrate the cultural periods of early man in different areas would involve us
in detail unnecessary to our purpose, as, generally speaking, there is a striking
similarity in stone-working in widely separated areas, and presumably, over
widely separated periods of time also. Therefore the methods presented can
be considered those universally used since arrow-head making began,
irrespective of time and place.

Surprisingly little time is needed by an expert to shape a tool from flint,
and the first task of the prehistoric worker in stone was to find suitable raw
material of the right size and shape. This would have been attained by experi-
mental work, and a search for the best source of stone of the requisite quality.

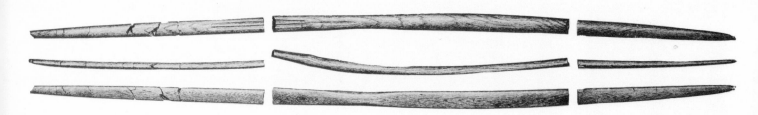

When a suitable cache was found a regular mining process began, and picks made from the antlers of deer were used to dig out the mineral. The actual material varied considerably according to availability; siliceous stones, the flint-like rocks, being the most popular. The advantage of flint is that it will fracture in any direction, in contrast to a stone like slate which splits in one direction only. It is therefore possible to calculate the effect of a blow before striking. Another widely used stone was obsidian, a volcanic rock which breaks somewhat after the fashion of glass, and is an ideal material for the manufacture of arrow-heads. The second task, and the first in the manufacturing process, was to strike off a flake from the main core of stone. This was usually performed by striking a blow with a primitive hammer, and the result was a thin, slightly curved, wedge-shaped piece of flint. The piece of flint might have been held in one hand, or rested on a stone anvil, or wooden block, or the knee, ready for this process. The type of anvil used has been shown to affect the result of the blow delivered by a hammer-stone, a wooden bar, or a bone. Combinations of striking tools with different anvils give a wide range of techniques for flaking, and during the Old Stone Age certain techniques can be distinguished as typical of particular human groups.

The next stage in the manufacture of a stone arrow-point required the greatest care, skill, and not a little patience. This was the problem of straightening and sharpening the edge of the flake, solved by the development of pressure-flaking. If a steady pressure is exerted at a slight down-

An elm-wood bow of the late Ertebolle culture from the Muldbjerg Settlement, Aamosen, West Zealand. The lower drawing shows the flat side of the bow, and the position of the hand-grip can be seen clearly. The upper view shows the convex side, or what was probably the "inside" of the bow when drawn. (From *Aabōger for Nordisk Oldkyndighed og Historie*.)

One limb of a yew bow excavated from the peat of Meare Heath, Somerset, and dated by radio-carbon analysis to approximately 2690 B.C. It is unique in that traces of sinew and leather bindings were found on it, the uses of which remain a mystery. When complete the bow must have measured 6ft 3in long.

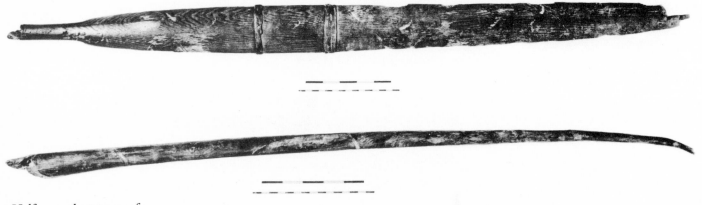

Half a yew bowstave, of a sophisticated design, from the peat diggings at Ashcott Heath, Somerset; dated to approximately 2660 B.C. It would originally have measured 5ft 2½in long.

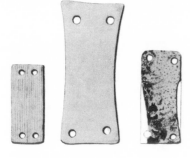

From prehistoric times archers have used some form of protection on their wrist against the slap of the bowstring. A great variety of materials have been used, slate, stone, bone, metal, leather and plaited fibre being the most popular. This illustration, after Buchholz, shows simple prehistoric bone bracers which were fastened by thongs.

wards angle at the edge of the piece of flint, a small chip flakes off, and by repeating this process at carefully selected positions the final shape of the arrow-head is obtained. The flake to be worked was sometimes placed flat in one hand, suitably protected by a pad of leather, and gripped firmly by the fingers. A flaking tool, perhaps consisting of a tine from the antlers of a deer, was now held in the other hand, and the downward pressure was exerted until each flake had been successfully removed. In later Stone Age times, with an increase in knowledge and skill in stone-working, the flaking implement was fitted to a wooden haft. Sometimes a final refinement to an arrow-head of stone were notches positioned so as to accommodate the sinew lashing round the arrow-shaft, and this was done with a stone hammer and bone punch. Advanced flaking techniques characteristic of the Late Stone Age in Europe, the Middle East and India, and in comparatively recent times among the Aztec Indians of ancient Mexico, are known as ripple-flaking: in this process long ribbon-like flakes are struck off the implement being shaped. Although in many cases other flint tools and weapons received a finishing process involving grinding and polishing,

The South West African Bushman, skilled in the use of the bow as a hunting weapon, remained in a primitive state well into modern times. This photograph shows a Bushman taking aim with a poisoned arrow.

Primitive archery is unencumbered by elaboration of weapon design or by the complications of extra paraphernalia. The "loose" demonstrated here by a native from the Sepik headwaters, New Guinea, is typical of primitive archers where they still survive. It is reasonable to assume that this was the method used by prehistoric archers.

Dumini, a fighting leader of the Chimbu, New Guinea, who killed at least forty-seven white people with bow and arrow in the late 1930s. A rare photograph taken in 1938 by David Skinner, senior.

One of the few surviving groups of primitive peoples are the Veddah of Ceylon. The detail shown here is taken from a photograph made in the late nineteenth century by Colombo Apothecaries Co.

arrow-heads were never accorded this final treatment. The most common method of attaching a stone arrow-head to its shaft was by inserting its base into a slot cut into the end of the arrow and securing it by binding with thong or sinew; or by setting it into a resinous or bitumastic cement; or both. Excellent examples of this process can be found among specimens of arrows from North America, as well as the surviving prehistoric relics.

It has been demonstrated that small, crescent-shaped flakes known as microliths, which can be shaped in seconds, can be fitted into slots cut in the wooden arrow-shaft without the use of gum, by virtue of their shape. Groups of these microliths, which represent the barbs of arrows, have been found in the skeletons of animals which escaped only to die later. Prehistoric arrow-heads were also fashioned from bone and antler, splinters of which were probably fastened diagonally to the extremity of the shaft to form barbs; and the ends of the wooden arrows themselves were sometimes shaped to form blunt heads, reserved for specialised uses. Wooden arrows with thickened ends dating from Mesolithic times have been found in sites on both the west and east coasts of the Baltic. It can safely be presumed that they were manufactured for the same purpose as the almost identical arrows made today by Eskimoes and other primitive tribes; that is, to stun birds and small fur-bearing animals without piercing the skin. As the victims fell they may have been retrieved by hunting dogs, for it was in this period that the dog was domesticated.

SURVIVING PREHISTORIC BOWS

In a paper published in 1963,* Professor J. G. D. Clark describes two remarkably well-preserved bows of the Neolithic period which were discovered in a peat bog in Somerset. These weapons are the most recent additions to a total range of about thirty prehistoric bows which have so far been discovered in north-western Europe. The bows, the first of which was found just over a hundred years ago, originate from several continental sites and provide fascinating data for the study of the craftsmanship of the prehistoric bowyer. Radio-carbon datings have established the respective ages of most of them; the earliest, dated to 2690 B.C., and the most recent, 1320 B.C., were both found in England. Of the total, twenty-five were made from yew (*Taxus baccata*), a long-lived and slow-growing tree that produced tough and resilient wood; four were made from elm; and one, from Sweden, from pine. Where the climate was too cold for the yew to achieve substantial growth, the other woods were used. Switzerland has contributed the greatest number, three

*CLARK, J. G. D., *Neolithic Bows from Somerset, England, and the Prehistory of Archery in North-Western Europe*, Proceedings of the Prehistoric Society, Vol. XXIX, (1963)

or four complete bows and fragments of fifteen others, including the important finds from Robenhausen and a child's bow, all of Neolithic date. The four yew bows from England date from the Neolithic period to the Bronze Age, and these include one magnificent specimen of extra large proportions. From Holmgaard in Denmark come two Mesolithic elm bows, and another from Muldbjerg, also of elm. From Germany come three of yew and one of elm of Neolithic and Bronze Age dates; two of yew from Holland and one example of pine from Sweden complete the list of known prehistoric bows in Europe.

The majority of these bows have carefully tapered limbs of "D" section and well-defined hand-grips, and they appear to have been fashioned by craftsmen with a mature knowledge of bowyery. The average lengths of these specimens is 155 cm. (60in.), those from Switzerland being the longest (170 cm.), and those from Germany the shortest (135 cm.). These prehistoric examples of the simple self-wood bow were the forerunners of a longer bow, designed on the same lines and having the same characteristics which eventually developed into the famed long-bow of the Middle Ages.

The techniques of bowmaking and the uses of archery were well established in north-western Europe by late Mesolithic and Neolithic times, and the skills of archery were regarded as a precious heritage by warriors and hunters. Their love of the bow is indicated by the frequent discoveries of bows and arrow-heads buried with their owners. This simple but devastating contrivance of stick and string became the hunter's most prized possession, and no doubt he constantly sought to improve its mechanical efficiency and prided himself on increasing accuracy with the weapon. A measure of the marksmanship of these long-forgotten bowmen can be judged from remains of beasts with

Stalking fish in the upper Juruena river of the Matto Grosso, this Erigbaagtsa Indian uses a primitive technique as old as archery itself. This scene must have been repeated countless times in every area of the world where the use of the bow was vital to human existence.

The easy dexterity with which a bow is strung is demonstrated by a primitive Krahó Indian from the Tocantins River in Brazil. The bow is identical in appearance to prehistoric examples known to have been used in many parts of the world.

arrow-points still embedded in vital parts. A flint arrow-head nearly penetrating a vertebra of a large mammal gives silent but vivid testimony to the perseverance of the prehistoric hunter and the effectiveness of his weapon.

ARROWMAKING AND FLETCHING

We can, with reasonable accuracy, assemble the tools of the ancient bowyer and fletcher and assess their manner of employment, and we can compile a brief catalogue of the materials they used. Bow design of surprisingly high standard and the symmetry of arrow-shafts clearly reveal the technical skill of these prehistoric craftsmen. The primary tasks which confronted the earliest bow and arrow makers were cutting and smoothing. For these purposes primitive yet effective tools were used. Sharp axes and curved knives of flint sufficed for the shaping of bow-staves and the whittling of arrow-shafts, and the final smoothing would have been done with sandstone rubbers. The straightening of arrow-shafts would have been achieved with a bone pierced with a hole large enough for the shaft to be inserted; by skilled manipulation

A group of beautifully made arrows
from New Guinea. The variation
in design of primitive arrows is
often deliberately contrived in
accordance with their intended
use.

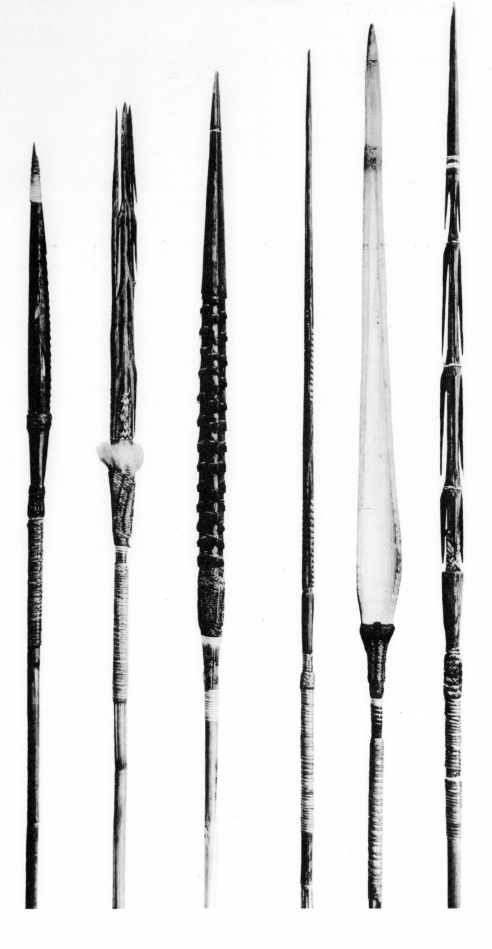

A fine example of a Scythian archer carrying the
distinctively shaped short bow of advanced
composite form. His action in drawing an arrow
ready for use, although businesslike, is delightfully
poised. A clay plate, *pinax*, from Vulci, signed by
Epiktetos, c. 520 B.C.

A Turkish mounted bowman, from a miniature of
the fifteenth century. This shows the typical
composite bow and splendidly decorated quiver of
arrows.

after the shaft had been warmed over a fire, it could have been made true.

There is evidence that from early times feathers were attached to the rear end of the arrow to steady it in flight. The numerous hunting scenes featuring archers depicted in the rock paintings of eastern Spain show that this was standard practice among the Neolithic peoples, at any rate of this region; and finds of arrows in Denmark bearing traces of binding where the fletchings would normally be located, provide evidence for the habit among peoples further north. Prehistoric fletchers followed the standard practice among primitive archers of splitting the quills of sections of comparatively straight feathers, preferably pinion feathers, removing the feathering for a certain distance from either end, and binding the projecting ends of the quill to the arrow with sinew threads. These were also used for the attachment of points to arrow-shafts and the reinforcement of arrow notches or "nocks".

The examination of prehistoric archery relics gives no indication of the exact material used for the bowstring, the vital component without which the bow would be useless. However we can assume that it was made of twisted sinew or long thongs cut from a hide, similar to those used with primitive bows of historic times, or perhaps plaits of twisted fibres, examples of which are found in ethnographical collections. The position of attachment of these strings, often marked by cut-away shoulders at the tips of the bow limbs and typical signs of wear at this point, can clearly be seen on existing prehistoric bows. The bowman's outfit would not have been complete without an arm-guard or bracer, to protect his forearm from the smart of the bowstring on release. Excellent examples of these bracers, made of slate or bone, have been discovered in the graves of prehistoric warrior-hunters still in position on the left or right forearm. These were simply flat plates made to fit snugly on the inside of the lower arm and tied there by means of leather thongs. When this accessory of archery was first used is unknown, but it is certain that it is of great antiquity.

The survival of several isolated communities of Stone Age peoples who use archery as an everyday adjunct to living, provides us with a useful means of studying primitive equipment; and, as they have not progressed beyond a prehistoric level of culture, we can add to our list of equipment and techniques used by our long-forgotten bowmen ancestors such items as pouches for spare arrow-heads and strings, bow-cases fashioned from pelts, game calls, and methods of fletching and stone-chipping.

STONE AGE SURVIVALS

Many of the tribes of Africa used the bow and arrow until comparatively recent times, together with the Veddahs of Ceylon, the primitive tribes of New Guinea, the Andaman Islanders, peoples of the still uncharted areas of

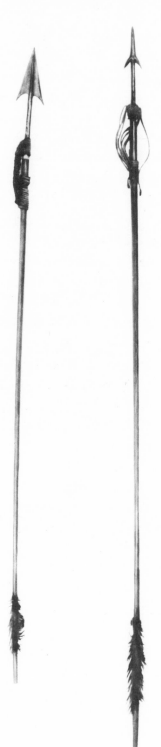

South America, the handsome archers of Bhutan, and those from parts of India and the islands of the Pacific. All these primitive groups have been subjected to ethnographical surveys which invariably include details, varying in scope and complexity, of the use of archery among them. Apart from local variations in technique and independently developed technical features attributable to individual requirements, the equipment, methods of manufacture, and shooting techniques of these modern primitives are remarkably similar to what we know of the bowman of prehistory. Numerous parallels could be cited to support the inclusion of a brief reference to these various tribes in a chapter devoted to prehistoric times, although in some respects they have replaced stone with metal. The survival of a primitive archery tradition among many of these groups who have in other ways progressed beyond a prehistoric level of culture is a curious aspect of their development, which serves to emphasize the deep-rooted popularity of the bow during several thousands of years before Christ.

Clear evidence of how prehistoric man fashioned his bows and how he used them can be drawn from studies of the rapidly dwindling tribes of central Brazil. The way of life of these Indians is simple and in all respects their culture is still that of the Stone Age. The tribes of the River Amazon area, for instance, still rely on the bow as their principal hunting and fishing weapon and it is clear that the archery methods used by them have been handed down over many centuries.

In recent years detailed studies of many of these groups were made by the late Harald Schultz, and from the wealth of information collected by him and other ethnographers and scientific pioneers in these practically untouched regions, we can piece together a fairly complete picture of primitive bowyery and the hunting methods of a genuine Stone Age culture. Generally speaking metal was completely unknown in this area until the coming of white men in comparatively recent times, and each process of making bows and arrows was carried out with knives of stone, shell or bamboo. Arrow-shafts of a special reed were straightened, as they still are, by manipulating the heated shafts in strong and capable hands. Fibre from lianas is the usual binding material for fastening arrow-heads or for string-making, and beeswax and resin are used for any task that requires adhesion or for protection against wet.

The hunting methods used by these peoples rely on the simplest of aids such as wooden fish decoys or game calls, and their wonderful knowledge of natural phenomena, animal habits and plant life has been accumulated over generations of necessity. The primitive hunter is also a keen observer, he has an inherent skill in the judging of distances and his mental and physical reactions leave little to be desired. No doubt he would be hard put to it to explain these and other intuitive attributes but, combined, they provide him with all that he requires in the way of food and clothing. The weapons them-

selves follow patterns which we have come to associate with prehistoric and traditional long-bow designs. The powerful bows are from five to seven feet long, tapering, sometimes flat in section and sometimes oval or semi-circular. Arrows were provided with stone points or, alternatively, sharp bone points were added to hardwood foreshafts. Archaeologists point to the existence of these tribes in Brazil for some 10,000 years, and much of their way of life has remained unchanged until the present day. A student of prehistoric bowyery and practical hunting methods with bow and arrow is recommended to delve more deeply into this fascinating area of study. There is undoubtedly much more to discover and correlate with the present theories of prehistoric archery.

This was the general pattern of archery which gradually spread across the continents, its secrets being lost and subsequently re-discovered from time to time, until the bow and arrow was established as an indispensable part of man's existence. Migratory tribes on their endless journeys into wild and unknown countries in search of new pastures took with them their accumulated knowledge of archery skills; in later chapters, we shall see how the design patterns of bows and arrows were adapted as living conditions altered, and how the use of raw materials changed according to local availability. In heavily wooded country, for instance, a short bow was easier to manage; and horseback riding raised the need for specialized carrying equipment. Scarcity of bow woods in certain regions encouraged the use of other materials such as horn and sinew, and special types of arrows were devised for different classes of game—blunt heads for small animals, harpoons for large fish, and barbed detachable points to rankle in the flesh of big game. We shall see how the character of the bow changed according to the people using it. In some cultures it became a weapon supreme in the hands of the common soldier, while in others it acquired significance as a religious symbol; laws were passed regulating its use, and at times it became a rare and exclusive plaything for kings and princes. As an implement of war it was often under-estimated by enemies—to their cost; and as a sporting weapon it still has much to commend it.

We have considered the possibility that the bow was used in a primitive and undeveloped form some fifty thousand years ago; the archaeological evidence which points to the bow being in constant use in North Africa for at least ten thousand years has been studied; and we have examined briefly the facts that indicate that it was by far the most important weapon in north-western Europe for a period of several thousand years from the ninth millennium B.C. This brings the story of the bow roughly up to the commencement of the Christian era, and the chapters which follow deal with its remarkable historic progress from this period onwards as a hunting weapon, a weapon of war, and as an implement of leisured recreation.

Harpoon arrows with heavy steel heads for use against large game. On impact the head would detach and embed in the beast and the shaft would foul the undergrowth, thus hampering escape and accelerating death. From the Belgian Congo, Africa.

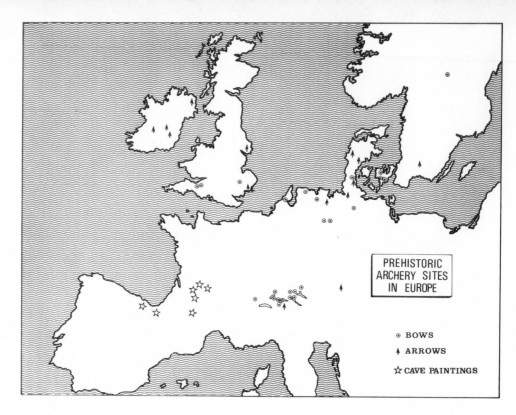

PREHISTORIC
ARCHERY SITES
IN EUROPE

⊙ BOWS

↟ ARROWS

☆ CAVE PAINTINGS

SELECT BIBLIOGRAPHY

Alimen, H., *The Prehistory of Africa* [n.d.]

Allchin, Bridget, *The Stone-Tipped Arrow* [1966]

Baumann, Hans, *The Caves of the Great Hunters* [n.d.]

Bibby, Geoffrey, *The Testimony of the Spade* [1956]

Blackwood, Beatrice, *The Technology of a Modern Stone Age People in New Guinea*, [1950]

British Museum, *A Guide to the Antiquities of the Bronze Age* [1920]

British Museum, *Flint Implements* [1956]

Clark, J. Desmond, *The Prehistory of Southern Africa* [1959]

Clark, J. G. D., *Derivative Forms of the Petit-Tranchet in Britain*, Archaeological Journal, No. 91, [1934]

Clark, J. G. D., *Neolithic Bows from Somerset, England, and the Prehistory of Archery in North-Western Europe*, Proceedings of the Prehistoric Society, Vol. XXIX [1963]

Cranstone, B. A. L., *Melanesia, A Short Ethnography*, British Museum [1960]

Cushing, Frank Hamilton, *The Arrow*, The American Anthropologist, Vol. VIII, No. 4 [1895]

de Morgan, Jacques, *Prehistoric Man, A General Outline of Prehistory* [1924]

Evans, Sir John, *The Ancient Stone Implements, Weapons and Ornaments of Great Britain* [1897]

Keller, Dr Ferdinand, *The Lake Dwellings of Switzerland* [1878]

Knowles, Sir Francis H. S., *Stone-Worker's Progress* [1953]

Lhote, Henri, *The Search for the Tassili Frescoes* [1959]

Mainguard, L. F., *History and Distribution of the Bow and Arrow in South Africa*, South African Journal of Science, Vol. XXIX [1932]

Oakley, Kenneth P., *Man the Toolmaker* [1949]

Piggott, Stuart, *Prehistoric India* [1950]

Schultz, Harald, *Indians of the Amazon Darkness*, Journal of the National Geographic Society [1964]

Smith, Regional A., *Flint Arrow-Heads in Great Britain*, Archaeologia, Vol. 76 [1926–7]

Sollas, W. J., *Ancient Hunters* [1915]

Stow, George W., *The Native Races of South Africa* [1905]

Troels-Smith, J., *An Elm-Wood Bow from Aamosen* [1959]

2 The Great Composite Bow – The First 2000 Years

Homage to you, bearers of arrows, and to you, bowmen, homage!
Homage to you, fletchers, and to you, makers of bows!

TAITTIRIYA SAMHITA

ONE of the most ingenious examples of man's technical skill was his adaption of such unlikely materials as animal sinew and horn to serve as components in the construction of his bows. By the addition of horn and sinew to simple wooden cores the bowyers of the East transformed the bow from a weapon of very modest performance, mainly suited to hunting small game at short range, to a superior arm of fearful accuracy and dreaded power, to be handled properly only after years of arduous and diligent training. The differences between these complex weapons and the simpler and more universal type of bow are many; the intricate construction, for instance, requiring the unification of several organic materials, is itself an art not easily mastered, while the design, following a more complicated pattern based on involved engineering principles, has been developed over many centuries of experiment and improvement. The shooting techniques for the composite bow, having their own characteristics and often involving a special kind of "loose", demand specialist equipment, which was evolved with Asiatic thoroughness in a unique manner. The mobilisation of the skill of the bowyer, the dexterity of the archer and the audacity of the warrior chiefs in the use of the renowned composite bow, won for the armies of the East shattering and decisive victories over many kingdoms, and left the survivors of overrun cultures drifting helplessly through Europe and Asia for centuries afterwards.

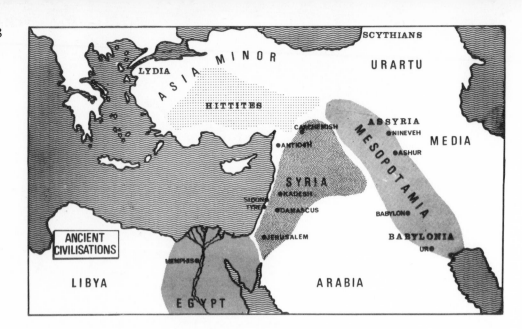

A sketch map of the Near East, showing some of the centres of ancient civilisations mentioned in the text.

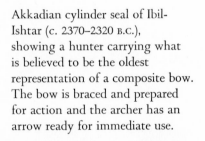

Akkadian cylinder seal of Ibil-Ishtar (c. 2370–2320 B.C.), showing a hunter carrying what is believed to be the oldest representation of a composite bow. The bow is braced and prepared for action and the archer has an arrow ready for immediate use.

In another form the composite bow became respected as the royal weapon of the chase, and in yet another guise it flowered into perfection as the most sought-after plaything of the Persians and Turks, who found pleasure in its exquisite design and joy in its superlative performance as a flight bow. Before we trace the history of this remarkable weapon let us first examine its unusual physical attributes and design.

THE CONSTRUCTION OF COMPOSITE BOWS

Whereas the longbow and other bows of self-wood construction were made exclusively of wood in one or more pieces, the oriental composite had limbs constructed of layered materials so arranged that the tension and compression in the bent limbs occurred in those materials best adapted to withstand these forces. Horn, which is compressible, was used as the belly of the bow—the side nearest the archer; sinew, which has elastic properties, was used for the opposite face, the back; and the whole was built up on a wooden core and covered with moisture-proof lacquers. When released, the horn belly acted like a coil spring, returning instantly to its original position. Sinew, on the other hand, contracts after being stretched, which is exactly what happens to the convex back of the bow. The combined pushing of the horn and pulling of the sinew straightens the bow, when the string is released, with much greater speed than could any known wood, and this ingenious arrangement enabled a shorter and faster-reacting bow to be constructed. Details of construction varied with the place of origin of the bow, the availability of materials and the use for which the bow was designed. The bowyers of some nations added extra reinforcing strips of horn, while others elaborated on the method of securing the sinew layers. All were designed with the same basic engineering principles in mind. The natural attributes of the layers of horn and sinew complemented each other in compression and elasticity, the wooden core serving only as an essential form on which the subtle shapes of the bow could be built. An Arab author of the late fifteenth century wrote:

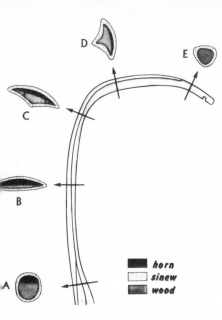

Various cross-sections showing the construction of a typical composite bow. The wooden core was usually made from several specially shaped pieces jointed together. The horn strip, glued to the 'belly' of the bow, was widest and thickest at the centre of the bow limbs and tapered to nothing at the stiff ends or 'ears'. The even layers of sinew can be clearly distinguished and the whole was wrapped in bark or parchment and lacquered.

A. Section through hand-grip.
B. Section through limb—note maximum horn layer.
C. Section through recurve—the wooden core is spliced.
D. Section through rigid section —the horn layer tapers off.
E. Section through 'ear'—only wood and sinew.

(Not to scale)

"The structure of the composite bow is not unlike that of man. The human body is made up of four basic elements—bones, flesh, arteries and blood. The composite bow has the same four counterpart elements—wood, its skeleton; horn, its flesh; tendons, its arteries; glue, its blood. Man has back and belly. So has the bow. And just as man can bend forward but is likely to damage himself by bending backward, so with the operation of the bow!"

The principles of mechanics controlling the release of energy which is momentarily stored in a drawn bow were thoroughly understood by the bowyers of ancient Asia, and this knowledge was ingeniously used in the development of the composite bow, in ways which are accepted as sound practice by modern craftsmen. From time to time additional features devised to improve the performance were added to these bows; such as, for instance, the long, stiff "ears" of the Mongolian bow, extending each of its limbs by nearly a foot and having the effect of giving extra thrust or "cast" to the projected arrow. A bewildering variety of devices with specialised uses were evolved, increasing the complexities of bow construction and making shooting techniques more difficult to master but giving a greatly improved performance. The story of the composite bow is a tribute to the skill of the Asiatic bowyers and their ingenious solution to the problem of being unable to procure sufficient bow-woods of the necessary length, straightness and texture.

A prince from the time of the Sassanid Empire (c. 225–650) in a hunting scene on a silver plate. Bows used by these peoples seem to have been of a well-developed composite construction, powerful and efficient both for warfare and hunting.

ARCHERS FROM MESOPOTAMIA

The victory stele of Naram-Sin
(twenty-second century B.C.), with
a splendid representation of a
composite bow. In addition to
what appears to be a most business
like weapon, the bow is shown
here as a symbol of power and
an emblem of victory.

At a time when the Neolithic population of Great Britain was being driven north and west by the megalith builders migrating from the Mediterranean, a great civilization was flourishing in Mesopotamia. A completely new form of bow construction emerged from this area, and although its actual birth is obscure the earliest evidence for its existence comes from Sumeria on the tiny cylinder seal of Ibil-Ishtar. Carefully carved in the stone is the figure of a hunter carrying a bow which is undoubtedly of composite design. This is dated to the twenty-third century B.C. and may slightly predate the victory stele of the Akkadian king Naram-Sin, from Susa, which shows the king firmly grasping a distinctive example of this weapon.

The Sumerians, a non-Semitic people who lived from 3500 B.C. onwards in the region between modern Baghdad and the Persian Gulf, and between the Tigris and the Euphrates, are renowned as the inventors of cuneiform writing, which was adopted by all the peoples of the Near East. The historical record of this multiplicity of city states, more often than not at war with each other, has been preserved in this unique form of script, and describes guerilla warfare with invaders from the east and battles with conquerors from the north. The power of Sumer was subsequently merged with that of the Semitic Akkadians of Babylonia, whose empire reached its height under the great codifier Hammurabi (c. 2200 B.C.). The Sumerians developed a system of warfare which was remarkable for its methodical and disciplined organization and for the use of the deep phalanx. This was the principle of advancing under the protection of rectangular shields, the spears of the warriors being thrust forward horizontally. The phalanx undoubtedly went into action in the immediate wake of the chariot charge, although this was possible only on reasonably level ground. Had the Sumerians added to this formation a long-range archery unit operating from the rear and the flanks, they would certainly be entitled to the credit of having achieved near perfection in the art of battle in open terrain. But it was their successors, the Akkadians, who contributed this decisive feature. Naram-Sin and his generals utilised the potential of the bow as a warlike weapon and conquered Mesopotamia and

One of the bowmen attendants of Ramesses III with a triangular bow and elaborately decorated quiver of arrows. From a coloured relief at Medinet Habu, XXth Dynasty (1192–1160 B.C.).

An Egyptian bow factory of the fifteenth century B.C. The bowyer on the left, with a hand adze, is shaping a bowstave, the worker next to him is using a saw to shape what is probably a wooden core. A fletcher on the right is sighting along an arrow-shaft and straightening it, and a bow is being braced, probably for testing, on the extreme right. A painting from the tomb of Menkheperra 'sonb at Thebes.

the Sumerians, even reaching the Mediterranean. The principle of co-operation between infantry and artillery together with the mobile striking force of the chariot became standard practice, and monuments commemorating long-forgotten battles show the phalanx of infantry armed with spears and swords, charioteers, and long-range archers, operating together in full co-ordination. One of the most important battles in early history, that between the Hittites and the Egyptians, was fought in this way, and is depicted in a monument to that event.

The composite bow was widely used in Mesopotamia in the Akkadian period, but by the beginning of the second millennium its use there was sparse. According to Professor Yadin* this was due no doubt to its complicated manufacture, which was beyond the capacities of the semi-nomadic tribes of Syria and Palestine. The armies of small kingdoms and the fighting men of small tribes, unlike the regular forces of rich empires, could not produce this type of weapon in mass quantities. The Egyptians, on the other hand, established special workshops for the manufacture of the bow, and the art of warfare in Syria, Palestine and Mesopotamia reached its peak in the first half of the second millennium B.C. This was when the bow began to come back into widespread use and, together with the chariot, it became the principal instrument used in battle. Fortifications had been improved and the battering ram had been developed. In no subsequent period, until the invention of gunpowder, did the armies of the world succeed in introducing on to the battlefield new methods or new weapons of war. Despite the slow development of the bow there is no doubt of its effectiveness, which is borne out by arrow-riddled bodies of warriors discovered in Egypt. In one case an arrow had gone right through the body from back to chest and protruded for a distance of 20 cm.

The exact materials used in the manufacture of composite bows of the period are itemised in the Ugarit texts:

"Let me vow birch tree from Lebanon,
Let me vow tendons from wild bulls,
Let me vow horns from wild goats,
Sinews from the hocks of bulls."

THE ANGULAR BOW

A sequence of composite bows was evolved in the Eurasian heartland; each of these in turn was adopted by a wave of nomads and thus transmitted to the civilizations of the marginal crescent. At the beginning of this series stands the apparently unsophisticated angular bow which usually appears as a shallow isosceles triangle with a wide-angled peak where the bow is gripped,

*YADIN, YIGAEL, *The Art of Warfare in Biblical Lands* (1963)

The middle sections of three bows
from the tomb of Tutankhamen,
two of which are elaborately
decorated with inlaid bark designs.
These bows, dating from
c. 1350 B.C., represent innovations
in design not found elsewhere.

and angles of about 30° formed by the string and the ends of the bow limbs. This was superseded by a bow with recurved limbs, easily recognised by the tendency of its arms to curve away from the string near its ends. There was inevitably some overlapping of periods when these early types were in use and sometimes they are shown together, as in a wall painting of Semites from the fifteenth century B.C. bearing votive offerings. The composite bow was a valuable piece of equipment and easily damaged by careless handling or, as some believed, by changes of weather, and so it was frequently kept in a special case. This was either slung at the archer's waist or fitted in a convenient position to the side of the chariot.

Before 2000 B.C. Egyptian culture and civilization had reached an advanced level, but the increase in the use of the composite bow was gradual. However, there is much evidence for the use of the simple bow during this period. As early as the beginning of the Middle Kingdom (about 2052 B.C.) the Egyptians had produced a self-bow capable of driving an arrow right through a man, but an even stronger weapon was introduced by the invading Hyksos—the composite bow. The Hyksos, who were probably Hittites with a following of Semitic tribes, by their conquest of Egypt *(c.* 1800–1600 B.C.*)* seriously interrupted that nation's development. The Hittite Empire, whose greatness has only recently been disclosed by archaeological research, was at its peak in about 1400 B.C. and had its centre in south-east Asia Minor (Cappadocia) and the Taurus Mountains. It was from here that the Hittites waged frequent war against the Egyptians and other powers. There were also scattered Hittite tribes in Syria and Palestine. These peoples were great users of the composite bow and many rock carvings vividly portray the typical triangular pattern of the early variety of this weapon being used in the hunt and in battle.

A painting from a Theban tomb dating from the XVIIIth Dynasty, (1567–1320 B.C.) of the New Kingdom, showing Egyptian archers under training. The bow on the right is a simple self-bow, most probably used for the elementary lessons, and that on the left a composite bow used in advanced training. Note the careful supervision by the two instructors.

A company of Nubian bowmen; well preserved wooden models from the tomb of Masahti, Assiut, in the Cairo Museum. Dating from the Middle Kingdom (c. 2100–1788 B.C.), the models clearly show the simple self-wood bows issued to the Egyptian armies of the south.

EGYPTIAN ROYAL BOWMEN

The expulsion of the Hyksos from Egypt (1500 B.C.) was followed by a great imperialist period, when Egypt conquered Nubia and Syria, and it was during this era that the Pharaohs of the New Kingdom won renown as archer kings. With the new and powerful composite bow they performed a series of astonishing feats, perhaps never equalled since. Tuthmosis III, whose arrows struck with such impetus that they would penetrate a copper ingot three fingers thick and protrude beyond three handbreadths, organised an elephant hunt on his eighth Asiatic campaign in northern Syria and killed 120 elephants. Even more spectacular were the shots of his son, Amenophis II.

He used a weapon so heavy that no one else could bend it, and, apart from duplicating his father's exploits with the copper ingot, he challenged all-comers to match his feat of driving an arrow into a target for seven-ninths of its length. On one occasion, from a distance of twenty cubits (a little over eleven yards), he drove four successive shots completely through copper targets a handbreadth thick. Still preserved in the Egyptian Museum in Cairo is his composite bow of simple curvature.

The histories of several other reigns catalogue the many extraordinary feats of archery performed by these princely sportsmen and Tutankhamen, perhaps the last to do so, sustained this hereditary pose of archer even though he died before the age of twenty. Amongst the most significant finds in his tomb, which had survived the ages virtually intact, were twenty-nine composite bows. From the notes of these finds,* carefully prepared by Howard Carter, we can study detailed measurements and learn of the materials and construction of these rare relics. But of even greater historical importance is the fact that this collection of royal bows, making up three-quarters of the total number of composite bows preserved from ancient Egypt, can be precisely dated to the reign of Tutankhamen, 1352–1343 B.C., and fifteen of them even have the king's name inscribed on them. Most of these bows are of the angular pattern, the early form of composite bow, so often depicted in wall paintings and sculpture. This was the bow introduced by the Hyksos, together with the use of bronze, the horse and chariot, helmets and body-armour, and it was the dominant arm throughout the Middle East for the period from about 1800 B.C. until about 500 B.C. The angular bow appears frequently in Hittite art in the fourteenth and thirteenth centuries B.C., as well as in Assyrian reliefs from the ninth century B.C. onwards. The bow has three outlines: when unbraced, when braced but not drawn, and when

*McLEOD, WALLACE, *Tutankhamen's Composite Bows* (from Howard Carter's unpublished notes), Journal of the Society of Archer-Antiquaries, Vol. 7, (1964).

A coloured wall relief from the south wall of the Great Temple at Abu Simbel showing Ramesses II (c. 1292–1225 B.C.), in his war chariot at the battle of Kadesh. The light chariot gave the bowmen of the Egyptian armies a special mobility.

A drawing from the reliefs at the palace of Sargon, Khorsbad (721–705 B.C.) showing an Assyrian archer ready to shoot, protected by a full-length, portable shield manoeuvred by a shield-bearer.

one post and its fellow. Then His Majesty appeared in a chariot . . . . he fully drawn. The most common shape to be seen in graphic representations is when it is braced, ready for action. It is then that its angular form is most pronounced. When the bow is fully drawn it forms a gracefully curving arc, nearly semi-circular, and when unbraced appears as two flat curves with the handle section forming a more pronounced peak, somewhat like a flattened letter "W".

Among other tomb finds which have included ancient bows were those of Ramesses II, c. 1300 B.C., whose bow had first been recognised as an important relic in the history of archery by C. J. Longman when he examined it in the Berlin Museum in the spring of 1893. Up to then it had been incorrectly classified as *a musical instrument*. This weapon was possibly of Hittite or Assyrian origin, from its resemblance to bows in the sculptures of these peoples. It may have been introduced into Egypt as spoils of war or carried by foreign mercenaries. It may also have been a relic from an Egyptian invasion of Syria by Ramesses when he captured Kadesh, the capital of the Khita on the Orontes. During the invasions and occupation of Egypt by the Assyrians their weapons must necessarily have been numerous in the land, and it would be remarkable if some should not have been preserved. Such bows may have been valued trophies, or have been acquired in a variety of ways, but in any case their complex and beautiful structure must have favourably impressed bow-using peoples like the Egyptians. Whatever the reason for their presence in Egyptian tombs we must feel grateful for it, since such very perishable weapons probably owe their preservation to careful interment.

EARLY MILITARY ARCHERY

The composite bow by this time appears in a very advanced form, the complexity of its construction a tribute to the skill of the bowyers of the period. It was now a standard item of military equipment and its mass production must have strained the resources and manpower of the nations using it. The time factor in completing the necessary stages of manufacture, the precise skill and overall supervision required, as well as the organization for the provision of large quantities of the necessary components, were some of the considerations which had to be taken into account. Arrows, too, had to be produced in large quantities, possibly in hundreds of thousands, apart from other necessary accoutrements such as quivers, belts and bracers. Egyptian arrows consisted of a fairly stout shaft of reed (an ideal substance– strong, pliant, easy to shape and easy to prepare) to which were added a hardwood foreshaft secured with bitumen-coated sinew, and three neatly cut feathers glued in place. The use of stone for arrow-heads continued for a long time and a common form, which was secured with composition, was provided with a wide chisel-headed cutting edge. Arrows fitted with this shape of head are frequently shown in ancient wall paintings and appear to have been much favoured. The usual form of Egyptian quiver was a long cylinder of leather provided with a shoulder strap and designed to carry twenty-five to thirty arrows. Although special quivers were fitted to chariots, additional supplies of arrows were sometimes carried in quivers on the backs of the charioteers.

It is clear that the training of bowmen was an organised affair. We learn from documentary and pictorial evidence that special ranges were provided where targets of wood were set up for normal practice and where targets of copper were used for special penetration tests. The novice began his training under close supervision using a simple bow, possibly a self-wood bow, and, when proficient, graduated to the more powerful composite weapon. Emphasis was placed on shooting from horseback or chariot, as the report on the archery prowess of Amenhotep II shows: "He [the king] entered into his northern garden and found that there had been set up for him four targets of Asiatic copper of one palm in their thickness, with twenty cubits between

grasped his bow and gripped four arrows . . . . so he rode northward, shooting at them . . . . his arrows had come out of the back thereof while he
was attacking another post. It was really a deed which had never been done
nor heard of by report: shooting at a target of copper an arrow which came
out of it and dropped to the ground. . . . "

BABYLONIANS AND ASSYRIANS

The Semitic peoples, who probably sprang from Arabia, occupied the
whole area from the mountains of Persia and Armenia to the Mediterranean,
a wide crescent of settled ground from Palestine through Mesopotamia to
the Persian Gulf, curving round the great desert whence Bedouin movements
continually erupted. In Babylonia the beginnings of civilization were as
ancient as in Egypt, and, as in Egypt, the development of this empire was
checked by a barbaric irruption—that of the Aryan Kassites (c. 1800–1200
B.C.). It was constantly torn by wars and internal strife, changing hands
over and over again, and was ruled by a series of conquerors which included
the Kassites and the Hittites, King Sargon the Akkadian, and the Chaldean
kings Nebuchadnezzar and Nabonidus. It included the famous Third Dynasty
of Ur, whose founder promulgated the earliest code of laws yet discovered.
During six successive dynasties from about 1150 B.C. Babylonia lived under
the menacing shadow, and at times actual domination, of her northern
neighbour Assyria, a rival kingdom, and on October 12th, 539 B.C., the
conquering armies of Cyrus, the Great King of Persia, marched into Babylon.
They held it for two centuries, until it fell to Alexander in 330 B.C.

Apart from Babylonians, the greatest of the Semitic peoples were the
Assyrians, who were beginning to be active about the fifteenth century B.C.
and were later to unite nearly the whole Semitic area under their rule. The
Semitic peoples drew their civilization partly from Babylon, partly from
Egypt, and linked the two. The Assyrians became the dominating factor in
the Near East from about 1000 to 600 B.C., the older powers of Egypt, Babylonia and the Hittites having fallen into decrepitude. The great age of Assyrian
history began with Tiglath-Pileser III (745), and reached its height under
Sennacherib (705) and Esarhaddon (681). These monarchs ruled over the
whole of Mesopotamia and Syria, thus uniting all Semitic stock outside
Arabia, and for a time they also occupied Egypt. One of the warlike and
pleasure-loving kings of Assyria was Assurnazipal, who is shown in sculptures
holding a bow of typical Assyrian pattern. This has a feature similar to that
found in the bow of the Hittites in that the string is attached simply by
fitting it into a nock cut into the bow for the purpose. A study of later patterns
shows that this arrangement becomes improved; the bows of Assurbanipal,
for instance, the last great king of Assyria, have the tips of each limb carved

Skirmish on a river bank; an original Bundi miniature (1800–50) in the author's collection. This shows foot archers with simple self-bows, mounted bowmen shooting composite bows and, in lesser numbers, tribesmen with rifles in the same minor incident.

An Indian thumb ring from the collection of Dr Charles E. Grayson.

An Indo-Persian arrow box, early eighteenth
century.
A group of beautifully made and elaborately
decorated arrows from Kashmir, Northern India.
From a chest of arrows presented to Sir Henry
Clinton (1771-1829), whilst Adjutant-General in
India from 1802 to 1805.

The Assyrian king, Ashurbanipal, offers a libation to celebrate a successful lion hunt. He carries the distinctive Assyrian composite bow as a symbol of victory and attending him, in pride of place, is his bow-bearer with spare bow and a liberal supply of arrows.

This Assyrian hunting scene clearly shows the special details of bows and arrows used in the chase. The diminutive archer may be a bow-bearer for the more impressive and well-dressed archer at full draw.

The Bearer of the King's Bow. An Assyrian relief from the central palace, Nimrud. The carved animal head bow-tip, found only in the Assyrian type of bow, is clearly shown.

in the form of a bird's or lion's head, over which the string is passed and then hooked on to the beak or snout of the animal. This was quite a big technical improvement as it had the effect of imparting extra cast or thrust to the arrow.

A bow and arrows found in a tomb at Thebes closely resemble the weapons depicted in Assyrian sculptures, and the date of this tomb corresponds with the end of the period of the Assyrian domination of Egypt at the rise of the XXVI Dynasty. The Assyrians sacked Thebes in the year 663 B.C., so there would seem to be little doubt as to the origin of this particular find. The composite bow of Seti I, although of earlier date, was similar in design to the Assurnazipal bow and this type seems to have been used throughout the Near East until the time of Cyrus, when it was superseded by a bow with recurved ends to its limbs.

Assyrian archers were often accompanied by shield-bearers, and sometimes a unit of three soldiers would fight together—the archer, his shield-bearer, and a swordsman. At other times we find a shield-bearer allotted to two archers and frequently these ancillary pavisers are to be found protecting bowmen fighting from chariots. Occasionally horse-archers were employed in pairs, one holding the reins and guiding both horses while the other used his bow. The arrows used by the Assyrians were, generally speaking, of finer make than, for instance, Egyptian examples from the same period. The shaft was of a slender reed about twenty-two inches long with another eleven inches or so of hardwood foreshaft carefully smoothed and finished. This was made to fit into the shaft for a short distance and was bound securely with sinew. The nocks were of hardwood or horn, and there were normally three feathers. The most important feature was the head of bronze, its shape and design selected for special tasks, making a deadly and effective weapon.

A wounded lioness from the royal hunting scenes of Ashurbanipal, providing vivid testimony of the efficiency of the Assyrian composite bow as a hunting weapon.

A group of bronze arrow-heads from Mesopotamia showing a variety of design and giving some indication of the excellence of manufacture of these expendable items. The earlier forms were flat and had short tangs. Later types were provided with well-formed tangs, central ribs and longer blades.

The kingdom of Assyria lay near to the southern limit of distribution of the composite bow, and was situated immediately adjacent to Media and Persia; the latter, together with Turkey, was the country in which the composite bow reached its highest perfection. It will be seen, therefore, that any specimens of the Assyrian bow which may be discovered would be particularly interesting as early examples of the development of the higher forms of composite bow. At the end of the seventh century B.C. the Medes and the Chaldeans united and rapidly overwhelmed Assyria, culminating in the fall of Nineveh in 612 B.C., and this great kingdom was more completely ruined than any other empire in history. However, neither the Median nor the Chaldean empires lasted so long as their predecessor; in the middle of the sixth century B.C. both were overthrown by Cyrus and incorporated by him in the vast Persian Empire.

The Scythians (a name then used to describe several aggressive nomad tribes both in Europe and in Asia) were perhaps the most celebrated archers in ancient times, and it was to them that Cyaxares, King of Media, applied for instructors in archery so that his youths might learn the art of using the celebrated composite bow. This king, the great-grandfather of Cyrus, among other military reforms adopted the bow as a weapon, having learnt the use of it during his wars with the Massagetae Scythians and other races. Cyaxares died in 594 B.C. but the bow remained in use, and became a national weapon and an emblem highly revered. During this monarch's reign the Scythians conquered and occupied Media, hence we can readily see that a northern type of bow may have been grafted upon that already familiar to the Medes and Persians, probably a type very similar to that of their neighbours the Assyrians. It would then be a question of time and usage before the refinements of the superior weapon became incorporated in the Assyrian type, superseding it, and producing a readily recognisable new form of bow.

ANCIENT PERSIA

The old Persian Empire, that great empire in the ancient world, only flourished for some three hundred years, from 600 to about 300 B.C. During the course of these three hundred years, however, there unfolded on the Iranian plateau and in the whole of the Near East a drama so fascinating, a spectacle so fabulous and incredible, that we cannot fail to be dazzled by the insane genius, the atrocious deeds, the extravagance, and also by the greatness of some of the Median and Persian kings. The Persian Empire was built upon the ruins of the former supremacy of the people we know as the Medes, who came from somewhere in south Russia. By traversing the mountains between the Black Sea and the Caspian they reached Persia and some of them trekked on further to India, while others settled in Iran. It was not long before they and their descendants were holding sway over the kingdoms of Babylonia, Assyria and Syria.

The first king of the Medes of whom we know was Deioces. He established Ecbatana, his capital city, on a hill, and crowned it with a temple which glittered in the sun. The city is said to have been enclosed by seven walls, the innermost of pure gold, the second of silver, the third of gleaming orange-coloured brick and the others of blue, scarlet, black and white. There is a curious similarity in the arrangement of these colours to those chosen for the rings of the universally used archery target devised in the eighteenth century. Like the centre of Ectabana the central portion of the target is gold, then follow rings of red, blue, black and white. Perhaps the colourful example of Deioces' capital provided the necessary inspiration.

The daughter of one of the Median kings married a Persian prince of a vassal state. Their son, Cyrus II, was to conquer the land of the Medes and become the founder of the Persian Empire. He subjugated Babylonia, putting an end to the Semitic domination of western Asia which had lasted for a thousand years. He laid his mighty hand on Bactria, Margiana and Sogdiana; and far away on the Jaxartes, to the north of modern Samarkand, he founded the powerful frontier fortress of Cyreshata. In the east, Cyrus protected his empire against the audacious raids of the Saka tribes of the Turanian Steppes. In a comparatively short time after the conquests of Cyrus, the triangular bow, common to Mesopotamia, was superseded by the recurved type which approximated to the form of the later Persian and Turkish bow, a pattern of bow which remained virtually unchanged until the eighteenth century A.D. Cyrus did not die in his bed. He threw himself into the fray against an in-

Persian tile work of about 500 B.C., which ornamented one of the walls of the palace of Darius, showing one of the royal archer-guards. These bowmen are known from the description by Herodotus of the Persian Wars.

A group of bronze arrow-heads from the Middle East.

Left:

  Assyrian, used for long range armour-piercing.

  Scythian three-bladed point.

  Greek point with socket and central rib.

  Greek point with tang.

Right:

  Luristanian point with barbs and long tang.

  Typical leaf-shaped blade from Mesopotamia.

vasion by Asiatic bowmen, the Massagetic horsemen of the north who had stormed out of the steppes of Turkestan, incited by the Scythians. In the course of his heroic struggle against this menace to Persia, Cyrus the Great died in the summer of 530 B.C., presumably a victim of the wily tactics and dangerous bowmanship of his steppe-riding adversaries.

Although Darius I was defeated at Marathon in 490 B.C. later it was he who, after putting down dangerous rebellions and instituting a rigid bureaucracy, reconstructed the huge Persian Empire. One wall of his palace was decorated with a magnificent frieze of polychrome tile work consisting of archers of the royal guard, who are known from the descriptions of the Persian war by Herodotus. The relief is dated about 500 B.C. and clearly shows the archers, in gaily coloured uniforms, carrying their bows with pronounced recurved ends secure in bow-cases slung on each left shoulder. This is the bow which was carried by the armies of Darius in their widespread campaigns northwards. Darius led his armies across the Bosphorus, through Thrace and as far as the Danube. He crossed the river with a force of between 70,000 and 80,000 men and marched off into the uncharted wilderness, under constant attack by Scythian horsemen. Darius was never able to inflict a decisive defeat on the Scythians despite the magnitude of his operations, but he was one of the greatest rulers in world history, an organiser of the first order and a better practical economist than any other king before him.

THE FALL OF AN EMPIRE

Cyrus and Darius built the Persian Empire. Xerxes inherited it and allowed it to decay in a welter of excess and extravagance. Under his successors we can trace its downfall, for it was with them that a fatal series of murders and assassinations began. The vast Persian Empire drowned in a sea of cruelty,

A Scythian archer in the act of bracing his bow. Since early times this method has proved satisfactory for stringing short and powerful composite bows. From a *kylix* by the Panaitios painter, after c. 490 B.C.

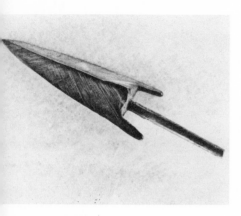

An arrow-head of bronze dating from about 1200 to 800 B.C., a type originating in Egypt and known as the rhombic point. Note the small triangular projection at the base of the blade, the use of which remains a matter for conjecture.

tears and blood, and Alexander had only to cut down something which was already rotten and internally decayed. In November 333 B.C., Darius III opposed Alexander at Issus with an army of perhaps 30,000 or 40,000 men. Alexander had only 20,000 foot-soldiers and 5,000 cavalry under his command, but what principally contributed to his victory was the oblique order of battle and the fact that, when he charged, Darius fled from the Persian centre in his battle-chariot, leaving his army leaderless. Old Persia was falling. This once glorious world empire had stretched from Egypt, via Palestine, Phoenicia, Phrygia, Ionia, Cappadocia, Cilicia and Armenia, to Assyria. It had extended over the Caucasus, Babylonia, Media, modern Persia and Afghanistan, Baluchistan, India west of the Indus, Soctria and Bactria, and reached as far as the steppes of central Asia. In this vast region people of many different races were ruled by a brilliant political organisation, they had to pay enormous taxes, and all males from their fifth to their twentieth year were instructed in horsemanship and archery.

A charming Amazon delivering a Parthian shot. A figure from the lid of a bronze *dinos* or cauldron of Etruscan origin excavated at Santa Maria di Capua Vetere, sixth century B.C.

An early Egyptian transverse or *petit-tranchet* arrow-head of stone with an unusual serrated chisel edge. The shaft is a modern reconstruction.

A lithe Etruscan bowman at full draw. This simple but effective statuette of bronze provides evidence for the use of archery during this civilisation in Sardinia, where it was found.

A bronze Etruscan "bow-puller" of 600–300 B.C. The precise use of these well finished but oddly shaped objects has puzzled archaeologists for many years.

THE ARCHAEOLOGICAL EVIDENCE

It is not surprising to find in the lands of these ancient kingdoms of the Middle East an enormous variety of archaeological material relative to archery. Arrow-heads of bronze, bone and obsidian, provided with sockets, tangs, ribs and barbs, in every conceivable arrangement of size and shape, provide ample material for study of the methods of the craftsmen and the equipment they produced. There are also, waiting for those curious enough to probe and learn, countless representations of archers shooting on foot, on horseback and in chariots, and relics of bows and arrow-shafts, bow-cases and quivers, armguards and all the other impedimenta connected with the art of toxophily.

For much of the period of the early composite bow it was the arrow-head of bronze that was used, and from the many archaeological finds of these interesting objects we can draw conclusions as to their development and use. However, the earliest arrow-heads of metal yet found in Egypt were made of hammered copper, and it is soon apparent that the "leaf-shaped" arrow-head was widely used over a vast area. Blades of a plain leaf pattern were found in the sand-bed of the temple of Sonkhkara dating from about 2000 B.C., but it is not until about 650 B.C. that the wider leaf-shaped blade of bronze appears, although the improvement of strengthening ribs occurs from possibly 1100 B.C. The usual method of attachment was by a tang inserted into the reed shaft, although an alternative to this was the provision of a socket into which a foreshaft of hardwood was inserted. Different forms of head were adopted for different purposes. For attacking unprotected flesh the wider forms with sharp blades were made, similar to the leaf type already noticed. The narrower forms were for penetrating clothing, and for piercing armour it was necessary to use small but heavy heads. The ribbed arrow-heads were generally cast and those with sockets were always made by this method. The mould was of two or three pieces according to the number of blades in the design, and after it was cast the point would have to be sharpened.

The vicious barbed head began in the simplest way, without any socket or tang for attachment to the shaft, and these have been found both in Greece and the Caucasus dating from about 1500 B.C. They must have been fastened to the shaft by some form of cement. By 1000 B.C. in Greece, tangs were added and this form with a long tang is common to Spain, Egypt and Persia. The provision of tangs gives an indication that reeds were used for arrow-shafts, added to which the considerations of cheapness, availability and ease of production support the probable universal use of this material in war in the Middle East. However, the use of tanged arrow-heads with solid wood arrows is noticed among the Saracens and later the Turks as well as in China. A peculiar head is sometimes found having a very wide edge; this would be designed for cutting through leather garments in preference to the long, tapering form which would lose its force by wedging in the leather. Another type of arrow-head which is found in great quantities is the so-called "three-tongued" style mentioned in the *Iliad*. This is an arrow-head of triangular form, sometimes with well-defined blades and frequently pyramidal. It seems to have originated in south-eastern Europe and to have a Graeco-Scythian origin, first appearing between 1000 and 300 B.C. Thence it spread west to central Europe, east to central Asia, north and north-east to Siberia. In Egypt this type is never found until after the great Scythian invasion of Syria (624–596 B.C.), therefore the Scythian source of those examples found in Egypt is quite probable.

A completely fresh invention dating from about 1200 to 800 B.C. was the interesting rhombic head. This was first found in the mortaring of a brick wall of Ramesses II at Abydos, and similar finds from Mycenae are of the same age. The cross-section, sometimes half as thick as it is wide, is rhombic and the outline is somewhat like the shape of a Gothic window-arch. There are barbs and a tang, but the most peculiar feature is a small triangular projection left at the base of the blade. This would act as a hindrance to penetration, yet the head was always barbed and was therefore expected to penetrate. It has been conjectured that this small knob was a useful stop to prevent the tang from retreating into the reed shaft, but it remains a puzzle.

Numerous other types have been found, and the variation of design and shape among these early arrow-heads is amazing. Only very occasionally are heads of iron found, such as those expended in the fighting round Fort Shalmanester when Nimrud fell. These were of Assyrian origin; simple leaf-shaped points with round tangs. Generally speaking the craftsmanship was excellent, some of the bronze heads which have survived being as keen as the day they were made. For items of an expendable nature they were manufactured with remarkable care, and by studying these relics it becomes apparent that the metalworkers of the two millennia before Christ had become highly expert in their craft.

During those twenty centuries western Asia saw the early composite bow develop as the dominant weapon in the constant sway of power between the kingdoms of early civilization. This weapon found its way to Italy and Greece during the early part of the first millennium at a period contemporaneous with the foremost period of its use by the Assyrians.

ETRUSCAN ARCHERS

The Etruscans emerged from the complex ethnic pattern of Iron-Age Italy as a distinct people in about the eighth century B.C. They enjoyed a period of prosperity gained from their exploitation of rich metal mines, and through the skill and enterprise of their sailors, who traded extensively with

Bowmen in a battle between Persians and Macedonians on the so-called "Alexander's Sarcophagus". Found at Sidon, Phoenicia, it possibly came from a workshop on the Peloponnese in Southern Greece and has been dated, on artistic grounds, to 330–320 B.C.

Greece and the Near East. From central Italy the Etruscan cities extended their dominion to the north as far as the Reno and Po valleys and in Campania; in the south, flourishing centres sprang up such as Capua, Pompeii, Sorrento and Salerno. The Etruscans were highly successful managers of their natural resources, efficient businessmen and, if the many tomb paintings accurately represent their habits, a gay and pleasure-loving people who lived out their lives in a straightforward devotion to hedonism. Nevertheless, their existence was dominated by a ritualistic religion, which seems finally to have degenerated into a morbid and fatalistic preoccupation with the future. The Etruscans played an immensely important role in the history of our western civilization. We owe to them the diffusion of writing by means of the alphabet they had themselves borrowed from the Greeks, and much of the civilization of Rome was founded on Etrusco-Italic beginnings. Their sculpture and painting reveal a unique quality of beauty and as artists in bronze they were brilliant.

The peak period of this civilization was the sixth and early fifth centuries B.C. but in the middle of the fifth century a decline set in, possibly due to a series of military defeats which Etruria suffered at the hands of her neighbours. In 504 B.C. land communication with Etruscan Campania was cut when the Latins, helped by Aristodemus of Cumae, defeated an Etruscan army at the battle of Aricia. Thirty years later Etruscan sea-power received a crippling blow from allied Greek naval forces off Cumae (474 B.C.). And finally the southern outposts of Etruria were conquered by the Sammites—Italic mountain tribes from the Appenines—whose invasion of Campania culminated in the overthrow of Capua in 423 B.C. Rent by internal social troubles and preoccupied by political rivalries, the Etruscan cities failed to make a common front against this relentless encroachment, and by the close of the third century B.C. Etruscan independence was virtually at an end.

The Etruscans undoubtedly borrowed the composite bow from the Greeks, and there is reasonable evidence to show that it was used by horsed archers of the Etruscan armies during the height of their power. A charming bronze *dinos* or cauldron, from the sixth or fifth century, in excellent preservation, has as ornamentation several mounted bowmen. These lively figures carry short recurved bows and are equipped with quivers for their arrows slung on their backs. The long-forgotten metal-worker who created these warriors faithfully recorded the ease and grace with which these practised horsemen turned in the saddle and, with their well-trained mounts careering on, delivered accurately directed shafts at the critical moment.

"BOW-PULLERS" OF ANTIQUITY

A number of finds of Etruscan bronze objects, having an unusual shape and unknown use, has set archaeologists a poser which has not, as yet, been satisfactorily answered. With only slight variation in design these objects consist of a plate from which project three spikes and which extends to incorporate two holes on either side of the spikes. Since the nineteenth century these curious objects have been variously assigned to uses which have included several archery applications. For many years they were authoritatively described as "bow-pullers"; they have been recognised as arrow-straighteners and cross-bow loaders, in addition to several non-archery uses such as spear-throwers, calthrops, various parts of harness, and even knuckle-dusters. A later theory ascribes to them a religious significance. They remain a mystery.

They are mentioned here as an example of one of the many peripheral studies connected with toxophily with the hope that the problems they pose, together with countless other incomplete aspects of archery history, will perhaps claim the attention of someone keen enough to unravel the mystery.

3 The Ultimate in Missile Weapons

An arrow from a warrior
Shot at an unbeliever
Counts more than many prayers
Said by a pious hermit.

ARAB ARCHERY

A Greek archer from a vase painting. His equipment is shown in intriguing detail. Note the quiver carefully positioned so as to facilitate the easy withdrawal of arrows. The fact that one arrow is being drawn whilst another is shown peeping beyond the bow suggests that the artist wanted to convey the impression of "rapid fire" in a form of animated cartoon. The accentuated classical shape of the bow is the result of composite construction or the use of animal horns for its limbs.

WHILE Britain was settling down to its late Bronze Age, many glittering chapters of military and naval history were being enacted in Greece, and from the sixth century B.C. the use of archery was a prominent factor in both sea battles and land warfare for at least four hundred years. Greece was composed of a series of separate city-states either warring with each other or becoming involved in hostilities or trade with many of the powers of the Near East. Much of the history of the race who called themselves Hellenes deals with the diffusion of an extremely advanced culture and philosophy, and a set of heroes who became immortal through a unique collection of legendary histories. The organisation of the Grecian armed forces was well-planned and very carefully administered. Regular bowmen in the Greek armies were properly mobilized and well equipped; their rates of pay were officially laid down; and their employment in epic battles such as Marathon, in the Corinthian and Peloponnesian wars, and in naval engagements between the Athenians and the Syracusans, seem to have been well controlled and of great military value. The drafting of reinforcements, orders relating to specific duties, and recommendations for their deployment all indicate that their commanders well realised the importance of bowmen used as support troops. Various extra-special duties were allocated to the archers, one being service with the Athenian "police", and Pericles mentions the use of mounted bow-men at the start of the Peloponnesian War.

A statue of Heracles as an archer in battle from the pediment of Aphaia temple, c. 490 B.C. A bronze bow and arrow were no doubt part of the original.

A silver stater from Cydonia, Crete, of 400–300 B.C., showing the hero Cydon bracing a bow. The contours of the weapon shown and the method of handling it suggests that it may be a simple wooden bow rather than one of composite construction.

The history of Classical Greece begins with the first Olympiad in 776 B.C. but at some unknown date long before this it seems that both Etruscans and Greeks emigrated from Asia Minor, having as forebears the mountain tribes of Indo-European stock. In their movement westwards, possibly over many centuries, it is likely that they carried with them the tradition and knowledge of composite bow construction and usage. In Crete, for instance, the composite bow seems to have been well established by 1500 B.C. The famed Cretan archers, however, according to Xenophon, were outranged by the Persians. The composite bow used in Greece was almost certainly very similar in design to that used by the Assyrians and Medes and by the tribes which reached the Indus valley and Arabia. The classical history of Greece ends in 133 B.C., the date when that nation, together with other powers in the Mediterranean, became a Roman province.

THE ROMAN EMPIRE

The Roman dominion at the beginning of the First Punic War in 264 B.C. did not extend beyond Italy. At the end of that war in 241, the Carthaginians were turned out of Sardinia and Corsica and from the western half of

A grim reminder of the superiority of the bow over primitive hand weapons. This shows the remains of one of the Iron Age defenders of Maiden Castle, in Dorset, a victim of an arrow from a mercenary bowman of Vespasian's 2nd Legion who captured and reduced the fort. The warrior must have died almost instantaneously.

Sicily—the eastern half continuing under the rule of Syracuse, a Greek settlement allied to Rome. Carthage, near modern Tunis, had been (traditionally, founded exactly a hundred years before Rome by the Phoenicians of Tyre) usually called Poeni or Puni by the Romans, and was therefore Semitic, so it seems safe to assume that the composite bow contributed largely to the power of this persistent rival of Rome. The Second Punic War began in 218, after the Carthaginians under Hannibal had besieged and taken Saguntum, now Murviedro, a city of Greek foundation on the Spanish coast, allied to Rome. They crossed the Pyrenees and the Alps and overran nearly all Italy, but failed to capture Rome and were eventually forced to retreat to Africa where they were decisively defeated in 202. The Third Punic War, 146, started when Carthage attacked Numidia, also an ally of Rome, and ended with the utter destruction

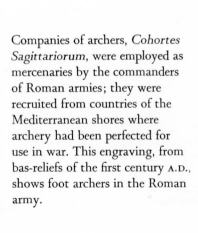

Companies of archers, *Cohortes Sagittariorum*, were employed as mercenaries by the commanders of Roman armies; they were recruited from countries of the Mediterranean shores where archery had been perfected for use in war. This engraving, from bas-reliefs of the first century A.D., shows foot archers in the Roman army.

of Carthage itself. Then, within a little more than three hundred years, the whole of the Mediterranean and half of Europe was swallowed up by Rome. Julius Caesar's brilliant military exploits added extensively to the growing empire; Britain, France, Palestine, Crete, parts of Syria and North Africa came under Roman rule. Finally, by the reign of Marcus Aurelius in A.D. 180, all of southern Europe and most of the Middle East and North Africa shared a common dictatorship.

The Romans attached far more importance to their enormous catapults, ballistas and other huge siege weapons than to the use of bows, and they developed the techniques of long-range missile weapons which were used to devastate strongholds well out of the range of arrows shot from a bow. For closer range missiles they put reliance on the *pilum*, the standard light throwing spear of which every legionary carried two or three, and the sling, which was used with great dexterity and effectiveness by battalions of specially trained soldiers. Although archery was not a feature of the Roman military organization, much use was made of mercenary bowmen drawn from the many nations within the Roman frontiers who were specially skilled with the bow. The weapon of these mercenaries, the *Cohortes Sagittariorum*, was the composite bow. Discoveries at Roman sites of arrow-heads of a solid, square or triangular section indicate that special importance was placed on the armour-piercing qualities of these missiles. It is therefore possible that the Roman commanders used archers for specific tasks as snipers, selecting the more valuable targets of enemy leaders who would have better armoured protection than the common soldier.

Throughout the whole of their turbulent history the Romans found themselves facing adversaries armed with the composite bow. It was used by the Etruscans and the Latins in their early struggles with the Romans, and

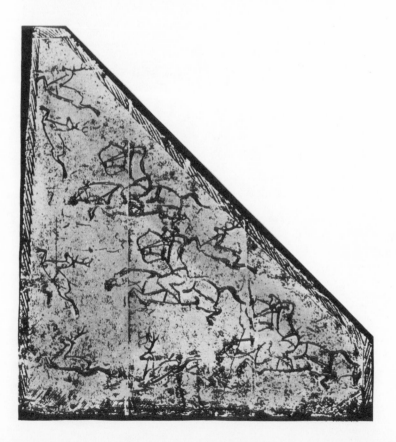

Chinese mounted huntsmen of the late first millenium B.C., using the bow as their principal weapon. From a decorated tile of the period.

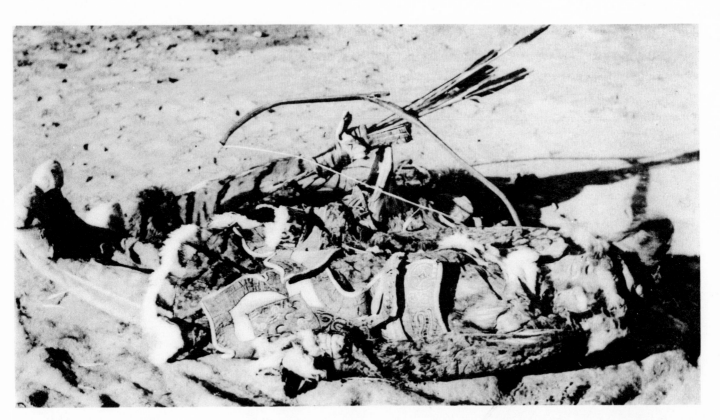

The well preserved corpse of a Mongolian warrior estimated to date back to the Yuan Dynasty (c. 1300) discovered in Chinghai Province in the lonely Tsaidam Basin. The extraordinary state of preservation was due to the dry and cold conditions, and the composite bow had survived more or less intact. There were also found eleven arrows whose steel heads were still razor sharp.

carried by the barbarian tribes during their invasions of Roman colonies. In their capture of Mesopotamia from the Parthians and their involvement in the Persian War, as well as in their actions against the Goths and during the ravages of the Huns in Europe, the Roman armies must have realised the potentiality of such a common weapon, and its dire effectiveness must repeatedly have been demonstrated to them. It is somewhat surprising, therefore, that it was not until the end of the Roman Empire in the west that Leo I (the Great), during whose papacy Attila was defeated at Châlons-sur-Marne by the Roman general Aëtius, emphasised the importance of the bow and attempted, rather belatedly and ineffectually, to introduce it officially to the armed forces. In his *Military Constitutions* he says: "You shall command all Roman youth, till they come to forty years of age, whether they have mean skill in shooting, or not, to carry bows and quivers of arrows. For since the art of shooting hath been neglected, many and great losses have befallen the Romans"; and in another place, " . . . but specially you are to have care of archers; and they that, who remain at home, and have vacation from war, hold bows and arrows in their houses. For carelessness herein hath brought great damage to the Roman state."

CHINA AND HER EARLY NEIGHBOURS

While the development of the composite bow was taking place in the Middle East and its use was becoming persistent among the nations of the

The young Buddha, who was an expert at archery, practising shooting. Traditionally he used a great bow that only he could draw, and successfully willed his arrows to pierce the target. From a Chinese silk painting of the eighth to tenth century.

western Mediterranean, another mighty civilization was becoming involved with the evolution of this weapon and making special contributions to its history. The prehistory of the Chinese is as ancient as that of any great civilization. Their ancestors lived 500,000 years ago, as the remains of the Man of Pekin testify, and the history of this vast nation of some seven hundred million people extends over several thousand years. The first Chinese dynasty about whose existence we have really reliable information had as forebears folk from the 5,000-years-old Stone-Bronze Age. This dynasty, known as the Shang, were familiar with the bow and arrow, as their pictograph symbols for hunting prove. Little is known of the archery of this early period; but at about the time that the Chinese say that archery came into perfection, equivalent to about 1200 B.C., the nomads of southern Siberia developed a new type of composite bow, in which the ears and grip of the bow were stiffened by the application of strips of unyielding bone. These features would improve the bow and make it even more efficient.

The land bordering China to the north, roughly the areas producing this improved weapon, were populated by the Huing-nu, a group of barbaric nomads, who for four hundred years laid waste the territories close to China's frontiers. These wild and warlike people eventually fulfilled the role of border guards to the Chinese, protecting their masters from other marauding barbarians. Every able-bodied man who could draw a bow was a warrior, and the Huing-nu were trained from an early age to ride and shoot. There is an interesting indication of the wide diffusion of specialised aspects of archery knowledge, in that certain influences of Iranian culture spread as far as these tribes by the second century B.C., particularly the introduction of the triangular arrow-head and the use of the extremely practical combination bow-case and quiver—the *gorytus*. The development of a short composite bow in the wastelands to the north of China was the natural consequence of two principle factors—the lack of proper wood for bowmaking, its growth being stunted by nature, and the requirement of mounted warriors for an easily handled and compact weapon.

The Huing-nu were gradually displaced by other nomadic tribes who were also well advanced in archery and, through centuries of contact with these horse archers of the semi-arid regions of mid-Asia, the Chinese themselves became skilled with the bow. Archery was eventually treated by the Chinese with that same respect and ritual which they accorded to so many important aspects of life. It was not only a powerful arm, deadly in war and in the chase, but it occupied an honoured place among their recreations. China's greatest philosopher, Confucius, was born during the feudal period of China in c. 551 B.C. in what is today the province of Shantung. As a young boy he quickly mastered the arts of bowmanship and music. Through his later writings he spoke of archery (unexpectedly, in view of its warlike nature)

An excellent example of a gilt-bronze thumb-ring of the Byzantine period.

Hunting scene from a hand-painted scroll by Fang Hsiao-ju after the original attributed to Li Hing Mien of the Sung Dynasty (960–1279). The horseman on the left is sighting down his arrow and straightening the shaft. Note the hawk on the shoulder of the huntsman in the centre. The other two archers are carrying typically high-strung composite bows.

and gave a list of the distances at which the various classes were to shoot, with a table of the targets assigned to each section of society. His spiritual teachings included the maxim, "By the drawing of the bow one can know the virtue and conduct of men". A certain mental calm is required for the best performance with bow and arrow, and the practice of archery can quickly reveal impatience or an undisciplined mental approach. It has been said that archery, in her many moods, can reveal the best, and the worst, in man. Confucius, in his keen and sensitive observation of human behaviour, must have recognised this delicate balance of the extreme qualities, and how a tendency one way or another could be revealed through the use of the bow.

Some two hundred years or so after Confucius, the Emperor Shih-huang-ti became impatient with the constant raiding on the Chinese borders and conceived the Great Wall of China as a defence against the nomadic Huns or Mongols, popularly called "the demons". This fantastic undertaking was commenced in 214 B.C., grew to a length of 1,500 miles, and had 40,000 defensive towers projecting from it. Shih-huang-ti intended that his empire should last for ever and that all emperors after him should be styled the second, the third and so on. His armies overran all the countries as far as Canton, and his influence extended into what is now Tonkin in North Vietnam. His monument is the fabulous Great Wall, still standing as the world's eighth wonder.

Thumb-rings from the collection of Sir Hans Sloane: above, Persian, green cornelian; below, Turkish, green jasper.

The Fustat ring. This elaborate thumb-ring, excavated south of Cairo in 1965, is now in the Islamic Museum in Cairo. It is dated c. A.D. 800 from which it may appear to be the oldest known ring from the Middle East.

THE MONGOLIAN BOW-RELEASE

The Han Dynasty followed, from 206 B.C. to A.D. 202, during which time a form of bow release came to be widely used which was to become classified as the Mongolian draw or thumb-lock. This involved the use of a ring or guard worn on the right thumb which was hooked over the bowstring to draw it back, instead of the more conventional method of hooking two or three fingers over the string. Locking the thumb over the string was done in a number of different ways, the draw itself could be performed in several fashions, and the actual release of the bowstring had many subtle variants; thus there were innumerable combinations of the methods by which a bow could be used. The Mongolian draw became the standard form of loose among the peoples of the major part of China, Mongolia, central Asia and Korea, and its distribution extended to India, Turkey and Persia. Various isolated instances of this method of releasing a bowstring can be found among other peoples such as the barbaric "X-Group" of Nubia, and a modified form of this special type of loose, also known and used by the Persians, was developed by the Japanese and remained peculiar to them. Thumb-rings have been found in tombs of the Chou Dynasty which ended in 256 B.C. Those from the Han period are made of bronze and are shaped to fit over the thumb, having on the inside a projecting tongue. This tongue gave additional protection to the ball of the thumb and fitted snugly to it. The string was held back by the hard ring, the thumb being locked in position by the index finger until the moment of release. The later patterns of Chinese rings, of jade, agate, glass, bone and metals, were of cylindrical pattern and had no tongue. Those

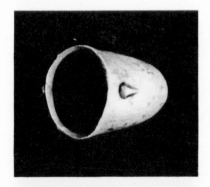

A rare type of Chinese bronze archer's thumb-ring of the Han Dynasty, c. A.D. 200, in position on the bowman's right thumb.

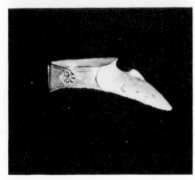

Detail from an Indian miniature painting, dated 1770, showing an archer's ring securely in position on the thumb.

from Turkey, Persia, India and Korea were made of horn, metals, and sometimes of semi-precious stone such as agate and jade, and all had a form of projecting tongue. In the later periods of these countries thumb-rings were occasionally elaborately carved or set with jewels and often worn only as ornaments. A bow released by means of a thumb-ring has a sharper and improved performance and the arrow's velocity and range is increased. However, the method is much more difficult to master than the more ancient and conventional loose normally used in the west, and endless practice is necessary for an archer to become proficient in this special technique. The Mongolian release is associated almost entirely with the composite bow, although in some areas where the composite bow has been developed this special method of loose has not been employed.

THE SCOURGE OF GOD

During the first few centuries of the Christian era the Huns, Tatars and many other bloodthirsty tribes pursued their widespread depredations, and most of eastern Asia was subjected to the brutality of marauding tribesmen from the steppes. History tells in full the story of Attila the Hun, called "the Scourge of God". Chronicles, tales and legends are full of the terror which beset men when the name of the Hun chief was mentioned. His hordes were made up of Turkestanis, Mongols, Kalmucks and Buriats, and men from tribes of the Herules, the Gepids, the Scyri, the Lombards, the Rugians, the Goths and a dozen other nations now lost in time. These dark, squat riders, with their high cheek-bones and narrow eyes, penetrated from the eastern end of Asia across the Urals, and swept unchecked to the gates of Rome. The Huns depended on their tremendous rate of missile discharge for the majority of their victories, and they were quite content to sit the saddle facing the enemy, discharging clouds of arrows, and howling uncouth war cries. Their horses gave them a mobility which was never successfully challenged, and these factors coupled with the psychological advantage of surprise made them an almost invincible force which would be hard to match throughout human history. This was the terror which inspired the prayer *A sagittis Hunorum, nos defende, Domine*—"From the arrows of the Huns, O Lord, defend us." Attila was killed on the Marne in 451.

The Huns carried the powerful composite bow which, in all probability, had remained unchanged over a long period. By now it had been developed to the extent that the backing, or sinew layer, had been firmly moulded to the shape of the bow, whereas there is a reasonable contention that the much earlier patterns were provided with sinew backing which was merely fastened to the bow-limbs by a system of tied thongs. This form of composite bow, known as loose-backed, is to be found amongst the Eskimo tribes of Asia

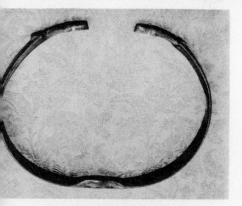

A particularly powerful Turkish bow, unstrung, c. 1850. This weapon is elaborately decorated with a painting of archer-princes on horseback.

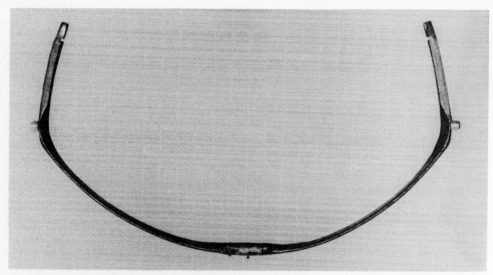

An unstrung Chinese composite bow which shows the typical outline of this type of weapon.

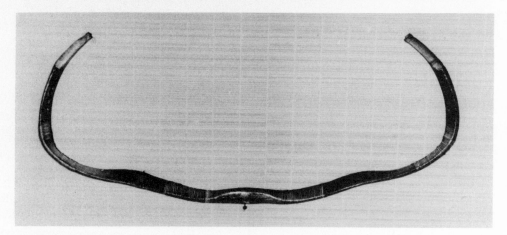

A good example of a composite bow from India in the unstrung position.

and America. There is substantial evidence that the strip of water known as the Bering Strait was dry land at some time in the very distant past. Anthropologists are certain that migratory tribes crossed this strip of land to become settlers in the north and on the west coast of America. This would give strong support to the assertion that the composite bow in its very primitive form was carried from Asia to the American continent. The loose-backed composite bow of the Eskimos, and a more advanced system of moulded backing used by some of the Indian tribes of the west coast of America, are undoubtedly survivals of these earlier migrations. The consequences of this vast drift of humanity to America are considered in another chapter, and it is sufficient to say here that these historical examples of the composite bow indicate the wide extent of the spread of this special knowledge.

MOUNTED BOWMEN OF THE STEPPES

Historians coldly eye Jenghiz Khan (about 1164–1227) as a conqueror with a taste more for blood than politics, and for pillage rather than authority.

The charges are true. For all his epic military conquests, the Mongol leader left no words for posterity, his people no significant cultural artefacts. Only the cold ashes of gutted cities marked his passing. But if Jenghiz Khan was ruthless, he was also brilliant—a leader whose genius for the martial arts surpassed the best that China, Korea and eastern Europe could throw against him. Seven centuries ago this illiterate son of the steppes conceived tactics which were to remain basic down through the ages. His concepts of battle were found eminently sound by Napoleon; they were used by Foch and Pershing, and re-employed by Rommel and Patton. Jenghiz Khan was the first to grasp that the horse-mounted archer was almost invincible, if he could somehow overcome the advantages of numbers and better armour which protected his foes. He set out methodically to discipline his wild plunderers, to mould them into a mobile striking force of loyal warriors. He introduced an order of battle and drew up his men into precise squadrons. The idea of war games—training manoeuvres in which his men could simulate combat and perfect their field operations—was enforced by the Khan, and he imbued his men with a sense of loyalty and devotion to his banner based on a code of honour—and also

Mongol bowmen attacking the famous warrior Takezaki Suenaga. From the Mongol Invasion Scroll (1293) attributed to Tosa Nagataka and Tosa Nagaaki, the Imperial Household collection, Tokyo.

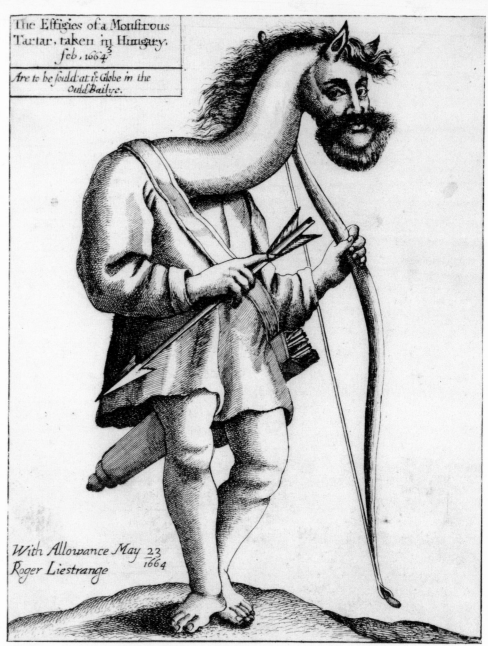

The Effigies of a Monstrous Tartar, taken in Hungary. feb. 1664¾

Are to be sould at ye Globe in the Ould Bailye.

With Allowance May 23/1664
Roger Liestrange

A pen and ink drawing by Andrew Geddes (1789–1844) of a Tatar archer protected against the bleak climate of central Asia and ready to take part in an imminent raiding party.

on the certainty that a fair share of the women and the booty would fall to their lot.

The Mongol riders carried seventy arrows designed to meet a variety of targets in different battle situations. These fearsome warriors carried armour-piercing arrows, their points tempered to steely hardness by immersion in salt water while hot; arrow grenades; incendiary arrows; and arrows designed for long-range shots. They even had a special arrow fitted with a head shaped like an open pair of scissors; it was said that this razor-sharp anti-personnel weapon could cut off a man's arm at the point of impact. All these arrows were carried in quivers, divided into compartments, slung at the right side of the saddle, the bow itself being carried in a leather case on the warrior's left. Jenghiz Khan saw in massed arrow-shot a tremendous psychological advantage as well as a powerful military weapon. With the powerful composite bow in the hands of his tough, disciplined and highly trained warriors, the Khan added the only remaining element needed for his plan of conquest—the right tactic. His enemies invariably advanced on a line, and so Jenghiz Khan evolved the wheeling, flank attack as the manoeuvre best suited to stop them. In an attack the Khan's commanders effectively deployed their men with signal flags; then at the right moment, masterfully, the drilled mounted units would swing round to exploit an enemy's weak point. They would ride in tightly massed ranks, and unleash a deadly cloud of arrows at selected targets identified by carefully directed whistling arrows shot by their leaders. When the enemy lines wavered under the missile attack and their horses were wounded and reeling, the Mongols would rush in with lance, battle-axe and curved short sword. Thus an overwhelming volley of arrows was combined with mobility—in effect, a *blitzkrieg*.

After interminable battles against numerous Tatar tribes, Jenghiz Khan was finally proclaimed Khan of the united Mongol and Tatar peoples. At this juncture, he declared that he had been called by heaven to conquer the world. This implicit belief communicated itself to his troops and he was able to lead them on from one victory to another. The land of the Uigurs in the middle of central Asia submitted to him voluntarily, and Jenghiz Khan became overlord of all the Tatars. In the year 1211 the mighty Khan led hundreds of thousands of Mongols against the Great Wall and, although he stormed the gate forts with ease, it took him five years, aided by an army of 700,000, to conquer China. Samarkand, garrisoned by a force of 110,000, was stormed, plundered and burned, as were Bokhara and many other towns great

After the battle of Igor Swiatoslaw (A.D. 972). An effective impression of the immediate after-effects of war by E. M. Vasnetsov (1848–1925).

The nomadic horsemen of the Steppes were renowned for their hard riding and expert archery.

An original watercolour of a Circassian chief equipped with Asiatic armour, bow and sword, ready for battle.

The Polish Rider, by Rembrandt van Ryn (1606–69). A splendid portrait study of a young cavalier of the Lysowski Regiment, originally the treasured family heirloom of Count Tarnowski. The warrior is equipped with a veritable armoury of weapons.

and small. He finally divided his empire, gained with bow and sword, between his five sons.

During the mid-thirteenth century the Mongol forces, which had already driven deep into central Europe, threatened to overrun and obliterate the Christian civilization of the west. Prince Batu, now the supreme commander of the Mongol army and future founder of the Golden Horde, pressed on even further towards realising the dreams of world conquest which his grandfather, Jenghiz Khan, had pursued so relentlessly. In the summer of 1240 the Mongols, from their bases in the Caucasus area, attacked what was then the southern-most region of Russia, and this campaign culminated in the fall of Kiev, the ancient capital. By now a great deal more was known in western Europe about these strange horsemen from the east, and Matthew of Paris, the chronicler, tells us that they were "–inhuman and beastly, rather monsters than men, thirsting for and drinking blood, tearing and devouring the flesh of dogs and men, dressed in ox-hides, armed with plates of iron, short and stout, thickset, strong, invincible, indefatigable, their backs unprotected, their breasts covered with armour.....they have one-edged swords and daggers, are wonderful archers, spare neither age, nor sex, nor condition." And, according to Sir John Maudeville, they regarded human ears "sowced in vynegre" as a particular delicacy.

THE MANCHUS

At the beginning of the seventeenth century a race of foreign overlords

A Chinese archery inspector instructing a bowman at Pekin. The original caption to this picture, taken from *The Sphere* of August 18th, 1900, concludes, "a great portion of the Chinese army is still armed with this type of bow".

A print of 1814 which shows a
Chinese standard bearer in full
regalia, complete with an
ostentatious display of archery
equipment probably signifying his
authority.

came out of the northern forests of what is now Manchuria, to fight their way
slowly down to Pekin. These Tungus tribes, who abandoned their native
forests for the silken cushions of the south, had as their leader Nurhaci, whose
military genius had previously been welcomed by the Chinese. During 1592,
when the Japanese under the great Hideyoshi invaded Korea, the Koreans
appealed to the Chinese for help to repel the invaders. In response to this
appeal Nurhaci offered to lead a Tungus battalion against the enemy, but was
not called on to fulfil his promise. However, the gesture earned for him the
title of General of the Dragon and the Tiger, conferred on him by a grateful
Chinese government. From 1618 Nurhaci waged war on the Chinese, and
this led to the conquest of that empire by the Manchus. In contemporary
illustrations he can be seen leading his armies of horse and foot archers, who
are armed with composite bows and massive quivers full of heavily fletched
arrows. In 1644 a Tungus Son of Heaven, the first of ten, was installed in the
Forbidden City. These eastern Tatars succeeded in establishing a reigning
house of China which lasted until 1912.

The great composite bow of the Huns can still be seen in use in the lonely
wastes of Mongolia, where the inhabitants of town and village include archery
among their national sports, together with horsemanship and wrestling. The
form of bow used by generations of these peoples is still being produced today;
perhaps it is not quite so powerful as of yore, and perhaps the old methods of
manufacture have been superseded, but the same components of horn, sinew,
animal glue and wood are used and the bowman of the present day, employing
the Mongolian release, still uses a thumb-ring to shoot these weapons.

BOWYERY PERFECTED

The Turks and Persians inherited their love of archery from their ancestors. Both had used the bow from necessity and in later centuries brought to

An incident during the siege of
Naples in 1191. The bowmen of
the army of the Roman Emperor
Henry VI (1165–97), make an
unsuccessful attack on the city.
From *Codex Bernensis* 120, folio
109, Petrus de Ebulo, *De Rebus
Siculis Carmen.*

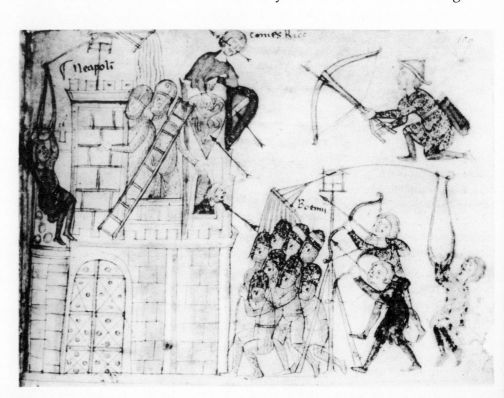

A fine study by Gentile Bellini
(1429–1507) of a Turkish janissary,
one of the regular professional
soldiers of the Ottoman Empire.
The proportions of his bow are
shown in good detail.

it a devotion which almost amounted to fanaticism. During the reigns of the sultans from Mohammed II, 1451, to Suleiman the Magnificent, 1566, Turkish archery reached the zenith of its achievement, the art of bowmaking became pre-eminent, and archery as a sport and pastime was highly regarded. The introduction of firearms during the conquest of Constantinople in 1453 marks the beginning of the decline of the bow as a military implement. The increase of its use solely for sport commences at about this time, and one of the objectives of the guild of archers formed at that time was to preserve the love of the sport among the people, even after it had been completely abandoned by the army at the end of the sixteenth century. Turkish archery as a pastime continued for about four hundred years and had a brief, but glorious, revival as a sport in the early nineteenth century. Encouragement for its continuation was given by many sultans and princes during this period, and a number of these exalted personages were noted for their prowess with the bow. The festivals and parades of the guilds of bowyers, arrowmakers, thumb-ring makers, archers and their instructors, were splendid affairs. Large public areas were set aside for bow practice, and elaborate stones were erected to commemorate great archery events and special long-distance records. The main event at archery meetings was the competition to shoot an arrow the furthest, and

A flight marker, having an inscription in ancient Persian script, in the Ok Meydan, "the place of the arrow", just outside Istanbul. A number of these marble posts still exist and they record the old distances of Turkish flight shooting, The zenith of flight shooting was between the years 1451 and 1566, and it enjoyed a brief revival between 1808 and 1839 due to the interest of Mahmud II.

Sultan Selim III, in the Old Seraglio, Constantinople, from a painting by Constantine Cyzikinoz. Selim (1762–1806) was deposed and killed by Janissaries.

the utmost skill of the bowyer and every subtle technique of the archer was used to force the last fraction of energy from the bow to project the slender ivory-tipped (and often parchment-fletched) shaft to the greatest distance. The distances shot in the past were truly remarkable, and many records exist giving us examples of the prowess of the Turkish master-bowmen. Princes and sultans, grand officials of the Turkish court, ambassadors and admirals have all reserved niches in the archives of archery history. The longest distance on record was shot in 1798 by the Sultan Selim, who is said to have shot an arrow which drove into the ground at 972 yards. Just four years previously, on the 9th July, the Secretary to the Turkish Ambassador in London, Mahmud Effendi, shot a flight arrow 482 yards in a field behind Bedford Square. His bow and arrows were preserved by the Royal Toxophilite Society, whose members witnessed this feat.

In the late seventeenth century, A. G. Busbequius* wrote of his travels in Turkey and describes the enthusiasm of the Turks and their keenness to excel in archery: "The Turks are wondrous expert at shooting at the bow; they accustom themselves to bend them from 7 or 8 to 18 or 20 years of age, and hereby their arms grow stronger, and their skill so great, that they will hit the smallest mark with their arrows. In the thumb of their right hand, they use rings of bone, on which the string lies, when they draw it. [They] gather themselves together in a great plain about Pera where, sitting over against one another cross-legged, they begin with Prayer (so the Turks begin all their enterprises) and then they strive, who shall shoot an arrow furthest. The whole contest is managed with a great deal of modesty and silence, tho' the number of spectators be very great. Their bows are very short for this exercise,

*BUSBEQUIUS, A. G., *The Four Epistles of, concerning his Embassy into Turkey*, *1560* (1694)

A Turkish Family. An engraving by Albrecht Dürer (1471–1528) which was undoubtedly drawn from life. At about the time of this study, the late fifteenth century, Dürer travelled Europe and, in all probability, came across this nomadic archer and his small family. The bow seems to be of the expected composite form and was probably used exclusively for hunting.

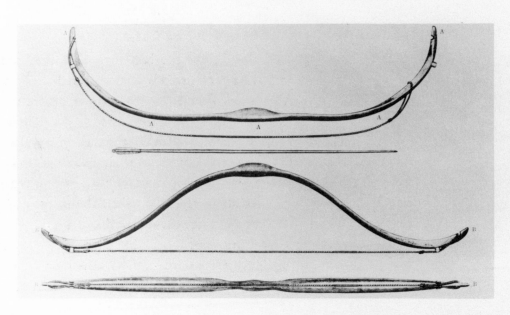

Turkish reflex composite bow estimated to require a pull of 118 lb to draw it fully. This is a good example of a well-made composite bow of the Asiatic type. Formerly in the possession of Sir Ralph Payne-Gallwey.

Sir Ralph Payne-Gallwey (1848–1916) author of *The Crossbow*, was an inveterate experimenter with all types of composite bows, crossbows and missile siege engines. He is here shown shooting his Turkish bow in the authentic fashion at a challenge match between bowman and golfer at Richmond, Yorkshire, in 1906.

and the shorter the better, so that they are hardly bendable, but by well practised persons. 'Tis almost incredible how far they will shoot an arrow; they mark the place with a stone, where the furthest arrow, for that year, was pitch'd. There are many such stones in the field, placed there time out of mind, which are further than they are able to shoot nowadays, they say. These were the marks of their ancestors' archery, whose skill and strength, in shooting, they acknowledge they cannot reach to."

At about the time when the sultans of Turkey were striving to shoot arrows the furthest, the shahs of Persia were organizing elaborate hunting expeditions and employing some of the most ornate and beautiful archery equipment ever made. The museums of the world often display quivers embellished with gold or silver decoration, full of arrows with ivory nocks and shafts covered with intricate lacquered patterns, and bows covered with beautiful painted designs from various regions of Persia and India as well as those from Turkey. These splendid weapons became implements of the chase for the princes of Persia and the rajahs of India. Some of the best examples of these richly finished masterpieces of the bowyer's art, together with quivers of exquisitely finished arrows, were often presented as official gifts to foreign ambassadors and royal visitors. All the skills of bowyery and arrowmaking, plus the artistic individuality of the East, was bestowed on these articles. Although the decorative aspect of these bows is immediately obvious they were nevertheless made for use, and the bowyer, who would have spent up to ten years in their manufacture, would guarantee their perfection as weapons. Individual bows would be named and the bowyer, proud of his workmanship, would often sign each weapon, sometimes adding a prayer to Allah for good measure.

THE BOW IN INDIA

The composite bow was first introduced to India by the wandering tribes from the Near East who settled in the Indus valley, which offers an environment not unlike that of Babylonia; in fact, the civilization which developed there clearly appears to be related to that of the latter, and there was certainly trade between the two regions. Luristan, primarily the area of the Zagros Mountains which provide the western physical boundary of Persia, is particularly rich in archaeological finds of fine quality bronze arrow-heads, and the early progress of the composite bow can be conjectured from the similarity of these early finds, in pattern and age, to those associated with the early types of Assyrian and Mesopotamian bows. The sites of the early Indian civilizations stretched along some 800 miles of the coast from the modern Persian frontier, and inland from the south of the Indus, through Sind and Punjab to the foothills of the Himalayas. It seems that a series of city states was formed in the Indus valley, and the absence there of advanced weapons of bronze or copper suggests the security of these cities and the absence of aggressors; but this military unpreparedness made them an easy prey to invasion when it came. The first major irruption was made by the warlike Aryan tribes, bringing horses and chariots and the composite bow from Iran. The Ayran tribes then moved eastwards across the Punjab and into the Ganges Valley. India was again subject to a great invasion in 326 B.C., when Alexander the Great invaded in the north-west; and within a hundred years or so a further series of invasions brought Bactrian Greeks, Sakas and other people of Iranian or central Asian origin into India, where they established kingdoms and were assimilated by the existing population. The Muslim conquest of India took two hundred years, until Muslim rule was established in Delhi in 1206, and in

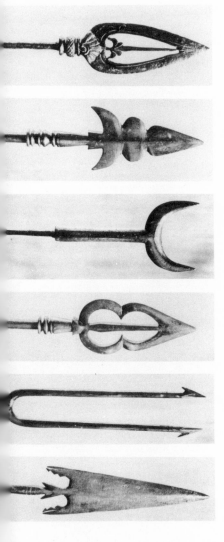

An interesting variety of different patterns of steel arrow-heads from Rajputana, dated to about 1750. A great amount of care and skill was lavished on the archery equipment of the princes and rajahs of India at about this time.

An excellent study of a fully equipped Russian cavalry archer, illustrating the fact that the horse was essential to wage the fast and mobile warfare of the great open Steppes.

the sixteenth and seventeenth centuries the Mongols successfully conquered and ruled the Indian peoples. The composite bow was, therefore, introduced to India in a long series of incursions by archer-peoples. Gradually its form became slightly modified, and we find main types evolving; those from the north and south, which vary only slightly, and the Sind bow, the so-called "crab" bow, which has a marked depression in the handle portion. Essentially the form of Indian composite bow remained exactly the same to that used further west. Latterly, in India as in Persia, this ultimate in weapons was used by the princely caste as an implement of the chase.

The survival as a sporting weapon of the composite bow in its original form up to the eighteenth and nineteenth centuries indicates a reluctance to give up the results of thousands of years of applied skills; and another factor, which had particular relevance in the areas of Islamic influence, was the exhortation by the Prophet Muhammad for its use. To be a competent archer was a matter of pride, but above all one could earn religious merit by practising with a bow. This noble weapon, designed initially as an entirely aggressive arm, was the result of careful handicraft and progressive technical improvement born in the vast regions of central Asia. In order that the lost arts of the Asiatic bowyers may be re-discovered and recorded for posterity, and in order to improve our knowledge of the evolution of these weapons, their detailed study has been undertaken by archer-scholars in recent years.

In the foregoing general outline of the story of the composite bow many landmarks in the history of the northern hemisphere have been discussed in detail, many have been dealt with briefly, and many have been omitted. It has been shown that the part played by this extraordinary weapon has been considerable and in some cases vital; its evolution represents a phase in the history of archery which has a particular fascination, and its further study cannot help but be rewarding. The Asiatic fondness for beautiful things and their love of the exotic is revealed in their special attachment to these essentially individual weapons, which are "elegant in form and wonderful in structure" in the words of an inscription on a fifteenth-century composite bow. This aura of femininity seems to have been associated with bows, particularly the composite variety, since time immemorial:

> The Bow brings grief and sorrow to the foeman:
>   Armed with the Bow we may subdue all regions.
> Close to his ear, as fain to speak, she presses,
>   Holding her well-loved friends in her embraces.
> Strained on the Bow, she whispers like a woman - this
>   Bow-string that preserves us in combat.

RIGVEDA HYMN VI 75
(Second millennium B.C.)

SELECT BIBLIOGRAPHY

Anati, Emmanuel, *Palestine before the Hebrews* [1963]

Balfour, Henry, *The Archer's Bow in the Homeric Poems* [1921]

Brinton, D. G., M..D, *The So-called "Bow-Puller" Identified as the Greek*, Bulletin of Science and Art [1897]

British Museum, *A General Introductory Guide to the Egyptian Collections* [1930]

British Museum, *A Guide to the Babylonian and Assyrian Antiquities* [1908]

Draeger, Donn F., and Smith, Robert W., *Asian Fighting Arts*, Ward Lock [n.d.]

Du Noyer, George V., *Remarks on the Classification of Bronze Arrow-Heads*, The Archaeological Journal, Vol. VII [1850]

Faris, Nabih Amin, and Elmer, Robert Potter, *Arab Archery* [1945]

Herodotus, *History of the Greek and Persian War*, trs. by George Rawlinson, New English Library [1966]

Klopsteg, Paul E., *Turkish Archery* [1947]

Larousse, *Encyclopedia of Ancient and Medieval History* [1963]

Livius, Titus, *The War with Hannibal*, trs. by Aubrey de Sélincourt, Penguin [1965]

McLeod, Wallace E., *An Unpublished Egyptian Composite Bow in the Brooklyn Museum*, American Journal of Archaeology, Vol. 62 [1958]

McLeod, Wallace E., *Egyptian Bows in New York*, American Journal of Archaeology, Vol. 66, No. 1 [1962]

Paterson, Lt Cdr W. F., *The Archers of Islam*, Journal of the Economic and Social History of the Orient, Vol. IX, Parts I–II [1966]

Paterson, W. F. and Latham, D., *Saracen Archery* [1970]

Petrie, W. M. Flinders, *Tools and Weapons* [1917]

Thucydides, *The Peloponnesian Wars*, trs. by Benjamin Jowett, New English Library [1966]

Vos, M. F., *Scythian Archers in Archaic Attic Vase-paintings* [1963]

Yadin, Yigael, *The Art of Warfare in Biblical Lands* [1963]

4 The Clothyard Shaft

Signal for England's archery
To halt and bend their bows.
Then stepped each yeoman forth a pace,
Glanced at the intervening space,
And raised his left hand high;
To the right ear the cords they bring,
At once ten thousand bow-strings ring,
   Ten thousand arrows fly!

SCOTT

THE history of the traditional long-bow is often confined to the fourteenth and fifteenth centuries, by which time it had become recognised by military commanders as an important supporting arm. Its superiority as a weapon remained unchallenged throughout the many classic battles of the Hundred Years War. This was the weapon of the simple man, the yeoman, the Tommy Atkins of the Middle Ages, who, by wielding his bow of yew and clothyard shafts, gained a totally unexpected immortality unique in the annals of medieval warfare—for at that time the lot of the common soldier was to struggle and suffer in complete obscurity. However, the evolutionary background of this great weapon reaches back beyond the days of the yeoman, beyond the Norman conquest of Britain, to the days before the Dark Ages descended upon Europe.

To have been such a significant weapon the long-bow must have had extraordinary qualities; let us therefore examine first the characteristics of its design which make it quite individual and distinct from any other bow. Its length is in the order of six feet and, gently tapering toward each tip, its "limbs" terminate in horn nocks over which the string is looped. In section it is somewhat rounded with a slight flattening to the face held away from the archer. The most individual aspect of long-bows is the use of the natural properties of yew *(Taxus baccata).* By skilled cutting and shaping the special

qualities of the sapwood and heartwood can be combined in an unusual manner. When a bow is drawn the inside face of the arc undergoes compression while the outer surface is stretched. The heartwood of yew is able to withstand compression and its sapwood is elastic by nature, both tending to return to their original straightness when unrestrained. By the craft of the bowyer the length of yew was arranged to present a face of sapwood on the outside of the bow and a solid D-section of heartwood on the inner face, thus ingeniously utilising the natural mechanical attributes of the wood. These principles were probably understood and used from a very early period in Europe, certainly by Neolithic English bowyers.

SAXON LONG-BOWS

In the centuries which followed the birth of Christ, when the Romans were still in occupation of Britain, while Attila the Hun was ravaging Europe, and China had experienced the end of the great Han Dynasty, there appeared in Europe a prototype long-bow remarkably similar to the weapon used by the English yeoman some thousand years later. Following the Neolithic period there was a gradual decline in the use of the bow in north-west Europe until the latter part of the Roman Iron Age, when evidence appears of a revival involving a superior weapon to that used previously. A series of splendid long-bows emerged from the three ancient and well-preserved Saxon galleys found in Nydam Moor in Denmark in 1863. Many of these were made of yew and they measured between five feet seven inches and six feet in length. Several other bows, similar to the Nydam finds, were discovered at Vomose in Schleswig-Holstein. All these bows have been scientifically dated to between A.D. 200 and 400, and all closely parallel authentic specimens of military bowstaves salvaged in 1841 from the wreck of the *Mary Rose*, which sank in 1545.

Another series of important finds which provides further evidence for the growing use of the new long-bow in Europe are the bows of yew found in a group of graves of A.D. 600 in Oberfracht, near the source of the Danube. They follow a design similar to that found in the earlier examples. Yet another link in the chain of archery history is the tenth-century bow found on the floor of an Irish crannogh in Ballinderry, County Meath. This long-bow from Ireland, again comparable to the traditional pattern, probably originated in Denmark, as the site at Ballinderry has been established as a Viking settlement. The Vikings have a traditional connexion with archery in the story of the martyrdom of St Edmund, who was shot by the Danish invaders in A.D. 870. In Anglo-Saxon Britain the bow was certainly used and, perhaps as a result of the repeated Danish invasions, began to play a more important part in later Saxon England.

THE CONQUEST OF BRITAIN

It is not surprising that William the Bastard included in his invasion force a large body of trained archers; and, as the Anglo-Saxons lagged behind European usage in such matters, it is understandable that Harold Godwinson's archers were relatively undisciplined at Stamford Bridge and almost non-existent at Hastings. The bowmen deployed by Duke William may have used a longer bow than that depicted in the famous needlework chronicle, the Bayeux Tapestry, for this fabled record of a momentous turning point in English history was designed, if not actually fabricated, in Canterbury, England, to the order of Bishop Odo of Bayeux. The bows depicted in the tapestry could well have been Saxon bows, familiar enough to local workers who may never have seen the improved models from the Continent. One chronicler,* whose accuracy is sometimes questioned by scholars, mentions the use of crossbows by the invaders. An examination of the battlefield indicates that whatever weapons were used to fling the final volleys high in the air, they must have been very powerful, for the distances involved could have been up to 400 yards. William could have known of the crossbow from his campaigns in the Near East, and it is therefore possible that at least some of his troops were so equipped.

The detailed progress of the Battle of Hastings, on Saturday October 14th, 1066, has been studied, thoroughly discussed and admirably described in a

*WILLIAM of JUMIÈGES, *Gesta Normannorum Ducum* (1070)

spate of modern books dealing with the subject; and the fascination of this great contest continues to claim the attention of scholars the world over. The events which led up to this conflict concerned the two boldest warriors of that age, both claiming the right to the throne, and both experienced soldiers who had fought together as brothers-in-arms. At Stamford Bridge only three weeks previously Harold, the elected king of the Saxons had, with his regular Housecarls and irregular Fyrd or Militia, fought off the threat of Viking invasion, and although the ancient sagas mention the use of bows and arrows by the defenders there is no indication that the archery talents of the Saxons were properly mobilised.

This was not the case with Duke William of Normandy, who gave considerable attention to army reorganisation, reform and rearmament in the years 1055 to 1058. It is during this period that we hear of the development of the missile weapon on a large scale, and it was largely due to the skill and training of his archers that William was victorious in his later campaigns. "Good pay and broad lands to everyone who will serve Duke William with spear, sword and bow" was the word in Normandy, and there is every reason to believe that the Conqueror himself was a skilled archer: "None but the Duke William could bend Duke William's bow" was the proud boast of his minstrels. To be of value a large body of archers had to be kept in constant training and practice, and it appears likely that such a body of troops was held constantly mobilized by the duke. It is no wonder then, that on that fateful Saturday in October 1066 the 60,000 or so invaders from Normandy, a large proportion of whom consisted of battle-hardened troops trained in archery, were able to out-manoeuvre the Saxons.

THE BATTLE OF HASTINGS

Harold had drawn up his army in order of battle on a rising mound, with his flanks and front protected by deep trenches, intending to sustain an attack but to avoid, if possible, the heavy-armed cavalry, a force in which he was inferior. The famous shield wall was manned by the Fyrd armed with pikes, pitchforks or any hastily secured weapons; few of them had swords, bows or axes. Behind this enthusiastic but ragged force were the cream of the army, the Housecarls, armed with swords and with the dreaded battle-axe which they wielded with devastating skill. Opposing them were the ordered ranks of William's army in three long lines. First were the archers and light infantry, second came heavily mailed men-at-arms, and the rear line was composed entirely of cavalry. The advantage in terrain was Harold's, and he stoutly defended a number of opening attacks which were preceded by archery which was quite ineffective. There had been several feints by the invader which, although they had weakened the defenders, had not defeated

A commemorative medal issued in 1966 to mark the ninth centenary of the Battle of Hastings. The scene is taken from the last stages of the conflict when Harold was struck down by the Norman cavalry.

The Battle of Hastings. Sketch map, not to scale, showing the disposition of the Saxon and Norman armies at about 9.00 a.m. on 14th October 1066. Where the tracks cross is approximately the site of the present town of Battle, Sussex.

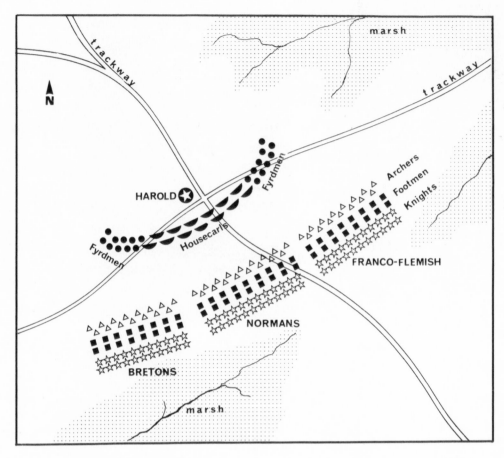

them. Up to the later phases of the battle each arm—archers, cavalry and infantry—had acted independently, and none had achieved a decisive result. A radical change of method was called for, and William applied the principle of co-operation. The archers were ordered to direct their arrows high in the air as a protective barrage for the final attack by foot soldiers and cavalry. "The arrows now flew thicker than rain before the wind." Did one of these wound King Harold, giving rise to the inaccurate rumour that he had been killed? This completely demoralised the Saxons and brought about the termination of the struggle. The traditional but quite apocryphal story of Harold's fatal eye wound first appeared in a poem by Abbot Baudri* some thirty years after the battle, and has spread the world over, to occupy an honoured place in every history book. Baudri described what he saw in the Bayeux Tapestry— one of a group of English knights with the word "Harold" above him grasping an arrow stuck in his face. Charles Gibbs-Smith† has explained that modern researches clearly show that the arrow is nowhere near the soldier's eye and in fact the character depicted is not meant to be Harold. The next scene to the right shows Harold being hacked to death by Norman horsemen who

*BAUDRI, Abbot of Bourguil (1099–1102), *Poem Descriptive of a Tapestry.*

†GIBBS-SMITH, CHARLES, *What the Bayeux Tapestry Does Not Show,* Journal of the Society of Archer-Antiquaries, Vol. 9 (1966)

were able to reach him as a result of the final arrow storm.

Had the bow been adopted previously as a general weapon in England, the outcome of the battle at Hastings might have been reversed and the course of history altered. It was many years before the lessons of this momentous conflict were put into practice on the same scale as the example set by the brilliant generalship of William the Conqueror.

TWELFTH-CENTURY ARCHERY

In 1188 Gerald the Welshman – Giraldus Cambrensis – accompanied Archbishop Baldwin, who was to preach the Third Crusade, through Wales. As a result of this journey he wrote his *Itinerary Through Wales* in which he describes the people of Gwenth as being "more accustomed to war, more famous for valour, and more expert in archery, than those of any other part of Wales". The Welsh of the twelfth century were a wild race given to hasty acts of aggression, and we can read of many instances of their impulsive actions producing reprisals to their disadvantage. William de Braose put to death a great number of Welshmen imprisoned in Abergavenny Castle in revenge for the murder of Henry of Hereford, after making an unsuccessful attempt

Several groups of Norman archers are shown in the Bayeux Tapestry, from which this illustration is taken. They are carrying short bows and drawing their arrows to the breast to reach the maximum range. The bows shown in the Tapestry are believed to be closer to the Saxon pattern than the longer Norman version.

From a fourteenth-century
miniature showing an assault on
Jerusalem, possibly illustrating a
chronicle of the Crusades. The
attackers include longbowmen who
appear to be using the Flemish
two-fingered loose.

to extract a promise, under oath, that none "should bear any bow, or other unlawful weapon". He realised that the bow in the expert hands of a Welsh-man was a weapon to be feared and respected. The same William de Braose testified that one of his soldiers, in a conflict with the Welsh, was wounded by an arrow which passed through his thigh, the armour with which it was cased on both sides, through that part of the saddle which is called the "alva", and mortally wounded the horse. Giraldus, however, was not over-impressed by the courage of the Welsh in battle, which, he tells us, "manifests itself chiefly in the retreat, when they frequently return, and, like the Parthians, shoot their arrows behind them". The "parthian shot", made famous by a tribe of Scythians who were a formidable challenge to the Roman Empire of the third century, was none the less no small feat, and a manoeuvre which used the element of suprise to its greatest advantage. Possibly the passage most often quoted from the writings of Giraldus Cambrensis, and which illustrates best the power of these bows from Gwenth, concerns an oaken portal "which was four fingers thick" penetrated by several Welsh arrows during one of the many sieges of those days. According to the chronicler the bows were "made of wild elm, unpolished, rude and uncouth, but stout; not calculated to shoot an arrow to a great distance, but to inflict very severe wounds in close fight".

Only a few years before the *Itinerary Through Wales* was written Richard de Clare, Earl of Pembroke, set out with his Marcher Lords to invade Ireland in the last of the Norman conquests; and it was from castles in South Wales that he and his private adventurers went forth. His chain-clad knights were supported by archers, whose skill was then the speciality of Wales, and it was these campaigns which earned him the soubriquet of "Strongbow".

The first mention of the use of massed archery by the English comes from Sussex, where in 1216 more than a thousand bowmen harassed the army of the French Dauphin Lewis and the rebel barons as they marched through the Weald; but it is not until 1298 that a really efficient use of archery in a great pitched battle was employed by an English king. This was at the Battle of Falkirk, where we are told that the greatest proportion of the king's soldiers were Welsh bowmen. However, before we discuss this battle in greater detail mention must be made of a great landmark in the history of English archery, the Assize of Arms of 1252.

THE ASSIZE OF ARMS

This statute directed that in a time of national emergency Commissioners of Array could select and impress men to serve as paid soldiers in the royal ranks. After ordering that the richer yeomanry who owned a hundred shillings in land should come to the host with steel cap, buff-coat, lance and sword,

Adam the forester is shot by a poacher. This drawing, taken from a roundel in the thirteenth-century miracle windows in Canterbury Cathedral, shows an unusual pattern of bow with sharply backward curving limbs. Artist's licence may have distorted the usual short and stiff contour of a Saxon-type bow, on the other hand there is a possibility that a primitive composite bow was used as a pattern.

FVR·FVGIE ·TS· GVTTV· R·PFORATIN SEQVENTIS·

Ladies using the bow in hunting scenes of the early fourteenth century. The weapons they are using appear to be fairly short and powerful self-wood bows.

the document proceeds to command "that all who own more than forty and less than a hundred shillings in land come bearing a sword and a bow with arrows and a dagger". Similarly, citizens with chattels worth more than nine marks and less than twenty are to be arrayed with bow, arrows and a sword. Even poor men with less than forty shillings in land or nine marks in chattels

should bring bows and arrows. By these means England obtained a reserve of amateur soldiers upon which she was able to draw for service in all her wars until the age of Napoleon. The Statute of Winchester of 1252 was the first official recognition of the importance of the bow in warfare, a great advance which was to prove of inestimable importance during the next two or three hundred years; and it was a welcome contrast to the earlier Assize of Arms of 1181, which did not mention the bow at all.

THE BATTLE OF FALKIRK

Edward I was an able soldier, and capable in devising new methods of war. His long experience in Welsh campaigns led him to introduce the scientific use of archery, much as had William the Conqueror at Hastings. The Battle of Falkirk, July 22nd, 1298, was the first engagement of real importance in which the bowmen, properly supplemented by cavalry, played a leading role. Edward's campaigns in Scotland alternately succeeded and failed according to the manner in which the English army was handled by its leaders. After a number of engagements Edward marched into Lothian, storming the

A Welsh archer of the thirteenth century; his elm bow is crude, but stout and powerful.

Medieval iron arrow-heads from the broad-bladed pre-conquest types to the solid, compact head of the Middle Ages, and barbed forms for hunting.

John Gower, the fifteenth-century poet, using a powerful looking long-bow and heavy barbed arrows.

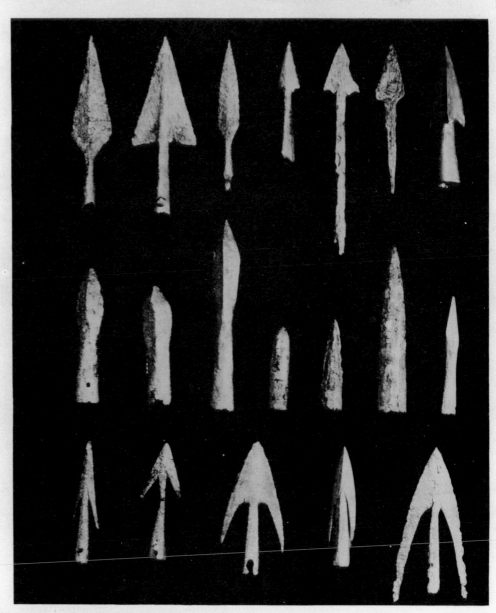

A gruesome medical reference chart used by military surgeons of the Middle Ages to indicate a variety of wounds and the vulnerability of the body to a selection of weapons likely to be encountered in battle. Note the arrow and quarrel wounds.

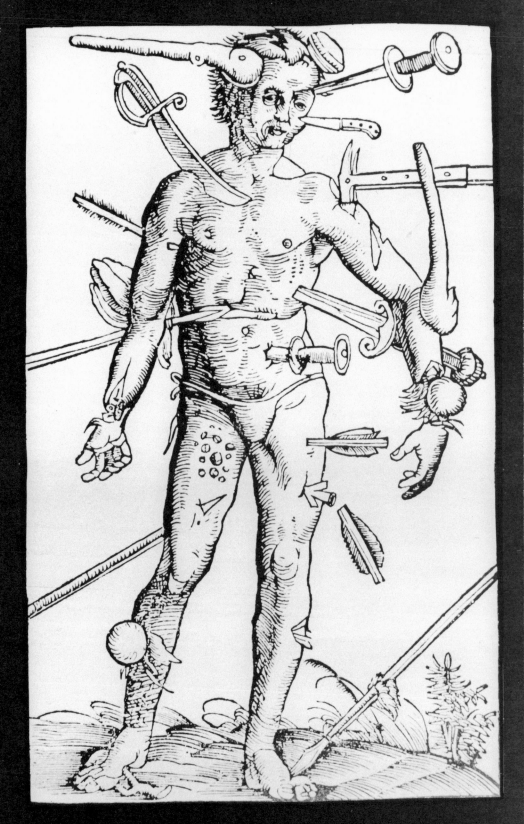

The accustomed method for dealing with barbed arrow-heads lodged in the flesh was to withdraw them in continuance of the direction in which they entered the body. This remained standard medical practice until the nineteenth century and was used by US Army surgeons during the Indian wars.

few castles which were defended against him. He spent so much time in this shire that his provisions began to run low and no more could be procured from the wasted countryside.

Wallace had gathered all Scotland to his banner and had withdrawn to the great forest of Torwood between Falkirk and Stirling. When Edward received news of the proximity of the Scots he decided to press his famine-stricken army on towards the enemy. Eventually the English came in sight of Wallace and his army occupying a strong position on a hillside about two miles south of Falkirk. Their front was protected by a broad morass; the Scots pikemen were arrayed in four great "schiltrons", and behind them were the thousand men-at-arms who composed Wallace's cavalry. On each flank and between the "schiltrons" were several thousand archers armed with the short bow. Wallace had fully deployed his troops and was prepared for a thoroughly defensive battle.

Edward drew up his men in three "battles", and almost immediately two cavalry corps began advancing simultaneously, skirting the morass from left and right in wide detours. These two masses of careering knights executed a headlong charge against each of the Scottish flanks. Wallace's archers were ridden down and scattered and his thousand men-at-arms rode off the field without striking a blow for Scotland, but the great "schiltrons" of pikemen flung back the rush of horsemen. This was the decisive moment of the day and Edward was quick to grasp the situation. The knights were ordered to halt and the bowmen were brought forward. They were ordered to concentrate their fire on fixed points in the enemy masses, and very soon they began to make a fearful slaughter. Then the command came for the knights to charge for the second time, and the rest of the fight was little more than a massacre—the survivors scattered into the woods, many thousands were killed and many more were drowned in the River Carron.

An archer of A.D. 1400 from a design, originally produced for a rifle shooting trophy, by Benjamin Wyon the medallist. This has been adopted by the Grand National Archery Society as their emblem.

The lessons of Falkirk were simple and very similar to those of Hastings: that even the best of infantry, if unsupported by cavalry and placed in a position that might be turned on the flanks, could not hope to withstand a judicious combination of archers and horsemen. According to many historians Robert the Bruce served on the English side at Falkirk; whether this is true or not he doubtless learned important lessons at this time which were to stand him in good stead at Bannockburn some sixteen years later. Whenever the English and Scots met in battle for the next two centuries the characteristics of the conflict at Falkirk were repeated—Halidon Hill, Neville's Cross, Homildon and Flodden were all variations on the same theme. The English longbowman might well boast that he "carried twelve Scots lives at his girdle".

BANNOCKBURN

King Edward I—"The Hammer of the Scots"—had long coveted the Scottish kingdom. After he had destroyed the Scottish army at Falkirk the country seemed to be at his mercy. Wallace was captured and executed in London in 1305, and Scotland was occupied from end to end. Whilst a foreign garrison lay in every town from Annan to Dingwall, Robert the Bruce was crowned King of Scots in 1306 at Scone; and in the following year Edward

The only guaranteed specimen of a medieval arrow, discovered in recent years in the Chapter House of Westminster Abbey. It measures 30½ in. long and still has an arrowhead in place.

This sketch map shows, diagramatically, the progress of the Battle of Bannockburn over two days, the 23rd and 24th of June 1314. (Not to scale.)

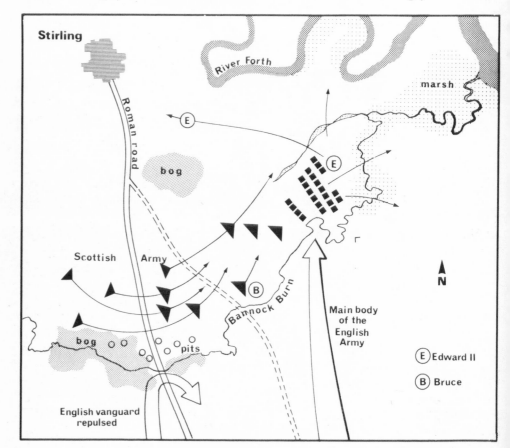

An illustration from *The Dress and Habits of the
People of England* (1796–9) by Joseph Strutt,
showing hunting habits of the thirteenth century.
The hunting bow of this period was probably
somewhat shorter than the one depicted and it was
in general use by country folk.

II succeeded to the English throne. The English domination in Scotland depended on the defence of a series of impregnable castles and strongholds. An average castle garrison would not much exceed a hundred fighting men comprising men-at-arms, archers and crossbowmen; but, providing it were adequately provisioned, such a garrison presented a formidable obstacle. Lochmaben, for instance, an important strategic point on the Annadale route, contained fourteen men-at-arms, sixty-five archers and twenty-five crossbowmen—yet it held out for years against the sporadic rampages of Edward Bruce, the brother of Robert. Stirling Castle was under siege from Lent until Midsummer in 1313 and it was only failure of provisions that forced its governor, Sir Philip Mowbray, to enter into a compact to surrender the place by June 24th, 1314, if by that time no army had come to his relief. At about this time Edward II was contemplating an advance into Scotland at the following Midsummer. By June 24th Stirling must be "rescued by battle" or it would have to surrender. Edward made up his mind to strike a blow which should not only relieve Stirling but finally crush the Scottish insurrection. By all rules and proper calculations the English host should have wiped the Scots off the ground. Estimates place the strength of Edward's army at approximately 20,000 including 3,000 heavily armed cavalry and a contingent of about 17,000 archers and foot. Bruce's followers could not have numbered more than 5,500 trained men. The result should have been a walk-over, but the example of Falkirk had been disregarded and no advance had been made in combining horse and foot, lance and bow. This was a mental gap which had never been bridged; if the horse were repulsed, all were repulsed and mere foot-soldiers were ripe for slaughter. This was not so with the Scots; each man felt that he had an equal chance and was of equal importance. It was a simple democratic army pitted against a much greater feudal assemblage of military might whose separate units enjoyed no real cohesion. The Scottish soldier had to provide himself with a protective basinet for his head, and a padded coat as protection against arrows. The archers had to provide, in addition, a long-bow and twenty-four arrows. The English were similarly equipped but the Scots had the advantage of time for combined training.

Bruce's forces lay astride the Falkirk–Stirling road with the Bannock burn or stream as a natural obstacle. This position was extremely well chosen: it covered Stirling and forced Edward either to attack frontally on ground unsuitable for heavy cavalry or to risk the left flank which was rough going for horse and dominated by the Scots' position. On the afternoon of June 23rd Edward decided on a frontal attack, and the "Great Van" of the English advanced across the Bannock burn, only to be driven back in disorder by the Scots. Bruce wisely called off any pursuit and re-manned his defences. A second attack by the English cavalry on the left flank was similarly repulsed, and the Scots stood firm. On the following day Edward planned a massed advance on Stirling; he was sure that Bruce, so inferior in numbers, would never dare leave his chosen position to attack him. However, low morale, lack of proper rations and the fact that the English had to spend an uncomfortable night in a "deep, wet, evil marsh" provided the ideal conditions for an attack from Bruce. "Now's the time and now's the hour, and Scotland shall be free" cried Sir Alexander Seton, and Bruce decided to attack at first light.

June 24th dawned fine and sunny, and the Scots advanced to within a few hundred yards of the English. Edward's bowmen drove off the few Scottish archers who covered the advance, and the Earl of Gloucester immediately ordered a cavalry charge. Both sides now became locked together so that archery support was impossible. The initial charge was broken and turned in confusion back into the main body. The Scots pressed on and engaged the whole army in a long, stern fight. At last the English managed to deploy a body of archers on the Scottish left flank and their arrows began to take effect. Bruce, seeing the danger, at once ordered a small body of mounted knights to drive them from the field, a manoeuvre they accomplished with complete success. The archers were badly cut up and decisively put out of action, some sheering off altogether, others rushing back upon their friends, who also swept them from their way in their eagerness to get forward. On these the Scottish archers, no longer outranged, now played with effect and, for once in their history, they had the field to themselves. The Bruce pressed relentlessly on, and the English archers in the rear found targets in the backs of their own troops rather than the Scots. With the retreat of their king the English began to disintegrate; the exuberant Scots pursued the defeated army, and the victory was complete. "The foe is chasit, the battell is done ceiss". At last the English learned the vital lesson; and later, on the fields of France, they showed, in their use of foot and archers in preference to the charging column of knights, how deep that lesson had been driven. "Poitiers and Agincourt were won under the rock of Stirling" said one historian, with very sound reasoning.

MEDIEVAL BOWS AND ARROWS

We can reconstruct, with absolute certainty, the bows and arrows of the Middle Ages, for a number of contemporary writings describe the equipment of the medieval archer in detail, in addition to giving vivid accounts of the sort of wound he could expect to inflict. One legal account, prepared at the turn of the fourteenth century, deals with an enquiry into the murder of Simon de Skeftington; it records how he received a fatal wound from an iron arrow-head tipping a thirty-three inch shaft of ash shot from a yew bow

An incident in 1418 when the
Earl of Warwick won two great
carracks in a sea fight. The picture
is full of interest. It was not
unusual for longbows, cross-bows
and cannon to be used in the
same engagement.

five feet seven inches long. The wound measured three inches long by two inches wide and was six inches deep, a terrible gash testifying to the effectiveness of medieval archery. The arrow was fletched with peacock feathers—not the gorgeous eye feathers from the tail but the stouter brownish-grey wing feathers which were highly regarded but naturally scarcer than the wing of the grey goose.

The English medieval war arrow, traditionally known as the "cloth-yard" although there is no evidence that it was so called before 1465, was perhaps produced in greater numbers than any other type of arrow in history. During the fourteenth and fifteenth centuries war or the threat of war occurred every four or five years, and amongst contemporary records can be found some clue as to the enormous quantities of arrows produced. For instance, on January 30th, 1356, King Edward III instructed fourteen sheriffs to supply, amongst other things, no less than 9,000 sheaves of arrows (a sheaf being 24 arrows); and in 1350 William de Rothwell was ordered to buy 240,000 good arrows and 24,000 best arrows. The Attiliator, who was the forerunner of a long line of Master Generals of Ordnance, was directed in 1338 to buy 1,000 bows, 4,000 bowstrings and 4,000 sheaves of arrows, no doubt in preparation for one of the many French campaigns, possibly Sluys or even Crécy eight years later. These enormous stocks of arrows and bows and other warlike materials were stored in the Tower of London and other fortresses, and were supplied on the King's directions to equip his troops as and when they were called up for service.

As an efficient weapon of war, capable of being mass-produced at low cost, the arrow proved itself over a long period. It was remarkably well made, considering the fact that it was expendable. A specification for production or measure of control over quality appears in 1405, when regulations for making serviceable arrow-heads were issued by Henry IV. This seems to be an indication that the standard had become poor and in fact there are recorded instances of bad materials and indifferent workmanship, benefiting only the war profiteer. The general pattern of construction does not seem to have varied much over a very long period, and we can date with some accuracy the material relics of these arrows—of which unfortunately only the heads remain, the shafts and fletchings having long rotted away.

MILITARY ARROW-HEADS

Early types of military arrow-heads had a broad, flat blade with a prominent shoulder, but by the thirteenth century a more compact type had appeared, a logical reduction in size as a result of the development of body armour. The trend was to produce an arrow with more penetrative power and the ultimate result was the famous Bodkin point—a square-sectioned chisel-ended arrow-head capable of piercing the stoutest leather, fine mail and even plate armour. The heads were made of iron, forged in one piece which included the socket and, complete with fletched shaft, cost fourteen pence per garb (sheaf) in 1341; without the shaft and feathers they were five-a-penny. The medieval war effort was a well-organised affair, and the arrowsmiths and fletchers had three distinct methods of disposing of their production. They could produce their wares and sell them as independent craftsmen, they could contract to sell their goods at an agreed price, or, on occasion, they were impressed to work at "the king's wages". Under the last arrangement William Lory, an arrow-head maker of the fifteenth century, was paid the princely sum of fourpence per day.

The length of the military arrow of the Middle Ages has never been satisfactorily decided although there exist many estimates. From the wealth of rather inconclusive evidence as to the length of these shafts only a generalisation seems to emerge. Out of all the millions of arrows that must have been made we have only one guaranteed relic to examine, 30½ inches long and found in the Chapter House of Westminster Abbey. This isolated example, interesting though it is, cannot be taken as a pattern for all arrows, and we must be content with an average length of between 28 and 36 inches. Suffice it to say that these arrows did their deadly work well and it matters only to an antiquary whether their lengths varied or conformed to a standard. Invariably there were three feathers to a shaft equally spaced, those from the goose being most common. These were tough, durable and cheap (1s 9d for as many as 4,000, according to one record) and, what was more important, they were in plentiful supply. The methods of fixing were binding, adhesion or a combination of both and they were left long, six to eight inches, to steady the stout shaft with its heavy point. They were usually cut straight and angular but the shape probably varied with the fletcher employed.

THE YEOMAN ARCHER

There is no doubt that the military archer of those turbulent days had confidence in his weapon and its missile, and this confidence must have contributed in no small way to the success of the campaigns which followed each other with relentless regularity in the reigns of Edward III and Henry V. What of the good yeoman "whose limbs were made in England"? Contemporary chronicles instruct us as to his liabilities for military service, his pay, the conditions of the campaigns in which he was involved, and, not least, his courage and enterprise. Lightly accoutred and unhampered by body armour or war horses, the archer of the fourteenth and fifteenth centuries was extremely mobile and could be deployed and re-deployed with ease. There were no problems of logistics or complicated manoeuvres confronting the commander of a body of medieval bowmen; movement was limited only by terrain and the speed of marching, or at best, by a furious dash from one battle position to another. The advance over corpse-strewn battlefields was not hampered by the military problem of lengthening lines of communication because, when further supplies of ammunition were required, arrows were hastily drawn from poor wretches who were already half-dead, as well as from corpses and the ground. For service as an archer in the fourteenth century the maximum daily pay was sixpence, and this was paid to troops from Cheshire, those coming from Flintshire in North Wales only receiving threepence. This may be the origin of the saying "There's many a good bow besides one in Chester". In action the archer would string his bow, keeping a spare bowstring handy for use in emergency, shake out his arrows and stick a few in the ground before him ready for use, then raise the bow and draw the shaft right back to his ear or breast. When he had exhausted his usefulness with a bow, he discarded it and fell to with hand-to-hand weapons. The Prince Louis Napoleon once said, "A first-rate English archer who, in a single minute, was unable to draw and discharge his bow twelve times, with a range of 240 yards, and who in these twelve shots once missed his man, was very lightly esteemed."

THE HUNDRED YEARS WAR

The reign of Edward III began in 1327 amid the darkest intrigue, with the grisly murder of Edward II a recent memory and with an inheritance of unrest in Scotland and enmity with France. It was during this reign that the most glorious period of the English long-bow commenced—the Hundred Years War. Described by Froissart* as a series of plundering expeditions by four generations of Englishmen, this conflict between England and France was never really concluded. No general peace treaty was signed and the English sovereign did not formally renounce his claim to the throne of the Valois and the Bourbons until the Peace of Amiens in 1802.

The factors which precipitated two great nations into a long, expensive and wearying war were complex. Edward's last possession in Gascony was coveted by the French king, who constantly aided the Scots in their own struggle against the English. In addition, Edward could not brook the French predominance in Flanders where important trade interests were centred affecting the export of English grown wool. At sea the English and French traders were perpetually cutting one another's throats. This all festered into a deep antagonism which could only break out in war, and preparations for the inevitable conflict were started in England. The freemen had compulsorily

*FROISSART, SIR JOHN, *Chronicles of England, France, Spain, and the Adjoining Countries*, trans. Thomas Johnes (1839)

been organised for training in military service on the principle of the Saxon Fyrd, brought up to date by the Assize of Arms. Edward made this campaign a national one. He raised an army by indentures made with local leaders under which they recruited, at agreed rates of pay, the precise number and types of fighting men required. The contingents thus raised were known as "retinues". An earl would contract to raise, say, sixty men-at-arms of whom ten should be knights and 120 bowmen, all equipped and with horses, for three months to a year "at the accustomed wages of war".

The long-bow was the prescribed weapon of the rank and file, and the archer rapidly grew in importance; the Muster Rolls of the Arrays of 1339 for the various counties in England show that archers already formed exactly half the foot soldiery, and in later years this proportion increased. The king himself was to be accompanied abroad by a bodyguard of personal knights and archers and a band of minstrels and for their services to morale these royal musicians ranked as archers. Everything was prepared, and now the most formidable and efficient invasion force history had yet seen gathered under its bright pavilions and banners in the Cinque Ports, ready to follow Edward to France in order that the claims and ambitions of the English throne could be decided in bloody conflict.

THE ENGAGEMENT AT SLUYS

Edward III's army set sail across the Channel, and the first notable action of the war was fought at sea off Sluys, a battle of nine hours, the course of which was to pave the way to the conquest of France. Forty thousand men awaited the arrival of the English fleet, including massed Genoese crossbow-

The Arms of Peace and the Arms of War of the Black Prince on his tomb in Canterbury. Those on the left are the famous Prince of Wales' feathers, the Arms of Peace which, by tradition, were won from the King of Bohemia at Crécy. The Arms of War on the right are the royal arms of England with the label of the firstborn son. The motto, with which Edward signed his name, reads "*Houmout*" and "*Ich dien*" –"High spirit" and "I serve".

men and men-at-arms, filling upwards of a hundred and twenty vessels and outnumbering the English by four to one. King Edward's ships fairly bristled with archers who, shooting from the ships at long range, cleared the shores and covered the invading troops. "This battle was very murderous and horrible," said Froissart; "archers and crossbowmen shot with all their might at each other and the men-at-arms engaged hand to hand . . ." The *Christopher*, which had been taken from the English the year before, was recaptured and the English "manned her again with archers, and sent her to fight the Genoese". The French fleet was defeated, and the following day the English king landed quietly in Flanders, ambitious and confident, and prepared to do further battle after having gained the first victory of the Hundred Years War.

For several years there was intermittent warfare on the frontiers of Gascony, without any decisive result, during which the archer gained in stature as a fighting man. From the experience of Scottish wars the army chiefs of Edward III had shaped a new method of warfare, combining the archer and the feudal knight in a single unit of battle, formidable alike for its missiles and its sword-play. When the archer's true value became fully recognised he was often supplied with defensive armour and a horse, so that the whole army of mounted infantry could scour through France on their raids. But all from king to scullion would dismount to fight if the occasion demanded.

In the spring of 1346 the English army was reconstituted, and new, carefully chosen levies, including 12,000 archers, landed at St Vaast in Normandy in July. The landing was forced under the cover of a rain of arrows which, once more, drove off the massed crossbowmen lining the quays of Cadzand Haven. There was a sharp fight on shore and the archers were posted on the flanks to protect the main body. The Bastard of Flanders charged the English but was completely routed by the irresistible hail of arrows from the flanks. The object now was the capture of Paris, and the English army thrust on to St Denis, where they were repulsed by the whole might of France. The retreat of Edward's forces over the Somme, where at Blanchetaque his archers again proved more than a match for the unfortunate Genoese crossbowmen, was the prelude to what Churchill has described as one of the four supreme achievements of the British Army—the Battle of Crécy.*

THE BATTLE OF CRÉCY

It is possible to stand today on the very mound used by King Edward as his command post, and the course of the battle of August 26th can be plotted

*CHURCHILL, WINSTON S., *A History of the English Speaking Peoples*, Vol. 1 (1956). The other three achievements were Blenheim, Waterloo and the final advance in the last summer of the Great War. (Written in 1939)

The Battle of Crécy. Sketch map showing the disposition of the French and English armies early on the morning of August 26th, 1346. Today the battlefield is essentially as it was in the fourteenth century. The small cross in the lower part of the sketch plan indicates the site of the memorial to the blind King of Bohemia who was slain in the battle.

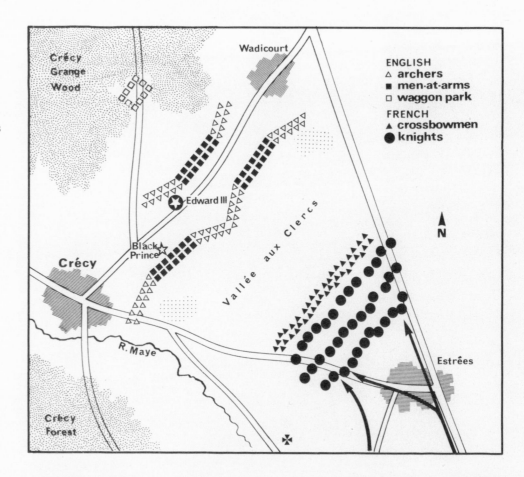

over fields which have hardly changed since 1346. The mound, on which there was a little windmill, stood on a low ridge facing south-west between the villages of Crécy and Wadicourt. Behind lay a wood—the Bois de Crécy-Grange—which, with the forest of Crécy on the right, provided cover in case of need. The ground sloped gently towards the Vallée aux Clercs* and to a track which led from the wood to the south-east, still known as le Chemin de L'Armée, along which the French army would presently advance.

More than half of Edward's 13,000 men were archers, added to which he could count on some 3,000 knights and men-at-arms. The marshals deployed the latter in three divisions, two of which were stationed a little way down the forward slope of the ridge, the remainder being held in reserve. The archers with Welsh spearmen in support, were arranged as four projecting salients on both flanks of each of the two forward divisions. This formation was described as a "herce" or harrow, from its rough similarity in pattern to that implement. In front the archers hammered in iron-pointed stakes and dug pot-holes to protect themselves from cavalry. Such a formation was calculated to force the attackers into two narrowing gulleys where they would have to contend with the English armour while being raked by arrows from the flanks.

*So named after the clerks compiled their casualty lists after the battle.

An early nineteenth-century representation of the Battle of Crécy at the height of the action, looking from the French left flank positions. Note the windmill, Edward III's observation post.

The sixteen-year-old Prince of Wales, later more familiarly known as the Black Prince, who had just received the accolade of knighthood from King Edward, was in titular command of one of the divisions; before the day was out he was to undergo his first major experience of battle and learn a military lesson which would eventually be put to good advantage when he commanded his own army. When all was ready the English waited and watched the vast French host slowly appear and take up their positions in the Vallée aux Clercs. The French army outnumbered the English by three to one and careful estimates give us a total of 40,000 men made up of men-at-arms, mercenaries, foreign notabilities and their personal followers, and the provincial levies. The mercenaries consisted mainly of some 6,000 crossbowmen from Genoa, who had already suffered heavily at the hands of the English archers during the past two days' fighting. The principal allies of the French included the gallant near-blind King of Bohemia, who was to be slain in the thick of battle and whose feathers were to become the personal emblem of the Prince of Wales; the turncoat brother of King Edward, John, Count of Hainault; King James I of Majorca; the Duke of Savoy; and various German mercenaries, all with their personal contingents of fighting men.

The vast French column moved on without proper control. The divisions were never properly sorted out from the start—still less towards the end of a long march—and contradictory orders of changes of direction, countermanded and then repeated, resulted in complete disorder. King Philip took command and, expecting the arrival of reinforcements, decided to halt while his footsore and weary main body rested and reorganized. But his commands were only partly obeyed. Impulsive French knights, supremely confident, ignored the order and pushed forward. The Genoese, who were in front, were jostled forward and had no option but to advance on the English in a hopelessly ragged formation. They slowly crossed the valley and started to ascend the slope until they were about 150 yards from the point where the English still waited. Now the story is taken up by Jean Froissart* in his lively chronicle: "During this time a heavy rain fell, accompanied by thunder and a very terrible eclipse of the sun; and before this rain a great flight of crows hovered in the air over all the battalions, making a loud noise; shortly afterwards it cleared up, and the sun shone very bright; but the French had it in their faces, and the English on their backs. When the Genoese were somewhat in order they approached the English and set up a loud shout, in order to frighten them; but the English remained quite quiet and did not seem to attend to it. Then they set up a second shout, and advanced a little forward; the English never moved. Still they hooted a third time, advancing with their crossbows presented, and began to shoot. The English archers then advanced one step

*FROISSART, SIR JOHN, ibid.

forward and shot their arrows with such force and quickness that it seemed as if it snowed. When the Genoese felt these arrows, which pierced through their armour, some of them cut the strings of their crossbows, others flung them to the ground, and all turned about and retreated quite discomfited.

"The French had a large body of men-at-arms on horseback to support the Genoese, and the king, seeing them fall back, cried out, 'kill me those scoundrels, for they stop up our road without any reason'. The English continued shooting, and some of their arrows falling among the horsemen, drove them upon the Genoese, so that they were both in such confusion, they could never rally again."

Assault after assault was launched by the French and a bitter hand-to-hand battle took place, but the English stood firm, the archers sending vast numbers of arrows into the mêlée and the Welsh and Cornishmen creeping forward with knives to butcher great numbers of dismounted French knights and men-at-arms who were wounded or rolling helplessly amid the press in their heavy armour. The English knights stood their ground and inflicted great losses on those of the enemy who managed to break through to their lines. One such party of French knights managed to get close to the young Prince of Wales and his safety being thus threatened a knight was sent to the king to ask for his assistance. King Edward, hearing that his son was not wounded or unhorsed, made his historic reply: "Let the boy win his spurs"; and the battle continued until nightfall. Soon after midnight the bitterly disappointed French king, himself wounded in the face by an arrow, was persuaded to leave the field, admitting the utter defeat of the might of France. Fifteen or sixteen assaults had failed and the flower of the chivalry of France lay dead on the field of battle; amongst them was the blind King of Bohemia, the reins of his bridle tied to those of his knights with whom he had charged. The remainder of the French melted away in the darkness; but there was no pursuit, for the English king, who had never once lost grip of the battle, had forbidden his men to break ranks. While the English losses were astonishingly light, the French were said to have lost 10,000 including no less than 1,542 knights and men-at-arms and eighty standards. As a permanent memorial to this battle Edward founded the Most Noble Order of the Garter, dedicated to St George and consisting of the king and twenty-four of his most renowned knights. For the badge of this illustrious Order the king chose a lady's garter dropped by mischance at a ball at Calais by the loveliest woman in England, the princess Joan of Kent, the wife of the Earl of Salisbury.

MOBILISATION AND TRAINING

After this decisive victory, due primarily to the mutual support of archers and men-at-arms under the brilliant generalship of King Edward, the road to

Calais lay open to the English, and they moved on sacking and burning the towns they passed on the way. An historic advance in the tactics of battle had been made and, to a large extent, the fortunes of England now depended on the provision of an inexhaustible supply of ready-trained archers. To this end the people of England were enjoined to practise with the long-bow so as to be ready in time of need. The practice at the butts behind the churchyard became the chief sport and excitement of village life, and Edward III, knowing the value of such training, encouraged it by royal proclamations insisting on regular archery practice under pain of fine or imprisonment. An example of such a statute was the one directed to the sheriffs of the counties of England in 1369, which read: ". . . . Cause public proclamation to be made that every-one of the said city [London], strong in body, at leisure times on holidays, use in their recreations bows and arrows . . . . . and learn and exercise the art of shooting; forbidding all and singular on our behalf, that they do not after any manner apply themselves to the throwing of stones, wood, iron, hand-ball, foot-ball, bandy-ball, cambuck or cockfighting, nor such other like vain plays, which have no profit in them or concern themselves therein, under pain of imprisonment. Witness the king at Westminster, the twelfth day of June."

In these times there was thus a formidable militia at the height of its efficiency which could be called out as required. From this large body of armed and half-armed freemen, a Commission of Array addressed to each shire picked a force to wage war overseas. First came conscription, eked out with volunteers, but as the French war went on the principle of compulsion was abandoned in favour of hiring private "companies" of professional warriors. These were long service soldiers, enlisted for pay by some noble or knight with whom the king could contract for their services, paying as much as half-a-year's wages in advance. Such a force was raised for a series of raids in France during the years 1355–7 (known as the Black Prince's "Grand Chevauchée"), a new phase in the Hundred Years War during which the prince found himself face to face with the French army at Poitiers. He could count on 2,000 of these dreaded bowmen, who represented about half of the total force under his command. The remainder of the English army was under the command of his brother, John of Gaunt, Duke of Lancaster, and the plan to join forces with him had miscarried. However, after a brilliantly executed tactical plan, which featured a strong archery support to cavalry charges, the day was again won by the English.

By this victory vast possessions in France were acquired and the French King John was ransomed for 3,000,000 gold crowns. Before the battle the Black Prince addressed his archers thus: "You have made it plain that you are the worthy sons and kinsmen of those for whom, under the leadership of my father and ancestors, the kings of England, no labour was too great, no place invincible, no mountain inaccessible, no tower impregnable, no host too

Opposite: the Battle of Poitiers, 1356, from a medieval illustration. The longbowmen press home their advantage and actively engage the enemy cavalry. Special targets were the horses, which the riders were unable to control if they sustained arrow wounds.

formidable . . . . . Honour and patriotism and the prospect of rich spoils of the French call you more than my words to follow in the footsteps of your fathers. Follow the standards, obey implicitly in body and mind the commands of your leaders. If victory shall see us alive we shall always continue in firm friendship together, being of one heart and mind. If envious fortune should decree, which God forbid, that in this present labour we must follow the final path of all flesh, your names will not be sullied with infamy and I and my comrades will drink the same cup with you." This royal recognition of the common bowman was indicative of the Black Prince's regard for the archer and his awareness of the great necessity of boosting morale before a battle, particularly when the odds were against his gaining the day.

JOHN DANCASTER, ARCHER

Up to this time King Edward had been kept busy in France by a long and arduous campaign. One incident which is worth retelling is the capture of the castle of Guines following the successful siege of Calais. The story, the principal character of which was one John Dancaster, an archer, was carefully chronicled by Geoffrey Baker;* it conveys the courage and resourcefulness of the hero as well as his licentiousness, which was only to be expected from a soldier of an expeditionary force of the fourteenth century. Dancaster had been captured by the French and, not being able to free himself by payment of the ransom demanded, was freed on condition that he worked among the French repairing the defences of Guines. Some of the occupying garrison of Calais meanwhile planned how they might overthrow the castle. Baker's chronicle goes on: "This fellow [Dancaster] chanced to lie with a laundress, a strumpet, and learned from her where there was a wall two feet broad stretching from the ramparts across to the edge of a ditch so that, being covered with water, it could not be seen . . . . . The archer (his harlot shewing it to him) measured the height of the [castle] wall with a thread." John Dancaster then made contact with those who wished to capture the castle and by using the secret information he had gained they planned to occupy the fortress by stealth. The plan was carried out and ". . . . they broke into the chambers and turrets upon the ladies and knights that lay there asleep, and so became masters of all that was within." The raiding party then released the English prisoners held there and bargained with the Earl of Guines for the purchase of the stronghold. John Dancaster and his private army of thirty dare-devils, being true patriots, would only surrender the keys to the King of England, which they did, ". . . the King of England bought it, indeed, and so had that place which he greatly desired."

*BAKER, GEOFFREY, *Chronicon Galfridi le Baker de Swynebroke*, Ed. by E. M. Thomson (1899)

Two archers of the fourteenth century preparing for action at the Battle of Newcastle. The bowman on the right is stringing his bow and his companion has a bow ready braced and the first arrow drawn from his quiver.

A military pass issued to William Jodrell, a Cheshire archer, who was on campaign with the Black Prince in France. He was allowed to return to England, possibly because of sickness. The translation reads: "Know all that we, the Prince of Wales, have given leave on the day of the date of this instrument, to William Jauderel, one of our archers, to go to England. In witness of this we have caused our seal to be placed on this bill. Given at Bordeaux, December 16th, in the year of grace 1355."

An exciting document which has survived since it was signed by the Black Prince on December 16th, 1355, is a leave of absence pass issued to William Jauderel, "one of our archers", authorising him to travel to England. The fact that a member of the rank and file was issued with a pass bearing the seal of the prince reveals his relative importance in the royal army. We also find that the Black Prince, although said to be ruthless as a commander, personally concerned himself with matters relating to the raising of archers, and in appreciation of the loyalty and prowess of the contingent of bowmen who came from Llantrisant, in South Wales, he gave to them and their heirs a large piece of land to be used as common pasture. The holders of this land became Freemen of the town and to this day such citizens are known as "The Black Bowmen of Llantrisant". Another grant of land, to encourage the young to practise archery for national defence, was made by Robert de Ufford, who fought at Crécy and Poitiers. He provided the villagers of Dedham in Suffolk with the "archery piece", and one of the ordinances of the Grammar School ran: "You shall allow your childe a bowe, shaftes, shootinge glove, brasser, and all things necessary to exercise shooting withall."

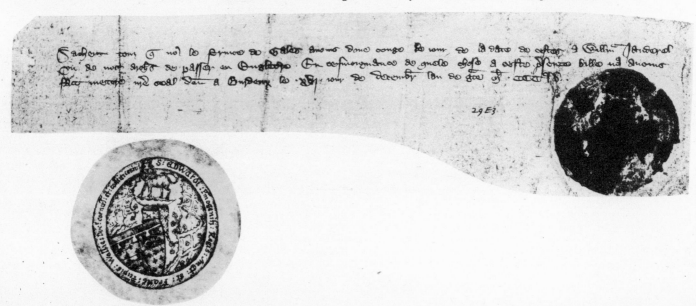

A fashionable bow-meeting c. 1835. The enthroned
figure in the tented pavilion is traditionally believed
to be Princess Victoria, shortly to become Queen.
The painting, by an unknown artist, is in the
possession of the Royal Toxophilite Society.

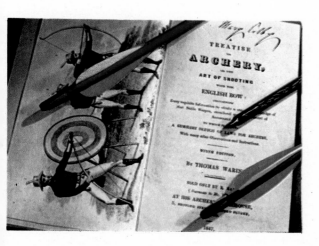

The last edition (1832) of Thomas Waring's
famous Treatise on Archery, with contemporary
ladies' target arrows.

Tametomo no Minamoto (1138–70), one of Japan's greatest archer-heroes. His bow was 8ft 6in long and very powerful. Many of his exploits are recorded in the legendary histories, in which he performs superhuman feats with bow and arrow.

A medieval pavise or shield of wood covered with hard leather and painted with the arms of the city of Ravensburg. This is of the type carried by pavisers to protect archers or crossbowmen.

During one of Edward III's many expeditions a young English soldier was taken prisoner by the French, and was subsequently freed, the King paying £16 towards his ransom. Previously employed as a page to Elizabeth, wife of the Duke of Clarence, the King's third son, he was to become the first great poet of the English language. His name was Geoffrey Chaucer. Following a career of diplomacy, and holding various official appointments and commissions, his life was spent close to the court and he spent much time in travelling abroad. Much of what he saw he used as material for his writings, and his portrait of a yeoman archer was certain to be accurate: ". . . . and in his hand he bar a mighty bowe" said Chaucer in the Prologue to his *Canterbury Tales*. "Upon his arm he bar a gay bracer . . . . A sheef of pecok arwes brighte and kene under his belt he bar ful thriftily: Well could he dresse his takel yemenly: His arwes drouped noght with fethers lowe." Chaucer was a keen observer, he knew the importance of keeping archery equipment—"takel" —in good order, and his mention of peacock feathers, listed sometimes in contemporary inventories, shows a critical insight into detail which another poet might have missed. It is also interesting to read in Chaucer's *Romaunt of the Rose* some reference to broad arrows which were "nokked and fethered a-right", as the notch in the end of an arrow is still known today as the "nock". His description of Turkish bows, which he must have examined carefully on a visit to foreign parts, is likewise accurate, and the detail would satisfy the most exacting of toxophilites.

The French were subjected to constant defeats by the indomitable longbowman and understandably they sought some form of defence from this terrible weapon. Increased body armour was soon penetrated by new designs of arrow-heads, and the once invincible cavalry charges were rendered impotent by the slaughter of horses in full tilt, falling victims to arrows with vicious, heavy points of steel. About the middle of the fourteenth century there appeared in battle the pavise, a specially designed form of shield carried by the French which, although somewhat cumbersome, gave some protection from the arrow hail. It became large enough to cover two men completely, the lower end resting on the ground and the upper supported by a prop or an attendant. The fashion for this particular contrivance spread and it was used by German, Spanish and English armies as well as by the French. It became a portable defence during siege operations for crossbowmen, who used its cover for their ponderous cocking and loading operations. However the pavise did not afford complete protection from skilfully placed longbowmen: cover from three sides and above would have been necessary to successfully neutralise English archery.

So the Hundred Years War dragged on, son following father at the butts to practise the skills of archery, each likely to be called up at any time for service overseas, each learning how to lay his body in the bow to coax the

In generacione ⁊ generacionem: an
nunciabimus laudem tuam.

Vi regis israel intende: qui
deducis uelut ouem ioseph.

Qui sedes super cherubin: manifesta
re coram effraym beniamin ⁊ manasse.

Excita potenciam tuam ⁊ ueni: ut
saluos facias nos.

Deus conuerte nos: ⁊ ostende faciem
tuam ⁊ salui erimus.

Domine deus uirtutum: quousque
irasceris super oracionem serui tui.

Cibabis nos pane lacrimarum: et
potum dabis nobis in lacrimis in

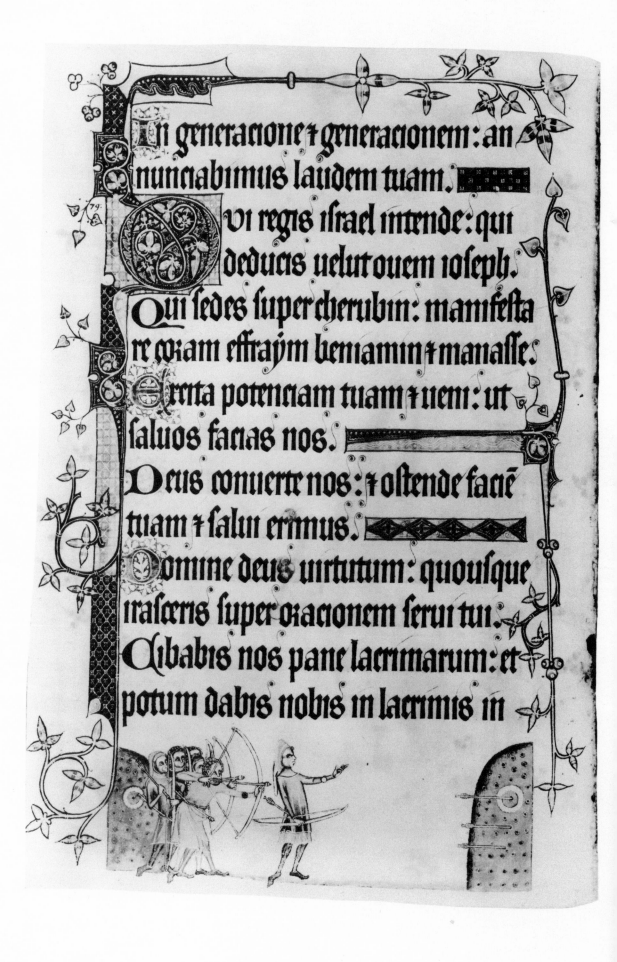

maximum length from each shot. Every minor aspect of technique was faithfully copied, and the handicraft of on-the-spot repairs to nock, string and shaft was eagerly assimilated by these practical English yeomen. The interminable expeditions and the consequent drag on the social structure of England by the incessant drain on resources of manpower and materials began to take its toll, and Richard II, recognising this war-weariness and anxious to enable the reserve of archers to be kept up to standard, ordained that no servant or labourer should have any arms other than bows and arrows. They were to practise with them on Sundays and they were to stop playing their favourite games. In addition the authorities kept a watchful eye on bowyers, stringers and fletchers, as the safety of England depended on the availability and the reliability of their wares. Henry IV had trouble with arrowsmiths who made broadheads of inferior metal, and during Richard III's reign at least one stringer was brought to court to answer for his "false and deceptive bow-strings . . .".

THE BATTLE OF SHREWSBURY

On July 21st, 1403, was fought "the sorry battaille of Schrovesbury between Englysshemen and Englysshemen", described by a French chronicler as "a battle unparalleled in history". It was certainly one of the decisive battles of the Middle Ages, deciding which should be the reigning family for the next sixty years. Henry IV had marched north with his army, having agreed to help the Earl of Northumberland to repel the Scots. By the time he reached Burton he was dismayed to learn that the Earl had turned against him and had taken sides with the Welsh chieftain Owen Glendower, and that they planned to join forces with the Earl's son, Harry Hotspur, in the vicinity of Shrewsbury. The King's son, later to become Henry V, was dangerously isolated at Shrewsbury with a force which had been carrying out a raid in North Wales. There was but one course open to the King; he must march with all speed to the help of his son, and this he did, just in time to prevent Hotspur from breaking into the town.

The two armies drew up in full view of one another, but beyond bow-shot, on the ground now known as the Battlefield, and after a pause during which the Abbot of Shrewsbury failed to negotiate a peaceful settlement, they engaged one another with the long-bow. As soon as the King's archers came within range the skilful bowmen from Cheshire let fly their deadly shafts; the royalists answered in kind, but, after a fierce exchange, broke ranks and streamed away down the hill. Hotspur, quick to see his advantage, sent his men-at-arms in pursuit. A general mêlée ensued, during which the Prince received an arrow in the face; and a little later in the course of this indescribable confusion, Hotspur, perspiring with the heat of battle, raised his vizor for air

116

and fell, his brain transfixed with an arrow sped by an unknown hand. The news spread with the inevitable result; the rebel line gave way and they quitted the field. While "the dead lay as thick as the leaves in Autumn" a merciless pursuit of the survivors was launched by Henry, and the victory was complete.

Ten years after the Battle of Shrewsbury, on Passion Sunday, while snow and sleet fell outside, Prince Hal was crowned Henry V, King of England and France and Lord of Ireland, in Westminster Abbey. Very soon it became clear that he was beginning to deceive himself into the fixed belief that he was the rightful heir to the throne of France. He followed his star with unfaltering courage. This arrogance, this sublime faith in his own triumphant destiny, protected him from ever realising the futility of his conquests, which were indirectly to lose his own son the throne of England. Henry V will always go down in history as a great soldier. His own sense of destiny did not hamper his actions or muddle the decisiveness of his thoughts. "Fair stood the wind for France"—now was the time to claim the heritage of the English throne, and Henry, reviving Edward III's pretensions to the French crown, set sail for Normandy in the year 1415.

Earlier the King had quietly prepared for the invasion of France while he pretended to negotiate with the Burgundians and Armagnac. France was broken by civil war while these two great factions see-sawed in and out of power, and each had offered various proposals to Henry in answer to his territorial and sovereign claims. While ambassadors passed from country to country, arrows and bows were being cut at top speed in London, barrels of brimstone were being stored in Poultney's Inn and at the Tower, and smiths were casting cannon. Every kind of steel instrument with which a man might maim or kill his fellows, every kind of ram, tower, pontoon and engine was being made. Ships were being repaired and built, oaks were being felled, nails and rigging prepared, foreign ships stolen and impressed. Writs were issued to master craftsmen, sheriffs and landowners ordering the supply of every war-like commodity. Such an order was sent to Nicholas Frost, bowyer, who was to provide, at the King's charge, workmen to make and repair bows and to collect wood from any place he liked except from land belonging to the Church. Frost, together with five other bowyers and a group of fletchers, eventually accompanied the expedition to France as part of the King's retinue of specialists, tradesmen and personal household.

War was a costly business, for the old days of feudal military service were gone. Henry had to pay his soldiers wages in addition to bearing the cost of sea-transport for man and beast. The range of wages varied according to the status of the men. A duke was given 13s 4d a day, an earl 6s 8d, a knight 2s; men-at-arms and archers had a sliding scale of 4s, 2s, 1s and 6d, which were comparatively decent wages when one considered that a skilled artisan then

The Battle of Shrewsbury, 1403,
between Henry IV and Sir Henry
Percy. Both sides employed archers
and during this battle the famous
Hotspur was slain by an English
arrow which pierced his breast.

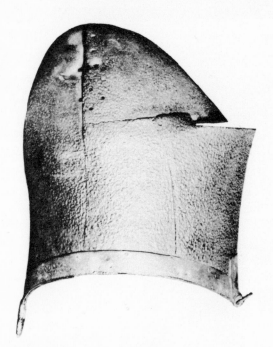

This helmet was, by tradition, worn by Henry V at Agincourt and for 500 years it has hung high over his tomb in Westminster Abbey, together with his shield and saddle. It was customary for the sovereign to wear a circlet of gold on his battle helm embellished with crosses and *fleurs-de-lis*. The dent in the helmet was caused by a blow from the Duke of Alençon during the battle.

drew a daily wage of only 5d. Beyond these expenses the King would have to pay for little else. Provisions were mainly taken from the conquered country and, according to old statutes, every man in England was compelled to have a certain amount of equipment always ready including a quilted coat, a helmet, gloves, a sword and a number of arrows and a bow. The protective clothing of the 8,000 archers in the English army was often limited to a leather jacket which sometimes, like those worn by crossbowmen, had plates of iron on the breast and at the elbows. A few archers, usually those who were mounted, had chain hauberks, and the black cloth jackets of others were lined with mail, but the majority of those who took part in the expedition of 1415 were without armour. It seems that most of them were also without the steel or chain skull-cap worn on previous campaigns, and wore instead conical hats made of boiled leather. All this vast army of men and their accoutrements, horses and wagons, cannon and other engines of war, were assembled at Porchester. Led by *The Trinity*, Henry's flagship, with the arms of St George, St Edward and England at her masthead, they finally sailed for a secret destination in France on Sunday, August 11th.

An early engraving of King Henry V (1387–1422), victor of Agincourt.

THE BATTLE OF AGINCOURT

The French expected the invasion at Boulogne but the King had secretly decided to make for Harfleur, an important port at the mouth of the Seine, within striking distance of Paris. Following a brisk engagement, not without serious loss to the English, the port of Harfleur fell to Henry, but the plan to advance on Paris became extremely hazardous due to a combination of various factors, and the King's War Council strongly recommended the return to England of the whole army. The season was getting late for campaigning; the King of France was assembling an army in the Paris-Rouen area which was likely to be formidable in numbers, and dysentery had taken a terrible toll of the English army. After a proportion of fit troops had been allocated to garrison duties at Harfleur there were only 900 men-at-arms and 5,000 archers available for field operations. Despite the recommendations of his council Henry decided to march on Calais, hoping to avoid interception from the French national army which was marshalling in the area of Rouen. A gruelling seventeen days followed during which time the English army marched no less than 260 miles, and, marching more or less parallel with them, crossing and recrossing their route, was the bulk of the French forces. Then, on the eve of St Crispin, the English came across the French host bivouacked astride the road to Calais, just short of the little village of Agincourt.

The French forces are estimated to have totalled at least 25,000. They were in high spirits and, although they had marched nearly the same distance as the English, the majority had been on horseback and were therefore much fresher. They now faced the weary and dispirited English army, most of them hungry and many still suffering from dysentery. They faced each other over a field newly sown with wheat. This open space, bounded by the woods of Agincourt on one side and Tramecourt on the other, narrowed towards the English positions, which had the effect of compressing the French as they advanced, restricting their movements and creating confusion and disorder.

There were three divisions of the English on either side of which were groups of archers thrown forward and outwards, somewhat like an opened triangle. When these divisions were drawn up flank to flank in one line the archers met, forming a series of wedges—the "herse". The English morale was momentarily raised to an unexpectedly high level by the King, whose powers of inspiration and leadership had never been more advantageously displayed; he now rode along the lines on a little grey horse, wearing a magnificent suit of shining armour and a surcoat embroidered with the leopards of England and the *fleurs-de-lis* of France. His harangue to the assembled troops included a reminder that the French had boasted that they would cut three fingers from the right hand of every archer they might capture in order that they might never presume again to shoot at man or horse. Four long hours of

The Battle of Agincourt, October 25th, 1415. The sketch map shows the opposing forces and the direction of the English advance. Note how the space narrows between the two forests of Agincourt and Tramecourt, which hampered any forward action by the French.

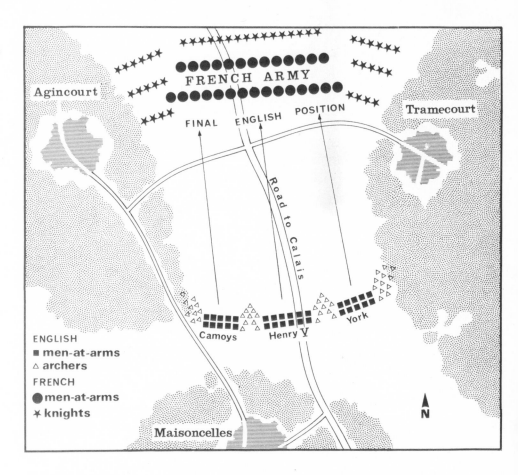

waiting passed, both armies holding their ground, the English bowmen becoming restless and impatient. As the morning wore on Henry's confidence began to waver. He had hoped to fight at dawn, or soon after, for his men would be incapable of fighting the following day being "very much wearied with hunger, diseases and marching".

The decision to take the initiative was soon made after a brief council of war between the King and the most experienced of his commanders. Edward Duke of York came to Henry and suggested that stakes should be planted before the archers, and accordingly every man took a stake of a tree and prepared it by sharpening it at both ends. Sir Thomas Erpingham was told to ensure that the archers were in their right positions. They were dirty and ragged, as well as hungry and tired. Their loose jackets were torn and mud-stained; many of them were barefoot, and some of them, according to one account based on uncertain authority, were naked, without even the hat of boiled leather, and wearing only a belt in which their arrows and clubs were stuck. When they were all arranged to Sir Thomas's satisfaction he threw his baton into the air and cried "Nestroque!"; interpreted as either "now strike" or "knee stretch". Sir Thomas was answered by a loud shout from the archers, and a few minutes later the famous order "Banners Advance!" rang out and the divisions moved forward, slowly, steadily and firmly, in fine order, with trumpets sounding, and shouts of "St George!" ringing through the autumn air. The shrewd Henry had detached a body of 200 archers and sent them behind the English army by a circuitous route to a concealed position in a meadow not far from the village of Tramecourt close to the French vanguard, with orders to lie low until the time for action came. At extreme bow-shot the advancing army came to a halt; the archers planted their stakes in front of their forward ranks, and started to shoot. Suddenly the "air was darkened by an intolerable number of piercing arrows flying across the sky to pour upon the enemy like a cloud laden with rain". This was probably calculated to provoke the French into advancing, and it had the desired effect. The cavalry lumbered into life and decided to charge the flank archers according to plan, and as they started to advance the men-at-arms also moved forward, probably without orders. The knights galloped forward bravely, keeping their heads down so that the arrows, which came flying towards them in a continuous stream, did not hit them in the exposed part of the face, and they rode straight at the fences of stakes. Those horses that were not impaled on the stakes were so infuriated by the arrows which tore deep in their flesh that they became unmanageable. Some leapt backwards, stung to madness, some reared hideously, some turned their backs on the enemy and others merely fell to the ground throwing their heavily armoured riders at the feet of the archers, who stabbed or clubbed them to death. In the meanwhile the small body of archers concealed on the flank were harrying the enemy from their left wing, and by the time the two armies met in hand-to-hand battle the French were so closely packed that they could not raise their arms to strike the foe. During the general mêlée which ensued the ranks of archers stood their ground and poured shower after shower of arrows into the tight mass of the enemy. The result was complete disintegration of the French army, the whole action taking little more than three hours. Their casualties, which included "the flower of all nobility of France", are said to have been between ten and fifteen thousand compared with the English dead of a few hundred. The tragic order given by the King to an esquire and two hundred archers, to cut the throats of all the prisoners, was to be remembered long after the event. In the heat of battle Henry had received news that his baggage camp had been attacked, added to which the French who had fled from the fight were reforming ready to counter-attack. There was, therefore, a serious threat that he might lose the battle if the enormous number of prisoners already taken were to rejoin these reforming units. So the King chose their wholesale extermination as a safeguard, an order carried out with much reluctance and considerable mis-givings. Despite this instance of cruel butchery the personal record of King Henry was a shining example of individual bravery and valour, a historical fact which is incontestable. When the battle was over, Henry asked what castle it was that he saw in the distance through the veils of rain which had

The monument to Richard Gilbert de Clare, 2nd Earl of Pembroke (d. 1176), named Strongbow, in Christ Church Cathedral, Dublin. The conquest of Ireland in 1170 was led by Strongbow whose followers included the Marcher Lords and Welsh and Flemish bowmen and men-at-arms.

begun to fall on the gruesome field, and he was told that it was Agincourt. "Then," he said, "let this day be called the Battle of Agincourt."

> *Agincourt, Agincourt!*
> *Know ye not Agincourt?*
> *Dear was the vict'ry bought*
> *By fifty yeomen.*
> *Ask any English wench,*
> *They were worth all the French*
> *Rare English bowmen!*
>
> *Anon.*

The Maid of Orleans. A drawing of the head of a fifteenth-century statue which is said to have been based on the sculptor's recollection of Joan of Arc.

JOAN OF ARC

France was now on her knees, and the claims of Edward III and Henry V were almost secure when, at the Siege of Orleans in 1429, Joan of Arc appeared. The story of The Maid is an astounding one surrounded by medieval mystery and wonder. The magnetic hold she had over the scattered and exhausted French welded them together and flung them victoriously at the English. The siege of Orleans was another typical study of defence and attack, siege and resistance, the English archers once more playing a vital role. However, they were no match for a French army carried forward on the tidal wave of religious fervour, and Joan, herself wounded by an arrow, no doubt gained special sympathy from the French by her bravery in battle, her feverish directness of purpose, and her courage in the face of impossible odds. Her inspiration continued and slowly, inevitably, England was pushed out of France. By 1453, with the capture of Bordeaux, hostilities finally came to an end, and only Calais remained out of the vast tracts which Henry had won.

* * * * * * * *

From the eleventh to the fifteenth century many soldiers saw in archery the decisive weapon; and this vast cavalcade of kings and princes, armoured knights and men-at-arms, and bowmen from the English shires and the Welsh marches in their hoods and liripipes, illuminate the pages of history with a special lustre. Millions of arrows must have rotted away, their carefully wrought points doomed to rusty extinction and their grey goose and peacock fletchings now nothing but dust. The sturdy yew bows have withered and disintegrated. But the passage of time cannot dim the glory of the victories they won for England.

William I, the ruthless conqueror, whose son was to die by the same weapon that gave his father England, moulders in Gothic splendour at Caen. Edward I, during whose reign the long-bow first became prominent as a weapon of war, caused the following inscription to be placed on his tomb in Westminster Abbey—*Edvardus Primus, Scotorum malleus hic est, 1308*. So great was his yearning to conquer Scotland that he required of his son that his bones were to be carried at the head of the English army till Scotland was subdued. Edward II, horribly murdered in Berkeley Castle, gazes unblinking toward heaven in Gloucester Cathedral. The third Edward, the tactician supreme, one of the greatest princes who ever sat the English throne, whose sword and shield that went with him to France once formed part of his monument in Westminster, rests now in the Confessor's Chapel in that Abbey. The Black Prince, whose terrible name was used by generations of French-women to quiet their disobedient children, sleeps in the great Cathedral at Canterbury, his tomb adorned with the plumes of the tragic blind king who

The splendid effigy of Edward the Black Prince (1330–76), in full armour of gilded bronze, sur-mounting his tomb in Canterbury Cathedral. On his surcoat can be seen the *fleurs-de-lis* of France quartered with the leopards of England and the golden circlet of princely dignity is still in place around his battle helm.

fell at Crécy; and Henry V—sometimes called the first modern general—lies in Westminster the legendary helm "that did affright the air at Agincourt" hanging in the darkness above, still showing the fearful marks made by the great sword of the Duke of Alençon. The arms of France and England conjoin in the achievements of these and other princes, as a permanent reminder of the long and bitter struggle between these two great monarchies.

Many hundreds of other knights, encased in sepulchres of stone, ride their spectral steeds for ever on clouds of glory. And the bowmen? They lie in mass funeral pits where they fell, covered, perhaps, with rough grey and brown and green coarse-spun hoods and capes, easily identifiable in the aftermath of battle, their fingers calloused from the constant friction of the bowstrings and their faces tanned from long months of hard campaigning. Their eyes were once bright and keen to spot and fix a target at 240 yards; their spirit was unquenchable, their loyalty unshakable. They obeyed without question the commands of their lords and princes, and found in the interminable expeditions to a strange land a spirit of adventure, pride and self-reliance which was handed on from generation to generation. Ignorant, bawdy, simple countrymen; yet this was a class of soldier as noble as any history has known. The mobilisation of home-bred talents and the introduction and skilled use of archery secured for the English victory after victory and established a pattern of warfare never before known, and never defeated by a weapon of that time. The lessons of Hastings and Bannockburn had been well learnt, and the place of the long-bow in the history of military arms was to be challenged only by the rapid improvement in the entirely new science of firearms.

A French archer of the fifteenth century, possibly serving in one of the Burgundian companies of archers raised in emulation of the invincible bowmen of England. The organisation of the French armies did not allow for organised support from their archers, who played no significant part in subsequent actions.

SELECT BIBLIOGRAPHY

Barclay, Brigadier C. N., *Battle 1066* [1966]

British Museum, *Guide to the Anglo-Saxon Antiquities* [1923]

Bryant, Arthur, *The Age of Chivalry* [1963]

Burne, Alfred H., *The Agincourt War* [1956]

Burne, Alfred H., *The Crécy War* [1955]

Butler, Denis, *1066, The Story of a Year* [1966]

Cambrensis, Giraldus, *The Itinerary through Wales and the Description of Wales*, Everyman [1908]

Chandos Herald, *The Life & Feats of Arms of Edward the Black Prince* (trans. Francisque-Michel) [1883]

Christison, General Sir Philip, *Bannockburn* [1960]

Cole, Thomas Holwell, *The Antiquities of Hastings* [1867]

Creasy, Sir Edward, *The Fifteen Decisive Battles of the World* [1851]

Dalton, O. M., *A Late Medieval Bracer*, The Antiquaries Journal, Vol. II, No. 3 [1922]

Davis, H. W. C., (Editor), *Mediaeval England* [1924]

Dillon, The Viscount, (Editor), *Pageant of the Birth, Life & Death of Richard Beauchamp Earl of Warwick K.G. 1389-1439* [1914]

Drayton, Michael, *The Ballad of Agincourt* [1606]

Elmer, Robert P., & Smart, Charles Allen (Editors), *The Book of the Long Bow* [1929]

Folio Society, *The Trial of Joan of Arc* [1968]

France, Anatole, *The Life of Joan of Arc* [1908]

Froissart, Sir John, *Chronicles of England, France, Spain, and the Adjoining Countries* (trans. Thomas Johnes) [1839]

Garmonsway, G. N., (trans.), *The Anglo-Saxon Chronicle*, Everyman [1935]

Hearne, Ethel H., (Editor), *The Sagas of Olaf Tryggvason and of Harald the Tyrant* [1911]

Hewitt, H. J., *The Black Prince's Expedition of 1355-1357* [1958]

Hibbert, Christopher, *Agincourt* [1964]

Lemmon, Lt Col Charles H., *The Field of Hastings* [1956]

Lindsay, Philip, *King Henry V, A Chronicle* [1934]

London Museum, *Medieval Catalogue* [1954]

Mackenzie, Agnes Mure, *Robert Bruce King of Scots* [1934]

Mackenzie, W. M., *The Battle of Bannockburn* [1913]

Miller, Rev Thomas, *The Site of the Battle of Bannockburn* [1913]

Milliken, E. K., *Archery in the Middle Ages* [1966]

Morris, J. E., *The Archers at Crécy*, The English Historical Review, Vol. XII [1897]

Nicolas, Sir Harris, K. H., *History of the Battle of Agincourt* [1832]

Oman, Charles, *A History of the Art of War, The Middle Ages from the Fourth to the Fourteenth Century* [1898]

Powick, Professor Sir Maurice, *The Battle of Lewes 1264* [1964]

Rickert, Edith, *Chaucer's World* [1948]

Rowse, A. L., *Bosworth Field* [1966]

Shakespeare, William, *The Life of Henry the Fifth* [Penguin 1959]

Stenton, Sir Frank, (Editor) *The Bayeux Tapestry* [1957]

Thompson, Peter E., (Editor) *Contemporary Chronicles of the Hundred Years War* [1966]

van Thal, Herbert, *Famous Land Battles* [1964]

Wrottesley, General The Hon. George, *Crécy and Calais* [1898]

5 The Decline of the Longbow

Let Princes therefore shoot for exercise,
Soldiers t'inlarge their magnanimities;
Let Nobles shoot 'cause 'tis a pastime fit;
Let Scholars shoot to clarifie their wit;
Let Citizens shoot to purge corrupted blood;
Let Yeoman shoot for th' King's and Nation's good;
Let all the Nation Archers prove, and then
We without lanthorns shall find virtuous men.

SHOTTEREL AND D'URFEY

BY 1453 France, with the exception of Calais, had been cleared of the English, and the virtual end of the Hundred Years War was reached, despite the fact that no peace treaty had been signed. The long-bow, however, continued to be used as a principal weapon by the English armies and, no doubt from lessons learnt during the past century or so, France decided somewhat belatedly to adopt the bow also. Sound arguments were not wanting, and a chivalrous respect for the bowman was now proclaimed by the highest in the land—"in battles, archers are the weight that turns the balance, and of archers, the English are the flower". Other battle tactics peculiar to the English had obviously impressed the French, as we also find that the Burgundian knights during the wars of Louis IX actually dismounted to fight. A contemporary historian said of them: "the noblesse fight always on horse and think it a dishonour to serve on foot . . . but . . . they all quit their horses . . . . . . so that the people might be the more encouraged and fight more valiantly; and this they learnt of the English." Sir John Smythe, the Elizabethan soldier, said: "the French king and some other princes, did in times past, establish laws and orders for the use of the long-bow, and our manner of shooting: that they might be able to encounter us with our own weapon: and to the intent that they should become good archers, granted unto all who became perfect in that weapon, great privileges and rewards." King John,

William le May, who was Captain of 120 archers of the King of France, Louis XI, and Governor of the city of Paris. By this time the Valois kings had adopted the custom of the English throne by appointing personal archer bodyguards.

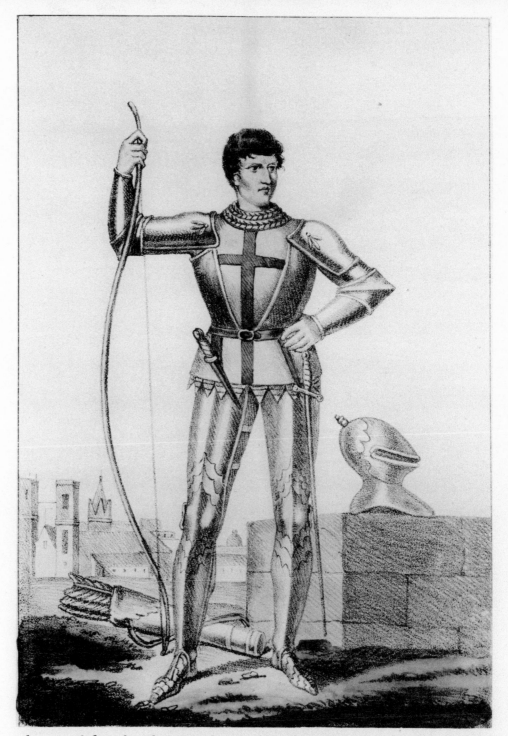

who was defeated and captured at Poitiers, had instituted the Order of the Star in 1365, but it was too freely awarded for "princes and the nobler sort to wear it"; so now, at the end of the sixteenth century, it was bestowed on the archers, no doubt as their privilege and reward.

However, the divisions of French longbowmen did not become an established part of the French military system, and we find the remnants of these bodies forming a guard at Henry IV's court. The royal household expenses include a payment of 720,000 crowns for the upkeep of 2,400 archers employed to wait on the many high-ranking officials at court. Part of this body consisted of Scots bowmen, employed no doubt as long-standing friends of France and because they were the ancient enemies of the English.

THE WARS OF THE ROSES

The English garrisons and armies returned home to a country torn by unrest and rebellion, conditions which soon fermented into the bitter conflict between the houses of Lancaster and York—the Wars of the Roses. The discontent in England had manifested itself in uprisings such as the Kentish rebellion of Jack Cade, a soldier home from the wars, who led 20,000 men to London after opposing Henry VI's army at Sevenoaks. His followers dispersed after they were driven from London and Cade was caught and killed at Lewes. The towns and villages of England were full of knights and archers accustomed to war and plunder, and fit for any mischief. The rival claimants to the throne, Edward of York, descended from Edward III, and the Red Rose of Lancaster, Henry VI, found ready support for their causes. The issue was simple, but the various factors which encouraged men to take sides were complex and confused; the stake was the throne of England and the balance of power depended on the two great armies massing for civil war. The conflict that burst over England in such battles as St Albans, Barnet, Towton, Edgecot, Losecoat Field, Wakefield, Mortimer's Cross, Tewkesbury, Bosworth, Hedley Moor and Hexham, were fought by the sons and grandsons of those same soldiers (and, perhaps, by some of the men themselves) who once stood side by side at Agincourt. Now they faced each other, equally armed with the weapon they had used to such advantage during the past two centuries. The tactics of these battles were those employed by the leaders in the recent French war; the archer still fought on foot, in line beside the man-at-arms, and the long-bow was still the lord of weapons. The men involved consisted partly of mercenaries and partly of tenants and private friends hastily called out. Every country gentleman kept in his pay a number of soldiers, and the services of archers were in great demand. Sir John Howard, contracting for the services of such a bowman, a man named Daniel, offered him £10 a year, two gowns, and a house for his wife to dwell in. As an extra inducement he gave Daniel a shilling, two doublets worth five shillings each, a new gown, and sent him off to a shooting match with twenty pence more jingling in his purse. The dignitaries of the Church, long acclimatised to sudden and violent action against their safety, likewise thought it expedient to arm; Bishop Wayneflete, for instance, stored at Farnham Castle amongst other irreligious implements "large barbed arrows, with peacock's plumage".

The first of the battles of the White and Red Roses was fought at St Albans in 1455, in which the Lancastrians were defeated, Henry VI taken prisoner and Richard Duke of York, great-grandson of Edward III and claiming the throne by descent, placed at the head of the governing power. Richard was killed at Wakefield, and his son, outstepping his father's ambition, caused himself to be proclaimed Edward IV. The Battle of Towton, which was fought in a blinding Yorkshire snowstorm in 1461, gave Edward his first great victory over the Lancastrians. The first incident of this battle was the capture of Ferrybridge by Lord Clifford, nicknamed "Black Clifford", and its recapture by the Yorkists, following the death of that bloodthirsty nobleman by a chance arrow finding its target in his neck.

THE BATTLE OF TOWTON

The main action was fought by two large armies, both well disciplined in arms. The Yorkists, taking advantage of the snow which was driving into the faces of the enemy, shot a flight of arrows into their ranks and then retreated a few paces. The Lancastrians, thinking their foe nearer than was the case, plied their arrows fast and thick against the blinding snow but with no result whatever, except to exhaust their quivers. Now the Yorkists replied and poured into the enemy a deadlier shower of arrows, their own store supplemented by those which had fallen harmless at their feet. The remainder of the battle was fought for a gruelling eight hours at close quarters, and it was equally balanced until the arrival of reinforcements for Edward's army; once they arrived, fresh and enthusiastic, the scales were weighed against the Lancastrians, and the battle ended in victory for the usurper.

ACTS AND STATUTES ENCOURAGING ARCHERY

It was now necessary for Edward IV to be prepared against the widespread followers of the Red Rose, as they were by no means subdued. In the fifth year of his reign an act was passed which directed that each Englishman, and Irishman dwelling with Englishmen, should have an English bow of his own height, which was directed to be made of yew, wych hazel, ash or awburne, "or any other reasonable tree according to their power". The next chapter directs that butts shall be made in every township, at which the inhabitants are obliged to shoot up and down on each feast day, under the penalty of a ha'penny when they shall omit this exercise. Local authorities took up this and other statutes and often amplified them to include minors. An entry in the Common Council book of the City of Chester sets forth that "for the avoiding of idleness, all children of six years old and upwards" shall be sent to school, and on Sundays and holy days to church, "and in the afternoon all the said male children shall be exercised in shooting with bows and arrows, for pins and points only; and that their parents furnish them with bows and arrows, pins and points for that purpose, according to the statute lately made for maintenance of shooting with long-bows being the ancient defence of the kingdom".

During their oft-renewed strife with England the Scots found good cause to dread the superiority of their old enemies in the use of the long-bow and it is therefore not surprising that in the early fifteenth century, in company with their allies the French, they found it essential to encourage its use by royal decree. James I, realising the paramount importance of archery, endeavoured by every means in his power to encourage the practice of it among his subjects. "That all men busk themselves to be archers, from the age of 12 years; and that in each ten pound worth of land there be made bow-marks, and specially near parish churches, where, upon holydays, men may come, and at the least shoot thrice about, and have usage of archery; and whosoever uses not the said archery, the lord of the land shall raise from him a wedder; and if the lord raises not the said penalty, the king's sheriff or his ministers shall raise it to the king." And ". . . yeomen of the realm betwixt sixty and sixteen years shall be sufficiently provided with bows and sheafs of arrows . . ." It is clear, however, that the Scots preferred the games of golf and football to acquiring dexterity in the use of the long-bow by shooting at the butts; ". . . the futball and the golf be utterly cryit doune" and "that bowe markis be made . . . and shuting be usyt ilk sunday."

The Lowland Scots never took kindly to the bow as a weapon of war, but in the Highlands it found favour with the clan warriors who subsequently brought it into the field of battle and used it to great effect. According to an ancient verse the Highland archer could only be properly equipped with:

Bow of yew Essrakin,
Feather from the eagle of Lochtreig,
Yellow wax of Balenageloun,
And an [arrow] head from the smith MacPeteran.

A rare archer's bracer of decorated leather, probably dating from the reign of Henry VII (1457–1509). From the design and inscription this may have been used by an archer in royal service.

TEWKESBURY AND BOSWORTH

After ten more years and ten more battles between the rival houses of York and Lancaster, the Lancastrians were again defeated at the battle of Tewkesbury on May 4th, 1471, and Edward IV was established as the Yorkist king of England. The action followed the now familiar pattern of warfare, with opening salvoes of deadly archery from each side followed by a fierce engagement at close quarters until, through the superior strength of one side, sheer exhaustion or near extinction, the other would turn tail and flee, to be pursued and relentlessly chopped down. During this battle the boy-prince, Edward of Lancaster, was made prisoner and barbarously murdered, many a knight of noble birth was slain and some 3,000 men met their death, many having being dragged from the sanctuary of the Abbey of Tewkesbury and driven towards a mill-pond where hundreds of them, bloody with wounds and with arrows sticking in them, were miserably drowned. The murderous and bitter feud of the Wars of the Roses continued to be fought out over the next decade or so, until finally at Bosworth Field on August 22nd, 1485, Richard III, Shakespeare's "crook-backed tyrant", was defeated and killed; the crown of England was retrieved from under a hawthorn bush, and the first king of the House of Tudor ascended the throne.

Throughout the reigns of Edward IV and Richard III enactments were made encouraging the use of the bow and craftsmen members of the Guilds of Bowyers and Fletchers, now well established, found ample work and profit in providing supplies of bows and arrows for the constant wars which occupied these monarchs. Supplies of suitable wood became strained to the utmost and an ingenious solution was found—an import duty in kind—merchants being ordered to bring into England four bowstaves with every ton of goods imported, and every butt of Malmsey wine brought in had to be accompanied by ten. This helped to counteract the increasing prices of the raw materials used by bowyers, the cost of bowstaves having risen from £2 to £8 per hundred. A measure of price control was also laid down—the maximum permitted cost of a finished yew bow, for instance, being 3s 4d.

A brief reference to artillery in one of these statutes can be regarded as a premonition of what was to come. The use of handguns, introduced into England by Burgundian mercenaries during the Wars of the Roses, was to become so general a practice as to oust the long-bow completely from its superior position as a weapon of English armies; and Edward IV, noticing the popularity of the new and novel weapon, directs that although the use of artillery was gaining ground "yet that of the bow and arrow was not neglected".

The first of the Tudors, Henry VII, sought peace and the enforcement of order; this cautious and thrifty king made no new orders as to the encouragement of archery, or, for that matter, relative to gunpowder or artillery. In the nineteenth year of his reign he forbade the use of the crossbow to all except nobility and the well-to-do, who had begun to use it in the chase, and confirmed the traditional use of the long-bow "whereby honour and victory had been gotten against outward enemies, the realm greatly defended, and much more the dread of all Christian princes by reason of the same". He also confirmed the price of bowstaves as 3s 4d and implemented the importation regulations by deleting customs duty on staves longer than six and a half feet. This encouraged the importation of good bowstaves of a suitable length.

We have seen how the long-bow became elevated above all other weapons by the English and how, against appalling odds, this nation subdued enemies of far greater strength by its use. We have also seen that the long-bow in the hands of equally matched opposing armies can, with skilful tactics, be turned to advantage. Kings and princes recognised the power of this weapon and manoeuvred their armies accordingly, and the rank-and-file yeoman archer reached a position of previously unimagined importance in the fourteenth and fifteenth centuries. Now, with the reigns of Henry VIII and Queen Elizabeth, the bow was to suffer a long and lingering decline, and a battle of words between adherents of the bow and supporters of the gun, unparalleled in the history of military writings, was to begin.

THE DECLINE STARTS

A member of the Toxophilite Society, speaking of the decline of the bow, said in his book *The English Bowman* (1801): "That our ancestors paid to the long-bow the highest veneration, and that their affection, or (as the introducers of fire-arms termed it) their prejudice, for the continuance of it was founded upon the most solid grounds, no one acquainted with the English history can for a moment doubt. It had long been the safety of the realm, and had led the English to the greatest and most extraordinary victories, that history had to record; securing their peace at home, and planting in the minds of their enemies a rooting terror, that did not terminate with them even in the grave; but survived, and was handed down to successive generations. It was the weapon of all others most suited to their genius, prowess and strength; with which they had been accustomed to form an acquaintance, very early in life; and it may, with truth, be said to have been the toy of their infancy, the pride of their manhood, and the boast of their old age."

When Henry VIII succeeded his father in 1509 he was eighteen years of age, a fine athlete, proud of his person (being immensely gratified when the Venetian ambassador told him that his calf was more shapely than Francis I's), a skilled tennis player, a great horseman who could wear out ten horses in a day's hunting, and a capital bowman. A contemporary, writing of the early years of his reign, said of him: ". . . . His Grace being young, and willing not to be idle, rose in the morning very early to fetch May or green boughs, himself fresh and richly apparelled, and clothed all his knights, squires and gentlemen in white satin, and all his guard and yeomen of the crown in white sarsenet. And so went every man with his bow and arrows shooting to the wood, and so repaired again to the Court, every man with a green bough in his cap, and at his returning, many hearing of his going a-Maying, were desirous to see him shoot, for at that time his Grace shot as strong and as great a length as any of his guard. There came to his Grace a certain man with bow and arrows and desired his Grace to take the muster of him, and to see him shoot, for at that time his Grace was contented, the man put one foot on his bosom, and so did shoot, and well towards his mark, whereof not only his Grace but all others greatly marvelled. So the King gave him a reward for his so doing, which person afterwards of the people and of them in the Court was called 'Foot-in-Bosom'.''

FLODDEN FIELD

Among his continental military ventures Henry VIII invaded France three times, but the only action at which he was present in person was the Battle of the Spurs. While he was thus engaged the French king tried to stir up the Scots to attack him in the rear. This resulted in the last general action ever fought by an English army consisting only of the traditional "bows and bills". On September 9th, 1513, three weeks after the Battle of the Spurs, the battle of Flodden Field was fought on the Northumbrian border. The victory at Flodden was due in a great measure to the archers. As the Scots gave way to avoid the storm of arrows poured on them the English were able to charge and break their ranks, which resulted in a complete rout. Some authorities say that there were altogether 10,000 Scots casualties against a loss of only 1,500 on the English side. Nearly half the peerage roll of Scotland were slain, and James IV was himself fatally wounded by an arrow. In commemoration of the battle the Earl of Surrey, the English commander on this occasion, was given the honour of displaying the demi-lion of Scotland pierced through the mouth with an arrow. In Archer's Hall in Edinburgh there is carefully preserved a bow known as the Flodden Bow which is reputed to have been used in the battle; ancient it no doubt is, and as an example of the bows of the period it provides a unique specimen, though whether in fact it was used in battle in 1513 has yet to be proved. Flodden is a landmark in the history of archery, as the last battle on English soil to be fought with the long-bow as the principal weapon, a fitting grand finale to a long and honourable service.

Some doubts as to the continued use of the bow were already being heard, and one of the earliest doubters was Lord Herbert of Cherbury, who asked whether the previous successes in battle could be expected again,

The Flodden Bow. This relic, associated with the Battle of Flodden (1513), was for many years kept hidden in a house close to the battlefield. It is a valuable and rare specimen from the early sixteenth century.

A section of the Flodden Window, in the parish church of St Leonard, Middleton; the window was erected in 1520 as a memorial to Sir Richard Assheton and his sixteen archers who distinguished themselves at the Battle of Flodden. Each archer, dressed in blue, carries a longbow above which is inscribed his name.

A contemporary woodcut of King James IV of Scotland (1473–1513) who was mortally wounded in the head by an arrow during the Battle of Flodden (1513).

"Especially since the use of arms is changed and for the bow, proper for men of our strength, the caliver begins to be generally received, which, besides that it is a more costly weapon and requires a long practice, may be managed by the weaker sort." These misgivings as to the efficiency of the bow in battle were laid aside, particularly when the first act of Henry's reign required every male (except ecclesiastics, judges, and people possessed of land to the value of two hundred marks a year) over seven and under sixty years of age to practise archery; the use of crossbows and handguns being forbidden. The King took exception to the use of the handgun against his deer, but allowed such weapons to be kept for the defence of all walled towns within seven miles of the sea.

THE FIELD OF THE CLOTH OF GOLD

By his personal example Henry demonstrated the benefits of archery practice and few men could, or would dare, match his attainments in the noble art. These special benefits were now to be shared by commoner and noble alike, and Henry VIII was to show that the weapon of the yeoman could also serve as the plaything of royalty. When Francis I of France sought to form an alliance with Henry against the Emperor Charles V, an elaborate meeting was arranged which became known as The Field of the Cloth of Gold. The kings of France and England staged a contest of a magnificence which was never to be equalled again. This glittering display of arms and pageantry included a morning spent in mimic warfare and then, at the particular request of the French king, Henry undertook to demonstrate his skill with the bow. After showing his paces a body of French went "to practise archery with the king of England, who is a marvellous good archer and a strong; and it was

right pleasant to behold". Another contemporary chronicler said: "No man in his dominions drew the great English bow more vigorously than Henry himself; no man shot further, or with more unerring aim." Undoubtedly the fact that the King publicly demonstrated his skill with a bow endeared him to the commoner; this was something novel, a sport which they could understand and one which they could enjoy to the same extent as their king. He was known to attend many archery matches and his household expenses show the receipt and payment of many wagers won and lost "at the butts". This form of gambling was emulated by the people—one record tells of a wager "shott in Fynsbere Feld . . . . of six men against six men, and one part had fifteen for three and lost the game". Finsbury Fields and Moorfields had become the chief resort of London archers and a favourite place for tournaments and competitions; these open spaces close to the City were to remain archery grounds for many years, until the last of the archery "marks" was removed to the headquarters of the Honourable Artillery Company in 1888. Arthur, the elder brother of Henry, is said to have been very fond of archery and became so popular among archers that the nickname "Prince Arthur" was given to any bowman who proved himself a particularly good shot.

Anne Boleyn, who had been present at the Field of the Cloth of Gold, often whiled away summer hours shooting with Henry, and he purchased quantities of expensive archery tackle for her. One item from the Privy Purse accounts reads: ". . . paid to Scawseby for Bowys, Arrowys, shafts, brode hedds, bracer, and shooting glove for my Lady Anne, 33s. 4d. The same daye paied to the King's Bowyer for four bowes for my Ladye Anne at 4s. 4d. a pece 17s. 4d." Her brother, Lord Rochford, was the king's constant companion at the butts and frequently won large sums off him. Within a year or so she was to be buried, headless, in a box of elm made for storing arrows.

ROYAL ENCOURAGEMENT

To control the quality of imported bowstaves Henry sent two experts abroad to select staves of the required quality: on one occasion they chose no less than 10,000, each of which was marked with the royal cypher of a rose and crown. The importation of a part order of 40,000 bowstaves from Venice was agreed and five bowyers, Henry Pykman, Thomas Bolley, William Ruckstead, John Snodon and Robert Patty, were paid a total of £200 13s 4d for making up 600 of these roughed-out staves into bows. The manufacture of archery equipment was still a thriving industry in early sixteenth-century England and numerous records list the cost of bows and arrows and wages for skilled labour of the period. The encouragement given to the general practice of archery was not confined to official statutes and royal decrees, for many public archery meetings were graced by the presence of King Henry and his retinue, and it was at any one of these, when Henry and his court at Windsor "caused sundry matches to be made concerning shooting with the long-bow", that the King dubbed one of his guard "Duke of Shoreditch" for his skill at archery. At the conclusion of this match, when only one man remained to shoot, the King remarked that if he should succeed in beating the rest he would be duke over all archers. The man, named Barlow, drew his bow and became the winner. The King kept his word and, discovering that Barlow lived in Shoreditch, named him Duke of Shoreditch. The title was revived from time to time in connexion with later archery matches in London, and a complete record of one of these elaborate meetings was published in 1583 under the title of *A Remembrance of the Worthy Show and Shooting by the Duke of Shoreditch and his Associates etc.* and was "set forth according to the truth thereof, to the everlasting Honour of the Game of Shooting in the LongBow".

THE FRATERNITY OF ST GEORGE

The suppression of the monasteries by Henry VIII had caused considerable unrest in various parts of the country and a general feeling of alarm and discontent prevailed. It was with the country in this unsettled condition that Henry, who placed great reliance on the support of the City of London, set his seal to the Charter which incorporated for all time the Guild or Fraternity of St George, for the better defence of the realm by the maintenance of "The Science and Feate of Shootinge" with long-bow, crossbow and handgun. This was the first body in England to receive official encouragement in the use of the handgun and this company of élite soldiery was to become eventually the Ancient and Honourable Artillery Company of London. The charter permitted members of the company to wear a uniform of any colour except purple and scarlet, and allowed them various special privileges not the least important being indemnification from murder: ". . . if it shall happen any person or persons, running, passing or going between any such shooter and the mark, shall be killed or otherwise hurt . . . then any such shooter shall not be arrested, imprisoned, sued, vexed, troubled . . . nor shall suffer death nor lose any member or forfeit any goods, lands or hereditaments" provided the archer "shall use, pronounce and openly speak . . . this word FASTE."

Previous to the incorporation of the Guild of St George there was undoubtedly a band or society of armed citizens of the better class intent on the preservation of peace and good order, and to enable them to enforce their authority they became efficient in the "Science of Artillery", which included the handling of long-bows and crossbows and, latterly, the use of handguns. These armed citizens were ready trained and qualified and had important connexions in commerce, trade and politics: what better body for the support of the King's endeavours? The patent granted to this exclusive and powerful corps was a shrewd act of statecraft ensuring the king of their support, in return for which they could now look forward to patronage from the throne for a long time to come.

NEW AND CRAFTY GAMES

Once universally practised, the general use of the bow in England began to wane. The people found other and more varied distractions, and the popular amusements of Tudor England were not designed to instruct the nation for war nor to prepare them against invasion. Henry VIII was acutely conscious of this fact, and a statute was passed entitled *An Act for Mayntenance of Artyllarie and Debarring of Unlawful Games*. According to this Act "subtle, inventative and crafty persons" were devising many "new and crafty games", one being shove-groat otherwise called slidethrift—the shove ha'penny of modern times. The owners of houses and alleys where this and other unlawful games were played or any persons benefitting financially from such games, as well as the gamesters themselves, were liable to a penalty of forty shillings for each day an offence was committed, a very large sum of money in those days. Meanwhile in all the villages of England the petty constables were supervising the maintenance of the butts, inspecting weapons and stopping such games as had been declared illegal. This ancient office of non-professional policeman, created by Edward I, was an annual stint, envied by none, but accepted as essential for the preservation of order, the pursuit of malefactors and for the general protection of the villages. Fortunately for modern researchers the work that had to be supervised was carefully recorded in parish accounts. The "Cost of Ye Buttes" at Cratfield in Suffolk, which included wages for four men and a boy, working for five days with full board provided, totalled 6s 2d. A homely touch is to be found in one churchwarden's account where it is recorded that "when the butts were made" the workmen were treated to bread and beer, and 4s was spent at Eltham in Kent for suppers "for all of them that worketh at the butts"; three trees for this work cost 12d and the fee of a bowman for an undisclosed service was likewise one shilling.

GUN VERSUS BOW

The gradual decline in the use of the bow continued, and the fact that it was in danger of being relegated to second place to the handgun now became an academic rather than a practical problem. The raging controversy between adherents of the bow and those who favoured the new-fangled gun was shortly to break out, the contestants being military writers and other prominent men, and various members of the newly incorporated Fraternity of St George were to play a vigorous and important part in the argument. Roger Ascham, sometime tutor to both the Princess Elizabeth and her half-brother,

Drawn & Etch'd by R. Bridgens.

Acquatinted by C. Hunt.

An aquatint of the early nineteenth century showing soldiers armed with the four principal weapons of the period: a halberdier, a pikeman, a musketeer with his new-fangled weapon which was soon to oust the bow as a military arm, and the bowman complete with bow, arrows and leaden maul.

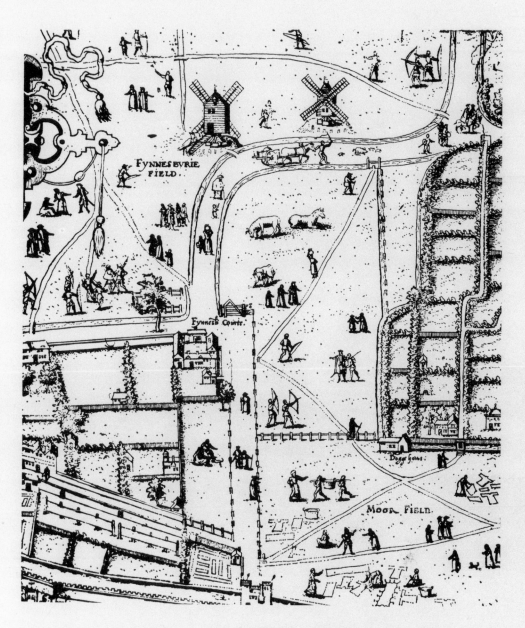

Archers and onlookers in Finsbury Fields in 1559. A detail from the earliest known map of London, attributed to Anthonis van der Wyngaerde.

the young Edward VI, wrote in 1544: "I have written and dedicated to his King's majesty a book, which is now in the press, 'On the Art of Shooting,' and in which I have shown how well it is fitted for Englishmen both at home and abroad, and how certain rules may be laid down to ensure its being learnt thoroughly by all our fellow countrymen." He formally presented the book, called *Toxophilus*, to the King at Greenwich and was promptly rewarded by a pension of £10 a year. This remarkable work, the first to be written in English on the subject of archery, sets down the pleasant talk of two college fellows, "Lover of Learning" and "Lover of Archery", as they discourse beside the wheat-fields in the neighbourhood of Cambridge throughout the long summer's afternoon, upon "the booke" and "the bowe". *Toxophilus* was presented as a specimen of a pure and correct English style, in the hope that the cultivation of the vernacular language by the scholars of the day would become as popular as the then exclusive study of Latin and Greek. The laudatory rhyme on the title page sets the mood of a true patriot:

> *Rejoice Englande, be gladde and merie,*
> *TROTHE ouercommeth thyne enemyes all,*
> *The Scot, the Frenchman, the Pope and heresie,*
> *OUERCOMMED by Trothe, have had a fall;*
> *Sticke to the Trothe, and euermore thou shall*
> *Through Christ, King Henry, the Boke, and the Bowe,*
> *All maner of enemies quite ouerthrowe.*

Ascham, himself an archer, and doubtless feeling deeply about his subject, manages to introduce into his work numerous arguments for the retention of the bow. It was "a pastime fit for the mind, wholesome for the body . . . worthy to be rebuked of no man . . . fit for all ages, persons and places".

THE BOWMAN BISHOP

The fall from popularity of the bow as a military arm was inevitable, and while it steadily declined the energetic but fruitless battle of theory and reason gathered momentum with a broadside directed against the followers of gunpowder from no less a personage than Bishop Latimer. Himself the son of a yeoman, Hugh Latimer was a popular prelate who well represented the moral aspect of the reformed English Church, and was noted for his rough and homely sermons given before citizens and courtiers alike. In a country torn by religious upheavals, when Protestants were burnt by the dozen, and the axe was as favoured a political weapon as the pen, when skullduggery and intrigue were the order of the day and the persecution of priests was as commonplace as brawling in church, the sickly boy Edward followed his father to the throne. He found in Bishop Latimer a friend, who by his honest outcry against the crimes of the Reformation did his best to redeem them; and his sermons, given before the young King on each Friday in Lent, 1549, contain a series of denouncements concerning the religious and secular conditions prevailing, the decline of archery being of sufficient importance to him to be featured in one of them: "Men of England in times past, when they would exercise themselves (for we must needs have some recreation, our bodies cannot endure without some exercise), they were wont to go abroad in the fields a-shooting, but now is turned into glossing, gulling, and whoring within the house.

"The Art of Shooting hath been in times past much esteemed in this realm, it is the gift of God that he hath given us to excell all other nations withall. It hath been God's instrument, whereby he hath given us many victories against our enemies. But now we have taken up whoring in towns,

Roger Ascham (1515–68). Latin secretary to Mary Tudor and Elizabeth I, he wrote *Toxophilus*, the first full length study of archery in English (1545). This is the only known likeness of Ascham, with Queen Elizabeth, after an eighteenth-century engraving by Michael Burgers.

Queen Elizabeth I (1533–1603), who was said to have been a skilful archer, in the unusual guise of Diana, the huntress. The attributes of this goddess are bow and arrows, hound, and the crescent moon, all of which can be seen in this painting which hangs in Hatfield House. Attributed to Cornelius Vroom.

instead of shooting in fields. A wonderous thing, that so excellent a gift of God should be so little esteemed . . . In my time, my poor father was as diligent to teach me to shoot as to learn any other thing, and so I think other men did their children. He taught me how to draw, how to lay my body in my bow, and not to draw with strength of arms as other nations do, but with the strength of my body. I had my bows bought me according to my age and strength; as I increased in them, so my bows were made bigger, for men shall never shoot well, except that they be brought up in it. It is a goodly art, a wholesome kind of exercise, and much commended in physic . . . in the reverence of God, let it be continued."

Edward VI found solace in the gentle art of shooting in a bow, as his successes and failures so carefully recorded in his diaries show. With Roger Ascham and Bishop Latimer as teachers he must have caught some of their infectious enthusiasm for archery. Ascham died of ague at the age of 43 and Latimer was to perish in the flames under the Catholic terror of Mary's reign

Youthful archers of Abshoven, in a Flemish School painting of the seventeenth century. A charming genre study of a rural scene which could be set in any village in England or the Low Countries.

and during the next five years we find no item of special note concerning our story excepting that the statutes of Henry VIII received confirmation and the experts shuffled their facts ready for the battle of words which was to reach its peak before another reign was finished.

The forty-five year reign of the Virgin Queen, Elizabeth, was a period of great adventurers, explorers and colonists; the country grew richer as commerce thrived, and the development of sea power gave the Elizabethans a naval superiority never before known. This was the period of English history that produced such great figures as Hawkins, Drake and Frobisher, the redoubtable Sir Walter Raleigh and a host of politicians, soldiers and churchmen of a unique quality. The Armada of Spain threatened, and Philip's beard was singed, the Bard of Avon began his incomparable comedies and tragedies, real theatres were built for the first time, and Gloriana led fashion by being the first to wear silk stockings. This was a lusty, extravagant, brutal and cultured period in which we can trace an even more marked decline of archery, despite a stubborn reluctance to change to gunpowder.

ELIZABETHAN ARCHERS

Elizabeth appointed a commission to move about England to supervise the use of the bow "which was much decayed", and William Harrison included an enthusiastic defence of the skill of the English archer in his *Description of Britain*. "In times past the chief force of England consisted in their long-bows. But now we have given over that kind of artillery . . . Certes the Frenchman, and Rutters, deriding our new archery in respect of their corslets, will not let, in open skirmish, if any leisure serve, to turn up their tails and cry: 'Shoot English!' and all because our strong shooting is decayed and laid in bed. But, if some of our Englishmen now lived that served King Edward the third in his wars with France, the breech of such a varlet should have been nailed to his bum with one arrow, and another feathered in his bowels, before he should have turned about to see who had shot the first." Harrison then grudgingly admits the new-found skills: "But, as our shooting is thus in manner utterly decayed among us one way, so our countrymen wax skilful in sundry other points, as in shooting in small pieces, the caliver, the handling of the pike, in the several uses of which they have become very expert."

From the middle of the sixteenth century the proportion of guns to bows in the muster rolls slowly rose, and from 1595 the government tried to get rid of the bow entirely from the ranks of the trained bands. The Elizabethan bowman and his equipment is admirably described in a contemporary manuscript: "Captains and officers should be skilful of that most noble weapon; [the bow] and to see that their soldiers, according to their draught and strength, have good bows, well nocked, well stringed, everie string whippe in the nocke, and in the myddes rubbed with wax—braser and shutting glove—some spare strynges, trymed as aforesaid; every man one sheaf of arrows, with a case of leather, defensible against the rayne, and in the same fower and twentie arrows; whereof eight of them should be lighter than the residue, to gall or astoyne the enemie with the hail-shot of light arrows, before they shall come within the danger of their harquebuss shot. Let every man have a brigandine or a little cote of plate, a skull or hufkin, a maule of lead, of five feet in length, and a pike, and the same hanging by his girdle, with a hook and dagger; being thus furnished, teach them by musters to march, shoote and retire, keeping their faces upon the enemy's . . . None other weapon maye compare with the same noble weapon."

Although England could not keep out the arquebus, the caliver and the musket, the persistent loyalty to the bow is one of the most striking examples of conservatism in English history. What lay behind it? Free from invasion and not involved in most of the wars which forced the rest of Europe to keep abreast of developments in the art of war until late in the sixteenth century, Englishmen could afford to let tradition and sentiment affect their choice of weapons. The bow was the weapon of the patriot, with which the pride of France had been toppled at Crécy, Poitiers and Agincourt. Then there were the various vested interests which favoured the bow. The bowyers and fletchers, naturally, did not want their trades to suffer and they stressed the superiority of their own products over the musket and ball. The landed classes, to preserve their lands from poaching, and realising that the long-bow was vastly inferior as a poacher's weapon to the gun, supported legislation which restricted the use of firearms to official butts. Arrows were cheap, and could be used in practice over and over again, while the ammunition for guns, to the despair of local authorities, literally went up in smoke.

THE GREAT CONTROVERSY

By 1588 the bow was distinctly obsolescent, though there were still many archers in the great mass of shire-levies that were called out on the threat of Spanish invasion, the approach of the invincible Armada. By this time, however, there were some regions where of all the men embodied there were no bowmen—only pikemen, and arquebusiers or caliver-men. In London not one man of the regular trained-bands had a bow, and in the Midlands and the north the proportion of bows to firearms was in the minority.

The great controversy between the admirers of the old weapon and the modernists who condemned it now began in earnest. The most important advocate of the bow was Sir John Smythe, who published in 1590 *Certain Discourses . . . Concerning the Formes and Effects of Divers Sorts of Weapons, chiefly of the Mosquet, the Caliver, and the Longbow; As, Also, of the great Sufficiencie, Excellencie, and Wonderful Effects of Archers*. His critical observations on the comparative performance between bow and gun were answered by *A Briefe Discourse of Warre* published the same year by Sir Roger Williams. These two books contained the essence of the argument which other writers took up, but it must be admitted that the theme of many of these military authors was somewhat backward-looking. "The myghte of the realme of Englande standyth the moste upon archers", said Sir John Fortescue, and the following lines by Alleyne indicate the stubborn persistence of yet another historian convinced of the bow's superiority:

> "*That the white faith of Hist'ry cannot shew,*
> *That e'er the musket yet could beat the bow.*"

Humfrey Barwick, a brother officer of Sir John Smythe, calling himself (in the title page to his book) "Gentleman, Soldier, Captain et encor plus oultre", wrote an impatient reply* to Sir John's observations on the use of

*BARWICK, HUMFREY, *A breefe Discourse, concerning the force and effect of all manuall weapons of fire and the disability of the long bow or archery, in respect of others of greater force now in use* (1594)

During the plague in
seventeenth-century London,
burials of the dead took place
outside the city walls, and it was
customary for such obsequies to
be attended by armed law
enforcement officials. This
contemporary print shows the
last rites of William Wiseman, a
plague victim, with longbowmen
in attendance.

the bow in which he declared: "that he had held conference with divers
persons, of sundry callings . . . wherein he found so many addicted to the
opinion of Sir John Smythe, touching the commending of the archery in
England . . . that many were thereby persuaded, that the long bow is the
only weapon of the world for the obtaining of battails and victories."

The main advantage of the bow, it was said, was that it would shoot
several times faster than the gun—six aimed shots a minute, claimed Smythe,
against only one from an arquebusier. The supporters of the gun claimed
that the impact of the bullet was much greater than that of the arrow. Bows
were more accurate, declared the archers, and the very sight of arrows darken-
ing the sky struck terror into the enemy's heart. The art of archery is much
decayed and archers can be as nervous in battle as arquebusiers, replied the
followers of the gun, and the real efficiency of the bowman depends on his
bodily strength, "if he have not his three meals a day, as is his custom at
home, nor lies warm at nights, he presently waxes benumbed and feeble, and
cannot draw so as to shoot long shots." At least, said the archers, they could

not be blinded by smoke or put out of action by the least drizzle of rain as was the musketeer; after all, they continued, the bow is a simple weapon and firearms very complicated things—the piece clogs and fouls very easily, is liable to breakage, and can only be repaired by a skilled gunsmith. Wet weather spoils the powder, windy weather blows out the match, or sends its sparks flying among the powder of horns or bandoliers. If bad weather is pernicious to firearms, came the retort, it is no less so to bows. Rain makes bowstrings slack and after a march in the wet arrow-feathers flake off.

So the argument went on. There were even attempts to bring the bow up to date by devising new methods of using it; William Neade suggested equipping a "Double-Armed Man"* with a bow attached to a pike, and another inventor made lavish claims for flaming arrows ignited by a fuse which was lit just before fitting them to a bow.† In the dedication to his book Smythe charges Leicester and others of the Queen's advisers with incompetence and corruption. These charges were brought to the Queen's notice, and she

*NEADE, WILLIAM, *The Double-Armed Man* (1625)

†BARTLETT, JOHN, *A New Invention of Shooting Fire-Shafts in Long Bowes* (1628)

One of the seven carefully drawn woodcuts illustrating William Neade's *The Double-armed Man* (1625), and described therein as "portraitures proper for the pike and bow".

A woodcut from *A New Invention of Shooting Fire-shafts in Long Bowes*, (1628), which shows a curious and rather dangerous-looking use of the bow in war. There is no record that this was officially adopted.

King James I of England (1566–1625) with his son Prince Henry who, at the age of eight, learned to shoot with bow and gun. At the same time this prince had an officer in his establishment who was styled Bow Bearer.

directed that all copies of the book be "called in, both because they be printed without privilege, and that they may breed much question and quarrell". Sir John was sent to the Tower a year or so later and kept there for two years for using seditious language and inciting some of the musters to mutiny.

The modernists had their way, and the verdict was finally given against the bow when the Privy Council, by their Ordinance of 1595, decided that archers should no longer be enrolled in the trained bands as efficient soldiers, but only arquebusiers, caliver-men or musketeers; all bows had to be exchanged for muskets and calivers, and vast stocks of bows, arrows and archery appurtenances found their way into dusty stores in the Tower of London and other armouries. This was the virtual death-knell of the bow as a military weapon in the hands of the English, although there are some isolated instances of archery being used up to the middle of the seventeenth century, when bodies of archers were raised for service during the Civil War. For years to come the occasional lone voice was raised in defence of the bow in the forlorn hope that it would again be in the front rank of the English armies. Gervase Markham, writing in 1634,* suggested that archers should be brought back into the trained bands; the Earl of Craufurd early in the eighteenth century recommended the adoption of archery in the British army as "an advantage to these nations . . ." and as late as 1776 Benjamin Franklin, in a letter to Major General Lee, gave six reasons for the re-introduction of the bow in the American regular army.

THE ROYAL ARTILLERY COMPANY

Some interesting survivals resulted from loyalty to the bow as a weapon. The Royal Artillery Company of London owed its origin to a number of noblemen of the court who formed themselves into a body-guard for the protection of Queen Elizabeth subsequent to the defeat of the Spanish Armada. These élite bowmen feared that the king of Spain would, out of revenge, send an emissary to attempt the life of the Queen. They were styled the Companie of Liege Bow-men of the Queene, and Dudley, Earl of Leicester, was their captain. This exclusive corps, which had many privileges, was distinguished by the splendour of its uniform and accoutrements. The company was disbanded and subsequently reformed at the Restoration under the title of the "Royal Company of Archers" and from this originated the Royal Artillery Company.

The old supporters of the bow now pressed their case for the continuance of archery for reasons of health and tradition. "Shooting . . . is a very healthful and commendable recreation for a gentleman; neither do I know any other comparable unto it for stirring every part of the body; for it openeth

*MARKHAM, GERVASE, *The Art of Archery* (1634)

the breast and pipes, exerciseth the arms and feet, with less violence than running, leaping etc . . ." said one sixteenth-century writer, and another declared: "But this sufficeth for the declaration of shooting, whereby it is sufficiently proved that it incomparably excelleth all other exercise, pastime and solace . . ." Thomas D'Urfey warms up on this theme and, after disdainfully rejecting the ignorant notion that archery is a dull and laborious pastime fit only for peasants, tells us that "this Noble Exercise" is perfectly suited for a gentleman and is "acknowledged by the Learned and Judicious to be not only a Sport fit for the brawny Commonalty, but the Generous Nobility . . . . it banishes growing Distempers from the Bodies of such whose destructive Idleness nourish their Diseases" and of course liberally bestows health, strength and courage on "all Worthy Practicioners of the Science".

PUBLIC ARCHERY MEETINGS

Although the use of military archery now rapidly diminished, the popularity of bow-shooting as a leisure pastime grew. One great meeting of 3,000 archers from London, each with a bow and four arrows, marched to Hodgson's Field for a shooting match which lasted two days. They shot at about 135 yards and the meeting terminated with a torchlight procession, a banquet and celebrations for all and sundry. Up to this point all shooting matches of any size had been held in London, but an interesting departure from this custom took place in 1582 when there was "a great shooting at York". This was a precursor of what was to be, some 250 years later and also at York, the first of many English Championship meetings. The following verses were composed by a patriot who made an unsuccessful plea for the Queen's presence on that occasion:

God save our Queene, and keepe our peace,
That our good shooting maie increase;
And, praying to God, let us not cease,
    As well at Yorke as at London.

God graunt that once her Majestie,
Would come her cittie of Yorke to see,
For the comfort great of that countrie,
    As well as she doth at London.

Yorke, Yorke, for my monie,
Of all the cities that ever I see,
For merry pastime and companie,
    Except the cittie of London.

152

A selection of silver medals which were formerly attached to a silver arrow shot for in competition at the University of St Andrews. Each year another medal was added by the winner.

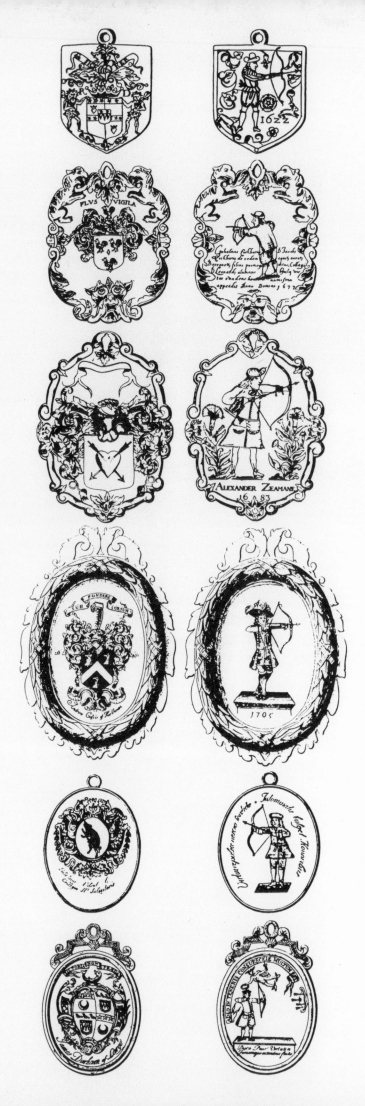

SHOOTING METHODS

At this time there were three chief methods of shooting: Prick or Clout, Butt, and Roving. Prick or Clout shooting took place at from 160 to 240 yards, the "mark" being eighteen inches in diameter, made of canvas stuffed with straw, and having a small white circle painted on it, the centre of which was a wooden peg; to "hit the white" meant to hit the white mark; to "cleave the pin", was to strike the peg. The object of this practice was to "keep a length" or shoot many arrows the same distance. Butt shooting required more accuracy; the butts, made of earth and covered with turf, were built from 100 to 140 yards apart. A paper disc, sometimes marked with concentric circles, was placed on these and to hit this disc was again called hitting the white. Roving consisted of shooting over open ground at unknown distances, except in the Finsbury and St George's Fields, for which printed guides existed showing the distance of each of the standing marks from the others.

An ingenious author of the nineteenth century sets out to give evidence of Shakespeare's practical knowledge of archery by analysing scores of terms, phrases, metaphors and similes in his works and suggesting comparable expressions used in archery.* This industrious Victorian savant draws freely on Ascham's *Toxophilus* and the many interesting comparisons he makes leave no doubt in the reader's mind that Shakespeare was, in fact, an archer of some experience. Shakespeare's plays were performed before audiences consisting mainly of the common people who could readily understand colloquialisms in the dialogue. The fact that Shakespeare recognised the value of including homely and readily understood references to archery (and, for that matter, other sports and pastimes) confirms his skill as a playwright and explains to a large extent the great popularity of his works in Elizabethan England.

KING JAMES AND KING CHARLES

At the end of the sixteenth century bows and arrows were undoubtedly in general use by "all sorts of persons without distinction of grade, age, or profession", and foreign observers were unanimous in their puzzlement that the stubborn English continued in such old-fashioned pastimes. Their bewilderment was tempered with some respect, however, possibly in memory of past history when so many victories were secured by the use of this very same stick and string. James I, whose son Prince Henry learned to shoot with bow and gun, encouraged the pursuit of archery as a pastime and appointed a Commission to survey and restore all old archery grounds that had been enclosed and built on. The growth of London had seriously encroached on

*RUSHTON, WILLIAM LOWES, *Shakespeare an Archer* (1897)

Left: The frontispiece to *The Art of Archery* by Gervase Markham (1650), in which Charles I is represented as an archer shooting in Finsbury Fields.

Finsbury Archer's ticket for the shooting of 1676: "All Gentlemen, lovers of the noble Society of Archery, are desired to meet at Drapers Hall in Throgmorton Street, on Monday the 24th day of July, 1676, by twelve of the clock precisely; and according to ancient custom of Finsbury Archers, to deliver to the Bearer hereof Mr William Wood, upon receipt of this Ticket, Two Shillings and Six-pence, that Provision may be made accordingly . . ."

archery fields these and conditions had been commented on by Stow* several years previously: "Why should I speak of the ancient daily exercise in the long-bow by the citizens of this city," he says, "now almost clear left off and forsaken? I overpass it, for by the means of closing in the common grounds our archers, for want of room to shoot abroad, creep into bowling alleys and ordinary dicing houses nearer home, where they have room enough to hazard their money at unlawful games, and there I leave them to take their pleasure." Charles I confirmed the order which prevented the fields near London from being enclosed, so as not "to interrupt the necessary and profitable exercise of shooting". The same Commission directs that bridges should be thrown over the dykes, and that all shooting marks which had been removed should be restored. Archery societies still in existence for more than a century afterwards continued to make occasional surveys on the north side of London to enforce such old enactments concerning the illegal enclosure of grounds used for archery practice. As late as 1746 a cowkeeper at Hoxton named Pitfield, whose name is preserved in a street in that neighbourhood, was compelled to re-erect a butt which he had removed, in commemoration of which it was inscribed with the words "Pitfield's Repentance" as a warning to others.

THE FINSBURY ARCHERS

For centuries Finsbury Fields had been one of the national centres for archery and the shooting ground of the Finsbury Archers. Little is known of the early history of this society but a list of their archery marks for rovers, giving the distances in scores of yards, was published in 1594 under the title *Ayme for Finsburie Archers*. They were closely connected with the Artillery Company for two centuries, and were revived after the Civil War in the same year as that body; they were frequently allowed the use of the Artillery Ground for practice, and many members of the Company were also archers. One of their most distinguished members was Sir William Wood, who as their Marshal received on their behalf the Braganza Shield, a silver badge weighing 25 oz, subscribed for by members of the Fraternity of the Finsbury Archers and dedicated to Catherine of Portugal, queen to Charles II. The shield is now in the possession of the Royal Toxophilite Society.† William Wood was buried in Clerkenwell churchyard with full military honours, and three flights of whistling arrows were shot over his grave. His epitaph reads:

*STOW, JOHN, *Survay of London* (1598)

†The Braganza Shield is on permanent loan to the Victoria and Albert Museum, London, where it is on public exhibition.

Sir William Wood lyes very near this stone,
In's time in Archery Excelled by none
Few were his Equals and this Noble Art
Has suffered here in the most tender part
Long did he live the honour of the bow
And his Long life to that alone did owe
But how can Art secure or what can save
Extreame Old age From an appointed grave
Surviving Archers much his Losse lament
And in respect bestow'd this monument
Where Whistling Arrowes did his worth proclaim
And Eterniz'd his Memory and Name.

During the seventeenth century the Artillery Company carried out official bodyguard duties to the Lord Mayor and were often accompanied by the Finsbury Archers, at that time commanded by Sir R. Peyton. They were then referred to as "a most heroic rarity; viz: gentlemen archers completely armed with longbows and swords, arrows and pallisades [stakes pointed at both ends for defence against cavalry], with hats turned up at the outside,

A contemporary portrait of Sir William Wood (1609–91), Marshal of the Finsbury Archers and famous for his encouragement of archery in the seventeenth century. The picture is one of a pair painted on panels which formed the doors of a cupboard in which the Braganza Shield was kept. The shield itself is proudly displayed in the picture. Both portraits are in the possession of the Royal Toxophilite Society.

The Catherine of Braganza Shield. Purchased by the Finsbury Archers by subscription and named after the consort of Charles II, this commemorative piece was held in the custody of Sir William Wood.

A print of a view of the north side of London by Wenceslaus Hollar (1607–77), which shows archers shooting in Finsbury Fields in 1665. A rare illustration which gives a good impression of the contemporary conditions of that area, famous for centuries as a shooting ground.

and tied with large knots of green ribbon". The Finsbury Archers held many of their annual meetings on the Artillery Ground and a newsprint of 1721 records a test of skill "between John Smith, Master of Archery, living near that ground, and Thomas Polington a Devonshire Gentleman, for a bowl of punch of half-a-guinea, where 'tis supposed most of the Proficient in that Art will be to see the Performance: Three Flights in Five are to decide the matter." Until 1738 the Court of Assistants of the Artillery Company gave permission to this body to erect two archery butts in their ground, and as late as 1753 targets were erected in Finsbury Fields during the Easter and Whitsun holidays, but little more is heard of this active and enthusiastic corps of bowmen and they appear to have become extinct as a society round about 1770. The few survivors became members of a new body of archers which was formed in 1781 and which still exists as the Royal Toxophilite Society.

The art of archery in England had now reached a significant point in its history; the great era of military archery had died a not unexpected death and the loyal continuation of the sport by a few enthusiastic but outnumbered supporters had slowly come to a halt. Apart from isolated instances of country gentlemen continuing to use the bow in memory of their fathers, the art was

During the eighteenth century shooting at the popinjay became a popular pastime among the leisured classes of continental Europe. Note the composite bows. From *The Ages of Man* by Nicolas Lancret (1690–1743).

Opposite page: The Archers. Thomas, Viscount Sidney and Colonel Ackland, painted by Sir Joshua Reynolds (1723–92). It appears that a competition is in progress between a traditional English longbow and an Asiatic composite bow. Both archers are using the Flemish, two-fingered, loose. The longbow would be rejected as a perfect example as, from observation of its tensed arc, it would "jar" in the hand on release.

popular no more; the butts were overgrown, the worms and moths found plenty to satisfy their appetites in bowshafts and feathers, and the skills of the bowyers and the fletchers were now half-forgotten. The sport was to slumber for a few years, but shortly it was to enjoy a revival of a magnitude never dreamed of in all its past history.

Gold medal of the Scorton Archers. On May 14th, 1673, this society began shooting for a silver arrow for which there is still annual competition. From *Anecdotes of Archery* (1845).

SELECT BIBLIOGRAPHY

Ascham, Roger, *Toxophilus, 1545*, Ed. by Arber [1895]

Barwick, Humfrey, *A Brief Discourse Concerning the Force and Effect of all Manuall Weapons of Fire, and the Disability of the Long Bowe or Archery* [1594]

Dallington, Robert, *The View of Fraunce, 1598*, Shakespeare Association Facsimiles, No. 13 [1936]

Gregory, Donald, *Notices Regarding Scotish Archery*, Archaeologia Scotia, Vol. III [1831]

Grose, Francis, *Military Antiquities Respecting a History of the English Army* [1786]

Holmes, M. R., FSA, *Moorfields in 1559*, HMSO [1963]

Latimer, Bishop Hugh, *Seven Sermons before Edward VI*, Ed. by Arber [1869]

Markham, Gervase, *Country Contentments* [1615]

Oman, Sir Charles, *A History of the Art of War in the Sixteenth Century* [1937]

Ormerod, G. Wareing, *On the Substitution of Firearms for the Long-Bow*, Transactions of the Devonshire Association for the Advancement of Science, Literature and Art [1885]

Oxley, James E., MA, PhD, *The Fletchers and Longbowstringmakers of London* [1968]

Rushton, William Lowes, *Shakespeare an Archer* [1897]

Ryan, Lawrence V., *Roger Ascham* [1963]

Smythe, John, *Certain Discourses . . . concerning the Formes and Effects of Divers Sorts of Weapons . . . Also of the Great Sufficiencie, Excellencie, and Wonderful Effect of Archers* [1590]

Somner, William, *The Antiquities of Canterbury* [1640]

Turner, Sir James, *Pallas Armata* [1670]

Wood, William, *The Bowman's Glory, or Archery Revived* [1682]

6 The Sporting Revival

It is an exercise (by proof) we see,
Whose practice doth with nature best agree,
Obstructions of the liver it prevents,
Stretching the nerves and arteries, gives extents
To the spleen's oppilations, clears the breast
And spungy lungs: it is a foe profest
To all consumptions.

BOWMAN'S GLORY

A rare engraving of Sir Ashton Lever, Bt. (1729–88), founder, in 1781, and first President of the Toxophilites, now the Royal Toxophilite Society.

SIR Ashton Lever was a remarkable man. Amongst other accomplishments he trained horses at Oxford; accumulated an aviary of 4,000 birds; hunted with a pack of beagles; hired a boat, sailed to France and brought home an enormous quantity of shells and, adding countless fossils and stuffed animals to the collection, formed a museum which people came from far and wide to see. He was persuaded to bring his collection to London and exhibited it at Leicester House. The speculation did not pay, however, and in 1785 it was disposed of by a lottery of 36,000 tickets at a guinea each. Attached to the museum, as its curator, was a Mr Waring, who contracted a disorder in his chest for which doctors were unable to find a remedy. At some former period of his life he had studied bowmaking under the elder Kelsal, of Manchester, whose family had been bowyers for several centuries, and he resolved to try archery as a cure for his ill-health. In a short while he found shooting did him so much good that he persevered, and with such good results that he was completely cured. Sir Ashton Lever, seeing the splendid results obtained by the self-imposed treatment of Waring, decided that he too would take up archery, and this he did, persuading a few friends to join him and meeting in the grounds of Leicester House which stood in Leicester Square. Before long a few remaining Finsbury Archers joined Sir Ashton and his friends and together they formed the Toxophilite Society in 1781. This gave impetus to the great

162

The original monochrome
water-colour drawing by Joseph
Slater from which James Heath
(1756–1834) made the popular
engraving, entitled "Archery".
The central figure is undoubtedly
a portrait of Thomas Waring
(1731–1805), famed toxophilite
who helped encourage the revival
of archery.

revival of archery in England at the end of the eighteenth century, the Toxophilites taking the lead and being practically the parents of all the archery
societies subsequently formed.

THE ROYAL COMPANY OF ARCHERS

Before the development of the English Revival is discussed in greater
detail, it is fitting that the aspect of archery as a sport in Scotland is considered,
with particular reference to one distinguished society which has a longer
history and an earlier origin than the Toxophilite Society, forming a unique
survival in its own right. From a fairly early date some isolated instances of
butt shooting in Scotland are recorded, among which references we find that
Mary Queen of Scots herself practised with a bow at Holyrood and St
Andrews, the velvet glove used by her on these occasions being mentioned in
one of the inventories of her effects. Another unique record of butt-shooting
is contained in the history of the University of St Andrews, possessor of

three arrows of silver for which the students competed annually between the years 1618 and 1751. In addition there are several other brief references to regularly practised archery dating from the sixteenth to the eighteenth centuries. However, in 1676, a momentous year for the history of archery in Scotland, a group of gentlemen in Edinburgh associated themselves to restore the practice of archery in that country. The following year their constitution was confirmed by the Privy Council who, in addition, gave them twenty pounds to purchase their first prize and sanctioned their title as The Royal (or King's) Company of Archers. Their most ancient trophy, the Musselburgh Arrow, has been competed for since 1603, which gives some indication that they existed as a less formal corporation before their official recognition. Queen Anne gave them a charter in 1704 which allowed them "free ingress and regress to all public butts, plains, and pasturages legally allotted both for shooting with the bow at random or at measured distances, and that freely, quietly, well and in peace . . ." The charter concluded by requiring the company to render "to us and our successors one pair of barbed arrows at the term of Whitsunday, if asked only . . ." This symbolic tribute, known as a "Reddendo", can still be demanded by the sovereign and consists of three beautifully made arrows tipped with silver broadheads and fletched with peacock feathers. The fact that three arrows are called a "pair" dates from the time when this number was carried, two only being for use and the third kept in reserve as a spare. Following a grant of letters patent in 1713, the style and title of this body became the Royal Company of Archers, and they applied to the Common Council in Edinburgh for the use of a piece of waste ground called Beth's Wynd. The Council, willing to encourage this laudable enterprise, not only granted them their request but, in 1719, gave them as a further encouragement a silver arrow to be shot for annually.

One of their most illustrious members was Sir Walter Scott, who was admitted in 1821, a year after he had written *Ivanhoe*, a novel in which there are many romantic but reasonably accurate references to shooting with bows and arrows. Scott's interest in archery dated from before his admittance to the

The Reddendo, a "pair" of arrows, (always three in case of damage or loss) traditionally provided with barbed heads of silver and fletched with peacock feathers, which are presented to the sovereign by the Royal Company of Archers on official royal visits to Scotland.

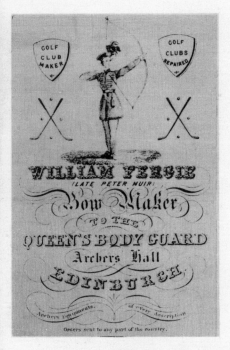

A trade card of William Fergie, official bowyer to the Royal Company of Archers, who took over the business of Peter Muir which had been established for about 150 years.

Royal Company, and he had previously referred to them as a society "amongst whom Jacobitism long found refuge". He does not seem to have joined in the shooting, but was profoundly interested in the aims and traditions of that historic body; and some say that he played a prominent part in their promotion to The Royal Body Guard, which confirmed their loyalty to the House of Hanover.

King George IV made a state visit to Scotland in 1822 and showed great interest in the company. The considerable patronage which he subsequently bestowed on it not only improved the status and prestige of its members but promoted the company itself to the dignity of an officially established institution, their full title now becoming The King's Body Guard for Scotland, The Royal Company of Archers. Up to this time the military ranks they used were purely honorary—they had never been, in any sense, recognised as a military body, and even after the royal recognition their actual status was a matter of uncertainty. George IV himself designed some of the elaborate uniforms which were proudly worn on various occasions, including a gorgeous dress coat, a field uniform and a mess coat which could be worn on the occasions of the quite frequent formal banquets. An earlier uniform had consisted of tartan trews trimmed with silver and worn with a black bonnet and white ruff. No club, lodge or guild has quite the same distinction of duty, history and dress as the Royal Company, and their mem-

The Royal Company of Archers shoot regularly in traditional fashion with longbows at a "clout" target. The uniform shown is the field dress worn on informal occasions, but a full dress uniform is worn for formal functions.

Left: on the occasion of Queen Victoria's visit to Edinburgh to unveil a statue of the late Prince Albert in November 1870 the Royal Company of Archers provided a royal bodyguard led by their Captain General, the Duke of Buccleuch.

bers, wearing their field uniform of green archer-cloth with eagle feathers in the bonnet, still attend upon the sovereign during official visits to Scotland.

THE CLOUT AND THE POPINJAY

The traditional form of shooting at a "clout", dating from the days of the first Elizabeth or earlier, is still regularly practised by the Royal Company of Archers. Another ancient and specialised variation of archery practice was shooting at the popinjay, or "papingo" as it is known locally, traditionally held to have been practised at Kilwinning as early as 1482 but never really popular in England. This consists of shooting at a "bird" made of wood, resembling a parrot; the wings were made "louse for shooting af" and this target was set on the end of a pole projecting from the top of the remaining tower of Kilwinning Abbey, some 100 feet up, in such a way that a slight touch could "ding her doun". The Ancient Society of Kilwinning Archers have records of the annual shoot from 1688 which has been continued each year with the exception of one longish break. This is a survival of a form of shooting which is rarely found elsewhere, despite the fact that shooting at the popinjay as well as butt shooting was popular in country districts for many years. In the burgh archives of Irvine for October 1532 there is an account of a "Walpynshaw"—or weapon showing—when the men of the district assembled and showed their skill in the management of the bow and other weapons; and in 1665 reference is made to the papingo set up by the magistrates of Irvine conforming to "old ancient practises so that the Burgesses might adres themselffs theirto with their bowis and arrows".

The Irvine Toxophilites was a society constituted in 1814, and the most important occurrence in its history was when sixty members served as a body-guard to Lady Seymour, the Queen of Beauty, at the famous Eglington Tournament in 1839. This event, which owing to torrential rain turned out to be a dismal failure and ended in sorry confusion, was a costly enterprise launched by Lord Eglington on the wave of the Gothic revival of early Victorian times. Special uniforms were designed for the archers consisting of tunics of green plush, with buckskin breeches, wide boots and a large hat with a plume. In recognition of their services the Earl presented them with a silver-gilt belt and quiver, set with carbuncles and worth £200, which was shot for annually for a few years, the competition consisting of Clout, Papingo and Butt shooting. The original Irvine Toxophilites have long since disbanded but in recent years the society was revived with a view to restoring the annual competition for the Eglington Belt. Two other groups of archers took part in the tournament, the Queen of Beauty having the added attraction of the Ballochmyle Archeresses in attendance, a society which was probably more elegant in costume than proficient in archery, while the Ayrshire Archers waited on the Lord of the Tournament, who was none other than the Earl of Eglington.

REGENCY BUCKS AND BOWS

The period of the revival of archery in England coincided with the regency, with a king whose sanity was suspect and whose court was a hotbed of gossip and conniving courtiers, presided over by the Prince Regent, the most flamboyant leader of fashion England had ever seen. Prince George was neither bad nor foolish; he patronised the arts, and his polished manners made him prince among his own dandies. But he was selfish and petty, and in an age of prudent virtue his debauchery made him unpopular. The period was one of contrasting opulence and poverty, twenty years of war with

For the Eglington Tournament of 1839 Lord Glenlyon, who appeared as the Knight of the Gael, raised and equipped a bodyguard of seventy-eight officers and men known as the Athole Highlanders. To commemorate the part they played in the festivities he presented his men with this silver medal. The Atholl Highlanders, as they are now known, are still maintained by the Duke of Atholl as the only private army in Britain.

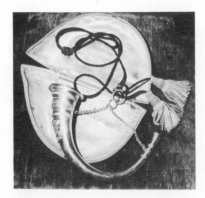

One of a series of silver bugle horns presented by the Prince of Wales to the Royal Kentish Bowmen and won by Edward Hussey on August 18th, 1794.

Revolutionary and Napoleonic France, Nash terraces and sumptuous marine pavilions, and rural England in all her unspoilt beauty standing on the brink of the Industrial Revolution. The pleasures of the lower classes now excluded archery; their enjoyments were to be found in the spectator sports such as horse-racing and prize-fights. The common people would travel miles to witness a match between two bare-fisted champions, and it was known for up to 20,000 to assemble at one time. The fashionable members of the aristocracy ran these meetings, hiring and backing pugilists and owning and racing horses. The duel was still popular, but whereas in the eighteenth century duels had been fought with rapiers, in the nineteenth century pistols were used. A singular account mentions a duel, in which bows and arrows were the chosen weapons, taking place between two gentlemen in Edinburgh in 1791, to decide a point of honour. They were accompanied by seconds in the approved manner, and had a surgeon in attendance. After a harmless exchange of three shots the parties retired, the point of honour, doubtless, being thus satisfactorily settled. The reporter makes no mention of the distance involved but adds, "If similar weapons were always employed in duelling this amusement would speedily become unfashionable, seeing that the seconds would run quite as great, if not a greater, risk than the principals."

Taking up a novel or unusual plaything, the latest fashion or a newly devised extravagance, was nothing new in the courts of Europe, and the nobility, with time and money to spend and eager to curry favour, would readily follow the latest caprice of their king or prince. When the leisured classes took up shooting with a bow and arrow the pastime became a lavish entertainment rather than a simple sporting pursuit, and apart from those slavishly following fashion, occasional seekers for "something different" came under the spell of archery. Such an individualist was Madame de Staël, wife of Louis XIV's Finance Minister, political opponent to Napoleon and a brilliant courtesan, who as a young lady developed a sudden passion for archery after seeing a new ballet called *Télémaque*. This was the only sport she was to master and, in company with her tutor, she endlessly practised target shooting clad as a nymph in a costume of diaphanous gauze.

ROYAL KENTISH BOWMEN

The revival of archery in England gathered momentum, at first following the example of the Prince Regent who, apart from being a patron of several archery societies, himself shot in a bow in the "Level" close to his fabulous seaside pavilion at Brighton. This example attracted the sycophants and the fashion-conscious smart set, who were quick to organise themselves into societies devoted to archery and social convivialities. The Royal Kentish Bowmen was one of the most exclusive, in addition to being one of the

Ladies' Head Dresses. | The Royal ARCHERS at their antient & Manly Exercise. | Fashionable Head Dresses.

A favourite device of the advertisers of fashion is to use some up-to-the-minute and popular activity as an eye-catching background for their wares. This engraving of the eighteenth century is an unsophisticated treatment of the same principle. Note the reference to "ancient and manly exercises". "Ancient"—conveying a sense of solidarity through long-established use, and "manly"—to set feminine hearts a-flutter.

earliest, of these élite clubs. It was formed in 1785 and "Prinny" took a special interest in their affairs, even finding time occasionally to shoot with them at Dartford Heath. Once again the Prince Regent showed his fondness for sartorial elaboration when he ordered for the society a uniform of "a grass green coat, buff linings, and buff waistcoat and breeches: black collar to the coat, uncut velvet in winter, tabby silk in summer, with yellow buttons, according to the pattern sent to Nuttings, 16 King Street, Covent Garden". This had to be worn by members at all meetings under the penalty of a fine of two shillings and sixpence.

Much of the manner in which these exclusive societies conducted themselves and the many special activities which they organised can be discovered in the records of the Kentish Bowmen, a typical society of the period. We read of the immense care taken with all the elaborate arrangements for a field day, the appointment of numerous officials with special duties, such as standard-bearers, laureates, cup-bearers and antiquaries, and the formation of committees of infinite variety. We can visualise their special meetings where, accompanied by the appropriate musical salutes, they displayed with extrovert pride specially designed banners and uniforms, their ladies graciously supporting their endeavours as "ornaments to the occasion". No amount of skilled attention was spared for quite the most important and indispensable feature of their gatherings—the banquet: this was followed by a ball, often

A French fashion plate of 1813.
The English revival of archery
rapidly spread to the Continent,
where it was considered an
elegant and genteel pastime.

A fashion plate of c. 1825 showing
a typical outfit for the elegant
"archeress" of the period, engraved
by Wm. Hopwood.

An engraving by Cook entitled "Archery at Hatfield", from *The Sporting Magazine* for November 1792. The print shows a meeting of the Hertfordshire Society of Archers, to whom the Marchioness of Salisbury gave her patronage. Her Ladyship is depicted with an arrow fully drawn and attended by other persons of quality.

in costume, always a glittering event not to be missed by the élite of the district or any social aspirants lucky enough to be invited. The aspect which received the least attention was the actual shooting. The rules were drawn up correctly and in great detail and the skill of the champions was rewarded by valuable prizes. Equipment was the best that money could buy and the archers were gathered together for the purpose of matching their skill against each other, but archery was abandoned if the weather turned inclement or when dinner was ready, or when, by general agreement, the competitors had had enough.

THE BLACKHEATH MEETINGS

Several reviews of archers were held at Blackheath, near London, during the early 1790s and most of the prominent societies sent companies to take part in these grand events, and also, if they were so inclined, to shoot. These were splendid affairs, up to 500 archers travelling from as far away as Yorkshire, Wales or Northumberland to compete. Many of the societies represented are recorded in a rare list* of forty-four preserved in the British Museum, which includes the contingents from the Honorable Artillery Company, who drew their Archery Division from members of the Toxophilite Society, together with a strong representation from societies in the Home Counties. In addition to the participants these gala days attracted enormous crowds of sightseers. Some idea of the elaborate and colourful spectacle which these meetings presented is contained in the following extract from Pierce Egan's *Book of Sports* of 1832: "On Wednesday 29th May, 1793, the general meeting of the Archers of Great Britain took place on Blackheath. About twelve o'clock, according to general orders, the bowmen entered the field with their band of martial music, and having paraded the enclosure, a signal was given for the archers to assemble at their respective targets, and the shooting instantly commenced, which the shooters followed up with prodigious dexterity, till three o'clock, amidst a vast concourse of genteel company; and then with their band playing, marched to their tents for refreshment. About half-past-five the shooting was given up by consent. The company, who were becoming too numerous having broke the line of order, and so deranged the shooters, that the Royal Surrey Bowmen could, towards the conclusion, seldom see their own targets."

In addition to the social arrangements which followed the actual shooting, many other activities took place not even remotely connected with archery. At the Royal Kentish Bowmen's Lodge, which was their headquarters at Dartford Heath, members took part in plays and entertainments which appear to have been remarkably well produced, although no records exist of the

*BANKS, MISS, Notes, Extracts, Cuttings from books, etc, relating to archery, and patterns of archery ribbons. British Museum ADD. Manuscripts 6314 to 6320.

quality of the individual performances. Prominent members featured in the programmes: "Mr Smart provided the Musick. He played the double Bass. His second son led the band. The Hon. John Spencer played the organ or Piano Forte," says one report; and during 1798 performances of *The Tempest*, *Who's the Dupe*, *The Children of the Wood*, *Henry IV, Part I* and a play called *Midas* were performed in the Lodge, all in four days. A really marathon evening was held in January of that year when *King John*, *The Dragon of Wantley* and a curious entertainment called *The Interlude of Silvester Daggerwood* were performed; one Mr Maddocks, in addition to being founder of this prominent and active society, taking part in all three plays. The Kentish Bowmen must have found the decision to hold a masked ball a welcome relaxation from all these exertions, and the exclusiveness of this occasion can readily be surmised when we read that tickets were a guinea each, a large sum of money in those days. A stern reminder to the romantically minded appeared on the foot of the notice for this ball: "No gentlemen admitted in Dominoes", which no doubt disappointed amorous young bloods anticipating a flirtation in disguise.

An engraving of Byron (1788–1824), when a boy aged seven, from the original picture by Kay. In addition to the fact that it was fashionable to pursue archery from a tender age, Byron's lameness and his delicate constitution probably prevented him from enjoying other outdoor pastimes.

THE MARCH OF ARCHERY.

As with so many other pursuits reserved for the gentry in the early nineteenth century, archery soon became a butt for lively caricature and ribald comment. This cartoon, in the possession of the Royal Toxophilite Society, is a fine example of contemporary humour. It was drawn by "Robin Hood' and published in 1829 by G. Humphrey.

It was customary for specially employed and properly trained markers to signal each shot at certain bow meetings. Note the convenient cache of refreshment.

Left: an unusual fashion plate of 1829. The central figure shows a uniform especially designed for the Royal Oak Archers. Dress regulations in many societies were rigidly enforced on penalty of fines or disqualification for non-compliance.

The Reverend W. Dodd, Usher at Westminster School, who was the appointed laureate to the Kentish Bowmen, found time to publish a volume of verse dedicated to the Prince Regent. This habit of producing laudatory or commemorative verse occurred in connexion with several other societies at about this time, and despite the inauspicious quality of the poetry the sentiments expressed were sincere and the energies of these amateur poets are

worth exploring. "If the following compositions, which, through the medium of a kind-hearted and early known friend have obtained the high honour of being dedicated to your Royal Highness, should draw forth one smile of approbation from the exalted Personage who deigns to patronise them, the primary object of their author will be accomplished," said the Reverend Dodd in his dedication. History does not relate whether or not his object was accomplished; however the following sample may have raised a wry smile from H.R.H.:

> In the circle of Fashion if Vanity leads,
>   Carol it, carol it, hey to the ditty;
> Extravagance loosens, and Folly succeeds;
>   Carol it, carol it, hey to the ditty;
> But in Archery's circle Economy guides,
> We have health to reward us and Vigour presides,
>   With derry down derry,
>   We're lively and merry,
> Sing derry down, derry down, hey down derry.

This volume of verse is curious to modern eyes. Many of the pieces are set to music; one, entitled "The Bowman's Dirge", begins "Come tune the solemn strain to the twang, twang of the Bowstring while slowly o'er the plain, we march our Yeomanrie," etc. Other and more lively airs, evocative of Robin Hood and his Merry Men, were sung at suppers and evening entertainments. "The Riband" was written to commemorate a whimsical occasion when a Lady (unnamed) sent a green and buff riband to a Bowman (also anonymous) to tie round his nightcap.

ARCHERY FOR LADIES

This period of the revival of archery also marked a significant step forward in the emancipation of women. In 1787 the Royal British Bowmen was the first society to admit ladies as shooting members and, although many other societies were reluctant to allow ladies the privilege of membership, there was no lack of encouragement for them to take up the exercise. "It has been said a reward was formerly offered to him who could invent a new pleasure," said Dodd. "Had such a reward been held forth by the ladies of the present day, he who introduced Archery as a female exercise, would have deservedly gained the prize." The act of shooting was recognised as being within the accomplishments of a lady, not over energetic, nor too coarse an amusement; after all, the best people practised archery as a pastime and one could look especially feminine and graceful whilst drawing a bow. Diana herself, archeress supreme, was goddess of love and beauty—what better model to copy, how

A meeting of the Royal British Bowmen in the grounds of Erthig, Denbighshire, on September 13th, 1822. The lively and interesting scene, which can be taken as an accurate if formalised representation of an exclusive bow-meeting, was drawn by J. Townsend from an original sketch by W. H. Timms and engraved by Bennett.

better to display the attributes of womanhood! This was the mood of the era of Romanticism, now in full swing, and those with leisure would harmlessly wile away the gentle summer evenings directing lightly aimed shafts in the general direction of a target. A famous opera dancer, so it is said, upon being taught the use of the bow, declared "of all the attitudes she ever studied, she thought the position of shooting with the long-bow the most noble and dignified".

There were those, of course, who raised objections to the adoption of the bow by the fair sex on the grounds that archery was "too masculine to accord with the gentleness of manner" of the ladies. This protest was rapidly demolished by the comments of several gallant writers, and Thomas Roberts,[*] a member of the Toxophilite Society, was one: "This censure seems to be somewhat unmerited and ill-timed; it is unfortunate, that there are few diversions in the open air, in which women can join with satisfaction: and archery seems to be an admirable antidote to the sedentary life which is incident to the general employment of their time." Popular journals now took

*ROBERTS, THOMAS, *The English Bowman* (1801)

176

up the theme and articles and prints appeared enthusing over the possibilities of archery as a ladies' sport. *The Ladies (Most Elegant and Convenient) Pocket Book*, for 1791, included a view of the Hertfordshire Society of Archers showing the Duchess of Leeds, the Marchioness of Salisbury, Miss Grimstone and Miss Seabright busy at the targets, and *The New Lady's Magazine* of the previous year published a popular historical account of archery which no doubt entertained and instructed many a sweet young thing on rainy afternoons. Reports of meetings now started to appear in other weekly and monthly magazines, and archery events became part of the social calendar. In 1801 the Toxophilite Society asked the celebrated Mrs Crespigny to accept the office of Lady Patroness, and this she did with the spirit and enthusiasm for which she was noted. Both she and her husband, who was subsequently created a baronet, were rich and entertained lavishly, and her archery fêtes were particularly attractive. At these meetings, held at Champion Lodge, matches were shot in which ladies, in addition to the gentlemen of the Toxophilite Society, participated, fines being levied on the losers and devoted to charity.

THE BOOK AND THE BOW

The first major work on archery to appear since Ascham wrote his famed *Toxophilus* almost two and half centuries previously, was published in 1792. This was *An Essay on Archery*, an interesting though somewhat disconnected history of the bow, offering for popular consumption a collection of facts never before assembled in one volume. Walter Michael Moseley, the author of this work, was descended from an ancient, respectable and opulent family in the county of Stafford, and was led to enquire further into the history of the bow than ever before attempted, although much of the material he used had been included in an admirable paper* read before the Society of Antiquaries of London by the Honorable Daines Barrington, in 1783. This work was followed, nine years later, by another book dedicated to the Patron of the Toxophilite Society, H.R.H. the Prince of Wales, and written by the aforementioned Thomas Roberts. *The English Bowman*, as his book was called, included a concise historical background to archery, a lengthy comment on the teachings of Ascham, extracts from the works of Sir John Smythe and a dissertation on the life of Robin Hood. Finally Roberts reprinted several notable accounts of archery meetings of the sixteenth and seventeenth centuries and completed this excellent treatise with a glossary and a bibliography. The publication of these books offered further proof of the growing popularity of archery and satisfied a yearning among many of its devotees who,

*BARRINGTON, The Hon. DAINES, *Observations on the Practice of Archery in England*, Archaeologia, Vol. VII (1783)

as a result of the growing interest in things archaic and heroic, wished to learn more about the traditions of the bow and arrow.

The Prince Regent continued his patronage of several societies and found time to shoot with them on their "grand days". There is no doubt of his deep interest in archery. He presented a number of trophies to be competed for, the most renowned being a series of silver bugles, several of which are still proudly possessed by the descendants of those who won them. His Highness sometimes presided in person at prizegivings of the societies of which he was patron, and on one of these occasions the Reverend J. W. Dodd, of whom we have already spoken, won one of the famous bugles. He later waxed rather more than ordinarily eloquent when he described the event: "The prize of Archery on the day of conquest, which the writer of this happily won, and which your Royal Highness was pleased in person to bestow upon him, has been carefully preserved ever since as the trophy of the day. It will remain with its present possessor through life—sacred and inestimable: and when it descends to future inheritors, must be regarded by all of them as an unalienable memento of princely grace and bounty to the victor who fortunately bore it away from his competitors."

THE PRINCE'S RECKONING

During these early years of revival the Prince Regent's influence was undoubtedly considerable; he restored to the bow and arrow a prestige which it had lacked since the days of Henry VIII, and he elevated archery to a level of importance greater than any other participatory sport. Ascham had regularised the method of shooting and now the Prince of Wales was to regularise the method of scoring—which up to this time had been extremely haphazard and arbitrary. This was an important innovation which would enable accurate comparisons to be made between shooters and would eventually provide a useful measurement for individual ability and improvement. He first standardised the coloured rings on the target, and then laid down scoring values for each. The coloured rings which received this royal notice had been used since 1754 at least, when the stewards of the Finsbury Archers were directed to "provide a target or square pasteboard, covered with cloth; round the centre of which should be drawn a circle, and about that circle four concentric rings, to be visible and exactly distinguished by colours". The circle in the centre called the Gold, which was then gilded, now scored nine; the next ring, the Red, scored seven; the Blue, at some time the Inner White, five; the Black, three, and the White, the outermost ring, one. These values have been known ever since as "The Prince's Reckoning" and have remained standard practice for target archery in Britain, America and elsewhere to this day. In addition to this novelty Prince George, realising that his new system of scoring would not work satisfactorily unless everyone shot at similar distances from the target, proceeded to standardise the target ranges. The resultant distances of 100, 80 and 60 yards became known as "The Prince's Lengths" and subsequently formed the basis of the York Round. The British Championship is still decided on the combined score of two of these York Rounds, an annual reminder of the wise and practical decisions taken by one of archery's most distinguished devotees.

A TEMPORARY SET-BACK

Many of the societies which were formed in the first flush of enthusiasm disbanded on the threat of war with France at about the turn of the century, and the following resolution, passed by the Royal British Bowmen, was typical: "That on account of the several military employments which many of the members of this society have entered into, and which will probably take them out of the neighbourhood, there shall be held only three bow meetings this year, and the meetings afterwards cease till peace be restored, and our bowmen more at liberty to attend to the noble science of archery." The indefatigable Dodd reported the dismal scene of former archery glories that was once the Lodge of the Royal Kentish Bowmen, which he visited some time after their disbandment: "All was dreary, forlorn and wild—the buildings untenanted, forsaken, and dropping fast into decay; and the grounds rude and uncultivated, like the adjacent heath beside them. What the scene once was, many must remember—what it now is, all liberal minds must deplore." These troubled years, however, created only a temporary set-back and, as times became more settled, and peace assured, the influence of the few remaining societies began to make itself felt. Gradually more and more accounts of archery meetings began to appear in the papers and magazines, and notices of the revival of old societies and the formation of new ones, occurred more frequently until about 1830 when archery was again established as a popular and fashionable amusement. The mood struck by writers was still one of enthusiasm for the revival, and gentle persuasion for those who had set aside their bows and arrows for sterner matters was not lacking: "Since archery has again raised its head, crowned with such distinguished honours, and offering so much pleasure and advantage: let us receive it with due respect: and pay our tribute, by continuing to cultivate the art."

There was no lack of response and this renewed interest provided a fresh incentive for the manufacturers of archery equipment to produce fine quality bows and arrows which were made to order by first-class craftsmen. Thomas Waring, junior, whose father's example induced Sir Ashton Lever to form the Toxophilite Society, opened an archery warehouse in Bedford Square and had an archery ground at Bayswater, extending to several acres, for

"The Toxophilites". A charming pen and ink sketch of 1840 by W. Murray which exactly conveys the refined pleasures of archery during a summer's afternoon among the upper middle classes.

prospective customers to try out their purchases. His little handbook *A Treatise on Archery* was published in 1814, and became so popular that it went into nine editions. The author was well grounded in the practical aspects of archery, and in his introduction, in a manner reassuringly persuasive, he invited the ladies to participate; it was "the only field diversion they could enjoy, without incurring the censure of being thought masculine", an important point at a time when the female sex spared no endeavours to remain feminine. An interesting section of Waring's book deals with the formulation of a set of rules, and he quotes examples drawn from the regulations of existing societies. Many of the restrictions thought necessary then would be totally unsuited to modern application: "care should be taken that every member's coat be cut from the same cloth" . . . "it is agreed and hereby declared, that if any of them [members] shall that day curse or swear . . . he shall forthwith pay down one shilling, and so proportionate for each oath" . . . "if any member marry he should pay a fine of £100 or alternatively treat the rest to a marriage feast" . . . "no children" . . . "no dogs" . . . "no smoking" and "perfect silence when others are about to shoot", being but a few of the rules readily acceptable at this time.

THE VICTORIAN ERA

The eighteen-year-old Victoria succeeded to the throne in 1837, and now England was to settle down to a long and largely peaceful reign until the end of the century. For nearly a hundred years after Waterloo there was no great war, and the Victorians began to enjoy a period of prosperity marked by strong religious feelings and a full appreciation of family life. Britain stood on the frontiers of science, and wonderful inventions began to emerge. Photography, for instance, which had its beginnings as early as 1827, was later acclaimed by an observer as "the greatest boon that has been conferred on the poorer classes", and the age of the camera had come to stay. The masses were beginning to enjoy other more material benefits such as seasonal holidays, easier travel and the purchase of a wider range of goods available through free trade and better communications. They were also able to shepherd their exceptionally large families round such public spectacles as the Great Exhibition of 1851; their working conditions were being drastically revised and they were realising a greater freedom than before. If they were so inclined the restless sections of the community could now settle in Canada, Australia and New Zealand.

The upper classes were still very rich and formed only a very small minority of the population. Their lives had not changed much since the days of George I and II. The influence of the noble and the wealthy had, no doubt, considerably stimulated the spread of archery and the Queen herself, when Princess, together with her mother the Duchess of Kent, had become a patron of the "Queen's" Royal St Leonard's Archers, and attended meetings of the Royal British Bowmen. As a young girl of twelve Victoria had been taken to watch the fleet in the Solent, and on the same visit spent time watching an archery meeting at nearby Carisbrooke. From a letter she wrote to Leopold I, King of the Belgians, it appears that she enjoyed the naval grandeur rather more than the quiet archery scene: "We went to Sir Edward Codrington's fleet, the day before yesterday, it was a most beautiful sight; and yesterday we went to an Archery-meeting at Carisbrooke Castle, which was likewise a pretty, but not half so grand a beautiful sight, as the fleet. . . ."

Thomas Hastings, a Collector of Customs, published *The British Archer* during the same year as Princess Victoria's visit and, no doubt in commemoration of that royal event, included a self-drawn frontispiece of an archer at Carisbrooke with the castle in the background. The verbose Hastings in his Conclusion improves upon the eulogies of Dodd, Roberts and Waring and tells us that a healthy body can be assured through archery which, in turn, produces a genuine cheerfulness of heart—"and a lively cheerfulness of heart is the sunshine of life, for it imparts its felicity to all around". He goes on to claim that even the worst of tempers can be improved, and gloom and despondency quickly dispelled, by "exercise in the field with an object in view". That the ladies should be encouraged once again to indulge in archery is the object of his final paragraphs: "We naturally look to the society of ladies, for everything that can endear the common scenes of life; they enhance the

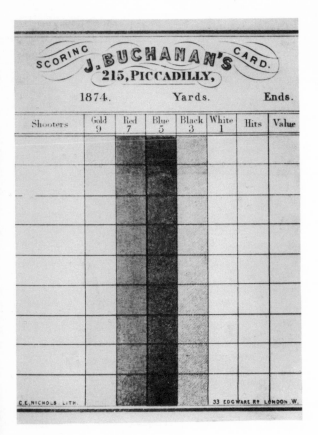

A selection of nineteenth-century ephemera concerning archery meetings.

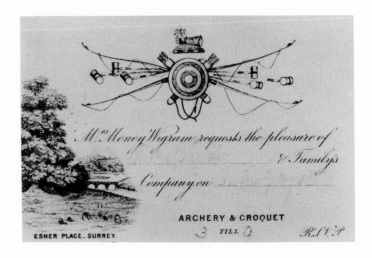

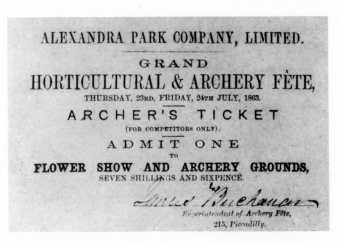

pleasures of general association: there is necessarily a blank without their enlivening presence, they are our homes, and who could debar them from the recreative pastime of archery. . . ."

ROYAL ARCHERY PRIZES

Upon her accession to the throne Queen Victoria was pleased to remain a patron of the Queen's Royal St. Leonard's Archers, and instituted the Royal Victoria Challenge Prizes of a gold inlaid arrow shawl-pin for the ladies, and a small gold bugle for the gentlemen. Additional royal prizes were presented in due course, consisting of a jewelled tortoiseshell comb and earrings, and a large silver winding horn. An annual gift of twenty guineas, which was usually spent on a gold bracelet, was continued for eleven years. As a singular gesture of her royal patronage to the sport of archery, Queen Victoria created a Master of Archery among her household officers, an appointment which has since fallen into disuse.

The early years of the nineteenth century saw the culmination of the delightful popular art of the coloured print—it ruled the mind and the imagination of the age, as photography, films and television rule ours. Favourite themes included cartoons, fiercely political and libellously personal, by Gillray and Rowlandson; incidents in the wars of all Europe, or topographical subjects, showing the homely dignity of great country houses or university towns. Also immensely popular were outdoor sporting scenes, from big-game shooting in India and Africa to the field sports at home. It is through these prints that we can best understand the spirit of the grand archery meetings of the period, and from these excellent examples of contemporary reporting we can recapture the atmosphere of the gracious archery fêtes held on the neatly cropped lawns of country houses. This was also the age of scrap-books laboriously kept by ladies equipped with scissors, gum and methodical minds, and the period when every country parson fancied his chances as a Poet Laureate. Some of the verse churned out by these clerics is in keeping with the age, to the modern taste execrable and fraught with pomposity, dullness and the wistful recollections of a long-lost childhood. However, it does on occasions provide us with a cameo of the secure, insulated, gracious and selfish life of the well-to-do, "playing" archery as an essential requirement for acceptance into the favoured social circle of the upper middle class. As a social accomplishment archery ranked equally with croquet and tennis, fit for genteel ladies, polite ecclesiastics, newly retired military gentlemen and the leisured rich—and occasionally, although as an exception to the rule, for an enthusiast taking the sport seriously. The mid-nineteenth century bred several archery giants whose feats with the long-bow have never been bettered. Such a legendary figure was Horace Alford Ford.

THE UNBEATABLE FORD

The son of a solicitor and "a lady of good birth", Ford was brought into the world in 1822, an addition to a family already large by modern standards. He had the education befitting a young gentleman and on reaching manhood managed the colliery which he jointly owned with his father. Horace Ford was a remarkable man in many respects and apart from his outstanding archery career he was proficient in a diversity of sports and accomplishments. At cricket he surpassed many players of repute, being a "capital batsman and a decent bowler", he excelled at billiards, especially pool, and became a brilliant exponent of chess. His musical talents were considerable and he exhibited a remarkable degree of skill as an instrumentalist on piano, violin and violoncello. He was a talented conjurer and a facile and fluent writer.

This tall, commanding man made his public debut in archery in 1848, at the fifth Grand National Archery Meeting which was held at Derby, although he had been introduced to the pleasures of shooting three years previously at Brighton. He speedily became adept with the bow and contemporaries speak of his unassuming manner with great enthusiasm. He became so keen to improve his performance that, in order to avoid trespassing upon the time claimed by more serious occupations, he frequently rose at four in the morning during the summer months and shot a round before breakfast. Although his religious persuasions forbade him the pleasures of archery on Sundays, he invariably visited the range and gazed at the target—no doubt contemplating upon the problems of shooting, and planning the chapters of his famous treatise on archery. Ford was a constant visitor at the residence of the Reverend Bramhall, a fellow enthusiast and his constant shooting companion, in whose house he wrote the greater part of the first edition of his book, and in whose grounds—which were accurately marked out and measured—he shot the long range scores reported in the second edition of his work. At the time Ford published *Archery, Its Theory and Practice* (1856), at first as a series of eighteen articles in *The Field*, there were no recognised teachings for the guidance of archers who wished to excel in this pastime, everyone being left to the resource of his own fancy as to the method of shooting, with the natural result that the methods adopted were as various as the characteristics of the individuals practising them. Ford's work, therefore, was very welcome and filled a long-felt want in archery circles. His approach was a fresh one and the result of logical and intelligent application of a series of simple principles to the art of shooting, regularizing the pattern and reducing the risk of inconsistency. A clue, revealing Ford's intellectual approach, is contained in his answer to a novice when he was asked, "Why don't I improve, I am always practising?" Ford replied: "Ah, that is the reason. You use your arms too much and your head too little; and so you go on repeating and confirming your faults, instead of mending them." Ford's

184

The unbeatable Horace Alford Ford (1822–80); twelve times Champion Archer of Great Britain, author of the classic *Theory and Practice of Archery*, and innovator of modern methods of shooting technique. From an old photograph.

Facsimile of Horace Ford's best score. The score card of the period was pricked according to the hits and colours scored and finally totalled at the end of a round.

treatise was popular for half a century, and the national reviews which heralded a posthumous re-issue confirmed its importance as a thoroughly competent and exceptional work of great practical value.

At the 1849 Meeting, also at Derby, Ford became Champion of Great Britain, a position he held no less than twelve times, eleven of which he won in consecutive years—a record which has never been broken. He featured in the prize-lists of forty-three major meetings and collected £618 12s in prize money over a period of sixteen years, until at last at Alexandra Park in 1864, for the first time, his name did not appear in the prize-lists. "They may beat me at this time; but will they beat my scores?" said Ford, and his query, charged with an uncanny confidence in his own superiority, remains to this day unanswered—for the recorded scores made by Horace Ford with a long-bow have never been bettered. However, he came back to win his twelfth title three years later at Brighton. It was said that he finally abandoned archery due to injuries to the muscles of his right hand, but Dean Hole, a contemporary and close friend, tells us in his memoirs* that "Ford expressed, in his later days, a sorrowful regret that he had spent so large a portion of his time in archery". There is some suggestion that religious strictures finally induced Ford to reject his favourite sport, but whatever his reason for giving it up this versatile champion of champions will be for ever remembered as one of archery's brightest stars.

THE PROMOTION OF ARCHERY

The meetings which Ford had attended were established in various parts of the country by energetic committees who sought an extension of the social activities of their societies, as well as feeling a genuine desire to promote the gentle art of toxophily. These meetings were invariably held in the choicest of situations and often included, as a final celebration to the proceedings, a full-dress ball. Archery notices in the journals and sporting magazines now began to share honours with racing, regattas, cricket, concerts and exhibitions: "Saturday May 30th 1840. A full dress archery fête at Beulah Spa; one of the most interesting and animating scenes imaginable" . . . "Archery meeting at St Leonards: On August 17th Her Majesty gives an annual prize to be contended for at this meeting of the Queen's Archers, St Leonards; it is most numerously and fashionably attended, and creates considerable interest" . . . "August 28th, The West Bucks Union Archery Club meet for a grand field day" . . . "September, the Brighton Archers have a grand meeting" . . . "A Grand Archery Fête, open to all England, at Lord's cricket ground."

*HOLE, S. REYNOLDS, *The Memories of Dean Hole* (1892)

An unusual and rare theatrical poster printed on silk, illustrating some of the special arrangements made to entertain the archers and their friends visiting York for the first Grand National Archery Meeting.

The invitation "open to all England" included in the last announcement underlines the trend of these grand meetings, and soon proper arrangements for championship meetings were under way. The idea of establishing a gathering of archers from all parts of the kingdom—"as likely to improve archery and as a social meeting to promote friendship amongst distant archers"— was suggested at a meeting of the Hull Archers in 1842 or 1843. After much preliminary correspondence and several committee meetings it was finally decided to hold a meeting in York, in 1844, to be called The Grand National Archery Meeting. The number of arrows to be shot was decided and target distances were settled, a standard system of scoring was agreed and a prize list drawn up; and thus on Thursday, August 1st, 1844, the Archers of the United Kingdom assembled on Knavesmire (the racecourse near York) where "with bended bow and quiver full of arrows" they matched their skills at shooting in a bow. Amongst those present were archers from Thirsk, Darlington, London, Salisbury, Richmond Hill, Nevill's Cross, Glasgow and Sherwood Forest, attracted by the promise of a pleasant day's shooting and, let it be admitted, the valuable prize list which, "owing to the spirited exertions of many citizens and others", totalled some £125. Despite heavy showers of rain and the annoyance caused by one spectator who insisted "as a freeman of the City of York" on standing in front of one of the targets, the meeting was so successful that it was decided to hold another the following year at which ladies would compete.

Each year a resolution was passed, by a self-elected committee, for the continuance of the meeting on an annual basis. Liverpool was chosen for 1861, the meeting being held at Aintree in very windy weather, close to the site of many other "Grand National" meetings, and there the Reverend Octavius Luard, whose name appears in the annals of English archery for more than forty years, proposed the formation of the Grand National Archery Society. This ensured the regular holding of annual target meetings and at the same time brought them more directly under the control of the great body of archers themselves. A set of rules was framed and the Society now had its permanent members. Other societies of a regional character were formed from time to time to organize championship meetings for their own areas: the Leamington and Midland Counties Meeting in 1854, the Grand Western Archery Society in 1861, the Northern Counties Archery Meeting in 1880, and much later in 1903 the Southern Counties Archery Meeting. It was at the Grand National Archery Meeting that the Champion Archer of Great Britain defended his title, and apart from the war years this championship has been held annually ever since.

The attraction of these meetings, where one could meet old friends and compete in friendly rivalry, and partake of the added pleasures of the ballroom and the dining-table, undoubtedly encouraged individual societies to organize

THEATRE-ROYAL, YORK.

Under the Management and Lesseship of Mr. J. L. PRITCHARD.

Late of the Theatres Royal, Edinburgh, Hawkins Street, Dublin, and Covent Garden.

THE LAST NIGHT OF PERFORMING UNTIL THE RACE WEEK.

This Evening, FRIDAY, August 1st. 1844,

The Entertainments are by Desire and under the Immediate Patronage of

THE GRAND NATIONAL

ARCHERY MEETING

NOW ASSEMBLED AT YORK.

When Her Majesty Queen Victoria's Servants will perform Mrs Centliver's celebrated Comedy of

THE WONDER !

A WOMAN KEEPS A SECRET !!

Don Felix ...... Mr PRITCHARD	Colonel Briton .... Mr HUTCHINGS
Don Pedro, *Father to Violante* .. Mr A. E. REYNOLDS	Don Lopez, *Father of Felix and Isabella* .. Mr MORGAN
Frederick ...... Mr EBURNE	Gibby, *a Scotch Footman* ...... Mr BRUCE NORTON
Lissardo, *Servant to Don Felix* .. Mr GOURLAY	Vasques ... Mr THORNHILL Servant .. Mr REEVES

Alguaziles .... Messrs Elsegood, Anson, Lingham, Patterson, Dewar, &c.

Donna Violante .... Miss WAVERLEY SCOTT	Donna Isabella .... Miss MATILDA ROSS
Flora, *Servant to Donna Violante* ...... Mrs GOURLAY	Inez ...... Miss VILLARS

The Pas de Polka, by Mr. Elsegood and Miss Clari Harcourt.

MISS VILLARS WILL SING "LAND OF THE WEST."

To be followed by a New Grand Ballet, written and produced by Mons. LE CLERCQ, entitled

Bacchus & Ariadne.

THE ARGUMENT.

Theseus having conquered the Minotaur, and extricated himself from the Cretan Labyrinth, by the aid of Ariadne, becomes her husband. At length weary of her society, he determines to revisit his kingdom. Ariadne is resolved to accompany him ; he (apparently) cheerfully consents, and they embark ; a storm arising, he makes it an excuse for their landing on the Island of Delos, where he ungratefully leaves her. Bacchus encounters her; Cupid playfully revenges himself for a supposed affront by causing a reciprocity of Love to be the result of the meeting of Bacchus and Ariadne. Hymen ultimately unites the lovers ; a Grand Bacchanalia takes place, and Ariadne becomes a Constellation by the power of Bacchus. The whole produced with *New Scenery, Dresses, and Decorations.*

Bacchus.. Mons. LE CLERCQ	Cupid.. Miss LE CLERCQ	Hymen .. Miss LOUISE LE CLERCQ
Ariadne.. Mad. LE CLERCQ	Theseus .. Mr SMYTHSON	Satyrs.. Messrs FRENCH & THORNHILL

Fawns .. Messrs ANSON, MORGAN, REEVES, and PATTERSON

IN THE COURSE OF THE BALLET—The Storm and approach of THESEUS'S GOLDEN GALLEY—The Landing of Theseus and Ariadne—His Departure—CUPID'S CARRIAGE CLOUD.——THE FLOATING VEIL.

A Pas D' Arcadie .. by Miss LOUISE LE CLERCQ, the Infant Dancer and Pantomimist.

Characteristic Entree of the Bacchante and Bacchanals.

Grand Bacchanalia Pas Seul ...... Mademoiselle LE CLERCQ.

Mons. and Mad. Le Clercq will dance their original Grand Pas Des Schals.

A GROTESQUE SATYR DANCE BY MR. FRENCH.

Grand Allegorical Finale by the whole of the Characters, terminating with a SPLENDID MYTHOLOGICAL GROUP !!

A POPULAR SONG, BY MISS SINCLAIR.

Mr. Hart will Sing "The Wolf."

A specially commissioned medal for the Grand National Archery Meetings which was designed by Benjamin Wyon (1802–58). This is a mint example of an early issue which was mounted in glass. These awards became known as Diana Medals and were issued in silver, silver-gilt and bronze. The Society's motto is on the reverse— 'Union, True Heart and Courtesie'.

regular programmes of practice and local prize meetings. The panoply of archery dress and the elaborate trophies, some of which were very valuable, provided a splendid theme for the convivialities at night after the shooting; and the targets gleaming with the Prince's Colours set in typically English surroundings made a suitably elegant backcloth for the daytime concourse of the socially conscious of the nineteenth century.

COUNTRY HOUSE SPORT

This wider interest soon encouraged the toxophilite with literary aspirations and ample leisure to turn to his chosen sport for inspiration, and a steady flow of works on every aspect of the subject now began to appear. Most of these books consisted of an abridged history of archery followed by practical instructions which varied according to the ingenuity of the author. The majority were popular handbooks, few were notable and most took the lessons of Ascham and re-wrote them. A number of histories were attempted, which contained little new research but a considerable amount of Victorian verbosity. The most important are listed at the end of this chapter. Part of the leisure of many country parsons in mid-Victorian times seems to have been spent in writing diaries, and some of these personal and meticulously written records preserve a unique picture of country life of the period. A classic example of such a diary was written by Francis Kilvert between the years 1870–9, in which he records his impressions of a number of archery and croquet parties which he attended. His simple and tender descriptions of leisure days spent with agreeable companions in charming surroundings leave little to be desired. "The targets were pitched in the long green meadow which runs down to the river [Wye] and the summer houses, one of the prettiest archery grounds I ever saw, the high woods above and the river below. It was a pretty sight to see the group of ladies with their fresh light dresses moving up and down the long green meadow between the targets, and the arrows flitting and glancing white to and fro against the bank of dark green trees." And on another occasion: "Crossing the river at Normanton Hatches we walked along the hillside through meadows and barley fields till we came to the hospitable Manor House of Great Durnford, where we found Mr and Mrs Pinckney, Mr Charles Everett and Major Fisher, the Champion Archer of England, at luncheon. After luncheon the archers went out to shoot at a beautiful archery ground by the riverside. The ladies sat watching under the trees while the arrows flashed by with a whistling rush . . ." Many such personal scraps survive, and faithfully describe the tempo of life among those who could afford to indulge in such pastimes; and this was a pattern which continued for many years with little change.

Meetings began to be reported in full in all the best provincial newspapers

This is believed to be the earliest photograph of a Grand National Archery Meeting. It became a regular arrangement for these meetings to move around the country and in 1866 the championships were held in Leamington where this picture was taken.

On Thursday, August 1st 1844, the Archers of England assembled on the racecourse at Knavesmire, near York. There took place the first Grand National Archery Meeting at which the championships of Great Britain were decided. Apart from war years this meeting has been held every year since.

and such important national media as *The Field, The Country Gentleman's Newspaper; The Telegraph; The Sporting Gazette; The Manchester Examiner; The Sunday Times* and *The Lady's Newspaper;* and one memorable morning the august *Times* appeared carrying a full leader on archery, extolling its virtues and, for good measure, including an admirably written and condensed history of the sport. Every journalistic novelty was employed to vary the descriptions of these events and well-drawn full-page illustrations began to appear; often several columns were given up to detailed reports of the meetings and descriptions of the social scene together with lists of those attending. In the *Leamington Courier* for June 1851, which referred to the National Archery Meeting held in that town as "the great event of the present season", six or eight columns were devoted to descriptions of the two days' shooting, the rules of the meeting, lists of the competitors and the prizes, and a history of the revival; and liberally sprinkled throughout can be found general notes on archery. This is a typical example of the laborious reporting of the day, which provides researchers and antiquaries with a mine of fascinating detail but would of course be unacceptable to modern readers. The site chosen for this meeting was the eight-acre cricket ground belonging to the famous firm of Messrs Parr and Wisden, and in addition to the two full days' shooting, which on its own merits attracted vast crowds, there was a "Pyrotechnical Fête" in the Jephson Gardens with a German band in attendance; luncheons were served in the Indian Pavilion, "which was as much admired for the spacious accommodation it afforded, as well as for its rich Oriental appendages"; the band of the 4th King's Own Regiment played in the afternoons, and the Grand Dress Ball, which was held in the Royal Assembly Rooms attended by some 300 guests, rounded off the occasion. "The elegant suite of apartments were brilliantly lighted, and towards midnight the ball-room presented a gay and animating appearance." (We can even study the "gems of the musical *repertoire*" played on this occasion.) Finally, at two o'clock in the morning, the prizewinners were declared.

TROPHIES AND AWARDS

The list of jewellery and plate confirms the opulence and the scale of this congress, the exhibited items including "Solid silver corner dishes, in sets of four; silver tea kettles; silver tea and coffee services, complete, of Chinese, convolvulus, Louis XIV, Victoria, medallion arabesque and melon patterns. There were also silver waiters of every pattern, from eight to twenty-four inches in diameter; claret jugs, some entirely silver and others of Bohemian

Four Victorian lady archers, from the *Illustrated London News* of 1855, at an archery meeting. They appear to have matters well under control despite the voluminous and fussy clothing which must have hampered the accurate management of a bow.

glass and crystal; a silver claret jug of colossal size, and antique Greek design, Tankards and cups, chased and engraved with rural, agricultural and Toxophilitic subjects; silver castor frames; silver inkstands, cake baskets and fruit dishes; cream ewers; toast racks; egg frames; clocks and candelabra in ormolu and bronze, etc. The Ladies' prizes included gold bracelets set with diamonds, pearls, carbuncles and ruby garnets; gold and enamelled watches in cases; jewel caskets in buhl, nacre, and oxidised silver work; tables and jardinières in buhl, together with an endless variety of brooches for morning and evening wear." This list, according to the report, "comprises but a tithe of the assortment to be inspected" and reflects the tastes of those wealthy enough to indulge in such pleasures, for the subscriptions required were high and the incidental expenses considerable.

During 1877, in *The World*, a fanciful account of a meeting of the Royal

The first grand meeting of the American National Archery Association in August 1879, at Chicago. There were a total of 54 gentlemen and 20 ladies representing 11 archery societies shooting for the newly instituted National Medals which were awarded for the principal competition.

Toxophilite Society was published in which many personalities were mentioned, thinly disguised as characters from the stories of Robin Hood. There were: T. W. Hinchliff, the author of *Over The Hills and Far Away*; the President of the Alpine Club, and publisher, C. J. Longman, who was British Champion in 1883 and who collaborated in the writing of the *Archery* volume of the Badminton Library, still a standard work; W. Spottiswoode, the President of the Royal Society; Spedding, editor of Bacon's works, and many others who regularly participated in this pastime now almost entirely reserved for the wealthy and genteel society.

THE PLEASURE GARDENS

The early Victorian pleasure gardens often provided facilities for practising archery and these establishments, natural descendants of Vauxhall and Ranelagh, became fashionable meeting places for those who could afford the admission fees. The Rosherville Gardens, just outside London, was one of the most lavish of all and consisted of an elaborate mixture of zoo, botanical gardens and fun-fair, laid out in the confines of disused chalk-pits near Gravesend. There were Swiss Walks, the Fairy Wilderness, the Terpsichorean Lawns, or the Choragic Temple to be contemplated to the strains of a brass band. One could dance, eat and drink, go up in a balloon, watch fireworks, peer into the camera obscura or shoot on the splendidly laid out archery lawns. The Reverend G. Crolly wrote a set of couplets enthusing over the diversions of Rosherville, in which he says that "friendship there was never chill" and that "archery could show its skill"—the suggestion being that a fair amount of archery was done by Cupid himself.

The latter part of the nineteenth century saw the sport becoming less the pastime of the *élite* and more of a pursuit attracting followers from every walk of life. The pleasures of archery were beginning to be enjoyed by a greater number of people from a wider cross-section of the community and undoubtedly the introduction of public meetings encouraged this increasing participation. Although it was still important to cut a dash, if you were a male, or to appear in a creation outdoing all others, if you were of the fair sex, more importance was given to the actual shooting than previously. Scores were more important, and prizes, although still excessively elaborate and, apparently, unlimited, began to relate to performance. The Challenge Trophy, as opposed to the prize that was won outright, was becoming more popular and in 1849 a Champion's Gold Medal was struck for the Grand National Archery Meeting; this medal, first won by Horace Ford, is still proudly worn by successive British Champions. Whilst archery had come to stay in England it had started to take deep roots in America, and the development of target archery in the States is an interesting and quite individual story—not connected in any way with the historic use of the bow over many thousands of years of that country's history by the American Indian.

THE REVIVAL IN AMERICA

One winter's night in 1827 two young gentlemen of Philadelphia, both well-to-do and of English ancestry, sat discussing the revival of archery in England and considering the possibility of instituting it on their own lawns. The following spring they were joined in their project by a third enthusiast who owned a large country seat on the banks of the Schuylkill River, called Fountain Green. These three, Dr Robert Eglesfield; Samuel Powel Griffitts, an apothecary and son of a distinguished physician; and his cousin Jacob Giles Morris, were joined by the brothers Franklin and Ramsey Peale, sons of the famous painter. On September 3rd, 1828, they organised themselves into the Club of United Bowmen of Philadelphia. These enthusiasts soon began regular shooting practice based on English methods, and experimented with distances from 80 to 125 yards. They quickly settled down to the standard range of the former, which has remained their official distance ever since. Soon other members were admitted, after being subjected to an initiation ritual which employed a system of cryptic identification marks for each member which were subsequently used in all their shooting records, their real names rarely being used. An order was dispatched to Thomas Waring in London for a complete set of archer's equipment, and in due course (some six months having elapsed before the consignment reached Philadelphia) the excited members of the United Bowmen unpacked a bow, twelve arrows, quiver, bracer, strings, etc, and a copy of Waring's *Treatise on Archery*. The total cost was $46.80, or £10 16s 6d, plus heavy customs charges. Before long these enterprising archers had mastered the complications of bowyery and the intricacies of arrow-making and were producing their own equipment— "for beauty, neatness, goodness and durability may be backed against any bow that Mr Waring ever turned out of his shop".

The United Bowmen moved around and shot in the grounds of various country houses, a "new ground back of State Penitentiary" and a field, belonging to a dairy farm, which they named Sherwood. Earthen butts twenty-one feet long and five feet high were quickly raised at each end of Sherwood, and it was here that they held their annual Prize Meetings. These were splendid affairs; the bowmen wore uniforms of iron grey frock coats with black braid, white duck trousers and a green cap with a black visor, and the general arrangements were modelled on English lines. Tents and pavilions with flags and bunting were erected, a military band was in attendance, and on a table "covered with a snow-white cloth, the prizes were placed, surrounded with delicately entwined wreaths of beautiful roses". *The Saturday Evening*

Post estimated that a thousand spectators attended the meeting of 1839 "composed of the beauty and fashion of the city".

THE THOMSON BROTHERS

By 1858 events which were to lead to the Civil War were already in train; and in the unsettled conditions of the day, matters more important than archery occupied the minds of the community. The serene pleasures of prosperous times departed, and the United Bowmen ceased shooting and disbanded. There are no shooting records from 1858, but it appears that social contacts were continued by several members up to the latter part of the nineteenth century. This serious attempt by a few dedicated toxophilites to introduce the art of archery to America was now forgotten until the upheavals of the Civil War receded in the memory of society—and until the Thomson brothers of Crawfordsville, Indiana, created a mass archery fever which was nothing less than phenomenal.

In 1844, the year in which the first Grand National Archery Meeting was held in England, Maurice Thomson was born in Fairfield, Indiana. His father,

Will H. Thompson of the Wabash Merry Bowmen, the first champion archer of the United States, proudly wearing the coveted championship medal.

Maurice Thompson, first President of the American National Archery Association, at the time of its formation in 1879.

the Reverend Matthew Grigg Thomson, was a Baptist minister who, apparently, liked to move around. Two years later Will was born in Calhoun, Georgia, and subsequently the family moved to Kentucky, and then to the Coosawatee Valley in North Georgia, where the father became the owner of a small plantation. The boys' mother, Diantha, was a student of literature, and with the help of hired tutors she gave both a good education. When the Civil War began the brothers enlisted in the Confederate Army, one seventeen and the other only fifteen; and at Cold Spring Harbor Maurice was wounded in the chest severely enough to keep him in delicate health for the rest of his life. At the end of the war Will helped his brother make the long and weary journey back to Georgia, where the Thomson house and the few acres adjoining had been devastated by Sherman's army in his campaign through that State. The house had been burnt to the ground and all movable property destroyed or stolen by the Union troops.

This was a time of despair: the brothers had no money and no immediate means of making a livelihood, and Maurice could not seem to shake off the effects of his wound. Their old doctor advised Maurice that on account of his thoracic lesion he should live in the open air, and so they went out into the wilderness for two years, from 1866 to 1868. They lived deep in Georgia's great Okefinokee Swamp and around Lake Okechobee in the Florida Everglades; and as they had been denied firearms because of their recent belligerency, they lived for the most part on game that they killed with the bow and arrow. It was a magic time for them; both had a kinship with nature, and the years benefited their spirits and healed their wounds. As boys Maurice and Will had been taught the use of the long-bow by a sort of hermit named Thomas Williams "whose cabin stood in the midst of a vast pine forest that bordered my father's plantation. My brother and I," said Maurice, "had, in a boyish way, been practising archery for some years before Williams gave us the lessons; but though we had of our own efforts become expert in the making and use of our weapons, we found to our chagrin that before we dared to call ourselves bowmen all we had learned must go for naught, and an art must be mastered, the difficulties of which at first seemed insurmountable." These boys had grown up in a family both cultured and refined, and both spoke and wrote a lovely, leisurely, classically correct language which was to stand them in good stead when they started to publish stories and verse of their past experiences with the bow.

THE WITCHERY OF ARCHERY

From 1873 to 1876 Maurice contributed a series of articles to *Appleton's Journal* and *Harper's New Monthly Magazine*, and in the meanwhile Will had been sending letters and articles to *Forest and Stream*, which appeared

The contingent from the West Kent Archery Society at the Grand National Archery Meeting at Cheltenham in 1887. The tallest of the ladies is Mrs Berens, who became an internationally famous archer; behind her is bearded William Butt, Secretary to the Royal Toxophilite Society and a well-known personality of the archery world for many years.

between the years 1874 and 1879. Then came *The Witchery of Archery* in 1878, which collected the best of Maurice's articles together; all dealt with hunting with the bow except the last, which described target archery. These gems of literary expression had an immediate effect on the folk of the 'seventies, who yearned for a release from the restricting post-war period with its decorous, hidebound, and narrow-minded society, in the throes of an extreme religious fervour, which suppressed the feelings of personal freedom in those who now eagerly read the adventures of the Thomsons from Crawfordsville. The opening lines of Maurice's first chapter on bowhunting read: "So long as the new moon returns in heaven a bent, beautiful bow, so long will the fascination of archery keep hold of the hearts of men," and as one turns the pages of this classic of archery literature it is not difficult to see why it brought a breath of freedom to a war-weary people with an almost complete lack of facilities for athletic exercise. "One day, not long ago, my brother and I were

At the Grand National Archery Meeting at Malvern in 1909; Captain Armitage, Secretary to the Society, measures a "gold". This was for a special award for the most central shot.

A moment in time at an archery meeting captured by a candid camera. Although earlier a regular mode of dress was *de rigueur*, fashion now decreed a more informal approach. As the twentieth century progressed a more uniform style of archery clothing can be observed.

practising at a target on a green lawn, when a miserably clad and hunger-pinched tramp approached us. Rags and dirt could not hide, nor could hunger and humiliation blunt the edge of a certain manliness of bearing as he touched his torn hat and paused near us. Could we give him a bite to eat or a few pence to buy him a cheap dinner? He was very hungry. The old story. We sent a lad who was scoring for us to my house to enquire if any cooked victuals were in the pantry, and then resumed our shooting. The tramp stood by watching us. Finally, as if impelled by an irresistible interest, he said: "Archery is a noble sport." We turned and looked at him in surprise. He waved his hand in a peculiarly graceful way, and in a sad voice said: "On Brighton sands I have seen good shooting. I have shot there myself." "In England?" asked Will. "Yes," he replied; "I am a gentleman." Will smiled doubtingly. "Would you let me shoot once?" he said. There was a sincerity in his voice. Will handed him his bow and arrow. He took them eagerly, almost snatching them. For a moment he stood as if irresolute, then quickly fixing the arrow on the string, drew and let fly. The movements were those of a trained archer. The distance was forty yards, and he hit the gold in the very centre . . . I mention this to clinch my theory, viz: that neither poverty, nor shame, nor hunger, nor dissipation, nor anything but death can ever quite destroy the merry, innocent,

Arcadian, heathen part of our nature, that takes to a bow and arrows as naturally as a butterfly takes to a flower."

GROWTH OF ARCHERY IN AMERICA

In the intervening years, since the days of the United Bowmen, the bow had not absolutely disappeared from private lawns and there may have been a few private clubs, but the excitement and interest created by Thomson's stories encouraged so many archery clubs to spring into existence that some old men reminiscing in the 1920s said they were to be numbered by the hundred. Paradoxically, so many tales of hunting with the bow did not send everyone off into the nearest forest to hunt and slay game; the urge to shoot found its outlet almost entirely in target archery. At first all the tackle and equipment had to be imported from England. Peck and Snyder of New York, quick to take advantage of the boom, announced that they had been appointed sole agents for the archery goods of Philip Highfield of Clerkenwell, and in a little booklet* published by them in 1878 they included a testimonial from Maurice Thomson which read: "No bows in this country, can equal those

*The Archer's Complete Guide, Peck and Snyder (1878)

The formal elegance and grace of the most fashionable archery meetings of the country are exemplified in this scene at the Ladies' Day of the Royal Toxophilite Society in 1904.

Opposite: A detail from a photograph of the Royal Toxophilite Society's Ladies' Day of 1903. Colonel Walrond, Secretary to the Society and author of numerous works on archery, can be seen (centre, wearing cap) supervising arrangements.

The climax of an archery meeting, particularly a full-scale one such as the Grand National Archery Meeting at Malvern in 1909, was the prize-giving. The "Lady Paramount" presided and presented innumerable valuable trophies and awards; many of these prizes are still competed for annually.

beautiful weapons made by Philip Highfield of London; he is maker to the Royal Families and Nobility throughout Europe etc etc." Their catalogue took up the whole of three pages, and the remainder of this lively little book included elementary lessons on archery, a collection of superfluous information about the sport and some curious observations which drew interesting comparisons between the English and American ideals of womanhood. "Those who have no experience in the matter, will, perhaps, be slow to believe that, in the short space of three months a most fragile young woman, by means of judicious archery practice, developed muscles that, when her arms were flexed, rolled up into balls like a blacksmith's biceps. . . ."

In addition to the bows and arrows brought into the country, tackle of excellent quality produced in America started to come on to the market, and within two years of the publication of *The Witchery of Archery* the Patent Office in Washington was flooded with applications relating to the manufacture of archery goods. E. I. Horsman, one of these "manufacturers of fine archery", published his eight-page catalogue as an appendix to a charming book written by Maurice and Will Thomson: *How to Train in Archery, Being a Complete Study of the York Round*. The techniques of bowyery had now been mastered and America could claim equality with the best bowmakers of England—that is, according to Maurice Thomson; no doubt partly motivated by gratitude to his publisher, he wrote to Horsman from Crawfordsville in May 1879: "I have given your bows the hardest and most merciless test imaginable: they stand better than English bows of the same class . . . they

are of better finish than English bows of the same material . . . your Snakewood backed, and Beefwood backed, are better than the same of English make." Will endorsed his brother's remarks and added that Horsman's arrows were "the best in the world".

THE FIRST AMERICAN CHAMPIONSHIPS

The same year, 1879, saw the first Championship Meeting at Chicago, organised under the auspices of the American National Archery Association, a body formed in January of that year. Both Thomson brothers shot at this meeting, Will becoming Champion Archer of the United States and Maurice lending his presence and influence to the cause as the Association's first President. But both were in poor shape during the three days' shooting, one having a serious attack of bilious fever and the other suffering from muscular strain. While the Thomson brothers were making archery history in America, Horace Ford was pursuing his scientific approach to shooting in England. It is interesting to note that Maurice developed independently a revolutionary system of shooting, afterwards recognising the similarity of his method to Ford's when he saw a copy of the British Champion's book. A contemporary report assures us that "the meeting was a gratifying success, and that archery may now be considered firmly fixed in the United States", but adds, "The shooting was, of course, not nearly up to the English standard"–which situation was to be radically reversed in the course of time. The history of this meeting is an interesting one; it was reported in the English *Archer's Register* and followed English tradition in almost every respect but one. The physical arrangements were such that it was more convenient for one line of targets only to be used instead of the traditional arrangement of targets in pairs facing each other at both ends of the range. The prize lists at the early meetings were even more valuable than those in England; the third meeting, for instance, in Brooklyn, had prizes to the value of $2,500, and a local newspaper reported that "some of the articles had to be returned to the donors, as there were too many".

NATIONAL ARCHERY ASSOCIATION

The formation of a national organisation for archery followed a precedent set in England where the Grand National Archery Society had been formed in 1861, the difference being that while the American Association became the governing body for the sport from its inception, the Grand National Archery Society was not recognised as such until over seventy years later. The nucleus of this great new interest in shooting bows and arrows was centred in the states of the north-east, those further west being fully occupied with lawless-

A scarce early photograph of the rural craft of target making. A long rope of rye straw was laboriously coiled and sewn to form a flat and circular "boss" about four feet in diameter, which was then covered with a canvas face on which was painted the coloured scoring rings.

ness and strife spawned by the Civil War and the resultant wide-spread dislocation of society which occupied the post-war years, and at the inaugural meeting in the mayor's office in Crawfordsville were delegates from other parts of Indiana, as well as from Illinois, Iowa, Pennsylvania, New York and Wisconsin.

The club in Chicago was represented by its Vice-President, A. G. Spalding, founder of the famous house of sporting outfitters, and its President, Henry C. Carver, and it was due to these two hustling characters that the inaugural meeting was called and the National Archery Association founded. It was not long before three major regional associations were formed, the Eastern Archery Association, which, with some minor lapses during hard times, has maintained a healthy life ever since; the Ohio State Association, which was very strong up to nearly the turn of the century and has enjoyed a revival in more recent years; and the Pacific Coast Association, centring around San Francisco, which for a long time ceased to function but is now firmly re-established.

The first five years of archery in America, from 1879 to 1883, were by far the best, for it was soon after this that archery declined as rapidly as it had expanded just a few years previously. A number of reasons have been given for this surprising turn of events: the cost of equipment and the difficulties of its importation, despite the newly founded manufacturers of archery goods; the competition offered in the fashionable alternative of lawn tennis; and the rival popularity of outdoor games such as rowing, baseball, football and golf, which reflected the desire for healthy and vigorous exercise by a nation emerging from years of restrictions and unsettled conditions.

The Fourth Olympiad of 1908 included archery as an event for the first time. This photograph shows the gentlemen shooting the York Round in Shepherd's Bush Stadium, London, in windy and rainy weather. The central figure in a light suit is the British gold medallist, W. Dod, of Welford Park Archers, Berkshire.

Whatever the reason the collapse was nearly complete, and only a handful of archers in each of the cities of Washington, Cincinnati, Chicago and Boston survived and shot through the rather dismal last years of the century; it was not until 1903, during the preparation for the World's Fair at St Louis, that the slumbering toxophilites of America were given a long-awaited shot in the arm.

The athletic programme had as its head none other than A. G. Spalding, by now well established as an important supplier of sports goods, and when he was asked to include archery on the list of events he did so with a willingness that was no doubt inspired by his earlier enthusiasm and former connexions with the Chicago Archery Club. The tournament, which was subsequently included in the Fair of 1904, was an unqualified success, despite dreadful weather conditions, and once more a wide and sincere interest in archery was roused amongst both those who had nearly forgotten its pleasures, and many new adherents. Since those days the sport has grown steadily in the United States, albeit spasmodically at times, until now an estimated six million Americans use the bow in some form or another, and the archery tackle business, from its doubtful start in the 'seventies, is reckoned today to be an important and thriving industry.

GRAND NATIONAL ARCHERY MEETINGS

In England throughout the remainder of the nineteenth century, archery steadily continued to attract more devotees, the number of clubs and societies grew, and bowyers and fletchers passed their skills on to sons and grandsons; an increasing number of expensive and elaborate trophies were instituted, many still being competed for annually, and different towns around England were being selected for the venue of the Grand National Archery Meeting. The choice of town was decided partly for the convenience of having suitable shooting grounds, partly for the ease of access and often for the attractions offered as fashionable resorts. A little later chauffeur-driven competitors would arrive in leisurely style at such spas as Cheltenham, Bath, Leamington and Tunbridge Wells, and at other towns currently popular such as Exeter, Shrewsbury, Hereford, Bristol, Worcester and Norwich; but it was at Oxford that this meeting was to settle down to an unbroken series for nearly half a century. Literally millions of arrows have been shot in the grounds of Worcester College in this ancient university town, within a hundred yards or so of two special relics which appeal to the lover of the book and the lover of the bow. Safely lodged within the sacred precincts of the college library are a fourteenth-century manuscript of the life of the Black Prince written by Chandos Herald,* who accompanied this valiant prince on his campaigns and shared many of his victories; and one of the rarest of archery books, a first edition of Ascham's superlative work *Toxophilus*. How can archers of today fail to feel proud with such splendid traditions of the long-bow in peace and war represented so close at hand?

The commemorative badge given to every competitor in the Olympic Games of 1908. The archery teams included ladies and gentlemen from England, France, Belgium and America. After a long lapse target archery is again to be included in the Twentieth Olympiad in 1972 at Munich.

THE TRADITIONAL LONG-BOW

Although shooting methods were modified from time to time and the arrangements for competitive shooting adjusted to suit the changing circumstances of mood and situation, the traditional long-bow itself did not change throughout the great revival of archery, both in Europe and in America. The original designs were retained and, despite an occasional experiment to produce a bow with greater efficiency, and trials of different woods, the basic lines of these beautiful weapons did not alter. A stiffening about the handle section had to some extent eliminated jarring in the hand, and this made bows easier to handle and thus more acceptable as a lady's weapon. Arrows, too, underwent minor modifications, but their pattern did not radically change over a century and a half. The long medieval feather, beloved by Edward III's fletchers, square-cut and capable of steadying a heavy bodkin point or broadhead, was inherited by the early revivalists and this pattern

*CHANDOS HERALD, *The Life and Feats of Arms of Edward the Black Prince*, subsequently translated into English by Francisque-Michel, (1883)

The lady competitors shooting the National Round at the 1908 Olympic Games. Target archery had now become internationally recognised and before long a series of world championships would be inaugurated.

remained standard until Horace Ford's day. Some interest was taken in arrow design at about this time and we can trace a reduction in size of feathers as about the only change. Some time later improvements to nocks were introduced and the introduction of mass-production encouraged the use of parallel points of brass or steel rather than the tapered variety.

The personal accessories of archers have not changed even to this day, except for one curious item—the "grease pot". This hung from the waist-belt and consisted of a small inverted container full of a mixture of suet and white wax. All the early manuals list this appendage as an essential item; to improve the "loose", the archer would occasionally dab some of this unlikely mixture on to his shooting glove or tab, and this would assist the string to slip more quickly off his fingers. The grease pot came into general favour at some undefined period of the eighteenth century and went completely out of use before the beginning of the twentieth. The other impedimenta of the bowman, in use since time immemorial, and consisting of the bracer or arm guard, shooting glove, tab or finger stalls, belt, quiver and tassel, are today little altered from the patterns evolved in earlier centuries.

OLYMPIC GAMES

The ultimate recognition of archery as a sporting activity on a level with other more commercially supported and widely popular mass pursuits came as a result of its inclusion in the Olympic Games. Although archery contests had taken place at the Second Olympiad in Paris in 1900, where the Exposition Universelle included popinjay events, crossbow competitions and a shoot for the French Championship, and at the Third Olympiad at the World Fair in St Louis in 1904, where the only competitors were from the United States, it was not until the games were held in London in 1908 that target archery became fully recognised. The invitation to the participating nations to provide teams of ladies and gentlemen for this Fourth International Olympiad was welcomed with enthusiasm. The Grand National Archery Society was approached and the proposals to hold such a competition met with its full approbation. The Royal Toxophilite Society, still virtually the ruling body for archery in Britain, was asked to appoint the necessary judges and officials and to make the arrangements for three days' shooting in the stadium at Shepherds Bush, London. One of these judges was Colonel H. Walrond, the co-author of the famous Badminton *Archery* and Honorary Secretary of the Royal Toxophilites. Conditions of competition were drawn up which were brief and to the point, and included a reminder of the niceties of conduct on the archery field surviving from the age of manners and the almost fervent regard for courtesy towards the opposite sex. Rule Eight reads: "Gentlemen will not be allowed to smoke at the ladies' targets . . ." The teams, limited to thirty each, consisted of twenty-five ladies and fifteen gentlemen from Britain, eleven gentlemen from France and a lone competitor from the United States. The first two days' shooting were taken up by a York Round for gentlemen and, with lesser distances, a double National Round for the ladies. The third day was a fifty-metre competition based on continental rules which at this time varied considerably from those used by English and American archers. The majority of prizes went to the British team but Mr H. B. Richardson, the Champion of the United States, succeeded in winning the bronze medal for the York Round. Although spirits were dampened by the weather, which was unusually wet and cold for July, and although the scene presented a dismal prospect unenlivened by spectators or the glamour associated with international sporting festivals of the present day, the dauntless teams of ladies and gentlemen turned out in their Edwardian finery, braved the elements and deliberately and precisely pursued their beloved archery with all the confidence and affection of true lovers of the bow. These few made history, and the long-bow, this weapon of the early settlers of Britain, of the stout yeomen of Crécy and Agincourt, of the warlike Harry and the gentle Ascham, of Prince George the Regent and of Horace Ford and the Thomson brothers, had reached the last years of a long and honourable life. The end of its history as a weapon of target archers was rapidly approaching with the introduction in the early decades of the present century of superior weapons of tubular steel; and finally, with the appearance of the modern composite bow made from a complex of fibreglass and plastics, both steel and yew were ousted as the archer's weapon *par excellence*. However, there is still something about shooting in a traditional long-bow of yew which captures the imagination, and a few sentimentally inclined arch-traditionalists even yet band together in quiet and peaceful surroundings to use this splendid and simple weapon of king and commoner.

SELECT BIBLIOGRAPHY

Andrews, William, *Historic Byways and Highways of Old England* [1900]
Andrews, William, *Historic Yorkshire* [1883]
Anstruther, Ian, *The Knight and the Umbrella* [1963]
Banks, Miss, Notes, Extracts, Cuttings from books, etc. ADD. MSS. 6314 to 6320.
Dodd, Rev. James William, *Ballads of Archery, Sonnets, etc* [1818]
Egan, Pierce, *Book of Sports and Mirror of Life* [1832]
Firth, W. P., *A Victorian Canvas*, Edited by Nevile Wallis [1957]
Fittis, Robert Scott, *Sports and Pastimes of Scotland* [1891]
Ford, Horace A., *Archery; Its Theory and Practice* [1856]
Grand National Archery Meeting, *Records, 1844 to 1871*

As the twentieth century progressed so archery became more and more popular and the importance of giving proper instruction to children was soon recognised. This photograph shows young archers practising, with obvious pleasure, to be future champions.

A nineteenth-century engraving of an Ainu
huntsman carrying his ready-braced bow. This
race formed the original population of the Japanese
islands but now only a few remain on Hokkaido.

Sasaki Takatsuna racing Kajiwara Kagesuye across
the Uji river in the attack by government troops
under Yoshitsune against his cousin the rebel Kiso
Yoshinaka (1184). From a c. 1890 wall scroll,
kakemono, by Go-un Tsunetatsu.

209

Hansard, George Agar, *The Book of Archery* [1841]

Hargrove, A. E., *Anecdotes of Archery, etc, etc* [1845]

Hargrove, E., *Anecdotes of Archery* [1792]

Harrison, A. P., *The Science of Archery, Shewing its Affinity to Heraldry* [1834]

Hastings, Thomas, *The British Archer* [1831]

Hole, Dean Reynolds, *The Memories of Dean Hole* [1892]

Kilvert, Rev. Francis, *Kilvert's Diary 1870–1879* [1944]

Latham, W., *Anecdotes of Archery* [1788]

Mason, Richard Oswald, *Pro aris et Focis, Considerations for the reasons that exist for Reviving the use of the Long Bow with the Pike* [1798]

Moseley, Walter Michael, *An Essay on Archery* [1792]

Paul, James Balfour, *The History of the Royal Company of Archers* [1875]

Peck and Snyder, *The Archer's Complete Guide* [1878]

Reeves, Boleyne, (Editor), *Colburn's Kalendar of Amusements for 1840*

Roberts, T., *The English Bowman* [1801]

Royal Toxophilite Society, *A History of the Royal Toxophilite Society* [1870]

Sharpe, J., Follett, T., Walrond, H., et al. (Editors) *The Archer's Register, 1866 to 1915*

Strutt, Joseph, *The Sports and Pastimes of the People of England* [1838]

Thomson, J. Maurice, *The Witchery of Archery* [1877]

Thomson, Maurice & Will H., *How to train in Archery* [1879]

Toxophilite, An Old, *The Archer's Guide* [1833]

Walker, G. Goold, *The Honourable Artillery Company* [1926]

Waring, T., *A Treatise on Archery or, The Art of Shooting with the Longbow* [1822]

Watts, Alaric A., (Editor) *The Cabinet of Modern Art* [1837]

Woodmen of Arden, *Records of Woodmen of Arden from 1785* [1885]

7 Warriors and Priests

One arrow to the target
The distance being right, a hit.

SENGAI

POPULAR notions of the part played by the bow in the history of Japan are often restricted to an impression of a body of charging, screaming Samurai on horseback, discharging battle-shafts with wild abandon at all and sundry. Or occasionally there may be some vague remembrance of the mention of a mysterious application of archery used by the adherents of Zen Buddhism in their rituals and training, highlighted perhaps by the sight of a ponderous museum showcase housing a strangely shaped but exquisitely decorated set of bow and arrows.

How true are some of the remarkable feats of bowmanship recorded in the ancient histories? Is it possible to unlock some of the inner mysteries of ceremonial archery? The answer to the second question is dependant on the study of the first. The symbolic as well as the physical power of the bow, a unique system of training in its use, the medieval feudal system of knighthood which involved deeds of incredible ferocity and an almost morbid sense of personal honour, the passion for creating objects of daily use of the most exquisite design and finish—all this amounts to *Yumi-ya no michi*—The Way of the Bow and Arrow. It was an art which reached a remarkably high degree of order and perfection, quite unique, and applicable to the Japanese alone.

The history of Japan is inextricably linked with legend and tradition, and fact and fiction are so intermingled that it is often well-nigh impossible

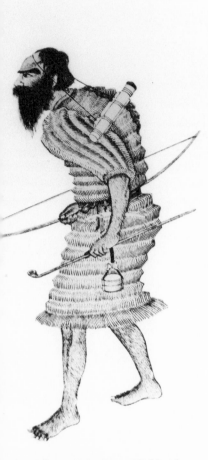

Ainu from Cape Sōya, Hokkaido, wearing bark costume and with the distinctive quiver of arrows slung from his forehead. From a silk scroll painting by Toyosuke Nagasaki.

to divorce one from the other. The history of archery is firmly woven into the history of Japan, and as we trace the progress of one within the other we learn of the special place reserved for the bow in the glorious military past of this once entirely warlike nation. Until comparatively recent times the warrior class were considered to be exalted beings apart, and tradition bestows divinity on Japan's princely soldiers from the earliest periods of her history. The bow became a noble weapon and a symbol of nobility, forbidden to other than the knightly class, and its use encouraged the founding of unique archery traditions which are upheld by many present-day Japanese toxophilites. Let us trace the fascinating progress of archery from the earliest times, even before the pioneers of the Japanese race ever set foot in Japan.

THE EARLIEST INHABITANTS OF JAPAN

Four large islands, 600 smaller ones, and 8,000 minute islets, many of them little more than mountain peaks sticking out of the sea: that is Japan. The last descendants of a dying race, the Ainu, live on Sakhalin, the large island at its northern extremity. These people, who were firmly established in all the islands when Japan's first emperor, Jimmu Tenno, came across from the island of Kyushu to the main island of Yamato in 660 B.C., have posed an ethnological problem which remains virtually unanswered to this day. They are related to west Europeans in physique, skull formation and colour of skin and it seems no less than fantastic that there should survive this isolated race of Caucasian stock. During the Neolithic period, somewhere between 3000–1800 B.C., the Ainu were already resident in Japan, and from a thorough study of bones and fossils taken from Neolithic graves it is apparent that this ancient stock had spread its culture over the whole archipelago before another race started to overrun the country. Their territory once extended over most of Japan and, according to national legend, there was a time when they could look out on their watery domain and exclaim, "Gods of the sea, open your divine eyes. Wherever your eyes turn, there echoes the sound of Ainu speech."

Sea-borne raids and invasion by the adventurous forebears of the Japanese were resisted time and time again by the Ainu, who were, to say the least, indignant that the safety of their homeland was threatened. There is some disagreement as to the exact origin of the invaders, but whether they came from the Asiatic mainland or from the islands to the south, they were certainly a more highly developed people than were the original Neolithic inhabitants of the land they were to conquer. Indignity and threats became humiliation and defeat, and eventually the Ainu were driven north and south. Ultimately those in the south were decimated; a remnant of these "Indo-Europeans" were left on Hokkaido and Sakhalin in the north. From that time they decreased in number, until today they are a tourist attraction exhibited as an ethnological miracle.

The ancient histories of Japan refer again and again to skirmishes with the Ainu, whose brave but ineffectual resistance continued for many hundreds of years. Undoubtedly the invader's weapons were far superior to the primitive equipment used by the original inhabitants, for whereas the latter were using stone points for their arrows the former employed well-made arrow-heads of bronze and later of iron. One of the finds among the Neolithic shell-mounds of Kyushu, the southernmost of the four major islands of the Japanese group, was an iron arrow-head under the rib-bones of one of the skeletons buried there. Its shape is approximately the same as others found in the proto-historic dolmens of Japan, and indicates a high degree of manufacturing skill in addition to a knowledge of the requirements of a specialised missile point. One of the two early chronicles of Japan,* dated A.D. 720, is said to mention bows, spears and swords in a legendary account of a migratory invasion by Japanese tribesmen—more than a thousand years earlier—of an island now thought to be Kyushu, and it is generally accepted that it was on this island that the earliest ancestral Japanese settled. The mute testimonies of bone and iron help to confirm the legendary histories of unsuccessful resistance by the Ainu.

BATTLES AND CEREMONIES

The methods of warfare can be imagined—a determined, well organised, barbaric invasion force, equipped with superior arms, taking by surprise a settlement of peaceable and bewildered aborigines whose archery was used more for hunting than for war. The advantage to the enemy of making a great number of small raids on targets scattered among the countless islands must have been immense, for this provided an opportunity of establishing strategic bases for incursions of even greater size. The early history of the Ainu is shrouded in the mists of time, and the details of wars and pattern of movement of these peoples among their innumerable lonely islands set in a hazy sea can only be conjectured. The existing survivors on Sakhalin, however, are living proof of the almost legendary references to these strange people and, fortunately for students of such matters, this pathetic remnant still keep alive their ancient beliefs and practise their primitive customs and ceremonies, although in somewhat modified form. An instance showing the symbolic importance of the bow to these people is its use as a sacrificial weapon in the climactic stages of their ancient bear-cult ceremonies. Primitive sacrifice was accompanied by a considerable amount of sacred ceremony and the gruesome implements involved, having a mystic significance, were specially

*The Nihongi

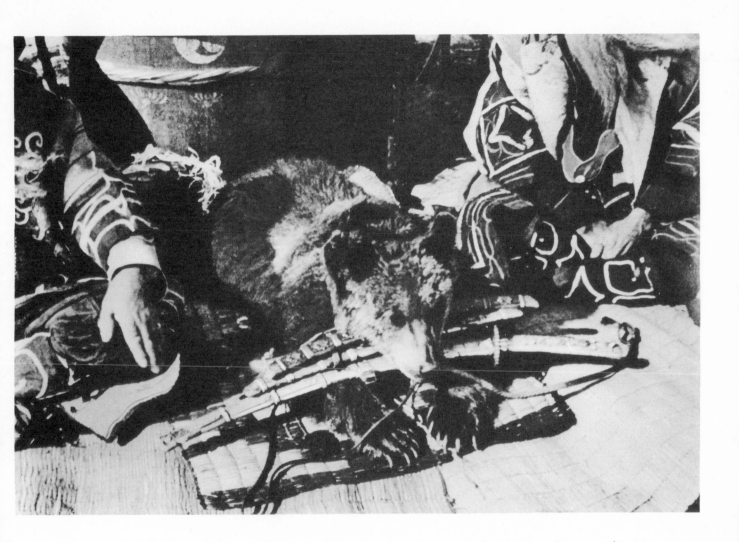

The last stages of the Ainu bear-festival. The body of the sacrificed bear cub occupies the place of honour whilst its soul floats up to the constellation of the Lesser Bear.

hallowed and cherished. A high-ranking functionary wielded these sacred weapons and performed the supreme act of the ceremonial: the sacrifice of the victim. The choice of an arrow to dispatch the unlucky bear cub to celestial bliss was not surprising. The Ainu, in common with many other primitive races, found that the bow was an important—well-nigh indispensable—adjunct to living. A long history of defending themselves against the invader (albeit less and less successfully) with crude armoury among which the bow was possibly the only missile weapon; plus, more importantly, a racial memory of thousands of years of searching out and killing game by the same means, must have implanted in the minds of this race a healthy respect for the bow and arrow which gradually grew to little less than a religious reverence. Archery began to have mystic qualities of which we shall hear more later. How better to unlock the gate to heaven than with a precisely delivered arrow?

The final stage of the bear-cult celebrations, after the beast had been fêted, fed, and its soul sent on its "happy" journey, was the shooting of a few more arrows into the air in a north-easterly direction. This gratified the superstitious beliefs of the Ainu, who were firmly convinced that spirits were lurking everywhere, perching and hovering on the breezes, waiting to delay the bear's soul on its upward journey. The arrows were loosed to protect the bewildered and newly disembodied spirit of the bear on the first stages of its unaccustomed progress.

BOWS, ARROWS AND POISON

When we study the bows, arrows and quivers of the Ainu it is immediately obvious that their design bears no relationship to the traditional pattern of Japanese equipment. It is rather more primitive. According to a traveller* who took part in a deer hunt towards the end of the nineteenth century, the bow used by the Ainu was a single stave of wood cut to length and shape, about four feet long, and quite stiff. Their arrows were rather short, measuring about eighteen inches long, the addition of poison being a special feature. The preparation of this poison was conducted with an air of great mystery, and was carried on in the sacred corner of a hut set apart for the use of the chiefs. First, and very ceremoniously, some roots of monkshood† were cut up and pounded to powder. The powder was boiled in about a quart of water until more than half the water was boiled away; the residue was then strained through a piece of rag, and evaporated further to a pulpy consistency. It was still far from ready—other bizarre and vitally important ingredients had to be added—the bodies of six spiders and the gall bladders of three foxes! These components were prepared separately with due ceremony and incantation, and the whole blended into a paste which was spread on to hollowed-out bamboo arrow-heads as required.

Quivers used by the Ainu today are of carved wood, with a curious pair of wing-like projections designed to keep the quiver in place when carried on the back. These act, so to speak, as stabilisers and prevent the whole contraption, which would otherwise be more or less cylindrical, from rolling about. A somewhat similar pattern can be observed in the design of wooden quivers often discovered in early tombs in the Gumma, Nara and Kyoto provinces, indicating the undoubted antiquity of this unusual shape.

INVADERS FROM ACROSS THE SEA

The Ainu play but a minor part in our story. We are more concerned with the invader who came across the sea to take the whole of Japan—ancestors of a remarkable nation now totalling over one hundred million souls. Experts'

*HOWARD, B. D., *Trans-Siberian Savages.*

†*Aconitum napellus* (Monkshood or Wolfsbane). The whole plant, and especially the rhizome, is very poisonous.

opinions are divided as to the origin of the Japanese race, and archaeological excavations have proved that Japan was peopled by immigrants not only from various parts of Asia but also from the South Seas. This drift to the Japanese islands may even be associated with the latter part of the mass Mongoloid migrations to the east some 15,000 years ago. Just why this enormous movement of people took place nobody really knows; perhaps the reasons lay in savage restlessness, an instinctive turning towards the rising sun, or in early over-population and barren earth problems. If some of these migratory tribes decided to settle in Japan then we must look to the mainland to the west for the ancestors of the Japanese. Wherever they came from, they brought with them basic skills from which were developed incredible techniques of manufacture and artistry.

After much tribal strife a group known as the Yamato emerged during the first three or four centuries of the Christian era, whose leaders are generally accepted as the ancestors of the present Imperial family. By the end of the fourth century contact was made between Japan and the kingdoms on the Korean peninsula. Through Korea, industrial arts such as weaving, metalwork, tanning and shipbuilding were introduced into Japan. Later the Chinese script was adopted, and in 538 Buddhism was brought to Japan from India by way of China and Korea. It is not unlikely that both the bows and the technique of Japanese use are of north-east Asian origin. One fact that points in this direction is that among certain proto-historic remains in Japan there have been found a number of turnip-shaped sound-making arrow-heads almost identical in design to similar arrow-heads common in Mongolia and formerly peculiar to the Mongolians. Several other interesting factors to support this theory will be discussed in due course. On the other hand, there is no evidence to support any contention that the Japanese bow is of southern origin. We know that the Malayans did not use the bow at all, and in Formosa the present wild tribes used a very primitive weapon, probably based on the bow used in China and Indo-China.

THE JAPANESE BOW

Curiously shaped and bearing little resemblance to any other bow the world over, the weapon used by the Japanese has not altered in design for over a thousand years. Its shape is not symmetrical, the arc being somewhat flatter at one end, and usually there are marked recurves—that is to say the tips curve slightly in the opposite direction to the main sweep. This recurving is more pronounced when the bow is unstrung. The most unusual feature, and one which is completely alien to good principles of bowyery, is the location of the handle or grip. This is positioned some two-thirds of the way down the bow instead of in the conventional mid-way position which is normal practice. This makes the limbs of unequal length, an unsatisfactory and unstable arrangement, which western archers would eschew.

From a number of ancient bows belonging to famous warriors of the past and preserved in various temples and shrines, it is apparent that the average length of a traditional Japanese bow has not altered for at least six or seven hundred years. There are some very long specimens, which are the exception rather than the rule, such as the one belonging to Yuasa Matashi-chiro which is eight feet nine inches long, and another, four inches shorter, which was used by Ihara Koshiro. Several bows preserved at the temple of Mishima average about seven feet seven inches, one of which was dedicated to the temple in 1363, while that which belonged to the famous Minamoto Yoritomo, in the temple of Hachimangu at Tsurugaoka, measured only six feet five inches. These bows must have been very powerful, and render less improbable the story that it took three ordinary men to bend the bow of Tametomo, which was eight feet six inches long. Minamoto Tametomo was the grandson of Yoshiiye (Hachiman Taro), and was very tall, his arms being so abnormally long that he could, as it was reported, draw a bowstring eighteen handbreadths—about five feet.

The construction of these bows follows basically the same pattern today as it did in ancient times. They are constructed of bamboo cut into strips and bonded with fish-glue into a filled-in box-girder formation. Some of the strips are laid edgeways on to the others, giving great strength to the bow. The sides are finished off with strips of *haze* wood, the wood of the wax-tree, and the shaped ends over which the string is looped consist of additional pieces of wood fitted in place and bound with rattan. There were slight variations of this arrangement, and a core of *sumac* or mulberry wood is sometimes found. Frequently the bow is bound at intervals with rattan, and invariably the whole is beautifully lacquered. Collectors of such items often assemble a number of thin slices of discarded bows, showing their cross-section, which are polished, carefully mounted, and attractively displayed to show off the pattern of laminations.

According to the *Buki ni-hiaku* there were five kinds of bows: the *Maru-ki*, or round wood bow; the *Shige-to yumi*, or bow wound with rattan; the *Bankui* and *Hankui*, similar bows, but of smaller size; and the *Hoko-yumi*, the Tatar-shaped bow. The last-named was probably a bow with pronounced recurves following a pattern which is common to Mongolia, and this bow sometimes had metal ends, or "ears". This possibly formed some sort of reinforcement as it is not unusual for the recurved tips of such bows to be rigid and inflexible. The *Otokane*, the metal-faced portion, was so positioned that when the bowstring slapped it, it produced a sound; and it is said that this effect was often used in signalling. This must have been a very localised signal, as the noise thus produced could not have been particularly loud; and

The Empress Jingo Kogo, of
mythological origin, who ruled
Japan in the third century, is often
depicted carrying the unique
asymmetrical war bow of Japan.

Japanese bow and arrow making, from an old photograph. The fletcher on the left, sighting along an arrow, has a bowl of prepared feathers in readiness. The man in the centre appears to be straightening shafts and the bowyer on the right expertly shapes a bow in a specially made block.

in fact it is recorded that when the Mikado required water for washing in the morning, three of his attendants made a signal to that effect by twanging their bows.

Modern Japanese bows, measuring seven feet two inches, are constructed on similar lines to those already described, and it is interesting to note that precisely the same arrangement obtains in respect of the position of the grip—two-thirds of the way down the bow, and the subtle curvature is still as it was centuries ago.

THE EVOLUTION OF BOW PATTERN

The construction and style of the bows used by the ancient Japanese prior to the dating of the specimens preserved in temples are not definitely known. We can make a shrewd guess that the pattern did not vary much from that which has been described, although the construction may have been from a single stave of wood. Many names are given in early chronicles and poems for both bows and the trees which supplied the wood. But although most of the trees are named, it is not certain to what species they belong. There is also no certainty that the development of these singular bows took place before or after the Japanese conquered their new homeland, and many theories have been advanced to account for the evolution of their asymmetrical shape. The contention that they were designed so as to be easily manageable on horseback is arguable. That the short stature of the Japanese demanded a bow which would clear the ground when held perpendicularly is not acceptable, because if the handle were set half-way down the bow it would still give ample clearance. The kneeling position of shooting, which was practised by armoured warriors, does call for a shorter lower limb to the bow, and this could conceivably be a factor that encouraged this practice of construction. An explanation involving the development of this weapon from the primitive sapling which, tapering as it did, needed a grip some two-thirds of the way down to effect some sort of dynamic balance, is intriguing and worthy of study. According to the Shosoin catalogue* there are preserved specimens of ancient bows made from a single stem of *azusa* (catalpa), the lower third of which has been somewhat worked down to increase the flexibility of the butt end of the stem. Later specimens show an improvement in design where two stems were used, spliced together, which avoided the necessity of working down the lower limb. Here was a chance to regularise the position of the grip, but even at that early date tradition was at work, and tradition called for a bow grip to be where it had always been. This would seem to be the simplest and possibly the most reasonable explanation for the unique form of the Japanese bow.

This was the mighty bow immortalised in the ancient chronicles of Japan. In their ceaseless pursuit of chivalric warfare the Samurai performed many deeds in battle which not only brought out the best qualities of personal honour and bravery, involving astounding acts of devotion and self-sacrifice, but also amply displayed an unrivalled prowess with the bow. Many of these exploits are fantastic by our standards and belief in them requires a feeling for the legendary aspect of history. A study of them reveals much of the character of the Japanese of those days. An elaborate ceremonial code involving the bow and arrow is closely associated with the rise of Japanese military domination, and present-day teachings in the art, which are described later in this chapter, are precisely similar to those evolved some 500 years ago.

FEUDAL JAPAN

In the sixth and seventh centuries an increasing interest in Chinese matters flowered among the Japanese. The application of a unique facility for

The Imperial Treasures in the Shosoin. (The Shosoin, literally "a storehouse", has been for 1,200 years the repository for ancient racial relics. It is located at Nara.)

altering, improving and adding a Japanese characteristic to borrowed skills and knowledge began to occur, and adopted Chinese cultures existed side by side with ancient Japanese feudal and religious customs. This is a special feature of so many things Japanese, from their simple handicrafts to complicated manufacturing processes, and even involving language, writing and administration. In all probability archery underwent this transformation, the specialised knowledge and techniques of the Tatar archers having been brought to Japan by the sea-borne barbarians at a much earlier date.

A theory worthy of consideration, claiming knowledge of Japan by China, concerns the ideographs which make up the Chinese character for "eastern barbarians". When separated these ideographs mean "large" and "bow". It is interesting to speculate on the identity of these eastern barbarians. The distribution of the ancient Chinese race was, of course, quite different from what it is at present, and although we do not know definitely who the users of this large bow were, it may be that these barbarians living in the east (of China) were also the same invaders who carried with them the large bow so completely identified with the Japanese.

Evidence is not wanting that the organisation of a feudal autocracy was being set up in the very early days of Japan's history, and one ancient institution was the *Be* or *Tomo*, sometimes translated as "clan" or "guild". They seem to have been instituted on many pretexts and to have differed widely in their memberships. What is interesting to us is that, as early as 480, in order that the memory of his three childless consorts should be kept alive for ever, the Emperor Seinei established three sets of *Be* in every province. They were named the *Be* of Palace Attendants, of Palace Stewards and of Palace Archers. This indicates the special importance given to the bow from an early date, and already we can discern emphasis on its use by a privileged few of the upper class, organised into clans similar to the hereditary guilds of the later Roman Empire.

One other example which will suffice to show the significance of the bow was its inclusion in a compulsory levy imposed as part of the Great Reform of 645. This reform abolished the old taxes and forced labour, and introduced a system of commuted taxes. Among levies there was the commuted house tax: all houses had to pay twelve feet of cloth and each 100 houses were required to contribute one horse of medium quality, or if the horse was of superior quality, it served as the contribution of 200 houses. Each person had to contribute a sword, armour, bow and arrows, a flag and a drum. Whereas the contributions of a sword, armour and bow and arrows would seem to be on a reasonable scale for equipping a military body, the overwhelming flags and drums must have encumbered the troops and hampered operations considerably.

A mounted samurai wearing a voluminous *horo* or drapery guard designed to deflect arrows. In later periods this item became purely an ornamental accessory. Re-drawn by C. Halls from an old print.

THE LEGENDARY HISTORY OF JAPAN

Many legendary stories of archers have been handed down, and one of the earliest* concerns Fujiwara Hidesato. In the year 940 he was sent to suppress the rebellion of Taira no Masakado. At the battle of Kushima, Masakado was hit by an arrow, fell from his horse and was beheaded by Hidesato. Then we learn that Hidesato changed his name to Tawara Toda, and it is under this name that he figures as the hero who slew the gigantic *mukade*, or centipede. There are different versions of the story, varying in details, but all agree that when the monster appeared Hidesato had only three arrows, two of which glanced off the creature's head; but wetting the point of the third in his mouth, he pierced the monster's eye and it fell dead. The exploit is commemorated by a chapel near the bridge of Seta, the scene of the adventure, and it is popularly believed that a centipede can be killed by keeping its head wet with human saliva.

The first permanent capital of Japan was established in Nara at the beginning of the eighth century, and for the following seventy-four years (710–84), emperors reigned from there with a growing authority over the country. In 784, however, a new capital was established in Kyoto, modelled after the Chinese capital of those days, and the Heian period occupies the next four centuries, until 1192.

Japan's contacts with China were interrupted at the close of the ninth century, and subsequently her civilisation began to assume its own particular

The Nihon o dai ichiran.

222

Wash drawing from a long scroll
signed by Ch'ien Hsuan (c. 1235–
1300) and dated 1290, depicting a
young nobleman on horseback
with his bow.

form and characteristics. In some ways the Heian Period was an age of elegance; an example was set by the highest in the land, and soon it became
fashionable to indulge in the arts and sports of the nobility. The Emperor
Toba II, for instance, who lived from 1103 to 1156, was said to be "at once
poet, musician, swordsmith, a great hunter, and many other things besides.
A great patron of cock-fighting, horse-racing, of the wrestling ring, of archery
with fugitive dogs as moving targets; he was also addicted to betting and
gambling: in short, he had all the vices and not a few of the virtues of what
is known in the slang of certain modern circles as a 'good sport'."*

THE STRUGGLE FOR POWER

As court officials whiled away the time with elegant banquets and games,
local clans gradually came into power on the strength of their armed forces.

*MURDOCK, JAMES, *A History of Japan* (1925)

They ignored the orders of the central Government, and low-ranking military clans in the Government service began to gain influence. There were two important military families, the Minamotos and the Tairas, descendants of separate emperors, and after a series of internecine struggles for power the Minamotos annihilated the Tairas in 1185. The legendary histories of these battles are full of incidents involving archery and, according to these reports, the Japanese warrior was no mean shot. He was also superbly equipped and a fearsome sight in full battle array, positively bristling with swords, spears, bows, and quivers full of arrows, and dressed in a complicated armour of lacquer plates held together by silken cords, embellished with elaborate ornament. All this was worn with a studied correctness. However, the final ostentatious blossoming of the Japanese medieval knight in his full panoply was to come later.

Minamoto Yoshiiye, the first Japanese archer of national renown, who lived in the eleventh century, once shot through three sets of strong armour as they hung from a tree. His descendant, Tametomo, an equally famous archer, distinguished himself in one of the battles of his day, a quarrel between the Emperor Goshira-Kawa and the ex-Emperor Shutoku in 1156, by shooting through the armour and body of the opposing general; the arrow, its force still far from dissipated, then mortally wounded the general's brother who, equally well armoured, was standing just behind. Tametomo was captured later in this battle, and the enemy, after disabling him by cutting one of the sinews of his right arm, exiled him to Oshima. However, his wound seems to have healed as he led a revolt on the island and with his arrows sank a boat-load of enemy soldiers sent to arrest him.

THE ARCHER AND THE FAN

During one of the last battles between the Tairas and the Minamotos, on March 21st, 1185, orders were issued for the evacuation of Yashima. All the Taira clan took refuge on board the fleet. The palace and fortress were burned before their eyes, and the Minamoto army showered arrows on them from the beach. At this time, a trivial but picturesque incident did much to disconcert the Tairas. On his visit to Miyajima in 1180, the Emperor Takakura had presented the temple with thirty fans, each emblazoned with the *Hi-no-maru*—the sun's disc. When his son Antoku Tenno was taken there in the course of his involuntary wanderings, the priest gave him one of these fans, assuring him that the disc thereon was the spirit of his father, the late Emperor, which would cause the arrows of the enemy to recoil on them. The Tairas now placed this fan upon the top of a pole erected in the bow of one of their junks, and a lady of the court dared a Minamoto to shoot at it. At Yoshitsune's request, a certain Nasu no Yoichi Munekata accepted the challenge.

Riding as far into the water as he could, he took cool and careful aim and launched his shaft. To the consternation of the Tairas the arrow smote the fan on the rivet, and brought it down in fragments. Omens and portents were of great consequence in those days, and this incident perhaps did more to take the heart out of the Tairas and their partisans than had the loss of their best captains a year before at Ichi-no-Tani. Claiming to be descendants of Munetaka, the Sasake family used as their cognizance, or *mon*, a fan with a black disc on it.

THE HORO

At about this time the *yumitori*, or bowmen, sported a novel accessory known as the *horo*. This was a drapery guard designed to balloon out behind the horseman, and its purpose was to deflect or catch arrows, especially those shot down from an eminence. The *horo*, made of silk, was fastened at the shoulders and waist and so arranged as to fill with air as the samurai rode forward. In twelfth- and thirteenth-century picture rolls depicting battles of the time the *horo* appears like a balloon behind the mounted warrior. This curious item of dress fell out of favour in the thirteenth and fourteenth centuries but enjoyed a revival in the sixteenth, when it was worn over a basket-like frame attached to the backplate. It was thus given a permanent shape.

In 1192 Yorimoto, head of the Minamoto family, established the Shogunate (military "camp" government) at Kamakura, thus marking the beginning of six hundred years of feudal government. The new regime remained in power until 1338, and this reign is known as the Kamakura Period. During these years emphasis was placed on stabilising the country by strengthening the ties of loyalty between the Shogun and his vassals. At the same time they tried to prepare for emergencies by encouraging chivalry. Thus *bushido* (the way of the samurai or Japanese chivalry) prevailed. The military government was temporarily interrupted by a period of Imperial rule, but was soon restored by the Ashikagas, who established a Shogunate at Muromachi in Kyoto. This period, known as the Muromachi Period, ended in 1578.

THE FOUR SCHOOLS OF JAPANESE ARCHERY

It was these first four hundred years of feudal Japan which saw the flowering and perfection of so many military skills. The swordsmiths, the armourers, the bowyers, the fletchers and arrowsmiths, all became pre-eminent in their trades, and fortunately for us many fine examples of their crafts have been preserved in museums and private collections. The oldest of the four schools of Japanese archery, the Heki school, was inaugurated during the Muromachi

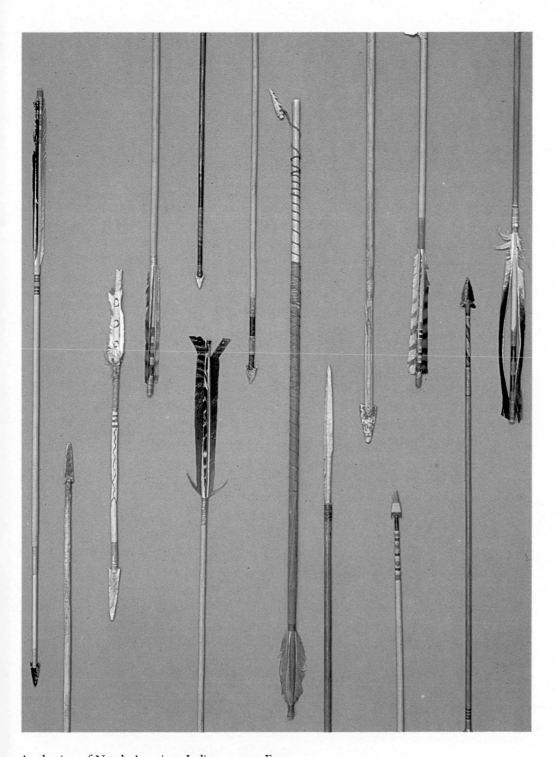

A selection of North American Indian arrows. From
left to right: Hupa Indians, Northern California,
obsidian point; (bottom) Plains Indians, crude iron
point; Sioux medicine arrow; (top, two) Northern
Californian Indians; (bottom) Sioux; (top) West
Coast of America; Point Barrow Eskimo, sea otter
harpoon arrow; (bottom) Kodiak, Alaska Peninsula,
carved walrus ivory point; (top) Alaskan peninsula,
sea otter arrow, walrus ivory and iron point; (top)
Hupa Indians, bird arrow, great horned owl feathers;
(bottom) Hupa Indians, ceremonial arrow; Klamath,
Northern California; (top) Plains Indians, eagle
feathers.

A Prussian nobleman of Friedland in fanciful costume of about the eleventh century, in his ownership of the crossbow enjoying a privilege denied to common people.

Samurai warrior in action. The management of a complicated armour and the competent control of a spirited war-horse, whilst shooting a bow with a high degree of accuracy, called for considerable dexterity. This was the result of years of critical training amongst the warrior class of Japan. From a film still.

period and the founder, Hekidanjo Masatsugu, who lived in about the middle of the fifteenth century, was a noted philosopher as well as an archer. The idea of teaching *Sharei* or ceremonial archery, which tends to stress form and mental attitude, was originally introduced from old China, and the teachings of Masatsugu were probably inspired by the five cardinal points of classic Chinese archery. These *Sharei* practices have now grown to be purely Japanese, although Confucius indicates their origin in one of the oldest books of China, the *Li-Ki*, when he says: "The archers, in advancing and in retiring, in turning or in making any other movement, were obliged to conform to the ceremonial rules."

THE SAMURAI BOWMEN

The *samurai*, whose code of chivalry became known as *bushido*, recognised warfare as a special art. From the few examples of battles already described it will be seen that individual accuracy rather than massed flight was

The horrific aftermath of an enemy archery attack. The long, slender, viciously pointed arrows of the Japanese bowmen possessed excellent penetrative qualities, piercing both the laminated plate-armour of the warrior and the tough, unprotected hide of his mount.

the accepted use of archery in battle, and all training and practice was directed with this in mind. These select and highly respected (and feared) warriors first appeared in the twelfth century, and an author of a slightly later date speaks thus of them and their ways: "Their ponderous bows are *San-nin-bari* (a bow needing three ordinary men to bend it) or *Go-nin-bari* (five-men bows); their quivers, which match their bows, hold fourteen or fifteen bundles of arrows. They are very quick in their release, and each arrow kills or wounds two or three foemen, the impact being powerful enough to pierce two or three thicknesses of armour at a time: and they never fail to hit the mark. Every *Daimyo* (owner of a great estate) has at least twenty or thirty of such mounted archers, and even the owner of a small barren estate has two or three. Their horses are very excellent, for they are carefully selected while yet in pasture, and then trained after their own particular fashion. With five or ten such excellent mounts each, they go out hunting deer and foxes, and gallop up and down mountains and forests. Trained in these wild methods, they are splendid horsemen who know how to ride but never how to fall. It is the habit of the *Kwanto-Bushi* that if in the field of battle a father falls, the son will not retreat, or if a son be slain, the father will not yield, but stopping over the dead they will fight to the death."

Further insight into the high ideals of courage and personal valour of the *samurai* is illustrated by an episode in the protracted siege of Kanazawa. In the camp of Yoshiiye, who strove to imbue his troops with a sense of discipline and a proper respect for military virtues, orders were issued for a singularly unusual arrangement. Special seats were set apart for the brave and for the shirkers, and after each assault the warriors were assigned to their places according to their deserts. A youth of sixteen, a certain Kamakura Gongoro, a Taira by birth, received an arrow in the eye in the course of one of the assaults. He merely snapped off the shaft, and then returned his enemy's fire and brought down the man who had hit him. When he took off his helmet he tumbled to earth with the barb still in his eye; and when a friend, in extracting it, put his foot on his face to give himself a purchase, the youthful warrior swore he would have his life for subjecting him to such an indignity, for to trample on the face of a *Bushi* was an outrage that could only be expiated by the blood of the offender.

The military spirit of the Kamakura period was in complete contrast to the fastidious taste of Heian times and, although it originated far earlier, it was under Minamoto no Yoritomo (1145–95) that *bushido* took on its own permanent form. Moreover Zen Buddhism now gave it its metaphysical and religious bases, and it became a philosophy of death practised in life. The principle of the Japanese knightly ethic is represented by the bow and the sword—symbols of inner purity—for the *samurai* perfected a technique for transcending death in the hour of death, and regarding it objectively. This

Warrior in full battle regalia
during the Three-Years War.
From the Later Three-Years War
Scroll, late thirteenth century.
Artist unknown.

was the art of enlightenment for the warrior; by making no distinction between life and death *bushido* eliminated the gap between them.

The importance of dying an honourable death preoccupied the minds of these philosophic warriors, and sooner than die in dishonour they preferred to die of their own free will. Death on the battlefield was natural and inevitable but must needs be honourable, and this tenet was interpreted in many ways which to Western minds have a curious and unfathomable quality. For instance, an arrow intended to be used against a general had to be of superior and more elaborate design than that shot at a private. This was taken to extreme lengths by the provision of two special arrows, known as *Wuwagashi* (upper arrows), in a standard set of twenty-four. These were reserved for shooting high-ranking warriors, and if such an officer was killed by a bow-shot intended for a lesser rank his fate was regarded as "death by a stray arrow".

WAR ARROWS OF THE JAPANESE

Military arrows used by the Japanese were beautifully finished examples of the arrowmaker's and fletcher's crafts. We can study their exact patterns in a great variety of designs by handling actual specimens, searching through contemporary drawings and paintings and reading accounts which include descriptions of arrows and arrow-heads. The arrow-shaft was made of mountain bamboo. Specially selected, carefully matched and made perfectly straight, it was then often permanently stained in a mixture of chemicals. Each part of the arrow was named and received its own particular share of a manufacturing technique to ensure its final perfection and uniformity. Some of these arrows were long by comparison with other war arrows; a pair in the author's collection measure 38½ inches, but a more normal length would be 33 or 34 inches. The nock was usually cut from a piece of hardwood or horn in the form of a plug and fastened to the rear end of the arrow by glue and silken bindings.

Next in importance to the arrow-head itself was the fletching, and the choice of feathers, their arrangement and final cut shape were especially significant, being related to the rank and status of their owner. There were usually three vanes, made from feathers of the pheasant, eagle, hawk, falcon, wild duck, owl or crane. So great was the demand that eagle feathers were imported from primitive peoples living in the north, and there seems to have been a shortage of this commodity even in recent times. C. F. Hawkes, in speaking of his travels in Sakhalin at the beginning of the present century,

Part of the superb collection of decorative Japanese arrow-heads belonging to James Goodspeed. Much of the delicacy of workmanship and intricacy of design of these *yano-ne* can be studied from such a group of specimens.

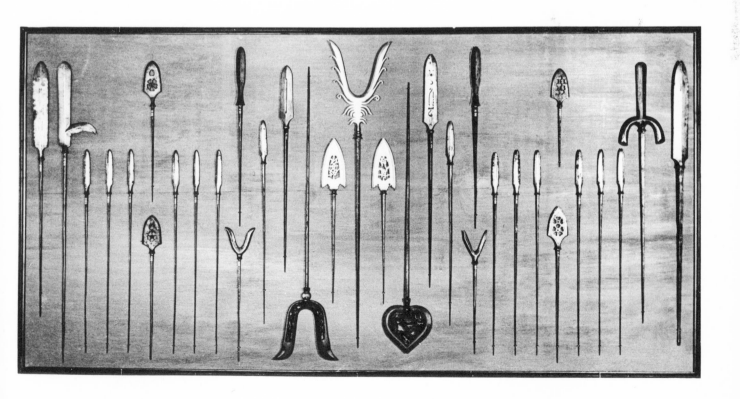

A group of Japanese *yano-ne* made for practical use. Other and more elaborate examples were intended only for decorative and ceremonial purposes.

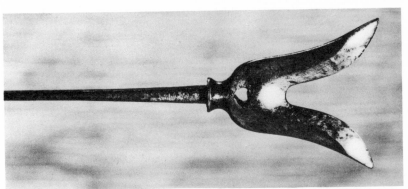

mentions the Gilyaks who pressed him to shoot white-tailed eagles for their tail feathers "for which they declared the Chinese gave them three dollars", and relates that the same people removed young eagles from the nest and reared them in the hope of selling the tails to the Japanese. A similar practice was reported by an eighteenth-century traveller in the Kuriles, where there was hardly a yurt without its eagle, fed constantly to provide feathers needed for fletching arrows or for trade to distant islanders, presumably Japanese.

The feathers were set on straight, that is to say parallel with the shaft as opposed to a spiralled setting, glued in position and always very neatly trimmed. They were cut into a long rectangle or a shape with gently curving edges. The matching of exquisite feather patterns and the use of dyes to obtain colour arrangements beyond the resources of nature were refinements which the dextrous and artistic Japanese soon developed, and early picture scrolls containing drawings of feather patterns and designs in a bewildering variety would need a volume of their own to describe. Although three feathers was the standard arrangement the *Wuwagashi* arrows, already mentioned, often had four vanes, two of one variety and two of another, set alternately.

JAPANESE ARROW-HEADS

One of the most rewarding aspects of toxology is the study of arrow-heads, and those from Japan are particularly rich in variety and interest, from the prehistoric points of stone to the elaborately pierced steel points, chiselled in relief and damascened in gold, of the later fifteenth and sixteenth centuries. Many of the dolmens or graves of rulers and noblemen are regarded as sacred and few have been opened. In those which have been examined many personal items and weapons have been found, including bullet-shaped or chisel-pointed arrow-heads of bronze. Additional valuable information as to the early pattern of these points has been gleaned from the study of *haniwa* figures or "tomb attendants". These coarse pottery figures of warriors, retainers and horses were buried with a great lord or emperor in place of the actual people who would have been buried with him. Their clothing and accoutrements are faithful copies of the items of the period. The early bronze arrow-heads are lozenge-shape in section with a central rib on both sides forming sharp bevelled edges, the basic outline being similar in shape to a Gothic window or bishop's mitre. They were provided with a tang which became the standard form of attachment for Japanese arrow-heads. The form was well developed, the design being so arranged as to give the maximum cutting potential. The metal and chemical content of various sample heads were studied some years ago,* and the results show a high proportion of copper, a considerable amount of tin and traces of antimony, nickel, iron, lead and

*CHIKASIGE, MASUMI, *Oriental Alchemy* (1936)

arsenic. From an early date the Japanese had a detailed knowledge of metal-lurgy and these analyses tend to show that this knowledge was gained from China, as arrow-heads of the same period from that country show a very similar combination of metals. A number of shapes of bronze arrow-heads have been noticed, many examples of which can be seen in museums.

The war point of the *samurai*, made of high quality steel, became the most common type of arrow-head from about the twelfth century. Its standard shape, designed for armour-piercing purposes, was little more than 1½ inches long and was square or lozenge-shape in section, with a fairly blunt point. The tang was often quite long, two or even three times the length of the exposed head, and one way in which experts are able to assess the approximate date of the point is by examining the file marks on the tang. This was the military issue type of arrow-head, produced wholesale in tens of thousands at Nagoya, Kaga Province and Echizen, and still stored in arsenals at the beginning of this century. Variations of this standard shape included a long and narrow point; others were wider and heavier, and some had slightly curved cutting edges, each one displaying the same basic characteristics and of superb workmanship. These are known as *Yanagi-bu* (willow leaf) points. The many other shapes introduced by the Japanese can be divided into three main groups: the *Togari* (pointed) arrow-heads, generally flat and broad and terminating in a sharp point; the *Karimata* (flying goose), which were forked heads shaped somewhat like a swallow's tail; and the *Watakusi* (flesh tearer), which were the barbed heads.

Many diverse patterns of these four groups were produced, and Japanese fancy and adaptiveness had full play in designing arrow-heads from natural forms. Each different shape was named, and these titles were most suggestive: bamboo leaf, camellia leaf, trefoil, water-plantain, fish's head, mackerel's tail, crab's claw, dragon's tongue, sparrow's beak, frog's legs and wild goose beak are but a few, all of which exactly describe the shapes. Many arrow-heads were designed for special purposes, as offerings to temples perhaps, inscribed with prayers or names, and frequently we find the shape of the *Ino me*, or wild boar's eye, pierced through the blade. This is sometimes mistakenly identified as the petal of the cherry blossom. The wild boar is the crest or totemic emblem of the warrior clan, and its peculiar eye does not turn. It charges straight ahead, fearlessly and unswervingly. By embodying the *Ino me* design in arrow-heads it was hoped that some of the mystic power of the wild boar would transfer itself to the weapon, ensuring an aim both accurate and fatal.

The most fabulous designs are to be found in the more complex and intricate examples of the arrow-smith's art, the decorated *Yano ne*. It was usually the *Togari*, *Karimata* and *Watakusi* types of arrow-head which were glamorised into a bewildering variety of pattern and decoration. Some are purely geometrical or naturalistic designs, or incorporate the wild boar's eye singly or repeated in a pattern; others have characters spelling out poems, names or prayers, exquisite examples of the metalworker's art, with razor-sharp edges. Pierced designs, complicated patterns chiselled in relief, and fantastic shapes all occur—the products, one might say, of a whimsical and capricious armourer gone artistically berserk. The largest and most elaborate of these are nearly all of a later period when militancy gave way to lavish ornamentation for its own sake.

Several catalogues exist which list collections of these *Yano ne*, showing their outlines and giving their names and often the name of the swordsmith who fashioned them. Some of the great swordsmiths specialised in making these unusual and beautiful objects, and Umetada, the Taiko's swordsmith, is regarded as perhaps the first artist of *Yano ne*, since he was as renowned for arrow-heads as for his sword blades. His speciality was open-work chiselling, and the same chiselling in relief in runnels and grooves as on his sword blades. By the inscriptions and signatures one may date *Yano ne* precisely, but as a general distinction those with square tangs are the earliest, originating from the twelfth century onwards, while those with round tangs date from about the fourteenth and fifteenth centuries.

WHISTLING ARROWS

As to other types of arrow-heads, some mention must be made of the *Hikimeya*, arrows provided with whistling heads. These heads were hollow, egg-shaped and made of wood or horn, pierced with holes arranged so that when they were in flight they would give a shrill whistle. They were said to be used as a signal in battle when one side or the other was ready to start hostilities. They were also shot by expert bowmen in the *Hikime* ceremony, which was a service performed to disperse evil, prevent calamity, bring peace and render happiness. A larger type of whistling arrow with a blunt or padded head was used in the dog hunt already mentioned in connection with the Emperor Toba (page 222). A number of dogs were let loose in an enclosure and the mounted archer endeavoured to single out and hit the animals with these blunt-headed whistling arrows. The dogs would suffer no injury from the blunt point, but no clear explanation has been given for the whistling— perhaps it was considered fair to warn the beast of the oncoming danger. Occasionally a whistling head and a decorated point were mounted on the same shaft; although their use is not absolutely clear these arrows were probably reserved for use by a high official, or prepared for special ceremonies.

The Momoyama period, 1578–1603, was a time of transition which saw civil wars, the breaking of the power of the Buddhist monks and the persecution of Christians. Korea was invaded twice, though not very successfully, and a series of great castles was built on an unprecedented scale of magnifi-

Typical examples of whistling arrow-heads. The four heads in the top row are of Japanese origin and are made of carved and lacquered wood. Those below are Mongolian and are fashioned from horn.

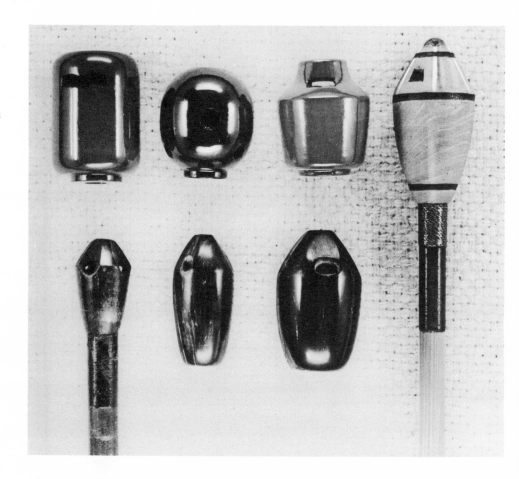

cence. Towards the end of the sixteenth century a chaotic situation was created all over the country owing to strife among local clans. The country was finally pacified by Hideyoshi Toyotomi in 1590. His work was consolidated by Ieyasu Tokugawa, founder of the Tokugawa Shogunate, and when he became the virtual ruler of Japan in 1603 he established Edo (now Tokyo) as his seat of government. From that time until the Imperial regime was restored in 1868 Japan was administered by the Tokugawas; this was a police state which lasted longer than any other in history, and was known as the Edo period. The Tokugawas closed Japan's doors to the outside world and it was during this period that the art of the swordsmith flourished, decoration became very elaborate and the arts were encouraged. The status of the artisan and commercial classes began to improve. This was the high period of the decorated *Yano ne* and of elaborately finished bows, quivers, and other archery impedimenta. A dainty indoor game with tiny bows and toy arrows dipped in coloured powders became popular with ladies of leisure. They used bows made of willow wood which folded into three, and miniature blunt-headed arrows with gilded shafts and ivory nocks, which were shot at pretty targets at short range. Sets of bows and arrows, quite lethal in performance but miniature in size, were carried in palanquins for personal protection. The bows, called *Rimankyu*, were made from one piece of horn cunningly shaped into an exaggerated replica of a traditional bow. Arrows, complete with perfectly made quarter-size arrow-heads and fletchings, were arranged in an open quiver with the bow, and the whole was beautifully finished and decorated with the owner's *mon* or crest.

THE MASTER BOWMEN OF JAPAN

The great feats of archery in warfare gave way to greater feats in archery practice and display. The schools of ceremonial archery thrived, and three special types of archery were cultivated, each having its own ceremonial procedure. The Ordinary School pursued straightforward target archery, used normal equipment, and shot at a series of standard targets at distances from about 28 to 60 metres. The Low Trajectory School practised shooting at greater distances but within a building which restricted the height of the trajectory of the arrow. This called for a special and quite remarkable technique. To avoid fouling the low roof, special arrows with finely adjusted points of balance were used in conjunction with bows of considerably more power than those normally employed. Some fantastic records of devotees of this school are available. The western veranda of the temple in Kyoto, called *San-jusan-gen-do*, the Hall of the Thirty-three Pillar Spans, is 384 feet long with a ceiling of 16 feet. In 1686 an archer named Wada Daihachi shot continuously for twenty-seven hours, discharged on an average one arrow every

A lively drawing showing a mounted bowman about to deliver a decisive shot. One of the archery games enjoyed by the nobility of Japan was a dog shoot in which whistling arrows were shot at a number of these animals let loose in a circular enclosure.

twelve seconds, and put 8,133 of his shafts down to the other end of the corridor without fouling the roof. In a similar building in Tokyo, used exclusively for archery, another more recent record was made by Masatoki who, in the fourth year of Kaei, the fifth month, and the nineteenth day (May 19th, 1852), started shooting at seven o'clock in the evening and ended at three o'clock the following afternoon, having shot all through the night by torchlight. In the twenty hours he let fly 10,050 arrows, which gives an average of one every seven seconds. When one remembers that in getting the shaft down the full length of the corridor the trajectory was limited by the 16-foot ceiling, Masatoki need not be ashamed of having made a total score of 5,383 clean shots.

The third school of ceremonial archery is the Horse-riders' School and this method of shooting, called *Yabusame*, is perpetuated at an annual ceremony at the famous shrine of Hachiman at Kamakura. This is the most spectacular and possibly the most difficult method of shooting in a bow. Special targets include three diamond-shaped targets in a row, a hat woven of rushes set on a post, and the captive dogs already mentioned in the *Inu-oi* shooting.

TRADITIONAL CEREMONIAL ARCHERY

Ceremonial shooting with the bow and arrow has a venerable history; for instance, there is evidence that during the early days of the Imperial court in the fifth century, ceremonial target shooting was practised. This was called *Sharei*, and was later designated as an official ceremony to celebrate the arrival of the New Year. This ceremony was performed annually at court during the period between the eighth and eleventh centuries. From the thirteenth century, when this ceremony was taken over by the warriors, the New Year celebrations, called *Onmatohajimo*, became the greatest annual event of the Shogunate family.

The bow and arrow ceased to be the great weapon of war with the introduction of firearms to Japan in 1542, but the archers continued to provide the guard of honour, a *corps d'élite*. Etiquette ordered that the bowmen should be placed at the left, the musketeers to the right, and a battle was formally opened by a shower of arrows. It is therefore quite easy to see how the special schools of ceremonial archery became firmly established, and how they became exclusive and important organisations the membership of which was an exalted and jealously guarded privilege. Members of these schools were called upon to perform the many obscure rites which accompany every important function and significant occasion in the life of the Japanese. As recently as 1960 court officials performed a ceremony in honour of the newly

Opposite: a group of Japanese arms from the Victoria and Albert Museum including a pair of bows and a quiver mounted ready for travelling, another type of quiver full of arrows, and two *uchi-ne*, or throwing arrows, bottom left.

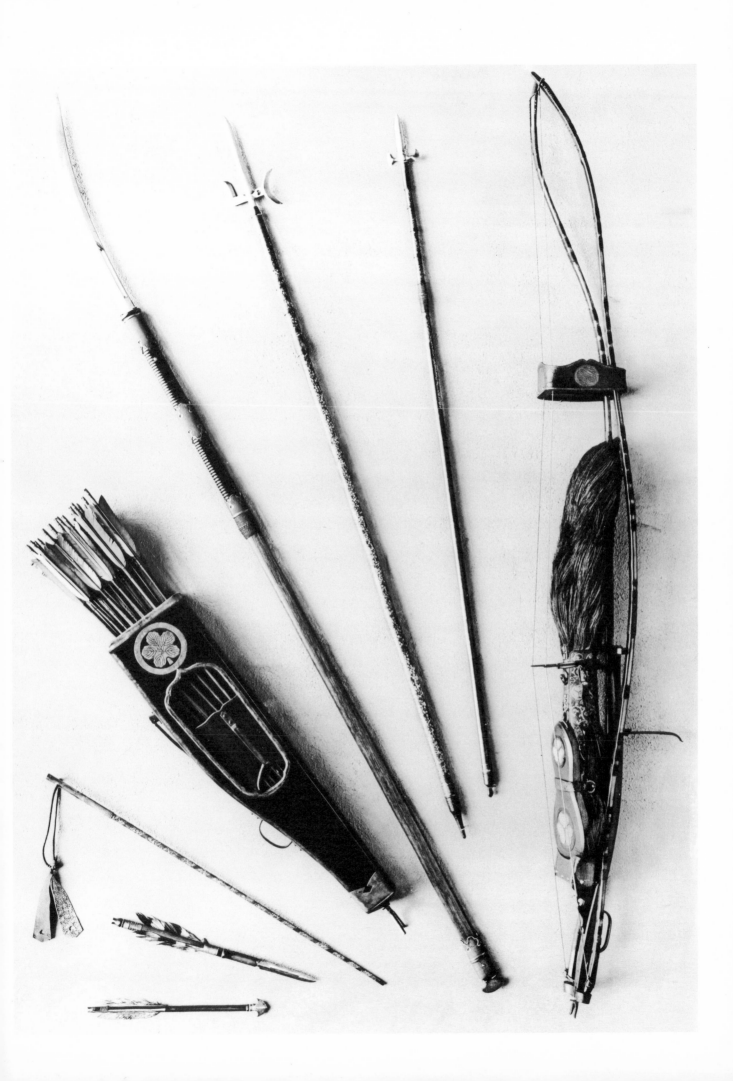

A delicate painting of the late nineteenth century showing Japanese nobility practising *Sharei* or ceremonial archery. The complicated ritual which accompanies this form of archery has been handed down over the centuries and many archers of Japan still shoot in this traditional fashion.

Opposite, the famous *Yabusame* archer, Takahashi, with his son dressed in classical costume, which dates back over the centuries. The *Yabusame* school of archery, one of the four types of traditional Japanese archery still practised in modern times, consists of shooting at special targets whilst on horseback at full gallop.

born crown prince, twanging their great war bows to ward off evil and to bring good luck to the new heir to the Imperial throne.

ZEN AND THE BOW

Some remarks on the influence of Zen Buddhism in medieval Japan have already been made, and the application of archery to Zen training has been briefly mentioned; to understand further the way in which archery aids the Zen master and his pupil some explanation of the precepts and feeling of Zen will be necessary. Zen was rooted in China by Bodhidharma, who came from India in the sixth century, and the philosophy was carried eastwards into Japan by the twelfth century. It contains many elements which are purely Chinese, or which were well developed in China before Buddhism was introduced there.

The essence of Zen is not something the Westerner can grasp easily. It is not a philosophy in the European sense, but rather a metaphilosophy. It is not rational, nor yet related to mysticism despite its origin in Indian yoga. It is not a theology and possesses no formal creed or doctrine. We can follow Zen and at the same time be Buddhist or Christian, scientist or plain labourer; it is something to be experienced in every field of man's spiritual activity. It depends essentially on a contradiction that cannot be grasped by formal thought, for something would have to be expressed which is simply inexpressible.

Above, the ceremonial shooting
of a whistling arrow, *hikimeya;*
and, *right*, the *Hikime* ceremony in
which special arrows with
whistling heads are discharged.
From ancient times shooting such
arrows was believed to disperse evil,
stop calamity, bring peace and
render happiness.

An archer of the close shooting school, *Chikamato*, shooting at 28 metres. An indispensible element of traditional archery practice in Japan, in addition to the physical and mental training is the artistic beauty of movement and the dignity of the shooting attitude.

A rare photograph of the late Eugen Herrigel, the author of *Zen in the Art of Archery*, taken during an informal practice session, c. 1935.

What differentiates Zen most characteristically from all other teachings is that while it never goes out of our daily life, and despite its practical and concrete nature, it has something in it which makes it stand aloof from the scene of worldly sordidness and restlessness. Training in Zen is rigorous and strikes one as utterly soulless, and much patience is needed to acquire the high standard of discipline which in turn paves the way to enlightenment. The Japanese call this enlightenment *Satori* and it is emancipation–moral, spiritual, as well as intellectual. It is strength–concentrated, universal, utterly free, gained by completely emptying the consciousness; it is life, inwardly enlightened and fulfilled; it is absolute inner freedom, perfectly dispensed at any moment.

All that Zen does is to awaken the primal consciousness hidden within us which alone makes possible any spiritual activity. Japanese Zen Buddhists never speak of what it is that moves them inwardly, nor do they feel urged to make confessions. Their secret can be approached only by one who is on the way to experiencing it himself.

THE WAY OF ARCHERY

Two archers, one American and one German, studied at different times the applications of archery to Zen, and after many years of patience and heart-rending practice they both wrote their experiences. There is so little literature in the English language on this very special subject that their books* are classics in their own right. We can read that every minute detail of their training was supervised by a master. The American was privileged to have as his master Toshisuke Nasu, a descendant of the famous Nasu no Yoichi, the archer who, in the twelfth century, shot at the Taira's fan (page 223); and the German was accepted as a pupil of another Zen master of note.

The Zen sect believes that one can obtain enlightenment solely through one's own efforts. They admit no distinction between mind and matter or mind and body, whence follows the idea that one may act upon one's mind or spirit directly by means of physical practices, and reach any desired state of mind or spiritual plane entirely through exercises of the body. One essential requisite, which is carefully taught, is systematic breathing and this is combined with the practice of one of the fine arts or the military arts. These arts are known as "ways", and so we find the Way of the Bamboo (flute playing), the Way of Painting, the Way of Calligraphy, the Way of Tea, the Way of Flowers, and among the military arts the Way of Pliability (judo), the Way of the Sword, and the Way of the Bow. The sole idea is the acquisition of poise, the development of character, the control of the mind and spiritual training.

*ACKER, W. R. B. *The Fundamentals of Japanese Archery* (Tokyo, 1937)
HERRIGEL, EUGEN, *Zen in the Art of Archery* (1953)

Kazuo Kaneko giving a display of *Sharei*, ceremonial target archery, in 1962. He is wearing the *monpuku* and *hakama* and traditionally strips bare one arm and shoulder as a display of manliness and strength.

By perfecting these arts the devotee begins to be "one" with the perfecting of his skill. The archer ceases to be conscious of himself as the one who is engaged in hitting the target which confronts him, and hitter and hit are no longer two opposing objects but are one reality. Eventually *Satori* is reached when something of an indefinable quality takes over and It takes aim and It shoots. "It" is a name for something which can neither be understood nor laid hold of and which only reveals itself to those who have experienced it. "It has been said that if you have Zen in your life, you have no fear, no doubt, no unnecessary craving, no extreme emotion. Neither illiberal attitudes nor egotistical actions trouble you. You serve humanity humbly, fulfilling your presence in this world with loving kindness and observing your passing as a petal falling from a flower. Serene, you enjoy life in blissful tranquillity. Such is the Spirit of Zen."*

Through the practice of *Sharei* (ceremonial archery) many of today's 600,000 archers in Japan strive for *Satori*; for them, hitting the target is secondary, but the integrated beauty of form and undisturbed dignity are indispensable for the attainment of perfection and unity of mind, body and bow. The Way of the Bow reveals much that would otherwise be hidden; the story of Japan begins and ends with the mystery of the bow, and it has been shown how its power has influenced the history and culture of this great nation.

SELECT BIBLIOGRAPHY

Acker, William R. B., *The Fundamentals of Japanese Archery* [1937]

Batchelor, Rev. John, *The Ainu and their Folk-Lore* [1901]

Culin, Stewart, *Games of the Orient*, Charles E. Tuttle [1958]

Gilberson, *Japanese Archery and Archers*, Transactions of The Japan Society, Vol. IV [1898]

Herrigel, Eugen, *The Method of Zen* [1960]

Herrigel, Eugen, *Zen in the Art of Archery* [1953]

Ichikawa, Shoichi, *Kyu-Do 'The Way of Archery' in Japan*, Natural History, Vol. XXXIII, No. 2 [1933]

Lissner, Ivar, *The Living Past*, trans. by J. Maxwell Brownjohn [1957]

Morrissey, Frank R., *Samurai Archery*, Archery [1960]

Murdock, James, *A History of Japan* [1926]

Neya, K., *An Introduction to Japanese Archery* [n.d.]

Reps, Paul, *Zen Flesh, Zen Bones* [1957]

Ross, Nancy Wilson, *The World of Zen* [1962]

Scidmore, Miss Eliza R., *The Japanese Yano Ne*, Transactions of the Japan Society Vol. VI [1904]

Watts, Alan W., *The Way of Zen* [1957]

*REPS, PAUL (Compiler), *Zen Flesh, Zen Bones*. Tokyo (1959)

8 Redskin Archers

The Arrow sings to the Bow—
I am alone.
If we were married
We would go out early.
We would kill a deer.

SERI INDIAN SONG.

LOST in the cold emptiness of a vast continent, groping their way dimly through wind-tossed glacial mists, the first Americans arrived, so we are told by anthropologists, some 20,000 years ago. After the first Ice Age man crossed the narrow bridge of land that almost certainly connected Siberia and Alaska (now the Bering Strait), migrations and infiltrations from Asia started which continued for thousands of years. No one knows how many times America was discovered by peoples of the Old World, people of resolute courage and incredible endurance, and perhaps the last of these nomads arrived only a few centuries before Columbus; but it is certain that at some time during these continued migrations the bow was brought to the New World and, undoubtedly, the bow-using habits of these wandering tribes were gradually adapted to the new environments into which they found themselves settling. Whereas the traditions of Asiatic archery are reflected in the use of the primitive reinforced bows of the Eskimoes (which represent the earliest stage in the development of the composite bow) and can also be recognised in the more advanced types of backed bow used by the Indians of California and the western plains, no positive date for their introduction to the continent of America can be assessed. The fact that the skills of archery, to a large extent, were carried from Asia to America is not surprising, and the enduring nature of these skills was assured by the efficiency of the bow as a hunting weapon,

Chippewa Indians, from the great plains of Canada, hunting large game from their birch bark canoe. Deer or moose travel more slowly swimming in the river than they do on land and this enables the hunters to approach within close range.

because the survival of the American Indian during the long period of his prehistory depended to a large extent on hunting and killing game.

THE NORTH AMERICAN INDIAN

No primitive man on earth ever fired the imagination of the fiction writer as did the American Indian. From the romantic novels of the nineteenth century, in particular, he has emerged as an athlete, skilled hunter, statesman, orator, warrior, relentless enemy and staunch friend, able to endure with unflinching fortitude hunger, cold—even torture to the point of death. The "noble savage" became a stereotype figure allocated to one of a dozen or so of the more popularly known tribes, his monosyllabic existence enlivened by pow-wows, war dances, festivals to the innumerable deities of his pantheon of pagan gods, and poker-faced interludes while peace-pipes were passed around. Above all, his performance with a bow and arrow was regarded as superlative. The legend that has grown up around the Red Indian is not easy to dispel.

The migrations that dispersed themselves over both North and South America thousands of years before the Christian era gradually fragmented into a multiplicity of language families, and became grouped according to widely diverse patterns of living. Each of these groups evolved its own individual culture which was adapted, modified or improved according to its location, hunting methods, domestic habits and many other factors; and eventually a vast pattern of the aboriginal American Indian emerged, speaking upwards of five hundred languages and pursuing many cultures of enormous diversity and individuality. For the purpose of studying the history of the bow amongst this complex of peoples it will be found convenient to divide them under several basic headings representing the leading culture groups of North America, coinciding with general areas of use of different types of bows.

An historic picture taken during the last great Indian Council held in the valley of the Little Horn, Montana, September 1909. The photograph, taken from *The Vanishing Race* by Dr Kospeh K. Dixon, is symbolically entitled, "The Last Arrow".

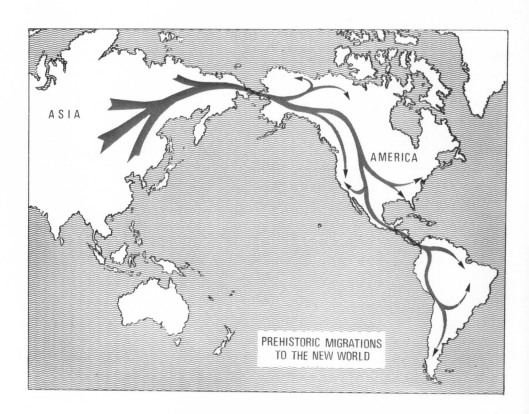

PREHISTORIC MIGRATIONS
TO THE NEW WORLD

CULTURE GROUPS OF AMERICA

The woodland country stretched north and south from Maine to Florida, and extended to the Great Lakes and the Mississippi valley. This was the area of the great forests, and among the scores of tribes who lived in this vast region were the Chippawa of the cold northern woods and the Atlantic seaboard tribes such as the Massachusett, the Peguot, the Mohican, the Delaware and the Powhatan. Close to the Great Lakes were the mighty Iroquois and the Conestoga, and in the southern states were the Choctaw, the Cherokee, the Creek, the Shawnee and many others comprising most of the major language family known as Algonquin. The vast open prairie land to the west which covered most of central America was the home of the Plains Indians, who made up the Siouan group and consisted finally of a number of tribes who did not populate this area until some four hundred years ago. During the sixteenth century the Conquistadors brought horses to New Mexico. Tribe after tribe of Indians stole horses from the Spaniards or got them honestly by trading, then moved into the rich prairie land from all directions. The Sioux and Cheyenne came in from the east, Blackfoot from the north, Ute from the west and Pawnee and Comanche from the south. The famous tepee was invented by the Plains Indians, and the buffalo became the universal provider of food, clothing, furnishings and general economic prosperity. Arizona and New Mexico in the south-west contained Indians who were primarily village dwellers. These villages grew up quickly, the growing of corn became impor-

A nineteenth-century engraving
of a female of the Arawak Indians
from the West Indies. The bow, for
hunting and warfare, was normally
reserved for the exclusive use of
the men of the tribe and it is rare
to find females carrying this
weapon. Occasionally, as in
South America, female Indians
together with children use the
bow for fishing.

tant and the south-western culture was essentially peaceful and democratic. After the agriculturalists were driven out by more warlike tribes this became the land of the Pueblo Indians, the Zuñi, the Hopi, the Pima, Mohave and Yuma. The Indians of the south-west included the Navaho and Apache, who were the wanderers, and probably the most recent arrivals in this area.

The great region comprising California and stretching north to include Southern Alaska was the home of another group, the culture of which competes with that of the Arctic for the status of being the most distinctive and at the same time the most foreign in North America. In many respects it affiliates more closely with north-east Asia than with the rest of North America. Here lived the Tlingit of Alaska, the Tsimshian, Haida, Kwakiutl and Nookta of Canada, and the Chinook, Makah and Puget Sound tribes of Oregon and Washington. Here was an abundance of fish and game, and men of the tribes which settled along the rivers became expert fishermen and hunters. The last major culture area is contained in the great northern Arctic belt which stretched from Greenland to the Yukon, including 15,000 miles of coastline and embracing most of Canada and Alaska. This was the land of the Eskimo, a hardy people subsisting on the barest of necessities and forced to an existence of improvisation, who developed a culture which mainly depended on fishing and the hunting of the now much reduced caribou, seal and whales. The western Eskimo, in particular, has been much influenced by the cultures of Siberia.

The hundreds of named tribes which make up the great Indian nation, with their widely differing customs and ways of life, have provided unlimited material for research and study by archaeologists, ethnographers, scientists and historians. The complete history of the American Indian has yet to be written, and to endeavour to search out an historical sequence applicable to the history of archery would be a task both unnecessarily complicated and inappropriate for our purpose. It is fairly safe to say however, that every Indian tribe had the bow in one form or another, and that their use of the weapon varied according to custom, preference and geographical environment. Tribes of some areas also used other weapons which almost excluded the bow, such as the spear (often used with the *atl-atl* or throwing stick of the Aztecs), the club, possibly the oldest of weapons, and the sling, bola and blow-gun.

SELF-BOW AND BACKED-BOW

The bow made of a single piece of wood without any sinew backing, called the self-bow, was used wherever archery was known except in the central and eastern Arctic. In this region wood was so scarce that suitable pieces for bowmaking were unobtainable. It was necessary to splice together

from two to six pieces of wood, horn or baleen to make a bow large enough to be effective. The sinew wrappings and backings were absolutely essential to such a bow which, without them, would have broken to pieces at the first pull. The only other large area where bow staves were made of several pieces is a region of the western Plains where mountain sheep horn and, later, cow horn was occasionally used in this manner; however, the majority of bows on the eastern Plains were self-bows. It is not known whether the horn bow of this western area is an independent invention, or whether knowledge of it was derived from the Eskimo and ultimately from Asia, where such bows were common.

There were two distinct kinds of sinew backing applied to bows. The Eskimoes and some of their immediate neighbours, as well as a few tribes in the south-west, first twisted or braided sinews into cords, and then laced the cords back and forth on the back of the stave from one end to the other, a few transverse lashings serving to hold the longitudinal cords in place. The second type of backing, sometimes called sinew lining or close-backing, was made by glueing individual threadlike sinew fibres on to the back of the bow. At even a short distance the sinew fibres blend with the stave and appear to be an integral part of it. The sinew lining occurred on the north Pacific coast, the

A horn bow of the American Indians. This type of bow, made from the horns of the Rocky Mountain sheep, the antlers of the elk or antelope horn, was used in North America up to about 1870, and they were reputed to be very powerful.

A special form of bow, of Eskimo origin, which has a loose backing consisting of a complex arrangement of sinew cords. Undoubtedly this had the effect of improving the performance of the bow in addition to making it more durable.

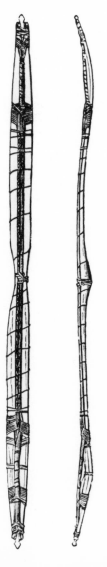

A restoration of a throwing-stick or *atl-atl* of the cliff-dwellers of S.W. America, after Cushing. These implements were used to propel a spear or feathered dart in the same way that other forms of spear-throwers were used in many other parts of the world.

western Plains, in California and down to the Mexican border. The variations of these types were almost as numerous as the tribes, and although these variants were governed to a large extent by the raw materials readily available they were usually developed to meet the particular needs of the area in which they were used.

The bow was nearly universal in North America at the time of European contact in 1492. It was absent, however, among the Eskimoes of Smith Sound (Polar Eskimoes) and East Greenland, and despite a brief revival in 1864, when it was reintroduced by visiting Eskimoes from Baffinland, it was rejected in favour of the gun in 1894. The principal animal hunted with the bow by the Eskimoes was the caribou, and the extermination of this creature would account for the disappearance of the bow in East Greenland. Among the Polar Eskimoes the disappearance of the bow was probably due to the abundance of summer birds, which were more easily obtained with clubs than were caribou or musk-ox with the bow. The bow was also lacking or little used among the Aztecs. The principal weapon of their armies was the spear-thrower, the *atl-atl*. This was also true of the Chibcha of Columbia, the Incas of Peru and among the Ciboney and Sub-Taino of the West Indies.

SIXTEENTH-CENTURY INVADERS

Beginning with the first voyage of Ponce de León to Florida in 1513, sixteenth-century historical and descriptive material on the Indians of the south-east is continuous, and more abundant than for any other portion of America. From the colourful accounts of the early French, Spanish and English explorers, rich details of the customs and manner of life of the native inhabitants are revealed. By the time de León visited Florida, during a voyage which he had absurdly undertaken in order to discover a fountain of youth, the bow had displaced the spear, which had been the principal weapon up to the beginning of the fifteenth century. Florida was conquered by the Spaniards in 1539 and plundered by Francis Drake in 1585. It was invaded by the British in 1702 and again in 1740, finally being ceded to the British crown in 1763. Eventually it was retaken by the Spaniards in 1781 and became part of the United States in 1820. The Indians who greeted de León and Hernández de Córdoba, another Spanish navigator and adventurer, were probably the Calusa, who occupied the southern part of the Florida peninsula. Of powerful

An eastern Eskimo bow made of several pieces of reindeer horn. In other specimens driftwood is introduced in the centre section. This shows the ingenious use of the limited materials available for bow-making in the Arctic regions of America and Asia.

In 1585 John White, the artist, accompanied Ralegh's first colonising expedition to Virginia and this water colour of an Indian chief was included in the graphic record he made of the trip. The primitive self-wood bow of this period remained unchanged for centuries.

physique, the warlike Calusa were the fiercest fighters of the New World. Without preliminary palaver, these natives fell upon all Spanish ships which visited the peninsula—so fiercely, in fact, that no permanent landings could be made for many years. They drove back all European attempts to enter their country, until eventually their numbers were greatly reduced by the introduction of European epidemic diseases. Before the end of the eighteenth century they had virtually ceased to exist as a tribe.

An early explorer to this area, wishing to test the power of native archery, offered a young Indian captive his liberty if he could shoot through a coat of mail. The garment was hung on a wicker basket and the Indian, standing 150 paces distant, shot a flint-headed reed through the armour. A second coat of mail was put over the first, and the Indian shot an arrow with great force through both. After this the Spaniards held their armour in contempt and devised a protection of felt or padded cloth which shielded them and their horses much better then chain or steel corselets. Some of the situations in which the early colonists found themselves were grim, especially when they were faced by husky Indians armed with bows and arrows, and many personal experiences recorded by these adventurers were punctuated with hair-raising incidents such as those which befell John Nicol and sixty-six other Englishmen in the Caribbean during the early seventeenth century. "All this time neither Harry, Peter Stokesley's man, nor myself was shot; but as we thought desperately to burst through them into the narrow path, there came an arrow and pierced quite through his head, of which he fell suddenly, and I ran to lift him up, but he was dead without speaking one word to me at all. Then came there two arrows and hit me in the back, the one directly against my heart, the other through my shoulder blade . . . ." Nicol then ran into a group of Indians and found one of them ". . . with an arrow in his bow drawn against me, who stood until I came very near to him, for he purposed to have sped me with that shot, which when I espied it coming, I thought to have put it by with my sword, but, lighting upon my hand, it passed through the handle of my weapon, and nailed both together. Nevertheless I continued running at him still and before he could nock another, made him and all the rest turn their backs and flee into the sands again. . . ."

INDIANS OF THE SOUTH-EAST

Another series of colonising expeditions to America was undertaken by Sir Walter Ralegh during the reign of the first Elizabeth. In 1585 John White, an illustrator of great charm and exceptional ability, accompanied Ralegh to Virginia, and the delightful watercolours which he produced have fortunately survived in excellent condition. His painting of an Indian warrior splendidly

arrayed in full battle attire reveals much to interest the archer-historian. The half-naked and painted Virginian wears a fringed apron-like breech-cloth of leather and carries a long-bow a little taller than himself. If the shrewd eye of John White enabled the bow to be correctly depicted, it would be from five feet nine inches to six feet, a self-bow, and almost identical in pattern to an English long-bow. Arrows are carried in a tubular quiver slung at the bowman's waist, and he wears a leather bracer on his left wrist. Another sixteenth-century work of considerable fascination is *The History of America* by Theodor de Bry. In it can be found drawings of the Indians fighting the Spanish invaders and, although the musket is shown as the principal weapon opposing the Indians, the bow can be seen well in evidence, being used by both sides in the conflict. Other illustrations from this work show archery equipment similar in many respects to that recorded by White. The Delaware Indians, who occupied a region which included the land on which New York City now stands, were dressed similarly to the tribes further south and they, too, carried six-foot bows together with quivers containing flint, bone or antler-tipped arrows, and the fearsome war club, carved of wood, with a ball-shaped head set at right angles from the handle which became the popularly used tomahawk of later centuries.

The Indians of the south-east killed deer and other game with the bow and arrow and often hunted in large companies, as the bones of various

An early representation of an Indian of possibly either the Calusa or Timucua tribal groups on the Florida peninsula. From what appears to be small game hanging from his waist and the fact that his bow is unstrung it would appear that the Indian is returning from a successful hunt.

An engraving of an Indian from Virginia after Theodor and Johann de Bry, late sixteenth century. Many contemporary representations of Indians of America are to be found in the illustrations of the travels and adventures of the early explorers of America in Bry's *Grands Voyages.*

animals, so common on their old kitchen refuse heaps, clearly prove. They also used the bow for shooting fish, as well as catching them in seines and gill nets and harpooning them. Together with the waging of war, hunting was the duty of the men of the tribe. Among the exhibits in the American Museum of Natural History is one which excellently illustrates the effect of the use of the bow in Indian warfare. The skeletons of three Indian warriors were excavated at Burial Ridge, Staten Island, in 1895. In the first skeleton, it was found that two arrow points of antler and one of bone had pierced the body and lodged near the spinal column. Another point of argillite had been driven between two ribs, cutting a notch in each. Four more points of antler were found amongst the remains, but the most interesting wound of all was one where the antler-tipped arrow had ploughed through one side of the body and fully one-third of the point had passed through one of the ribs, making a hole in which it remained. The second warrior was also terribly injured. The left femur showed an elongated puncture near the lower end made by an arrow point. Among the ribs was the tip of an antler point, and another of yellow jasper was among the ribs on the left side of the body. Three other points were amongst the bones. The third skeleton likewise demonstrated the results of old-time bow play; twelve arrow-heads were found amongst its bones. The positions in which several of the points were found certainly speak well for the great force which propelled them; the long-bows of the Indians must have been formidable weapons indeed. Taking into consideration the number of arrows which must have been embedded in the bodies of the warriors, it is probable that many of the projectiles were driven into the victims at close range after wounding.

INDIAN ARROW-HEADS

The general types of arrow-head from this region include stemmed, notched and triangular forms. The former are by far the most abundant, and while these are usually made of the nearest local rock possessing the necessary qualities, in some cases they are of bartered material brought from a long distance over established trade routes. The triangular type has long been regarded as the type used in war, the argument being that as it has no stem it was necessarily but loosely fastened in its shaft and, if shot into the body, would be very liable to become detached and remain in the flesh if any attempt were made to withdraw it by tugging at the shaft. Bone arrow-points, usually hollow and conical in shape, have been found but they are rather rare due to the fact that conditions are not suitable for their preservation in most regions. The manufacture of the head of the arrow and its various parts involved a knowledge of bone, ivory or horn, and also a familiarity with stone and stone-working. The primitive arrow-maker was a mineralogist; he not only knew

256

A Californian Indian arrow-head of obsidian embedded in the anterior surface of a human lumbar vertebra. The arrow passed directly through the abdomen and despite the severe wound that this must have caused, it did not cause the death of the Indian victim. Any infection cleared up naturally and fresh bone growth can be detected close to the arrow-point.

A fatal wound from an arrow which obliquely pierced the chest of a Central Plains Indian, its stone head lodging in a thoracic vertebra. The absence of any bone change would indicate that death was almost immediate.

the qualities of rocks but also their best methods of working, as well as the best conditions in which they existed for his purpose in nature. Arrow-heads from the greater part of America have been made of every variety of quartz, chalcedony, agate, jasper, horn-stone, chert, novaculite, slate, argillite and obsidian. In rare cases even quartz-crystal, carnelian, amethyst and opal were used. Detailed studies of the making of these fascinating artefacts reveal the care with which the savage craftsman must have exploited the proper materials, probably after long experimentation. Every Indian boy learned how to make a bow, and every man had a certain amount of skill in the art, spending much of his leisure in the repair and improvement of his bow and arrows. When he became old (if the fortunes of his hazardous existence afforded him such a blessing) and could no longer take the field, he kept his hold on his tribe by becoming a bowyer. First, then, comes the boy, struggling through his primitive institute of technology, then the warrior or hunter, skilful in making a bow and arrows and practised in their use. Last of all, the old man spends his closing years in making arrows for his sons, as did Longfellow's ancient arrow-maker:

The ancient arrow-maker
Made his arrow-heads of sandstone,
Arrow-heads of chalcedony,
Arrow-heads of flint and jasper,
Smooth and sharpened at the edges,
Hard and polished, keen and costly.

The Indian tribes from the eastern regions of America were users of hardwood self-bows. The Cherokee, for instance, came from Georgia, Carolina and Tennessee, where the finest oak, ash and hickory grow, and used every variety of available elastic wood for their bows, the toughness of which they improved by dipping them in bear-oil and warming them before the fire. In the north-east, walnut, hornbeam, sycamore and dogwood, in addition to oak and ash, are to be found as materials of the Indian bowyer; and in the Mississippi valley any of the many species of hardwood were used. The Iroquois tribes close to the Great Lakes, who used these self-wood bows, were among the first to receive firearms from the early settlers, and on this account they soon abandoned the bow and arrow which, by 1727, had been entirely laid aside. It is fortunate for our story that the gun did not replace the bow so quickly in most of the rest of North America; and we can now pass further westward, to the heart of the continent, where much of the history of American colonisation was written.

INDIANS OF THE PLAINS

The Plains, between the slopes of the Rocky Mountains on the west and the twenty-inch rainfall line on the east, and stretching from north of the Canadian border down almost to the Rio Grande in west Texas, was one of the greatest grazing areas the world ever knew. The land at first defied farming and it was not inviting to people without horses or metal, but it was the home of the buffalo, which ran wild on a scale almost beyond belief. With such a food supply there were bound to be communities of human beings, but the area was only very sparsely occupied. The Spanish explorers of 1540 and after spoke of the Indians who lived there in skin tents, who used dogs as beasts of burden, and hunted. They saw one Indian put an arrow through a buffalo, and remarked that this exhibition of primitive marksmanship would have been good work even with a musket. The horses which the Spanish brought into New Mexico ran wild and spread eastwards. From northern outposts in California, also, horses escaped, and multiplied in Oregon. Rapidly the increasing equine population was captured and trained

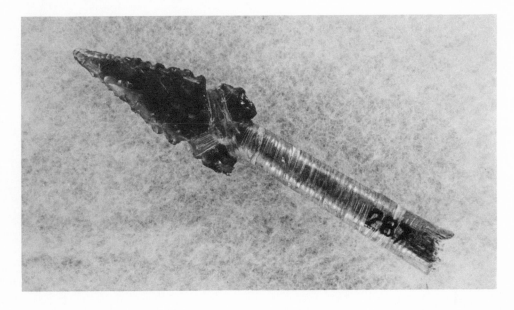

A beautifully fashioned arrow-head of obsidian, from the Californian area, in position on the foreshaft of an arrow. The binding is of sinew which, after soaking or chewing to soften, was wrapped and left to shrink, thus tightening the union.

by the Indians of the north-west and traded to the east; and in the eighteenth century, one by one, the tribes surrounding the buffalo country learned to ride. Several major groups of Indians concerned with warfare amongst themselves pushed eastwards. The Sioux and the Cheyenne, all by now mounted, abandoned their farms and moved west. The Blackfoot, Crow and Comanche all turned to the new life, centred on the buffalo, which the domestication of the horse now made possible. By 1800 the cultural revolution was in full flower; the Indians had settled into a new way of life, and were now ripe for the greatest revolution of all—the coming of the white man. Throughout the whole of these vast upheavals the warriors and hunters of North America had carried bows and arrows which had remained unchanged. Apart from the use of new materials such as iron and bottle-glass for arrow-heads, the traditional form and construction had been maintained.

The Indians of the Plains possibly contributed most to the history of the United States in the mid-nineteenth century, and it was the tribes of this huge area of open prairie which came under the greatest scrutiny by pioneer travellers, explorers, military reporters, amateur ethnographers and scholars and artists attached to officially sponsored missions. Whereas it was from the early colonists and adventurers that we drew our knowledge of the Indians of the eastern woodlands, it is from the robust and colourful pioneers of the nineteenth century that we can assemble a picture of the Indian archers of the Plains. The tendency of many of these characters, however, was to exaggerate their accounts of the Indians' prowess and accuracy with the bow, and it is for this reason that such tales should be regarded with a certain amount of caution. In 1810 Z. M. Pike published his account of the exploring expedition of 1806–7, during which he had reached the Plains and named them "The Great American Desert". His suggestion that the territory should be reserved for the Indians was adopted by Congress; but the white settlers who were pressing westwards soon found that the Plains were not desert at all, but good farming and grazing land. The fact that a remote authority in Washington had allotted the territory to the Indians did not prevent the newcomers from claiming land and building their homes there.

GO WEST, YOUNG MAN!

The story of American colonisation of the nineteenth century is a breathless one. The first great rush of population to the west was drawn to the mountainous regions. Gold was found in California in 1848, in Colorado and Nebraska ten years later, in Montana and Wyoming in the 'sixties and in the Black Hills of Dakota in the 'seventies. Attracted by the discovery of silver mines in the Rocky Mountains in the eighteen-seventies, thousands of pioneers travelled westwards. "Go west, young man, and grow up, with

A group of arrow-heads of several varieties of stone from North America. These examples are typical and show a few of the principal shapes which have been discovered in widely dispersed American Indian sites. These are the more sophisticated patterns from later periods; earlier examples would be simpler and, in some cases, more crude in finish.

the country" encouraged Horace Greenley, and speeding this process were the railroads. The Union Pacific pushed its track from Iowa, and at the same time the Central Pacific began to build eastwards from Sacramento towards an undetermined junction point. They finally met in Utah on May 10th, 1869. At this time the frontier line followed generally the western limits of the states bordering on the Mississippi River, bulging outward to include the eastern sections of Kansas and Nebraska. Behind this thin edge of pioneer farms was still much unoccupied land, and beyond that stretched the unfenced prairies, merging finally into the sage-brush plains which extended to the foothills of the Rockies. Then, for nearly a thousand miles, loomed the huge bulk of mountain ranges until, on the Pacific side, more plains and deserts stretched to the wooded Sierra Nevada and the ocean. Apart from the settled districts in California and some scattered outposts, this vast inland region was peopled by Indians. Following the Civil War came the cattle boom, which reached its peak by about 1885. Not far behind the rancher creaked the prairie schooners of the farmers, bringing their womenfolk and children, and by 1890 the wild west had given way to settled communities, the frontier had disappeared and virtually all the country had been carved into states and territories. The Indians, believing that they had been betrayed by the government in Washington, went on the war-path, and from 1820 to 1890 the United States had an Indian problem. Raids on the settlements and stage-coach routes reached such proportions that Washington had to send troops to protect them and to fight the Indians, who were often called the most formidable savage warriors ever encountered by white man.

Although the Indians' lack of numbers made it impossible for them to engage in disciplined assaults they developed the art of guerrilla warfare to a very remarkable degree, using stealth and cunning to make up for their deficiency in manpower. Their instinctive talents as hunters were now turned to the even more vital matter of self-preservation and, although their bows were supplemented by illegally obtained firearms, the bow and arrow remained the predominant weapon in early warfare. The use of the bow rather than the gun had the irreplaceable advantage of silence and, another vitally important consideration, there was no shortage of ammunition. "We could not even distinguish the officer from his men. Each body was pierced by from twenty to fifty arrows, and the arrows were found as the savage demons had left them, bristling in the bodies." So reported General George Armstrong Custer, a famous name in the history of Indian warfare who, in a short time, mastered the battle tactics of the Indians as had few other regular officers of the United States Army. His memoirs contain many vivid eye-witness accounts of the conflicts between his troops and the Cheyenne, the Sioux and the Delaware Indians.

GENERAL CUSTER AND THE INDIANS

On one occasion Custer and his men were surprised at dawn, and his description of the initial attack by the Indians is a classic example of on-the-spot reporting: "'O Heavens, General, look at the Indians!' Well might he (the guide) be excited. From every direction they dashed toward the band. Over the hills, from the west and the north, along the river, on the opposite bank, everywhere and in every direction they made their appearance. Finely mounted in full war paint, their long scalp locks braided with eagles' feathers, and with the paraphernalia of a barbarous war party—with wild whoops and exultant shouts, on they came . . . a number of young Indian boys from fifteen to eighteen years of age crawled up and shot about fifty arrows into the circle in which the scouts lay. One of these arrows struck one of the men, Frank Herrington, full in the forehead. Not being able to pull it out, one of his companions, lying in the same hole with him, cut off the arrow with a knife, leaving the iron arrow-head sticking in his frontal bone; in a moment a bullet struck him in the side of the head, glancing across his forehead, impinged upon the arrow-head, and the two fastened together fell to the ground—a queer but successful piece of amateur surgery. Herrington wrapped a cloth around his head, which bled profusely, and continued fighting as if nothing had happened." On another occasion, while engaged in rescuing two white girls, Custer and his men confronted a group of Indians without a shot being fired. A tense situation developed which could have exploded into a bloody incident if one false move was made or one indiscreet word uttered. Custer admitted that he could recall no other experience with the Indians so exciting. "Near me stood a tall, grey-haired chief, who, while entreating his people to be discreet, kept his cocked revolver in his hand ready for use, should the emergency demand it. He was one of the few men whom I had determined to hold. Near him stood another, a most powerful and forbidding-looking warrior, who was without firearms, but who was armed with a bow, already strung, and a quiver full of iron-pointed arrows. He stood apparently unaffected by the excitement about him, but not unmindful of the surrounding danger. Holding the bow in one hand, with the other he continued to draw from his quiver arrow after arrow. Each one he would examine as coolly as if he expected to engage in target practice. First he would cast his eye along the shaft of the arrow, to see if it was perfectly straight and true. Then he would with thumb and finger gently feel the point and edge of the barbed head, returning to the quiver each one whose condition did not satisfy him. In this manner he continued until he had selected perhaps half-a-dozen arrows, with which he seemed satisfied, and which he retained in his hand, while his quick eye did not permit a single incident about him to escape unnoticed." A tense situation indeed; but, happily, the girls were rescued without bloodshed.

The urge to investigate and enquire into the ethnography of the Indian who was, after all, still primitive in the nineteenth century, was not lacking. Officers of the United States Army whose duties took them into the heart of Indian territory, learned professors who had an almost untouched field of studies opened up for them, and amateur anthropologists and collectors whose respect for the Indian as a craftsman was unconcealed, all immersed themselves in the fascination of Indian ways. Their observations, official reports and meticulous accounts of the Indian at close quarters were published in a number of works which reveal the enthusiasm of these early toxologists and the thoroughness of their enterprise. These efforts to record a virtually dying race remain as an original and invaluable contribution to the history of archery. The ubiquitous Lieutenant Ray conscientiously produced detailed accounts of Indian archery from the Arctic to California; Captain John Bourke carefully reported on the Apache; Murdock, Mason and Wilkes added valuable contributions to the growing collection of knowledge, and investigations into specialised aspects of arrow-head making, bow-making, hunting methods and many other intriguing techniques were undertaken by various other enthusiasts.

APACHE BOWMEN

Writing at the end of the eighteenth century, an early traveller described the results of Apache bowmanship, which nearly parallels the best penetration of the medieval long-bow of England. "The Apaches are incomparable archers, and seldom miss; their arrows, when let fly by a strong arm, have more power and effectiveness than a bullet from the best musket. As a proof, I wish to cite only one example, to which I myself was a witness. A mounted soldier was

The Comanches, from the prairie lands of northern Texas, were expert horsemen and this drawing by Catlin shows one of their agile battle manoeuvres. They would hang at the side of the horse's flank and, while moving at full speed and carrying bow, shield and lance, they would shoot arrows or throw the lance at the enemy as they passed.

dispatched by his captain with letters to the captain of another garrison. His cloak, tightly folded up lengthwise, lay before him on the saddle and fell down part way over his left leg. Covering the cloak and the same leg hung his shield, made of three-ply, very thick oxhide, which hung down a little over the horse's belly. The soldier rode past a mountain where some Apaches lay in ambush and was struck by one of their arrows, which passed through the shield, through the many folds of the folded cloak, through the leg of the soldier, finally through the leather cover, and penetrated almost a quarter of an ell deep into the body of the horse. A bullet would scarcely have such force. When the soldier, fortunately saved by his swift mount, arrived at the place where I then was, I myself saw with amazement what had happened."

The Apaches were typical of the Plains Indians and their archery equipment was of a high standard of manufacture and finish; their arrows were especially well made. Their excellence was primarily due to the fact that the main part of the shaft was made of the reed, called in the Apache language *klo-ka* or "arrow grass", which needs no straightening, whereas those arrows made by other tribes in the locality had to be straightened by a process which involved much labour and loss of time. Every Apache kept in the roof of his *jacal* a collection of these reeds to dry for making arrows, together with an extra mulberry bow. Edwin A. Barber described in the *American Naturalist* nine different kinds of arrows used by the Apache, and said that often several shapes would be found in the same quiver. Although the Apaches generally used barbs of obsidian, which could be made in five to eight minutes, or of sheet iron, they also made them simply of triangular pieces of hard wood, in all respects resembling those first seen by Columbus upon reaching the continent.

THE INDIAN BACKED-BOW

Whereas the Indians of the eastern woodlands used self-wood bows, those from the western Plains and Sierra Nevada region of the west used bows of ash, mulberry, osage orange, yew, cedar and other woods, reinforced with animal sinew. This improvement consisted of a layer of shredded sinew, often chewed by the womenfolk to soften it, carefully arranged and glued to the back, the convex face, of the bow. Occasionally the long fibres of animal sinew would be additionally secured with a series of cross-lashings. Shorter and more powerful bows were the result. Another type of bow, found amongst the Sioux, can be described as a compound bow. It consists of several pieces of cow horn, mountain sheep horn or elk antler fitted

Apache hunters from the deserts of the south-west using their short and powerful bows. A rare photograph of c. 1870.

264

One of the last Red Indian warriors. The war chief of the Kiowas, a tribe from the Central Plains, photographed by the United States Army immediately after his capture by them in 1870.

together in a shape recalling the conventional "Cupid" bow of artists. The compound bow is also found among the north-eastern Eskimo. The bow of Pandarus, as described by Homer, appeared to be of this construction:

'Twas formed of horn, and smoothed with artful toil,
A mountain goat designed the shining spoil.

In such a vast area overrun with so many different tribes some overlapping of bow types was inevitable, and definite areas of demarcation are not practicable. It will be sufficient to say that the sinew-backed bow, suggestive of an early form of the more complex composite bow of Asia, was introduced by tribes from the western side of the American continent. Its form became modified according to the wood available, regional development and custom. Some experts declare that the occurrence of hardwood in the Great Interior Basin and of yew and other soft woods on the western slopes gave rise to the wide, thin bow in the latter area, and the long, ovate-section bow in the Basin. On the other hand some of the central Californian sinew-backed bows are narrower than many of the western Plains bows; and, in addition, bows made of hardwood and up to four inches in width have been found as far east as Minnesota and Oklahoma. The narrow bow, however, usually occupies the greater area of the western Plains and was the weapon of many of the warring tribes during the nineteenth century.

The Apaches laid down rules for making their bows and arrows which are interesting as an example of (literal) "rule-of-thumb" measurements; these rules were no doubt handed down from father to son. "The length of the bow, or rather of the string, should be eight times the span from thumb to little finger of the warrior using it. The curvature of the bow was determined almost entirely by individual strength or caprice. The arrow should equal in length the distance from the owner's armpit to the extremity of his thumb-nail, measured on the inner side of his extended arm; the foreshaft should project beyond the reed to a distance equal to the span covered by the thumb and index finger. This measurement included the barb when made of sheet iron. The iron barb itself should be as long as the thumb from the end to the largest joint."

The techniques used in making bows and arrows were often jealously guarded, and much of the work was accompanied by secret ceremony to endow the weapons with special powers. A detailed description of the manufacture of Omaha bows and arrows was written by Francis La Flesche,* who was specially privileged to observe one of the last of the bowyers of this tribe pursuing his skilled craft. Experience taught these craftsmen the best green-wood to use, the most expedient time for cutting it, and the exact amount of drying necessary; but the material which the bow-maker preferred was young ash killed by a prairie fire, because the wood was then thoroughly seasoned and set so that dampness and rain did not affect it. The bowstring was made from the sinew taken from either side of the spine of the buffalo, and men who were skilled in bowstring-making were employed solely in this occupation. The wood for making the arrow shaft was chosen with as great care as the wood used in making the bow. The saplings of a species of dogwood were preferred as they were straight and almost free from knot, but ash, cut in suitable lengths from a mature tree, was also used. After ten weeks seasoning the selected shafts were straightened, shaped and

*LA FLESCHE, FRANCIS, *Omaha Bow and Arrow Makers*, Smithsonian Report (1926)

smoothed. The nock had then to be cut, and the next process was grooving the shaft. There has been considerable discussion as to the meaning of these longitudinal grooves, usually three in number, which can be found on many types of Indian arrows. One reason given for these grooves was so that blood could run easily from a wound, another was that they acted as an aid to prevent warping of the shaft, but the most probable explanation was that they had a mystic significance, likening the grooves to lightning. The feathers were now added, fastened to the shaft with glue made from the shell of a soft-shelled turtle, bound in position with fine strands of sinew and trimmed to shape. The tangs of flat, barbed arrow-heads of sheet-iron were pushed home in slots cut for the purpose and secured with sinew binding. All that remained was the colouring of the shaft, black and red, representing night and day, the symbol of precision.

THE BUFFALO HUNT

The sinew-backed bow, a short hard-hitting weapon easily managed from horseback, was ideal for the buffalo hunting which occupied much of the time of the Plains Indians for the two centuries or so following the introduction of horses. However, the horse was not common to the Assiniboin, who occupied the area of the northern Plains through which the Canadian-American border now runs. Despite this lack they still managed to hunt buffalo successfully and in large numbers. Their method was to construct a pound and, after driving a herd of buffalo into it, by a concerted effort from their bowmen, they would slaughter all the beasts thus captured. So that individual marksmanship might be recognised, every arrow had its particular mark of ownership. The acquisition of the horse by the Plains Indians made the herding of big game and their subsequent killing much easier, and replaced other methods such as driving the animals over cliffs or into man-made enclosures similar to those employed by the Assiniboin. They used their skill as horsemen to gain close contact with the buffalo, speeding alongside the great mass of animal as it thundered across the prairie while loosing arrows at vital spots from around ten yards range, continuing alongside the beast until, as a result of the arrow-head rankling in the lethal wound, it would falter and drop. An examination of the dorsal vertebra of a buffalo which had been struck by an iron arrow-point reveals that there was enough force to drive the arrow through the thick hide covered with matted woolly hair, several inches of flesh, through ·55 of an inch of solid bone, and to protrude, beyond the bone, more than half this distance again. This was the concentrated power, unleashed from the short bow of the mounted Indian, which brought the huge bulk of the buffalo to its knees. Further evidence of the penetrative force of Indian arrows is not lacking; stories of arrows piercing

An engraving of the nineteenth century, after Catlin, which illustrates the method of hunting buffalo described by him. By clever horsemanship the hunter would move in close to the running buffalo and discharge arrow after arrow at very short range.

pine trees to a depth of six inches, of men being penetrated at three hundred yards, of shafts sunk up to the feathers in the giant cactus in Arizona, even of headless arrows mortally wounding Government soldiers—these and other awesome and equally romantic tales can be quoted to compare the power of the bow with other primitive missile weapons.

It is only comparatively recently that opinions of the North American Indians have risen above the old and popular idea that "the only good Indian is a dead Indian"; and if there are any doubts remaining of their true qualities one has only to read the fascinating notebooks of George Catlin to be convinced of their true nobility. The Indians of the Plains enjoyed centuries of peaceful existence before the white man destroyed their traditional way of life, and Catlin, self-taught artist of remarkable merit and diarist of note, made a comprehensive record of the life of many tribes in their unspoiled and primitive state. "I have visited man in the innocent simplicity of nature," he said, declaring his opinion of the Indians of the Great Plains of the West, after wandering and living alone amongst approximately forty-eight tribes in the days before the white man's civilisation had been imposed on them. This was between 1830 and 1836, during which time he painted and drew the Indians at their pursuits of hunting and warfare, games and dances, tribal ceremonies and many other activities. This most engaging documentary record of a race which was soon to be swallowed up by the unfeeling advance of civilisation contains much of interest to us in the study of archery. Possibly Catlin's action pictures, rather than his portraits, are those which convey best the spirit of the Indians. Many of these depict the exhilaration of the

His-oo-san-ches, one of the leading warriors of the Comanche tribe in the Red River Valley, from a portrait of him drawn by George Catlin, c. 1845. He is shown fully equipped for battle with long animal skin combined bow and arrow quiver, bow, arrows, shield and 14-foot lance.

chase and vividly illustrate the personal observations, full of minute detail, recorded in his *Letters and Notes*.* He gave us the first eye-witness account of the dramatic buffalo hunt: "The Sioux are a bold and desperate set of horsemen; and great hunters . . . he generally strips himself and his horse of his shield and quiver and every part of his dress which might be an encumbrance . . . grasping his bow in his left hand, with five or six arrows ready for instant use . . . the horse is trained to approach the animal from the right side, permitting the rider to shoot his arrow to the left; bringing him opposite the heart, which receives the deadly weapon to the feather . . . he sheers away to prevent coming on to the horns of the infuriated beast . . . these frightful collisions often take place, notwithstanding the sagacity of the horse and the caution of the rider."

"A Comanche on his feet is out of his element and comparatively almost

*CATLIN, GEORGE, *Letters and Notes on the Manners, Customs, and Condition of the North American Indians* (1841)

awkward," said Catlin, "but the moment he lays hand upon his horse he gracefully flies away like an entirely different being." Among the most impressive feats of horsemanship practised by this tribe, as well as by the Pawnees further west, was their way of throwing themselves down on the side of their horses while riding at full speed in the heat of battle. This effectively screened the rider from the enemy's weapons and in this position he was able to use his bow or lance in attack. "This is a strategem of war learnt and practised by every young man in the tribe," continued Catlin, who observed that other tribes practised this feat but none could match the Comanche warriors. Some experts were able to perform the remarkable feat of shooting an arrow from under the horse's belly with deadly effect.

Catlin's notes, made while with the Blackfeet and Crows, give a description of the weapon used by them. "The bow with which they are armed is small and apparently an insignificant weapon, though one of almost incredible power in the hands of its owner, whose sinews have been from childhood habituated to its use," he wrote. "The length of these bows is generally about three feet and sometimes not more than two and a half. They have no doubt studied to get the requisite power in the smallest compass possible, as it is more easily used on horseback than one of greater length. The greater part of these bows are made of ash and lined on the back with layers of buffalo or deer sinews to give greater elasticity. There are many also (amongst the Blackfeet and Crows) which are made of bone, and others of the horn of the

A study of a Navaho Indian about to draw his bow. These Indians, from the desert areas of Arizona, developed a simple and effective form of composite bow with a backing of layers of sinew.

270

mountain sheep. Those made from bone are decidedly the most valuable and cannot be procured short of the price of one or two horses . . . and their arrows are headed with flint or bone, of their own construction, or with steel, as they are now chiefly furnished by the Fur Traders. The quiver which is uniformly carried on the back and made of the panther or otter skin, is a magazine of these deadly weapons, and generally carries two varieties. The one to be drawn upon a human enemy, generally poisoned and with long barbs designed to hang in the wound after the shaft is withdrawn, in which they are but slightly glued; and the other is used for their game, with the blade firmly fastened to the shaft and with the barbs inverted, that it may easily be drawn from the wound and used again."

PRACTICE FOR WAR AND THE CHASE

The use of the bow was part of the education of a boy; he was trained in archery from infancy and whilst still young was taught to make the best bow he could. Boys were often called out to shoot for prizes, and a great part of their leisure was taken up with constant target practice and fighting sham battles which were spirited imitations of the successes of their elders. A favourite competition for the menfolk was the Game of Arrows. In this each contestant would add his wager to a winner-take-all prize. One by one each man would shoot his arrows into the air, endeavouring to see who could put the largest number in the air before the first struck the ground. Frequently as many as eight were put up before the first one fell. During the eighteen-forties the United States Exploring Expedition witnessed Indian boys exercising with the bow; an extract from the official report read: "They obtained an exhibition of the archery of the Indians by putting up a button at twenty yards [more probably feet] distance, which one of them hit three times out of five; the successful marksman was rewarded with it and a small piece of tobacco." Close range accuracy, not as easy as it sounds, was an essential requirement for the Indian of the Plains, and this early training prepared him for the traditional life of the hunter, when he would have to match his skill and dexterity with the bow against the desperate reactions of a cornered beast in the age-old contest for survival.

The use of the sinew-backed bow extended over the Rockies to the west coast and reached as far south as the Mexican border. Many of the sinew-backed bows found east of the Rockies may have been obtained by trade from sources further west and those of the great central valleys of California were invariably made in the mountains and traded over a wide area. One area close to the border was occupied by the Chiricahua tribe, and it is there that bows are found with sinew cords tied on the bowstave longitudinally as well as those with the sinew glued in place. This is an isolated example of the same arrangement of bow backing which was used by the Eskimoes, and this singular appearance of the loose-backed bow in the south-west has yet to be satisfactorily explained.

The finding of Indian arrow-points, whether by the amateur or the professional archaeologist, brings the past somewhat closer to the present. Countless thousands of these points have been found in the American south-west, reminding us that the early agricultural economy, based on corn, beans and squash, was substantially supplemented by hunting. In addition to the use of the bow for hunting, the finding of arrow-heads embedded in human bones and occasional evidence of mass burials, are ample indications that life was not entirely peaceful in the early south-west. A brief look at one particular weapon other than the bow is important to fully appreciate the development of the arrow in this area.

ARROWS WITHOUT BOWS

The spear-thrower of the Mexican Indians, called the *atl-atl*, was used to project a dart up to three hundred feet. It usually consisted of a narrow, flattened stick of hardwood about two feet long. Two loops were provided for the fingers of the hand to ensure a better grip and the dart was laid along the stick, its butt fitting against a projecting spur at the end. The *atl-atl* and dart were held together over the shoulder, the arm was then quickly brought forward and the dart released simultaneously to be propelled towards the target. The dart was longer and heavier than an arrow. A completed *atl-atl* dart measured from between fifty and seventy inches long and had a main shaft made of a pithy-centred wood, such as willow or reed or, according to some authorities, yucca. Added to this was a foreshaft of hardwood provided with a chipped stone point. Three wild goose or hawk feathers were attached to the butt end and the shaft was decorated with simple bands or spirals of red and black. Variations in the provision of a point, such as a fire-hardened wooden tip or a blunt head of wood, or bone, to stun small game, parallel exactly similar details in arrow construction. The distribution of the *atl-atl* in the south-west is generally restricted to New Mexico, Arizona, Colorado and Utah, and it belongs to the prehistory of this area; one example was dated by radio-carbon method at over 7,000 years old. By A.D. 700-900 the *atl-atl* fell into disuse as a true weapon and it was replaced by the bow and arrow, which were unknown in the south-west before this time. Very soon the bow became the principal weapon for propelling projectiles, its portability, accuracy and range no doubt being the main reasons for its replacing the *atl-atl*. A number of ingeniously reasoned connexions between the spear-thrower of the Indians of the south-west and the archery bow, which were supported by a profound etymological hypothesis, were produced by F. H.

Cushing in his paper* published in 1895. In this work Cushing sets out to unravel the evolution of the bow and, if his theories are not entirely sound, his work is one of curious interest.

SOUTH-WESTERN FARMERS

The early Spanish explorers had contact with the area of the south-west, and many of their writings describe the weapons carried by the Indians they encountered. In 1540 Coronado reported that the Indians living near to the present-day Pueblo tribe of Zuñi used arrow-points of bone. The arrow from this area, a descendant from the *atl-atl* dart, was not always tipped with bone, however, and not always with stone. Sometimes hardwood, bone or antler was used. Some 4,000 arrows found in one cache in south-west New Mexico yielded only eleven notched to hold stone points, the remainder being sharpened wood. Arrows were decorated in much the same way as the *atl-atl* darts, although in some areas these decorations became more elaborate and perhaps more meaningful. It has been suggested that arrow decoration helped the hunter choose from his quiver the arrow which was best suited to kill the game he was stalking. Arrows painted with "coded" designs would allow the hunter to withdraw a blunt-pointed arrow for birds and small game, larger, stone-pointed arrows for deer and antelope, and so on. Others have thought that decorated arrows helped to identify the owner of the game that had been killed.

The bows of the south-west were rather crudely made in comparison to the well-made arrows from that region, although in his description of a cliff-dweller's bow from Arizona, Saxton Pope† of the University of California declares that he found the workmanship excellent. This particular bow, some 1,000 years old and showing signs of long usage, is made of juniper or cedar and is about four feet nine inches long. It has several narrow sinew bindings up and down the limbs and the handle is wrapped with buckskin strips apparently slightly padded with red woodpecker feathers. Bows from this area were often decorated with bands of red, black and green, and in section they varied from round to oval. From an assessment made of the strength of the bow of the south-west it would appear that they were generally weak. "I doubt that such a bow could shoot more than two hundred yards", said Pope, in a generous estimate, and the nature of these weapons suggested that the Indians from the south-west were content with close-range archery, with the exception of the Apache, who had some very effective bows.

*CUSHING, FRANK HAMILTON, *The Arrow*, The American Anthropologist Vol. VIII, No. 4 (1895)

†POPE, SAXTON T., *A Study of Bows and Arrows* (1923)

Many records exist of a bewildering variety of ceremonies and dances performed by the American Indians. Perhaps the most extraordinary event was that enacted by these great plumed arrow dancers of the Navaho. A feature of this was swallowing a complete arrow up to the feathers. After drawings made by Brooke in 1884.

The Spanish explorers of the sixteenth century, making their way through Mexico and the south-west, encountered Indians who had wandered from the far north and who had settled in this rugged country. The men found they could sustain an existence by working unirrigated land and specialised in "dry" farming, while the women developed an unusually high proficiency in basketry and pottery making. In the course of time these people learnt silversmithing from the Spanish, and became the silver-workers of the south-west. One such tribe of these wandering farmers was named by the Spanish "Apaches de Nabajú". Later the Apache part of the name was dropped and they became known as Navahos, one of the most famous of all tribes today. The Navahos, who were farmers, were also warriors and raiders, and used the familiar sinew-lined bow. Their arrows were similar in many respects to those used by the Indians of the Plains. They developed a series of ritualistic rites connected with their legends and myths, which included the curious arrow-swallowing performance, which was put on as a special act, or *alili*, during the last night of the Mountain Way celebrations. Undoubtedly this strange, and no doubt uncomfortable, rite had a deep symbolic significance. A similar practice was observed by Don Pedro Sarmiento de Gambos who, whilst travelling in Patagonia during the sixteenth century, saw an Indian swallow an eighteen-inch arrow right up to its feathers.

INDIANS FROM THE WESTERN COAST

The sinew-lined bow extended to the coastal plains of California, the Sierra Nevada up to the north-western states on the North Pacific coast, through Oregon and as far as British Columbia. Many of the bows found in Alaska exhibit pronounced recurved tips to their limbs, and this feature is present in some form or another in bows from the western coast down as far as southern California. The composite bows of Asia invariably embody this feature, and its appearance in North American bows may possibly be due to a diffusion of knowledge or experience at a period later than the spread of the bow's influence from eastern Asia. The Indians who lived, hunted, farmed, and warred in this area produced a well-developed bow, broader and flatter than those used further east and made of softer woods such as yew, several varieties of juniper, spruce or maple. The use of sinew for backing bows was general except in lower California where the self-wood type of bow was used, made from various woods including the root of the wild willow, cottonwood and bois d'arc, commonly known as laburnum. A feature found on the bows of Californian Indians, together with those of the Sioux and the Shoshonean tribes, was the refinement of extra padding to thicken the handle of the bow. In many cases, in addition to this, the bows were painted in several colours; the marking of geometric figures and additions of bead-work made them quite fine specimens. The decoration of bows in this fashion manifests itself among coastal tribes who have exceptional artistic talent in basket-making and other work. Among the Yurok, bows and arrows were made by old men skilled in the art. One specimen examined by Saxton Pope proved to be extremely well made but had an indifferent performance. "In action," said Pope, "this bow is soft, springy, bends in the hand, is flabby in cast and kicks." Toxophilites will agree that this is probably the worst set of faults a bow could have, and a modern bowyer, producing a weapon to such specifications of performance, would very soon be out of business. Notwithstanding the conclusions arrived at by Pope these bows proved capable of killing man and beast over many centuries, and their efficacy was largely due to the use of excellent arrows.

Iowa Indians brought to England in 1844 by George Catlin giving a display of archery at Lord's Cricket Ground, London. This was the first Indian encampment in England and their display of archery was not so successful as various other activities, such as dancing, games and tribal ceremonies. From the *Pictorial Times*.

Unquestionably the arrows of the Indians of California were the finest of any in North America. Each was a work of precision. The point was extremely well made of obsidian, jasper or some siliceous rock, the edges chipped to a deadly, sharp miniature saw-blade, and having carefully worked notches for attachment to the shaft. It has been said that by means of the stone used, the shape and the artistic skill with which it was wrought, the edges, the tang, and the method of attachment to the shaft, arrows can actually be attributed to the tribe of origin, and even that individual makers within a tribe can be distinguished by their idiosyncracies. The shaft itself was beautifully straight and smoothed to a glassy finish, and a colouring according to established tribal custom was applied artistically and skilfully. The feathers, carefully selected for uniformity, size and colour, and with due regard to the symbolic power they were expected to transmit to the finished missile, were added neatly and trimmed to a long and slender pattern. Finally, each binding of sinew, at nock, feathers, the joint between main-shaft and foreshaft and where the head was secured, was made smooth and trim.

THE HUPA TRIBE

Warfare among the Hupa, from north-western California, consisted largely of feuds between their own kin groups or with corresponding groups in neighbouring tribes. The principal weapon was the bow and arrow. These were carefully and skilfully made and the finest were produced by specialists who took great pride in their work and sold their products for a good price. The points of war arrows were not poisoned, but stone from certain places was regarded as particularly deadly. A special variety of flint obtained from a quarry on Mad River was considered "deadly poison" and "broke off in a wound, making it inflamed". This flint was never used on hunting arrows because it was "too powerful". Arrow-points were given supernatural power through special treatment and the recitation of magical formulas, and feathers from a small kind of hawk were believed to make arrows more accurate. Bows and arrows were strictly cared for and, when not in use, were carried in skin bow-cases slung under the left arm. Moss was stuffed in each case to serve as a cushion for the arrow-points.

Cunning, treachery, ambushing and surprise attacks played an important part in Hupa warfare. Pitched battles occurred only when two enemy parties met face to face or when one was forewarned of an impending attack; once the fighting began, no order was observed and each man fought as he wished. A skilled fighter was able to dodge arrows either by watching his opponent's bow or the arrow itself. The ability to dodge flying missiles was developed from an early age when rough boyhood games included duels in which the contestants threw oak balls, bits of wood or other objects at each other. It is said that a good warrior watched an enemy's bow, observing which end moved, because the arrow was thrown in that direction, and he might then dodge the opposite way. The arrow was observed in flight and, if not aimed directly at a man, it could be seen in the sunlight and avoided. Womenfolk sometimes joined in the fight with clubs and stones, and both women and children ran about picking up arrows. The duration of the conflict was fairly short and, as Hupa weapons were not particularly deadly, casualties were few.

THE LAST WILD INDIAN

At dawn on August 29th, 1911, the workers in a slaughterhouse close to the town of Oroville in California were wakened by the barking of dogs to find a man crouching in the corner of the adjacent corral. This pitiful creature, desperate with hunger and in terror of the white murderers of his family, had wandered in exhaustion from his native hills down to this valley town in search of food. Promptly labelled a wild man by the townsfolk and carried off for safe keeping to the local gaol, he was finally identified as a Yahi Indian by an anthropologist from the University of California. Named Ishi, his own Yahi word for man, he was subsequently brought to San Francisco and lived there for the rest of his life under the protection and care of the staff of the Museum of Anthropology. The story of Ishi is an extraordinary one and provides an essential link between the wild, stone-age world of aboriginal North America and the present day. Fifty years old or thereabouts when he was discovered, cold, hungry, terrified and torn between self-preservation and suicide, it was through the patient and humane treatment he received from Professor Alfred Kroeber, who subsequently became his trusted friend, that Ishi completely adjusted himself to civilised living. For five years he cheerfully demonstrated age-old Indian techniques of arrow-head making, bowyery, fire-making and hunting, and had not Ishi been prepared to exhibit his skill in this way, such special details of Indian life could have been lost for ever. In 1912 Dr Saxton Pope, a member of the teaching staff of the University's medical school, knew Ishi slightly as a patient, and this doctor-patient acquaintance might have remained that and nothing more had not Pope one day glanced out of a window which opened on to the grounds and seen Ishi absorbed in the fashioning of a bow. He joined Ishi outside, where he could observe him closely, and persuaded him to demonstrate his shooting stance, his hold, and method of release. Watching, he became filled with a desire to learn, from one who had lived by the bow and arrow, the technique and the folklore of archery, pursued not as a pastime but as a way of life. So began Pope's mastery of the art of the bow. Archery, hunting big game with bow

An action photograph of Ishi, the
lone survivor of the doomed
Yahi Indians, taken in 1914 and
showing an unusual shooting
position.

and arrow and perfecting his knowledge, performance, and form was the
passion of Pope's later years. The results of Pope's careful archery studies and
the intimate details of the techniques of the bow and arrow which he learnt
from Ishi were published in due course,* and they remain as a unique and
valuable record of the Stone Age of the North American Indian.

*POPE, SAXTON T., *Yahi Archery*, University of California Publications in American
Archaeology and Ethnography, Vol. 13, No. 3 (1918)

To participate in the cycle of manufacture of a bow as Ishi made it was to journey back into Neolithic human history with Yahi overtones. Once blocked out, the bow-to-be was placed for seasoning where it would be constantly warm and damp. During this time it lay horizontally face up. Indeed the bow was laid, carried and shot face up—otherwise the arrow would not go true to its mark. For making the bow proper, the whole array of flint and obsidian knives and scrapers in Ishi's tool cache was used. The final finishing was done with sandstone. Ishi's bows have an elegantly curved line at the ends of the limbs, and so symmetrical are they that it is surprising to learn how simply he achieved these curves: first, by working the end to be recurved back and forth over a heated stone until the wood was pliable, then by pressing it against the curve of his bent knee, protected with a pad of buckskin, and holding it there with a steady pressure until the wood was entirely cool, by which time the curve was "fixed". To get the sinew needed for backing and for the bowstring itself, Ishi stripped the long tendons from the hind legs and the finer tendons from the shanks of a deer. To "tease" these out, soak, chew and work them was a tortuously slow process. When ready for use the long tendons had become flat parchment-like strips, thin and even, which were glued to the back of the bow. The glue was obtained by boiling salmon skin. The shank tendons Ishi shredded by pulling them through and through his teeth until they were of the fineness of silk thread, which he then spun into a continuous string. Before the bow was strung, it was again laid carefully in the sun and allowed to season for days or weeks. Then came the final smoothing, finishing and stringing. Although Ishi was content to wrap his bow in a piece of buckskin for a covering, he considered a mountain lion tail the truly correct bow cover. He was particular that when his bow was not in use it should lie and not stand. Standing, it continued to work, to sweat and become weak. Ishi's way of testing whether or not a bow was in good health and strength was to snap its string with his fingers. A healthy bow responded by giving a high, musical note. If the note was dull or dead in tone, the bow was no good, or it had been "contaminated". Perhaps a woman had touched it! Ishi would lightly snap the string of his bow, the musical note would follow, then he might put the bow to his lips and, tapping the string, coax from it a plaintive melodious song to accompany an old Yahi tale. He loved his bow as he loved nothing else he owned.

The same careful attention to detail went into the making of his arrows. He preferred the thin, straight stems of hazel to other wood for arrow-shafts. It was Ishi's custom to make arrows in groups of five; five were carried through the various stages of manufacture together, and only when they were completed and laid aside to season might another five be commenced. The hazel stick which was to become an arrow was first peeled of its bark; then, after it had been made hot by laying or rotating it in grooves in heated stones, any irregularities were straightened and it was held until cool, after which it was smoothed with sandstone, and given a final polishing by rolling back and forth across the thigh, the body oil contributing to its finish. Arrows were made to measure, the distance from the base of the breast-bone to the extended index finger with the left arm stretched along the arrow-shaft in shooting position; in Ishi's case, twenty-nine inches. Some, although by no means all, of Ishi's arrows were made with a foreshaft of heavier wood, about eight inches long. In order to fit the two parts of such an arrow together Ishi used a piece of bone ground to a sharp point which he placed upright on the earth and held in position with his feet. On to this he set the main shaft, perpendicularly, rotating it between the open palms of his hands until a tapered hole an inch or more in depth had been drilled out. He then cut a spindle at the end of the foreshaft to fit the hole, and secured it in the hole with resin or glue. The preferred feathers were eagle, but he used buzzard, blue jay and others. He mounted the feathers in sets of three, each set from a single wing, a custom generally observed by good bowmen everywhere. Precise details of the manufacture of stone points by this "last wild Indian" were carefully noted and described by Pope, and an examination of the surviving artefacts that were made by Ishi in true Indian fashion in the presence of his white friends will be sufficient to provide ample evidence of his skill as a primitive artisan.

ARCHERS OF THE ARCTIC WASTES

The last main group of North American Indians to come under our notice, as far as the history of their archery is concerned, are the Eskimoes, whose home for countless thousands of years has included the vast region of arctic wastes extending from Alaska to Baffin Island. The Eskimoes of Greenland, although not strictly American, are included for reasons of convenience and because their archery has so many similarities to that of the Eskimoes who are spread along the northern coasts of the American continent.

As a result of various Acts of Congress during the 'eighties, which directed research among North American Indians, official bulletins were published which have remained standard reference works for many of the tribes investigated. Such a report* concerned the detailed findings of the International Polar Expedition to Alaska in the years 1881-3. Though the main object of the expedition was "the prosecution of the observations in terrestrial magnetism and meteorology", full notes on the habits and customs of the Point Barrow Eskimoes were collected and made the subject of a special report. This full and factual account of a primitive race whose affinities to Asiatic stock were very close, and who, until 1826, had no general contact

*MURDOCK, JAMES, *Ethnological Results of the Point Barrow Expedition*, Ninth Annual Report of the Bureau of Ethnology (1892)

A Lapp and, opposite, two Samoyeds of the seventeenth century hunting on primitive skis. The forms of bow and the general application of archery of these northern peoples are similar in many respects to those found in Arctic North America on the same latitude.

with white men, deals with every aspect of their culture. Knowledge of these people was virtually non-existent and, in particular, the field of investigation into matters concerning archery was untrodden. The infectious enthusiasm that sparked off explorers, military reporters, doctors, anthropologists and archaeologists to inquire into the nature of bows, the techniques of primitive bowyers and the methods of hunting with bow and arrow, inspired John Murdock, the naturalist, to expand his knowledge to include a thorough understanding of Eskimo archery. As in the case of so many primitive tribes, one of the most important changes in the life of the Eskimo, as a result of his intercourse with white men, was the introduction of the gun. It is fortunate for us that the investigations into matters concerning our history took place before the gun completely replaced the bow.

The bow, which would project a missile to a greater distance than the throwing stick used by the Eskimoes and reminiscent of the *atl-atl* of the Mexicans, was used for hunting the bear, the wolf and the caribou, for shooting birds and, in case of necessity, for warfare. It was also developed as a specialized fishing weapon. Every boy had a bow for a plaything, with which he would shoot small birds and practise at marks, although Murdock tells us that "very few boys, however, show any great skill with it". The first mention of Eskimo bows with sinew backing will be found in Frobisher's account of his visit to Meta Incognita in 1577: "Their bowes are of wood of a yard long, sinewed on the back with strong sinewes, not glued too, but fast girded and tyed on." Due to the meagre natural resources of his Arctic home, a ready supply of proper wood for bow-making was not available to the Eskimo, and he had to devise a special form of construction for his bows which was unlike any other. The principle of arranging a complex system of sinew cords laced about the bow and tied to its back became known as loose-backed, due to the fact that the sinew was not glued to the bow as in other simple composite patterns. This form of construction was noted briefly by various authors. "Most writers have contented themselves with a casual reference to some of the more salient peculiarities of the weapon without giving any detailed information," said Murdock, and it was left to him to investigate fully this unique form of bow construction. His researches extended beyond the archery of the Point Barrow Eskimoes and included Eskimo bows from other regions. He declared that he had found three well-defined types of bows having a definite geographical distribution in western North America, all of which could be recognised as a slightly modified form of a simple original type found in Baffin Land. The differences in the three types, mentioned by Murdock, lay mainly in the way the fifty yards or so of braided sinew cord was hitched, twisted, lashed and tied off, the variation in size, and occasional additions of stiff "ears" to the spruce driftwood bowstave. Some strengthening by strips of rawhide from the bearded seal is found in some of these bows, and the combined effect of sinew cords, lashings and rawhide was to produce a very stiff, powerful bow capable of projecting an arrow with great force. Wood in sufficient quantity and of the necessary length was not always available and examples of bows made of several unequal pieces of driftwood, bone, horn, or antler riveted together are not unusual. Yet another method of over-coming the timber scarcity was by the use of pieces of the horn of the musk-ox spliced together, with, of course, the special loose-backing added. The Eskimoes of Greenland used a loose-backed bow similar in most respects to that used by the Eskimoes from the western Arctic, although, in addition, one made from whalebone arranged in layers was common in the northern coastal area of that vast island. The general techniques of bow construction employed by the Greenland Eskimoes follow closely those found among the Eskimoes throughout the Arctic regions.

ESKIMO ARROWS

The arrows of the Eskimoes show an individuality of invention compar-able with the best of primitive crafts the world over. Many varieties were made, all with their own specialised uses. Bear arrows had broad, sharp piles, often barbed and made of flaked flint; deer arrows were fashioned with a long, sharp, barbed point of antler, designed to fall off and rankle in the wound, while those for shooting gulls, geese and other large fowl were provided with

An Eskimo bow, quiver and arrows. This shows a type of bow in general use amongst the North American Eskimo tribes with a selection of typical arrows and a quiver, probably made of seal skin.

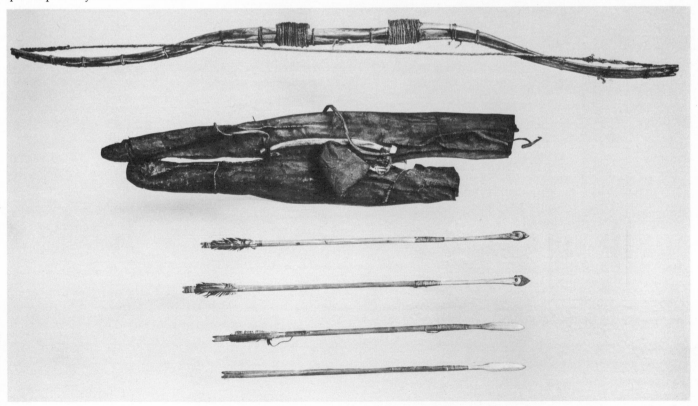

A Lapp woman accompanying her husband on a hunt with bows and arrows. A woodcut from a work of 1555.

slender points of walrus ivory having small barbs; and yet another type, used almost exclusively by boys to shoot small birds or lemmings, had a blunt head of bone or antler. The harpoon arrow, an exclusive weapon for hunting the sea otter, is the most elaborate and ingenious arrow known, and all its parts, in every specimen, are most delicately finished. The shaft is of spruce, gently tapering towards the nock, which is large and bulbous. Into the end of this shaft is inserted a foreshaft of bone, and into the end of this fits the barb. Three feathers, symmetrically trimmed, are seized at both ends with delicately twisted sinew thread. The barbed head is perforated and through these perforations is attached a braided line at least ten feet long. The other end of the line is attached to two points on the shaft by a martingale. When not in use the line is coiled neatly on the shaft and the barb is put in place in the foreshaft. When the arrow is shot, the barb enters the flesh of the otter, the loose fastening is undone, the line unrolled, the heavy bone foreshaft drops into the water, the wooden shaft acts as a buoy and the feathers are a marker to aid the hunter in tracing the animal.

The ancestry of the bow in America is an ancient one, and to tell the complete story of the North American Indian and his rich heritage of hunting and living by the bow would occupy many volumes. However, we have seen a little of the evolution of the bow among the complexity of Indian tribes, and we have shown how much the history of America, up to the nineteenth century, had been influenced by its use. The ancient crafts of bowyery, fletching and arrow-making reached a perfection amongst the Indians of North America difficult to match by any other primitive people. It was only the late arrival of the gun that finally replaced the bow and arrow as the universal weapon of the Red Indian and reduced it to a curiosity to be collected as a tourist trophy.

"Savages of Greenland", from an old engraving. The Eskimoes of Greenland and the Lapps have a history of the use of a crossbow of primitive form in addition to the use of hand-bows.

The fact that the number of active, adult bowhunters in America at the present day can be counted in tens of thousands is sufficient proof that the heritage of the past cannot easily be forgotten, and the same archery skills, applied previously to the matter of survival, are still used by a large-scale and thriving modern industry serving the enthusiastic toxophilites of today.

SELECT BIBLIOGRAPHY

Birket-Smith, Kaj, *The Greenland Bow* [n.d.]

Catlin, George, *Letters and Notes on the Manners, Customs, and Condition of the North American Indians* [1841]

Clissold, Stephen, *Conquistador* [1954]

Custer, General G. A., *My Life on the Plains* (Edited) [1963]

Driver, Harold E., & Massey, William C., *Comparative Studies of North American Indians*, Transactions of the American Philosophical Society, Vol. 47, Part 2 [1957]

Egede, Hans, *A Description of Greenland* [1745]

Ellsworth, Clarence, *Bows and Arrows*, South-west Museum Leaflet, No. 24 [1950]

Hibben, Frank C., *Treasure in the Dust* [1953]

Honea, Kenneth, *Early Man Projectile Points in the South-west*, Museum of New Mexico [1965]

Klopsteg, Paul E., *Bows and Arrows: A Chapter in the Evolution of Archery in America*, The Smithsonian Report [1962]

Knight, Edward H., *A Study of the Savage Weapons at the Centennial Exhibition, Philadelphia, 1876*, Smithsonian Report [1879]

Kroeber, Theodora, *Ishi* [1963]

La Farge, Oliver, *A Pictorial History of the American Indian* [1956]

La Flesche, Francis, *Omaha Bow and Arrow Makers*, Smithsonian Report [1926]

McCracken, Harold, *George Catlin and the Old Frontier* [1959]

Mason, Otis T., et al., *Arrows and Arrow-Makers*, The American Anthropologist [1891]

Mason, Otis T., *North American Bows, Arrows and Quivers*, Smithsonian Report [1893]

Mason, Otis T., *The Ray Collection from Hupa Reservation*, Smithsonian Report [1886]

Miles, Charles, *Indian and Eskimo Artifacts of North America* [1963]

Murdock, James, *Ethnological Results of the Point Barrow Expedition*, Ninth Annual Report of the Bureau of Ethnology [1892]

Murdock, John, *A Study of the Eskimo Bows in the U.S. National Museum*, Smithsonian Report [1884]

Oklahoma Anthropological Society, *Guide to the Identification of Certain American Indian Projectile Points* [1958]

Peckham, Stewart, *Prehistoric Weapons in the South-west*, Museum of New Mexico [1965]

Pope, Saxton T., *A Study of Bows and Arrows* [1923]

Pope, Saxton T., *Yahi Archery*, University of California Publications in American Archaeology and Ethnology, Vol. 13, No. 3 [1918]

Prescott, William H., *History of the Conquest of Mexico* [1901]

Skinner, Alanson, *The Indians of Manhattan Island and Vicinity*, Science Guide No. 41, The American Museum of Natural History [1947]

Wallace, William J., *Hupa Warfare*, South-west Museum Leaflet No. 23 [1949]

9 The Crossbow

And the crossbowman true and good
Thou shooter with the faultless wood,
Haste with thy stirrup-fashioned bow
To lay the hideous varlet low.

DAVID-AP-GWILYM

SOME explanation of the principal differences between the crossbow and the more familiar hand-bow are offered as an introduction to the story of this weapon. The crossbow was generally a portable weapon, but the principles of its operation were incorporated in heavier models for defensive warfare and in some of the massive siege engines of certain periods. As a personal weapon, however, its disadvantages rather outweighed its advantages; it was cumbrous and expensive, it had a slow rate of fire and the necessity for an involved loading procedure rendered the soldier handling it particularly vulnerable, although in its favour were the power and accuracy of its missiles. The performance of a crossbow was governed by the design and arrangement of the contrivance itself rather than by the skill and strength of the bowman who operated it. This fact was used in a laconic simile explaining the difference between testimony and argument: "Testimony is like the shot of a longbow, which owes its efficacy to the force of the shooter; argument is like the shot of the crossbow, equally forcible, whether discharged by a dwarf or a giant."

The principles of storing energy in a drawn bow apply equally to crossbows and hand-bows, but whereas to hold an arrow in a drawn hand-bow for any length of time, would soon exhaust the archer (apart from the awkwardness of the situation), a drawn and loaded crossbow could be kept ready

285

for use without effort. This was contrived in a crossbow by a mechanism which had the dual function of retaining the drawn string and, when activated by a trigger, releasing the string together with the missile previously set in position. We shall see that this mechanical release mechanism varied considerably in design, from a simple device comprised of a single working part to a complicated set of sears, pawls, springs, cams and articulated and pivoted levers. The bow itself, often conforming to the same method of construction as the hand-bows of self-wood or of composite form, was shorter, stouter and invariably more powerful than the conventional hand-held weapon. It was securely mounted at right-angles to a wooden stock which also housed the release mechanism. The missile, variously called a bolt, quarrel or carreau, was shorter and thicker than an arrow and had a heavier head. It was laid along the stock, often in a groove made for the purpose, and its blunt butt-end fitted neatly between the jaws of the mechanism which held the string back. On activating the trigger the jaws drop and allow the string to fly forward, projecting the bolt to its destination. Thus we see that the stock was substituted for the bow-arm of the archer and the mechanism for releasing the string replaced his fingers. Sometimes extra improvements were added, such as built-in aids for cocking the bow and a variety of sighting devices.

The more powerful the crossbow became the more difficult it was to draw back the string, and a variety of mechanical contrivances were devised to assist this operation. The greater the hitting power of the crossbow the more equipment was required to load and prepare it, and the more encumbered became the crossbowman. Personal mobility and consequent safety were sacrificed for hitting power. Although it served as a standard weapon in the armies of many nations, the crossbow never became a decisive arm as did the long-bow. It appealed to military commanders over a long period as a weapon with special applications, and even today armies of the Western world experiment with it occasionally as a potential infantry weapon. However, its use as a sporting weapon found favour with a wide following, and there are many interesting and unique survivals of this aspect of its history.

THE FIRST CROSSBOWS

The idea of mounting a bow on a cross-stave provided with a mechanical means for releasing the string occurred to the Chinese several centuries before Christ. There is some evidence that a form of crossbow, which used stones as missiles, was known to the Chinese as far back as the Shan Dynasty (c. 1500–1027 B.C.); and Sun Tzū, in his treatise* of the sixth century B.C., mentions the use of powerful crossbows for shooting fire arrows at the enemy. However, the principal source of our knowledge of early Chinese crossbows is

*Sun Tzū on the Art of War, Trans. by Lionel Giles (1910)

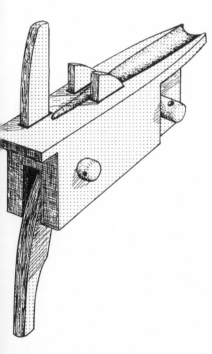

Bronze crossbow lock, or chi, from the Han Dynasty, fourth–third century B.C. The two jaws of the nut can be seen, behind which the cord is retained when the crossbow is prepared for action.

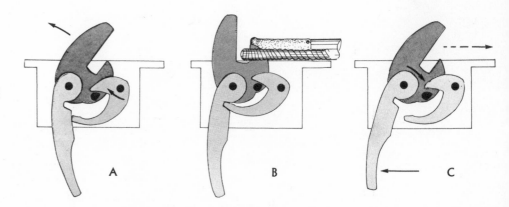

Diagrammatic representation of the mechanism of a Chinese crossbow lock or *chi*, of the fourth–third century B.C., from Chang Sha, Hunan.

A. The mechanism in the neutral position. To set the lock the cord is pulled back hard on to the latch.

B. The cord shown in position over the latch and the pawl engaged in the trigger ready for release. The bronze-sheathed base of the bolt is shown in position.

C. The release. By pressing back the trigger the whole mechanism is sharply activated and the string flies forward carrying with it the missile.

Detail drawn from the Admonitions of the Instructress of the Ladies in the Palace, a scroll painting on silk attributed to Ku K'ai-chih and dated to the sixth or seventh century A.D. In all probability this shows the earliest representation of a cross-bow in use.

taken from the Han Dynasty (206 B.C.–A.D. 220) and onwards. It was during this period that the crossbow came into regular use in China and, in fact, became as important in the stabilization of the north-west frontier as the Great Wall itself. They were considered so important by Ch'in Shih-huang-ti, the first emperor of the brief Ch'in Dynasty, that he had special automatic versions installed in his tomb. This was to ensure that anyone who desecrated his place of interment, under the Mountain of the Black Horses, met with certain death. The defence of the Wall from Han times was chiefly in the hands of infantry who were armed with these powerful crossbows, the most distinctive parts of which were beautifully made release mechanisms of bronze. A number of these ingenious *Chi* or crossbow locks, have been found in graves dated to as early as the fourth and fifth centuries B.C. Although the use of iron had been known from the seventh century and the chief weapons of bronze had been replaced by this metal, due to the intricacy of its design the crossbow lock continued to be cast in bronze. This contrivance was compactly designed and well made, its construction consisting of a box containing several moving parts held in place by carefully positioned pins. This box fitted flush into a wooden stock, and a trigger, projecting from its lower side, was positioned similarly to that of a conventional rifle. Two small jaws, behind which the string was held, projected through the top of the box. The bow itself was securely fixed to the end of the stock and when it was cocked the string was drawn back and held taut by the twin jaws of the lock. The bolt was then laid in a groove which ran the length of the stock, its butt-end resting against the restrained string. On pressing the trigger a series of moving parts operated, freeing the jaws; the pressure of the string forced them to fall clear and the bolt was propelled.

The stock, made of wood and often carved and lacquered, was sturdy enough to withstand the repeated shock of the discharge of a powerful bow held captive at its extremity, and so designed as to be comfortable to hold and operate. Rare examples excavated at Changsha in China, Lolang in Korea and Thanhoa in Viet Nam are each of a similar design, and all date from the Han period or a little earlier. A common feature of their design is a

287

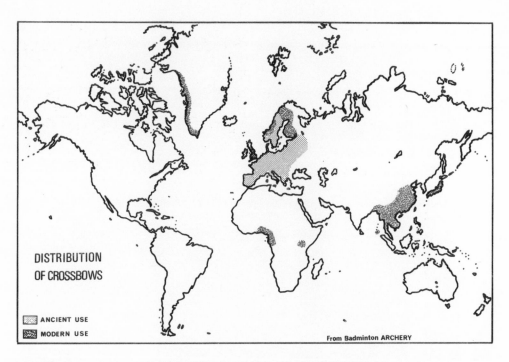

DISTRIBUTION
OF CROSSBOWS

ANCIENT USE
MODERN USE

From Badminton ARCHERY

thickening of the central lower portion, which is carved into a scroll. This no doubt provided a hand-grip, so that the weapon could be held easily and firmly. In addition, some of these excavated examples terminated in a projecting portion, somewhat like a pistol-grip, which would provide a second hand-grip. That these crossbows were used with both hands is confirmed by an illustration from a scroll attributed to Ku K'ai-Shih which shows soldiers using them in action.

The actual bow, sometimes referred to as the "prodd", was usually made of several laminations of bamboo, bound and glued together and covered with carefully lacquered silk. This was about three feet long and fitted snugly into an open slot at the front end of the stock. Other excavated examples were found to be of composite construction which followed, and no doubt improved upon, the earlier bamboo patterns. The strength of the crossbow is measured in the same way as that of a hand-bow, being the number of pounds required to draw the string to the extent required. In the case of the English long-bows used in war this probably amounted to 75 pounds; the heavier Mongolian bows of composite design ranged from 80 to as much as 100 pounds, and the target weapons of today draw only 35 to 40 pounds. The performance of the weapon did not necessarily improve in relationship to an increase in its weight. So many other aspects would affect its efficiency: the cast, or energy imparted to the arrow, is an important factor, and so is the design of the bow; the arrow itself and the method of release are other prime considerations. Generally speaking the crossbow projected a missile with enormous power, especially over the shorter distances. The energy imparted to the bolt, although initially very great, was quickly expended;

such a missile, therefore, was capable of crippling penetration up to a limited range, thereafter rapidly decreasing in potency.

BOLTS AND THEIR PENETRATION

The Chinese were the first archer-peoples to use a classification of weights for their bows, and amongst armoury records of the Han Dynasty we can read of crossbows with weights from 190 to 380 pounds. The bolts used with

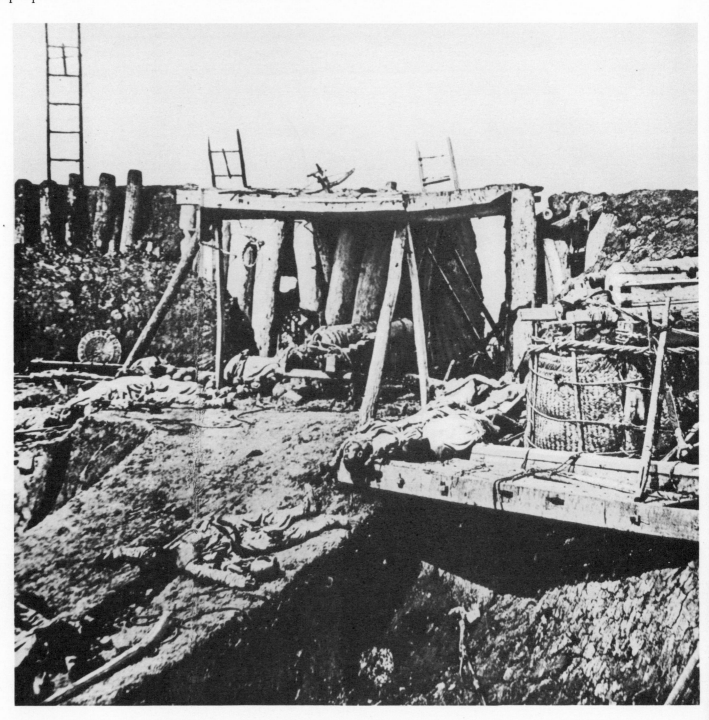

The scene of devastation and death in one of the forts at Taku, North China, after the surrender in 1858. The defenders used repeating crossbows, one of which can be seen discarded on the parapet.

Robin Hood has frequently been used as a figure of derision and scorn to reduce archery to nothing more than immature amusement. This lively cartoon of 1833 develops the theme to a ludicrous level.

"The Archers", a whimsical print published by R. Ackermann in 1802.

The Prince Regent, thinly disguised as Telemachus, being enticed by Lady Hertford's Calypso; an unpopular and publicly criticized attachment. Note the tiny Cupid precariously balanced as he aims his bow.

these powerful weapons had to withstand an enormous initial shock and, to be effective, had to be provided with a suitably efficient war-head with armour-piercing qualities. These crossbow bolts had straight, stiff shafts up to twelve inches long, and socketed three- or four-sided heads of solid bronze or iron capable of puncturing tough leather, padded and quilted tunics or armour of metal. To further strengthen them against the violent and sudden thrust of the string these bolts often had bronze ferrules fitted to their butt ends, which sometimes had, as a final refinement, small projections like spurs into which the string was engaged. The ingenious and original crossbow lock together with the occasional finds of associated relics such as bolt-heads and remains of wooden stocks have provided us with a tantalizing glimpse of the use of the crossbow for some 500 years of China's history.

In the absence of earlier evidence it would seem most likely that the credit for having invented the crossbow must go to the Chinese. Its precise provenance is unknown, although there is some suggestion that it spread northwards through China from south-east Asia, in which connexion there is an interesting link in the traditional use of a primitive type of crossbow among the peoples of Vietnam, Thailand and Burma. The basic components of crossbows of later periods, and from other parts of the world, varied only in design and arrangement from those already described in the context of the Chinese models. Probably it was conceived as a siege weapon, in which character it serves admirably, rather than as a weapon of offence, in which rôle it has many shortcomings. The disuse of the crossbow as a standard military weapon in China occurred in the centuries soon after the Han Dynasty. The reason for this has not been revealed to us but possibly the strategy of war changed and the demand for defensive planning diminished; commanders in favour of the crossbow may have given way to those unconvinced of its superiority, or possibly a very early use of gunpowder as an incendiary material was being enthusiastically received as the latest in weapons. Whatever the reason, the crossbow did not feature in the armies of China in the early centuries A.D., other than in a very special form.

THE REPEATING CROSSBOW

The Chinese repeating crossbow is possibly the most curious of all crossbows, and it dates from a very early period of Chinese history. It has been assigned to the first century A.D., and was still in active use during the war between China and Japan, 1894–5. No other nation developed a weapon which would enable a crossbowman to discharge ten bolts every fifteen seconds by a simple but cleverly devised mechanism needing no previous training of the man using it. The advantages of such a weapon are immediately obvious; for example, a hundred men equipped with repeating crossbows could send one thousand arrows into their opponents' ranks in a quarter of a minute. The effect of such a bombardment would be considerable, from both psychological and practical viewpoints, and this rate of discharge, if maintained, could be used with immediate military advantage.

The bolt shot from this crossbow was light, slender and often without flights, although some examples were provided with a spiral fletching consisting of very short feathers. Some authorities claim that the sharp pyramidal or square-sectioned points of these bolts were poisoned, so that their slight penetrative power was offset by the greater chance of an infected scratch becoming fatal. A specially constructed magazine, which held about ten or twelve small bolts, was so hinged that it could be moved back and forth along the stock. The magazine, which in fact formed a crude barrel, had lengthwise slots cut in both of its sides through which the bowstring passed. By moving the magazine forward the string was engaged in a notch at the rear of the slots, and when it was pulled back it cocked the bow and a bolt was fed in position from above. At the extremity of its backward movement a small wooden trigger was automatically forced upwards to push the string out of the notch and along the slot taking the bolt with it. This simple pumping action was repeated until the supply of bolts in the magazine was exhausted. The whole apparatus was simple and almost crudely made of wood, neither painted or lacquered, and the bow itself was formed of the familiar bamboo laminations about three feet six inches long. The effective range of these Chinese weapons was about 80 yards and their extreme range from 180 to 200 yards.

A splendidly decorated Chinese repeating crossbow reputed to be in the Musée Cernuschi, Paris.

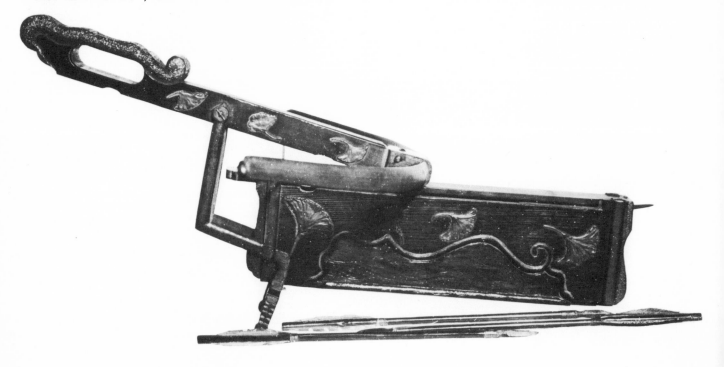

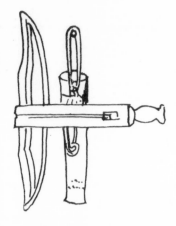

A drawing of the detail of a Roman tombstone from Polignac-sur-Loire, on which is carved in low relief a representation of the hand crossbow, or *gastrephretes*, of the Roman mercenaries.

ROMAN CROSSBOWS

From Asia the crossbow passed to Europe at some unspecified date. There is the barest minimum of evidence to indicate that it was employed by the Romans; Pitiscus, for instance, assigned its introduction to the Roman armies to the time of Constantine or a little earlier. Vegetius is inclined to consider the *scorpio* to be the same as the crossbow; he speaks of scorpions which, he says, were also called *manuballistaes* and in the works of later writers the weapon is sometimes termed *scorpio manualis*. Other classical authors make reference to a projectile weapon known as the *gastraphenes*. This was undoubtedly a portable weapon and very likely described the crossbow as used by the armies of Rome. The scant evidence provided by two tombstone fragments from France is sufficient to show the crossbow as used by the Romans, which seems to have been of a straightforward design, in all probability incorporating a composite bow. The stone fragments from Puy and Polignac-sur-Loire lack exact detail, particularly of the trigger mechanism, but this probably consisted of the "nut" featured in most crossbows of Europe. The nut consisted of a skilfully shaped block of horn or bone provided with a lip so arranged that it could be retained in one position by a catch. An integral part of the design was a pair of jaws, reminiscent of the Chinese pattern, between which the bolt fitted and behind which the string was retained when the bow was made ready for shooting. On pressing the lever, the nut was allowed to revolve on its retaining pin, releasing the string and shooting the bolt. The nut was a component which became a standard item of crossbow mechanism and, although improvements and variations in the method of triggering were introduced from time to time, the basic design of the nut did not change. Two of these nuts, made of bone, were discovered during the excavations of an early lake dwelling in Ayrshire and from a site in Wiltshire. Although other material found there tended towards an Anglian sixth- or seventh-century date, a number of items were obviously much earlier, and could be late Roman. The principles of crossbow construction and operation were utilized in the Roman engines of war, the balista, in particular, being a heavier and more powerful type of crossbow mounted on a giant wooden frame. Specialist crossbowmen may have been employed by the Romans as mercenary troops in the same way that bowmen from the Middle East served as support battalions.

Hengist and Horsa, when they invaded Britain in A.D. 457, were traditionally accompanied by soldiers armed with crossbows. The details of the story of these Frankish invaders from Europe are uncertain and no positive support can be given to the supposition that they were users of the crossbow. It is not until brief references occur in the early eleventh century that we can with certainty begin to trace the history of the crossbow in Europe and

Drawing taken from a fragment of a Roman tombstone from Puy, in Southern France, showing a crossbow.

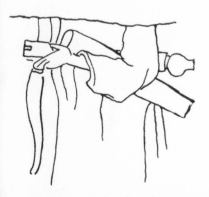

assess its value as a military weapon. The invasion army of Duke William of Normandy, which succeeded in defeating Harold of England near Hastings in 1066, could well have included crossbows amongst its armament. That hand-bows represented a principal weapon on this occasion there is no doubt, and documentary evidence from the period suggests that the use of crossbows by the Conqueror would be a reasonable assumption.

About a year after the Conquest, in 1067, Guy of Amiens mentions crossbows which were used, he says, by the *balistantes* of William's army, in a poem* commemorating the battle. In 1085 the Domesday Book, ordered by William the Conqueror to survey property in England for taxation purposes, mentions lands held in Yorkshire by the rent of a crossbow, and several *arcuballistarii*, captains of crossbowmen, are among the tenants-in-chief. Finally William of Tyre, in his chronicle of 1098, also mentions the weapon. Whether or not the Conqueror brought crossbows to Britain among the armament of his invasion forces is a question for further research. We do know that the earliest Crusaders were not without crossbowmen, though they did not at first understand how to employ them properly against the Turks. The description of the Crusader's crossbow by Anna Comnena (1083–1148), is probably the earliest full description of this weapon in the West which we can refer to. "That hitherto unknown engine, the Tzaggra", she says, "is not a bow held in the left hand and bent by the right, but can only be spanned by the bearer stooping and placing both feet against it, while he strains at the cord with the full force of both arms. In the middle it has a semi-circular groove of the length of a long arrow, which reaches down to the middle of its stock; the missiles, which are of many and various kinds, are placed in the groove, and propelled through it by the released cord. They

*GUY of AMIENS, *De Bello Hastingensis Carmen* (1067)

The army of the Roman Emperor, Henry VI (1165–97), parades before the conquest of Sicily (1194). Detail from *Codex Bernensis* 120, folio 131, Petrus de Ebulo, *De Rebus Siculis Carmen*.

The Turks besieging the Crusaders, from a medieval illustration. Three crossbowmen are preparing for action. One at the rear is setting a bolt in position and the other two are spanning their bows by means of belt and claw and a cranequin device.

pierce wood and metal easily, and sometimes wholly imbed themselves in a wall, or any such obstacle, when they have struck it." Recent inspections of the walls still remaining of some of the Crusaders' castles in the Middle East have revealed bolt-heads still lodged in the stonework.

THE CRUSADES

The use of the crossbow became widespread in twelfth-century Europe, and mercenary crossbowmen were used in the armies of William II (whose death in the New Forest has for many centuries been traditionally associated with this weapon), of Henry I, who conquered Normandy in 1106, of Stephen and of Henry II. For the first time since the Roman domination the foot soldiers of Italy again rose to prominence, and companies of soldiers from that country, skilled in the use of the crossbow, appeared at every siege and battle in the Mediterranean. Of all the peoples in Europe none were so proficient in the use of the crossbow, and none gained such a high reputation as marksmen, as did the Italian foot-soldiers, and especially the Genoese. Within a few decades these mercenaries were to be found fighting in the French service at Coutray, Sluys and Crécy. In 1139 crossbows were prohibited by Pope Innocent II, as being ". . . deathly and hateful to God and unfit to be used among Christians", although their use against unbelievers was condoned. In spite of this interdict, they were used in most of the Continental wars. Richard I, King of England for the period 1189-99, greatly encouraged crossbowmen in his armies, and they were employed to great advantage in his crusading battles all over the Middle East. It was probably through his enthusiasm that the crossbow was re-introduced, after years of unpopularity as a result of the papal decree against its use.

John Brompton, a monk of Jervaulx writing in the fifteenth century, said of Richard I: "Truly this kind of shooting, already laid aside, which is called crossbow shooting, was revived by him, when he became so skilful in its management that he killed many people with his own hand." At the siege of Acre King Richard's personal marksmanship was noted: "One of the Turks, boastfully wearing the armour of the aforesaid Alberic Clements [previously captured, stripped and killed by the Turks], was showing himself on the highest part of the wall to the annoyance of our men; but King Richard inflicted on him a deadly wound, piercing him through the heart with a cast of his arbalest [crossbow]." The Third Crusade, possibly the most glamorous and certainly the most historically important of all the Holy Wars, particularly involved Richard, who dominated the Christian allies opposing Saladin. The anonymous author of the *Chronicle of the Third Crusade*, thought to be a Norman "trouvere" who accompanied Richard to the Holy Land, frequently mentions crossbows together with all the other weapons of a medieval armoury. "What army was ever assailed by so mighty a force? There you might have seen our troopers, having lost their chargers, marching on foot with the foot-men, or casting missiles from arbalests, or arrows from bows, against the enemy, and repelling their attacks in the best manner they were able. The Turks, skilled in the bow, pressing unceasingly upon them; it rained darts; the air was filled with the shower of arrows, and the brightness of the sun was obscured by the multitude of missiles as if it had been darkened by a fall of winter's hail or snow." The chronicler repeatedly commented on the penetrative power of well-directed bolts, which even the best of armour could not withstand: " . . . no matter how close the armour fitted, nor if the coat of mail was twofold, it availed little to resist the bolts from the arbalests." While he laid siege in 1199 to the castle of Chaluz, near Limoges in France, the prize of which was to be a vast treasure recently

An aquatint of the early nineteenth century representing a crossbowman and his paviser of 1432. The use of the shield or pavise as protection for crossbowmen became popular in Europe during this period.

discovered, Richard Coeur de Lion was wounded by a crossbow bolt which bit deeply into his left shoulder close to the neck. The wound was aggravated by the necessary cutting out of the vicious head, and gangrene set in. Richard ordered the archer who had shot the fatal bolt, and who was now a prisoner, to be brought before him; he pardoned him and made him a gift of money. Nevertheless, after the well-loved king died the archer was flayed alive.

MERCENARY CROSSBOWMEN

The crossbowman continued to occupy the place of importance among the infantry of Europe until the middle of the thirteenth century, and King John employed a considerable proportion of them in his army. He maintained great numbers of both horse and foot arbalesters among the mercenaries who were such a curse to England. Their evil memory is perpetuated in the clause of Magna Carta which binds the King to banish " . . . from the kingdom all the foreign knights, crossbowmen, their attendants, and the mercenaries

The French attack the town of
Duras and take it by storm,
c. 1375, after an illustration in
Froissart's *Chronicles.* "The
men-at-arms made themselves
ready, and the crossbowmen, well
shielded, advanced to the town."

that have come to it; to its harm." During the reign of Henry III, although the long-bow was beginning to become more prominent, the crossbow was still considered the superior weapon. At the battle of Taillebourg in 1242, when Henry III was defeated by Louis IV, a corps of 700 crossbowmen in the English army were considered to be the flower of the infantry. Their popularity with English commanders rapidly diminished as the power of the long-bow was realised, and by 1415 we find that only 38 crossbowmen were listed by Rymer in the muster-roll of Henry V's army of 8,000 at Agincourt. It is an interesting fact that after this battle, in which the long-bow played such a decisive part, the French continued the use of the crossbow; and Henry V, as Duke of Normandy, confirmed the charters and privileges of the *balistarii* who had been long established as a fraternity in his city of Rouen.

Despite the decline in the use of the crossbow in the English armies it continued in favour with the forces of the Continent for a much longer period, and was in common use in European campaigns from about 1200 to 1460–70. For 250 years crossbowmen were considered to be the *corps d'élite* of the army and were always placed in the front of the battle line. Most of the nations of Europe adopted the crossbow and regarded it as a weapon of some significance. Some time in the thirteenth century it found its way to Switzerland, probably thanks to Swiss mercenaries serving under the Hohenstaufen emperors. The old Swiss confederates made good use of this weapon in warfare, and detachments of crossbowmen were employed in raiding and reconnoitring, and in any operation in which the element of surprise was important. In France the crossbow was particularly popular and was in active service until at least 1515 when, at the battle of Marigliano, Francis I defeated the Duke of Milan and the Swiss, having among his bodyguard 200 mounted crossbowmen who rendered signal service. The French army favoured the employment of mercenary crossbowmen, especially the Genoese. The history of the battle of Crécy relates that no less than 6,000 of these hired soldiers faced the English in the van of the army of France, and the manner of their defeat has been told in another part of this book. The famous General Cortes had a company of Spanish crossbowmen in his army at the capture of Mexico in 1521, and employed them in defence and assault as freely as he did his soldiers armed with hand-guns. The small band of about a hundred adventurous Spaniards who sailed from Panama in 1524 under Pizarro, to explore Peru, consisted solely of crossbowmen. The Continental crossbow had become such a costly weapon and one of such importance in warfare that in Spain, as early as the close of the fourteenth century, the crossbowman was even granted the rank of knight. The position of "Master of the Crossbowmen" was one of great honour in France, Italy and Spain, and was only bestowed on persons of high consequence and title.

To span a crossbow by the "belt and claw" method, the claw, which is attached to a waist belt, is hooked over the string, and by pressing down with the foot in the stirrup the bow can easily be tensed. The bowstring is then held back by the jaws of the nut ready for immediate discharge.

LOADING MECHANISMS

The manner of loading, or cocking, crossbows developed from a simple manual method to a complicated mechanical process the ingenuity of which outweighed its advantages. To load crossbows which became progressively heavier and more powerful, cumbrous additional equipment was required, often extending to a detachable mechanism of awkward size. The extra accessories encumbered the crossbowman, who, in using them, had extra tasks to perform to prepare his weapon for action, with the result that the whole process became slower and consequently less efficient. The use of the portable block and tackle, the windlass, had a direct effect on the rate of fire that could be expected from a crossbow. During the time it took a crossbowman to attach the windlass, wind the string on to the nut, remove the windlass, and aim and press the trigger, the longbowman had six arrows in the target. The earliest method of cocking a crossbow was by pulling back the string by means of hand pressure alone, but the added refinement of a stirrup fitted to the front end of the stock, into which the crossbowman placed his foot, enabled the whole contrivance to be held steady while the string was drawn back. Another method used in conjunction with the stirrup involved attaching the string to a hook hanging from the waist-belt, and using back and leg muscles to draw a more powerful bow. This was known as the "belt and claw". A variation of this method, which would provide extra purchase, was known as *turni balistarii* or *arbalest à tour*, where the cord was doubled back over a pulley hooked on to the string. As the strength of the bow was increased, with a view to acquiring a longer range and the use of a heavier bolt, so the contrivance for drawing back the string had to be developed, and the fifteenth century saw the introduction of the "screw and handle". This was a method more rarely seen, but it represents a further stage which may have suggested the much more convenient "cranequin" which followed it. The principle of the screw and handle involved a long, built-in, threaded rod on the end of which was a hook by which the string was drawn back. The end of the rod protruded through the rear of the stock and was wound up by means of a handle.

A crossbowman spanning his bow by hand. A carving on a medieval misericord seat from the Abbey of St Lucien, now in the Cluny Museum, Paris.

The French cranequin or "rachet-winder", sometimes also called the "rack and pinion", although efficient and simple in operation and lighter to carry, was considerably slower to use than some of the other means of cocking crossbows. Its mechanism was precisely similar to that of the old-fashioned lifting jack of the timber yards, consisting of a winder operating a large and a small cog which engaged in a rachet bar having at one end the hook for the string. This was the only crossbow winder which could conveniently be used on horseback to bend a powerful steel bow, and was probably designed with this special application in mind. Another method of spanning a crossbow which could have been used by mounted crossbowmen using light weapons was the "goat's foot lever". This ingenious mechanism operated on the principle of leverage about two specially located studs incorporated as part of the design of the stock. It was a rapid and easily operated method which was popular over a long period. The last method of crossbow loading we shall discuss is the famous "windlass", which was used with the perfected military crossbow. In one form or another the windlass had been used for bending the bow of the Roman balista for centuries before it was applied to the crossbow carried by hand. The windlass or "moulinet" comprised a bracket carrying a double hand-crank which wound up a pair of ropes running over a series of pulleys terminating in a claw to engage in the string. The whole apparatus fitted on to the rear end of the stock and was detached when the bow was in use. By means of this block and tackle system a very powerful bow indeed could be drawn back and prepared for action. The extremely powerful siege crossbow, which would have to be cocked by means of this method, needed a strain of 1,200 pounds to draw back the string a matter of seven inches, sufficient to propel a heavy armour-piercing bolt to a distance of 450 yards.

TYPES OF CROSSBOWS

The various types of crossbows used in medieval Europe began with a light military model, utilizing a bow of solid wood such as ash or yew and bent by drawing its string to the catch of the lock by means of the hands alone; this dated from the tenth or eleventh centuries. This was followed by those weapons fitted with composite bows and drawn with some mechanical means, such as a cranequin. These bows, in use from the thirteenth century onwards, were likely to have been introduced by the Saracens, who were famed for their bow construction techniques. In a list of crossbow makers compiled by the Baron de Cosson,* the name of Peter the Saracen appears, crossbow maker to the King of England in 1205. In that year the constable

*de COSSON, BARON, *The Crossbow of Ulrich V, Count of Wurtemburg, 1460,* Archaeologia, Vol. LIII (1892)

A fully-equipped medieval crossbowman. Slung round his waist is a belt and claw for spanning his bow; a supply of bolts is stored, point uppermost, in a quiver, and the crossbow itself is hooked on to the back of his belt. A pavise is also slung across his back.

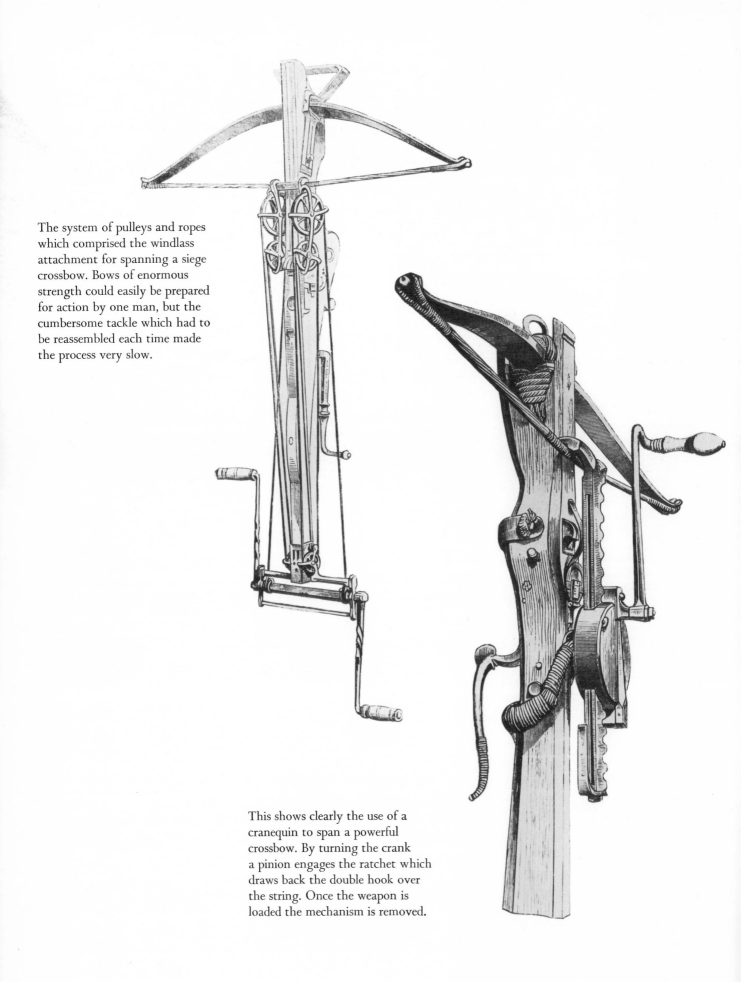

The system of pulleys and ropes which comprised the windlass attachment for spanning a siege crossbow. Bows of enormous strength could easily be prepared for action by one man, but the cumbersome tackle which had to be reassembled each time made the process very slow.

This shows clearly the use of a cranequin to span a powerful crossbow. By turning the crank a pinion engages the ratchet which draws back the double hook over the string. Once the weapon is loaded the mechanism is removed.

301

A modern reconstruction of a
medieval crossbow being
demonstrated by a member of the
Medieval Society. This clearly
shows how such a weapon is held
and aimed.

of Northampton received orders to retain this craftsman and another with
him, for the king's service, and to allow him ninepence a day. A document
dated 1358, describing the materials supplied for making twenty-five bows
of composite construction, lists 25 pieces of yew, 25 staples, 25 crossbow
nuts, 25 stirrups, 25 keys (that is triggers), 12lb of hempen string, 1lb of wax,
½lb of resinous pitch, 4lb of tallow, some charcoal, 4lb of glue, 4lb of ox sinew
shredded out like lint, 1lb of varnish and 12 rams' horns. The yew core, sinew
back and horn belly, glued together and varnished against the climate, would
conform exactly to the early examples of composite bows as we know them.
Such a weapon, fitted with a composite bow, once belonged to Ulrich V, Count
of Wurtemburg, and is accurately dated to 1460. It was described for the
Society of Antiquaries by the Baron de Cosson in 1892,* and can be assumed
to be typical of its type.

It is uncertain when crossbows were first fitted with steel bows, but this
improvement is noticed by the end of the fourteenth century and, after the
composite bow was rejected, continued in use into the nineteenth century.
The bow itself was made of well-tempered steel; it was extremely powerful,
that is in the military models, and required the assistance of a windlass or
cranequin to draw back its string.

*de COSSON, BARON, ibid.

ACTS AND STATUTES

In England, in the early sixteenth century, so as to enforce the more general use of the longbow, now considered the superior arm, a proclamation was issued forbidding the use of the crossbow "not only for usyng and exercisyng of longebowes and maintaining of archery within this his realme, but also for puttyng downe and destroyeing of Crossbowes and hande gonnes and other unlawfull games". This Act forbidding the possession of the crossbow was introduced in 1508 and was reinforced by statute, mandate or proclamation five times between 1512 and 1534. In 1536 the Act was repealed and the use of this weapon was permitted, except in the king's parks and forests. This legislation was once more renewed in 1537 but this time licences were granted to various persons, such as foresters and keepers, to carry crossbows to kill game. This marked the beginning of the use of the crossbow solely as a sporting weapon, in which guise it enjoyed a further period of popularity in England and Europe extending to the early nineteenth century.

In 1542, the last statute against crossbows and hand-guns was passed by Parliament. This one imposed the heavy fine of £20 on any unauthorised person keeping a crossbow, and stated among other reasons for suppression of the weapon, " . . . that divers murders had been perpetrated by means of crossbows, and that malicious and evil-minded people carried them ready bent and charged with bolts, to the great annoyance and risk of passengers on the highway". From this time shooting with the crossbow became an activity to be enjoyed only by the leisured classes; noblemen, rich landowners and even church dignitaries were favourably disposed to its use, despite its warlike associations, and it became a fashionable sporting pastime of the hunting, shooting and fishing fraternity. In the summer of 1621 the Archbishop of Canterbury, George Abbott, was involved in an unfortunate incident concerning the sporting crossbow. He had been invited to a hunting party and, when shooting at a buck, His Grace had the misfortune to kill a gamekeeper. A coroner's jury exonerated him from blame and King James himself declared that "none but a fool or knave would think the worse of a man for such an occurrence", adding the comment that the like had often nearly happened to himself. The Archbishop was greatly distressed; he prescribed for himself a monthly fast and settled £20 a year on the unfortunate widow which, in the words of a contemporary historian, "soon procured her another husband". Another story of this period, in which the crossbow played the principal part, is the only suicide on record committed with this weapon. Francis Norris, first Viscount Thame, brooding over imagined affronts after having suffered the indignity of imprisonment, mortally wounded himself in the face and neck and died as a result.

A fine example of a sixteenth-century siege crossbow which was utilised by the Germans during World War I (1914–18) for throwing percussion bombs to a greater distance than by hand. It was probably found in Belgium.

THE SPORTING CROSSBOW

The fact that the crossbow rapidly became the hunting weapon of the wealthier classes encouraged makers to produce superb specimens embellished with ivory decorations, inlaid wood and carvings; and many of these richly finished crossbows of the sixteenth, seventeenth and eighteenth centuries are still preserved in museum collections the world over. Some of the finest examples of craftsmanship came from Spain, where a powerful crossbow was used for killing deer, wild boar and chamois; a lighter version was employed for smaller game using bolts smeared with poison, known in the sixteenth century as the Crossbowman's Herb. The method of preparation of this poison was as follows: "This decoction is made of the roots of the white Hellebore, which should be gathered towards the end of August as it is then at its best season and strength. The way to treat them is to take off all earth and any kind of viscous matter which may adhere to them and wash them well. After this they should be pounded and placed under a press to extract all their juice, which will have to be carefully strained and then put over a fire to boil. All froth and viscosity which may remain must be skimmed off the juice. When this is done, the juice must be strained again and then set in the sun from ten o'clock in the morning till the day declines. This process will have to be repeated for three or four days or more. Each day before the juice is set in the sun it must be strained, when it should be like syrup, and of the same colour but thicker. If you put a straw or a bit of stick in it, it should adhere to it, and that which gathers together most quickly and which if smelt makes people sneeze violently, is the strongest." This description of making poison is taken from a work on field sports of 1644.

In Spain the stone-bow, or pellet-bow, was particularly popular. This type of crossbow, designed to shoot stones and lead balls, appeared in the sixteenth century and was developed particularly for hunting small game. Those made for nobles and princes had splendidly carved woodwork and delicately chased steel fittings. These were light bows; some, intended for ladies, could even be held and aimed with one hand, and those of the seventeenth century were often provided with built-in cocking levers. The string

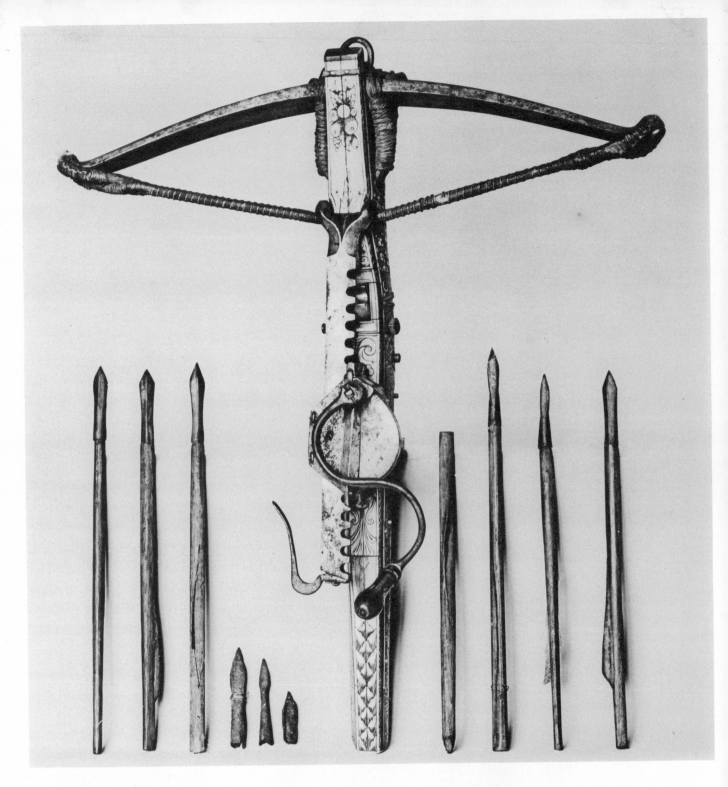

A beautifully decorated Tyrolese crossbow of 1556, shown with its cranequin in position and a selection of military bolts variously fletched with strips of wood, feathers and leather.

of a stone-bow was doubled, and incorporated a pouch of leather or woven string in which the missile was placed; and to some the refinements of sights were added. The triggers and locks of these crossbows were designed rather differently from those used in the more conventional types of weapon. The nut was replaced by a lever which incorporated a hook to retain the string, and this was tripped by a simple spring-loaded catch. The English bullet-shooting crossbow, a direct descendant of the earlier stone-bow, was a handsome and effective weapon sold by gunmakers in the early nineteenth century

R.B.del. N.Bonnart ruë S.t Iacques à l'Aigle, auec priuil.

The Princess de Guemene in the character of
Diana. This goddess was greatly admired by the
feminine nobility of Europe as, for one thing, she
represented a longed-for emancipation of her sex.

The traditional theme of Robin Hood as a poor man's friend; a poster issued by the Budget Protest League.

Detail of a woodcut by Johannes Stradanus (1535–1605), showing the use of a sixteenth-century stone-bow in a rabbit hunt. From *Venationes Ferarum*, 1578, which includes 105 large plates of sporting scenes.

for about twelve to fifteen guineas (now equivalent to about £75), and was used for rabbit shooting or keeping down rooks. This weapon was popular for about 100 years and, according to Sir Ralph Payne-Gallwey,* "Few people are aware how well and truly they were made, how accurately they shot or how much they were valued by sportsmen in former days." As sporting weapons the stone-bow and bullet-shooting crossbow enjoyed a popularity on the Continent similar to that experienced in England, as the writing of contemporary authors and artists amply illustrate. It was also in Europe that special forms of crossbow shooting descended from the ancient traditions of using this weapon, and one or two such survivals are singled out as being of particular interest.

CROSSBOW GUILDS

During the fourteenth and fifteenth centuries numerous companies of crossbowmen were formed in France and Belgium for the protection of their individual towns, and these companies of skilled, often knightly, crossbow-men were granted many rights and privileges. When the crossbow was re-placed as a warlike arm by the hand-gun it reverted to being used for sport, one application of which was target shooting. The mark chiefly used in

*PAYNE-GALLWEY, SIR RALPH, *The Crossbow* (1903)

A detail from a sixteenth-century painting showing a royal stag hunt. A group of nobles, armed with crossbows, pick off the game as it is driven towards them. Prominently shown are the two main types of bolt heads used for hunting, the crescent shape and the wide barbed point.

The crossbow became popular as a target weapon in Europe, where fraternities of archers were formed to take this form of shooting quite seriously. This painting, which is in the Luxembourg Museum, was painted by E. Buland.

The Archer, a Flemish engraving by Peter Serwonters, dated Antwerp 1574. The unusual angle of the principal subject admirably conveys a feeling of steadiness obtained by means of a carefully arranged stance. The archers in the background, shooting sky-wards, have a popinjay as their target, popular on the continent as an alternative form of archery practice.

crossbow shooting was the "popinjay". This peculiar form of practice dates from at least the thirteenth century, and from that time until the present day it has been a common amusement in some parts of the Continent. A former custom in France and Belgium was for each company of crossbowmen to hold an annual fête at which their "King of the Crossbowmen" or "King of the Bird" was decided for the ensuing year. The "king" was the best marksman of a company or the one who succeeded in winning the first prize of the meeting. Many records exist giving the details of a glittering cavalcade of royal crossbowmen, for monarchs and princes frequently took part in these contests and the patronage they gave to these companies was highly valued. We know from the chronicles of Brussels that the Archduke Albert readily took part in the recreations of the people and in 1615 his wife, the Infanta Isabella, was proclaimed "Queen of the Crossbowmen". The following, according to the account of Gerard van Loon, were the circumstances under which this event took place: "The Grand Confraternity of Crossbowmen of Brussels made great preparations for a match with a crossbow at a large

DeBoons Inuentor
Berwouter fecit.

leather popinjay, according to custom, at the cemetery of Notre-Dame du Sablon. On the 5th of May, the day fixed for the celebration, all eyes were turned towards the Archduchess, who, standing by the side of her husband in the midst of the crowd of crossbowmen, took the bended crossbow and after sighting for a short time let the arrow fly. Whether by luck or by skill, to the inexpressible delight of all present, she brought down the bird though it was set up as high as the steeple. A universal shout of joy rose to heaven more quickly than that happy arrow fell back again to earth. It seemed as if everyone imagined that he himself had struck the bird through the hands of his sovereign, who, in the midst of all that applause and without losing anything of her usual dignity, accepted the Kingship of the Confraternity and did not disdain to become a simple citizen among simple citizens. The lady was conducted in triumph to the high altar of the Sablon church and decorated with the insignia of her new dignity."

The Society of Crossbowmen of Dresden was another company with an ancient foundation whose members enjoyed shooting at the "Dresden Bird", a large, gaily-coloured wooden bird fixed to the top of a mast 136 feet in height. This target somewhat resembled the Imperial Eagle of Germany and was comprised of numerous pieces of different shapes and values. Each of some fifty pieces was named, and the crossbowman who brought one down was paid in accordance with its value as a prize. A special bolt with a blunt steel head, known as a *kronenbolzen*, was used by the Crossbowmen of Dresden. John Evelyn, when he visited Geneva in 1646, saw crossbow shooting and commented on it in his *Diary*. "A little out of the Towne is a spaceous field which they call Campus Martius . . . for here on every Sonday after the evening devotions, this precise people permitt their youths to exercise armes and shoote in gunns and in the long and crossebowes, in which they are excedingly expert, reputed to be as dextrous as any people in the world." The custom of shooting the crossbow for honoured titles has survived until today, the people of Switzerland still having their Federal tournament every five years and the cantonal and district competitions at more regular intervals.

Another event which has a direct link with the past is the contest between the crossbowmen of two towns on the borders of Tuscany and Umbria, San Sepolcro and Gubbio. These are the only two Italian towns which preserve the ancient practice of crossbow shooting, and each year they challenge each other to a feat of arms with these weapons. In 1151, when Gubbio was attacked by eleven surrounding towns, the holy Bishop Ubald Baldassini, later canonised, took matters into his own hands. He perfected the Gubbian crossbow of the time, taught his fellow townsmen how to use it and so saved the town from its enemies. To celebrate this event, and as a symbol of their preparedness to drive off further invaders, the good people of Gubbio each year publicly display their prowess with the crossbow. The festival is taken

Each year for centuries the crossbowmen of Gubbio, in Italy, have publicly displayed their skill by means of a feat of arms with their own special weapon. The contest is held primarily to celebrate the successful defence of their town in 1151 by the use of an improved crossbow.

seriously and care is taken to reproduce, as nearly as possible, the setting and mood of a medieval celebration of thanksgiving.

CROSSBOWS AMONG PRIMITIVE PEOPLES

Apart from Europe, the crossbow was used in a primitive and undeveloped form in various other parts of the world, sometimes brought there by traders or soldiers or, occasionally, handed down from ancient times as part of the heritage of the peoples using it. In Scandinavia, for instance, it was used in its simplest form as a weapon for shooting whales and for hunting other animals, and it also appeared in a similar form among the Greenland Eskimoes. The Norwegian weapon was equipped with a great bow of yew and shot a vicious bolt, sometimes poisoned, of a proportionately large size. An apparatus for cocking the bow, made of wood and approximating the "goat's foot lever" in design, was operated in a similar fashion to this device. The trigger mechanism, however, was quite unlike any of the methods considered so far. The stock was split in two horizontally for most of its length so that when the two pieces, joined by a hinge at the fore-end, were squeezed together in an action somewhat like that of domestic nut-crackers, a plug was forced upwards through a hole to dislodge the string from a notch to project the bolt. The mechanism was crudely arranged, but proved to be an efficient method of release although liable to accidental discharge. A form of crossbow, related to the Norwegian type and having a precisely similar release mechanism, is found, rather surprisingly, in a relatively small area of West Africa.

There is reliable evidence to show that some time in the sixteenth century European expeditions introduced the crossbow to the west equatorial region of the African continent. That the natives of Nigeria were the first to adopt it from these visitors, in the same way that they gained their knowledge of working bronze, seems to be a reasonable probability, and from there it was dispersed westwards to the Mandingo country and eastwards through the Cameroons district to the Gabon. The local varieties seem to be, for the most part, derivatives from one original prototype. The design of the African cross-

The use of the crossbow in West Africa. The wooden bow is mounted on a stock which is split into two levers, providing a primitive release device. Arrows, of thin slivers of bamboo, are poisoned with an extract from the seed of the *Strophanthus gratus.*

The crossbowmen of Gubbio, in medieval costume, drawn up in the town square in preparation for their celebration of thanksgiving. The great crossbows, which are authentic replicas of the original twelfth-century models, can be seen in detail.

bow became modified to suit the taste of the native craftsman and to comply with the artistic tradition of his tribe, in addition to modifications governed by the characteristics of his local materials. The stock became longer and thinner than the Scandinavian examples, the bow became shorter and stouter, and the bolts were finally evolved as needle-thin slivers of cane about a foot long, fletched with the segment of a green leaf, and smeared with poison obtained from the seed of a vine called by the natives "nea" *(Strophanthus gratus)*, which was said to remain effective for a month. The bolt, which

The crossbows carried by these natives of the Hill Tribes, Thailand (formerly Siam), are primitive in construction and simple in operation. The bows are of bamboo and the bolts are sharpened slivers of the same wood with dried grass fitted as vanes.

A Visit to the Armourer. An original treatment of the popular sentiment for the natural gentleness between extreme youth and old age. The miniature crossbow made as a toy for the children can be a killer, and many examples of pistol crossbows, which can be managed in one hand, have been produced by the crossbow makers of Europe. From the original picture formerly in the collection of William Webster.

was extremely light in weight, was held in position on the stock by a dab of wax, a supply of which was kept handy in a specially made depression under the stock. The natives were skilled in the use of these bows at ranges of up to about thirty yards, holding them somewhat like a rifle, and sighting along the length of the stock.

Although the distribution of the African crossbow, as a serious weapon, is so restricted, there are to be found outside the region of west equatorial Africa certain appliances in which the general principle of crossbow mechanism is adopted. Toy crossbows, for example, are found in districts far removed from where the crossbow proper is found; and there is also that widely-distributed appliance, the crossbow game-trap, varieties of which are to be found in many widely separated regions. These derivatives may have been independently introduced into Africa through Moslem influence after the Crusades. Another region where the crossbow was found in a very crude and

primitive form was south-east Asia, including Thailand, Burma, Vietnam, Indonesia and the Malay archipelago. Bamboo, indigenous to this area, was the invariable choice for the bow, and bolts with leaf fletchings were roughly made from the same material and merely sharpened to assist penetration. In this part of the world there are a number of interesting survivals of the crossbow, each having individual peculiarities of construction and operation developed by reason of environment and circumstance of use. To detail each one would serve little purpose other than to illustrate the lasting nature of the special knowledge of those archery skills which made their construction possible, spurned by some as a mechanical form of bowmanship and thus not true archery, while to others, providing material for a deep and absorbing study of a specialised form of missile projection.

That the crossbow does not demand the same personal effort and dexterity in use as does the long-bow, is not to be denied; but it does require a knowledge of engineering principles and an understanding of ballistics somewhat beyond that required for the hand-bow. The history of the crossbow is a remarkable one, particularly having regard to the fact that it is a mechanical contrivance which has altered little in basic concepts over possibly some 3,000 years. Despite the drawbacks which prevented it from becoming a weapon of the field of battle *par excellence*, it has served faithfully during its long career. As a sporting weapon it found its highest achievement and, as such, attracted standards of craftsmanship never before equalled, enabling it to stand on its own as a work of art in addition to its well-defined utilitarian purpose. Some mechanically-minded archers of the present day still find the crossbow an absorbing and challenging weapon, and find time to construct it from modern materials in the traditions of the past; and endless hours are spent by these enthusiasts in shooting their present-day equivalents of medieval crossbows, comparing their performance with that recorded from more leisured times.

SELECT BIBLIOGRAPHY

Alm, J., *Europeiska Armborst* [1946]

Balfour, Henry, *The Origin of West African Crossbows*, Smithsonian Report [1910]

de Cosson, Baron, *The Crossbow of Ulrich V, Count of Wurtemburg, 1460*, Archaeologia, Vol. LIII [1892]

Delaunay, L. A., *Étude Sur les Anciennes Compagnies D'Archers, D'Arbalértriers et D'Arquebusiers* [1879]

Giorgetti, G., *Le Armi Antiche* [1964]

Giorgetti, G., *L'Arco, La Balestra e Le Macchine Belliche* [1964]

Mann, James G., *A Crossbow of the Good King Rene*, The Connoisseur [1934]

Payne-Gallwey, Sir Ralph, *The Crossbow* [1903]

Powell-Cotton, P. H. G., *Notes on Crossbows and Arrows from French Equatorial Africa*, Man, Vol. XXIX, No. 1 [1929]

Viollet-le-Duc, M., *Dictionnaire Raisonné Du Mobilier Français* [1874]

10 The Symbolism of Archery

So long as the new moon returns in
heaven a bent, beautiful bow, so long
will the fascination of archery keep
hold of the hearts of men.

J. MAURICE THOMSON

THE study of myth, which has been described as "the gossamer cloak of folk memory overlaying the bare bones of prehistory", invites at least two alternative methods of approach; either by taking every story as falling into the category of children's tales or religious inventions, or by considering the myth as symbolical of good or evil according to the fashion of the period. The two aspects are interrelated as far as we are concerned. In his unsophisticated and naïve state primitive man marvelled at what he saw without understanding cause and effect, and, in observing the action of a bow, could reason neither why it projected an arrow nor why that arrow was able to become an airborne killer. That the bow and arrow did act in this way he knew, but being unable to reason why it did so he accepted these things as unfathomable mysteries to be treated with respect and awe. By the use of the bow and arrow man had filled his pot and defended his hearth for thousands of years, and his choice of this weapon as a symbol of survival is not to be wondered at. What, then, more natural than that it should be granted magical powers, and that the heroes of memory who wielded it should become supernatural?

To the person who has experienced that indefinable something which connects man and bow, or who can remember that perfect shot when the arrow leaves the bow effortlessly, almost under its own power and positive

316

Sagittarius, the zodiacal constellation of the Archer. The mythical Centaur was fabled to have been transformed into this constellation and, according to medieval romance, fought in the Trojan army against the Greeks. From *De astrorum scientia*, 1489.

in its direction, the choice of a bow and arrow as a symbol is easily understandable. Illuminating an archer's sense of one-ness with his bow is the long-hallowed (though now little heard) phrase which speaks of shooting *in* a bow, as opposed to *with* a bow. Then, Bishop Latimer, in his famous sermon,* spoke of "laying one's body in the bow".

The mythological significance of the bow and arrow is diverse and widespread and the implements of archery have been used as a symbol to denote good or evil for many centuries. Almost every nation can boast of at least one bowman-hero, many of them with a surprisingly similar story attached, from the myths of ancient Greece and sagas of Scandinavia to the medieval heroes of Europe and the folk tales of the North American Indians.

ELF BOLTS

In the latter half of the seventeenth century Dr Plot, writing a natural history of Staffordshire, makes one of the first references to the finding of flint arrow-heads in Britain. He tells us that in Scotland they were called elf-arrows—*lamiarum sagittae*—the belief being that they were dropped from the clouds. The Irish used a similar description—*aithadh*, or elf-bolt. A much older representation of an ancient arrow-head was described as a *glossopetra* (a stone said to have the shape of a human tongue). These strange objects, according to Pliny, were "thought by magicians to be very necessary for those that court fair women". He also mentioned that sleeping on arrows extracted from a body acted as a potent love charm. It was a common belief during the sixteenth and seventeenth centuries that to carry such artefacts was certain protection from drowning, and a guard against being struck by

*LATIMER, Bishop HUGH, *Seven Sermons Before Edward VI, 1549*, edited by Edward Arber (1869)

lightning. Often these elf-bolts were mounted as charms; they were frequently copied, the familiar shape being imitated and made up in some durable material such as bronze, and they were reproduced in semi-precious stones in France and Britain. Among the North American Indians arrow-heads were used as charms and amulets, the basic belief being that they were a potent charm against witchcraft, a good-luck token in fact, and as such they were carefully preserved as sacred relics. Before going into battle the warrior would ensure that the arrow-head amulet he carried had been blessed by the medicine-man who, according to tribal custom, would recite special incantations for the purpose.

The arrow itself has probably been imagined to appear in a greater variety of supernatural forms than any other weapon; it has been transformed into a bird in Alaska, and it afforded transportation in Arabia. In one story there is an arrow with eyes which flies anywhere it is sent without the benefit of a bow. Then there is the special arrow which strikes what it hears; the Hawaiians have a speaking arrow; and the Japanese, one that hums. Arrows play a

The Education of Achilles, after the painting in the Louvre by Henri Regnault. Achilles, one of the most celebrated characters in Greek mythology, was chosen by Homer to be the hero of the *Iliad*. His education in the military arts was the responsibility of Chiron, the centaur, who is seen here instructing his pupil in archery. Achilles was finally killed at Troy by Paris, who shot an arrow at his heel, the only vulnerable part of his body.

major rôle in legends from widely separated places and the "arrow-chain" motif appears quite frequently, being found in folk tales from America, Brazil, Ecuador, Siberia, Oceania and Africa, to name but a few. The typical theme is that the hero shoots a large number of arrows into the sky, one after the other, so rapidly that they form a chain up which he travels, usually to rescue a friend. Arrows were sometimes charged with magic power, as the writings of the ancient world show. This passage from ancient India for instance, is significant in its mystic meaning—"Cloud of arrows, sharpened with spells, fly forth discharged: go hit the adversaries, leave no single enemy alive." These special magical endowments were possibly secured through the intervention of Isu Devi, the arrow goddess to whom the ancient Indians made special supplications. The magical direction of arrows also appears to have been a favourite practice among many nations. Loha Penn, the Madras god of iron, steered the arrows of his followers against the enemy and even averted their countershafts. Saint Francis, one of the best known and loved of saints, was said to have personally diverted the arrows of the Scots at the Battle of Bannockburn, and at the Battle of Tri-Gruinard in 1598 a little man called Du-Sith, generally believed to be a fairy, was said to have been responsible for guiding by magical means the arrow which killed Sir Lachlan MorMaclean.

SYMBOLIC ARROWS

To the Japanese, practising archery as an adjunct to Zen Buddhist training, arrows took on special qualities. According to them the arrow shot from a

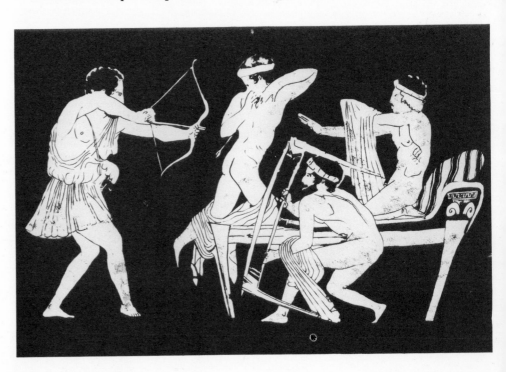

Odysseus, on returning home from his many wanderings, slays the suitors of Penelope, his wife. The use of a thumb release can be assumed from the arrangement of his right hand. From a red-figure cup from Tarquinii, fifth century B.C.

Superstitious country folk used ancient arrow-heads as magic charms. This fine example of a Bronze Age barbed and tanged point of flint has been mounted in a silver ring as a treasured possession having supernatural qualities.

bow should move as quietly as a breath, and "indeed, seeming to be a living thing", and this process of personification was used to excellent advantage by Saxton Pope in an expressive passage from his book *Hunting the Hard Way.* "The flight of the arrow is symbolic of life itself. It springs from the bow with high aim, flies towards the blue heaven above, and seems to have immortal power. The song of its life is sweet to the ear. The rush of its upward arc is a promise of perpetual progress. With perfect grace it sweeps onwards, though less aspiring. Then, fluttering imperceptibly, it points downward and with ever increasing speed, approaches the earth, where, with a deep sigh, it sinks into the soil, quivers with spent energy, and capitulates to the inevitable."

Since man could think for himself he must have been thankful for the precious gift of invention which gave him the bow, and it is only natural that it featured very prominently in his symbolism. The symbolic significance of the bow does not only reveal itself in myth and legend, however. For tribes in central India the arrow became a symbol of virility, personifying "man" in cult and tribal ritual, and it is featured in any number of betrothal and marriage ceremonies, such as the one practised by the Uraon, during which the following marriage song is sung:

The arrow which your bride has brought to you,
Take it, O brother mine, take it with you
To hunt, to kill the spotted deer,
Do take it with you, O brother, to the hunt.

The Jivaro of Brazil believed that their witch doctors could destroy or maim them by shooting mysterious, invisible arrows into their chest or neck, and

Two interpretations have been given for the arrows piercing this palaeolithic bison. They may imply a wish-fullfilment of the hunt to be, or they may represent fertility symbols. From a cave painting at Nieux.

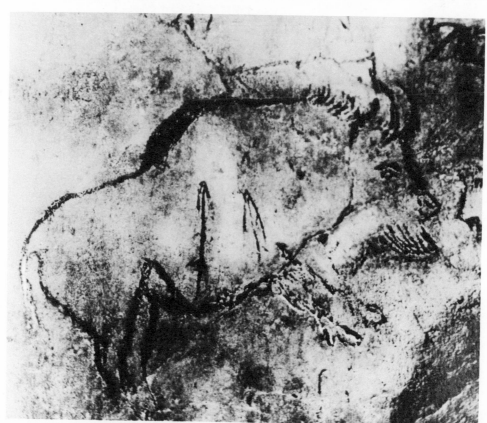

the shamans, sorcerers and magicians among many other groups of primitive archer-peoples frequently made use of the special magical powers of arrows or bows. Many are the forms of magico-religious ceremony in which the bow and arrow feature as essential apparatus, one of which was the use of homeopathic or "sympathetic" magic. Such primitive rites, which have been handed down over many thousands of years, possibly little changed with the passage of time, usually involved the primitive hunter, who, to ensure that the hunt or even the course of the battle would be successful, performed a ceremony which imitated the results he wished to obtain. In the great cave paintings of Europe this is vividly illustrated in many examples of mortally wounded man or beast, the hoped-for accuracy of the archer's shafts being well defined, leaving no doubt as to the intention of the hunter or warrior.

The invisible arrows of superstitious belief take many forms, perhaps the best known being Cupid's arrows of desire. We could quote numerous literary examples of the use of this delightful superstition, but one rather succinct example will serve to illustrate the not always successful attempts by the ubiquitous juvenile archer of love to score a hit. The sometime Principal and Vice-Principal of the Cheltenham Ladies' College have been immortalised, although rather unkindly, by a verse of the nineteenth century, which has a surprising modernity for the Victorian period:

Miss Buss and Miss Beale,
Cupid's darts do not feel,
Miss Beale and Miss Buss
They are not like us.

The use of arrows to symbolise the commencement of hostilities is frequently noticed among primitive peoples. This native from Papua pricks his arm with an arrow to show that his village is at war with a neighbouring tribe.

An old master engraving of Venus, one of the most celebrated deities of the ancients, with her son Cupid, the juvenile god of love.

FORTUNE-TELLING

Trying to divine whether or not our immediate future is to be blessed with good fortune has been an intriguing pastime, in which kings and peasants have shared, since time immemorial. Everyone, throughout history, has had a certain superstitious regard for the telling of fortunes, and the kings of the ancient Middle East were no exception. From the Old Testament we learn that the king of Babylon practised divination by arrows. This is described as "belomancy", and several interesting references to it can be found. A number of methods were used but the most normal seemed to be with two arrows kept in a case and produced by a priest when required—one marked "yes" and the other "no". Results were obtained by drawing an arrow at random or shaking them from the case. Sometimes a third, blank arrow was added, which would indicate that the inquirer should do as he pleased. This method of divination was in use by the Scythians, Slavs, Germans and Arabs as well as by the Babylonians, and in his *Essay on Archery* W. M.

Moseley tells of "a very mysterious custom in general use [among the Baby-lonians] which consisted in drawing omens from the appearance of the bright points of arrows, by the inspection of which the magician or priest discovered the intentions of fate". Arrows in flight were studied and their convolutions interpreted by the Mongol shaman for the purpose of divination or foretelling the future. The late and unlamented Aleister Crowley experimented with this form of belomancy and specimens of arrows made by him can be seen today in the Museum of Witchcraft, in the Isle of Man. He is reported to have said that he could never get the damned things to work! A variation of this practice consisted of attaching labels to a given number of arrows which were shot simultaneously by a group of archers, the advice on the label of the arrow which flew furthest being accepted and acted upon. Many other forms of belomancy have been practised in places as far apart as Africa and China. In Africa the arrows were poisoned and a selected victim underwent an ordeal, the results of which augered well or otherwise. The Chinese, on the other hand, used special arrows for divination which subsequently became changed into flattened strips of bamboo; from these strips the playing card in the form we know it today derived. A similar derivation can be found in the evolution of the stave-dice of the American Indians, the originals of which were arrows.

VIRTUES AND VICES

Geoffrey Chaucer, the father of English poetry, used bows and arrows to symbolise a range of virtues and vices in his *Romaunt of the Rose*. One character in this poem is described as a bachelor and has the unlikely name of Swete-Loking. He carries with him two Turkish bows and ten broad arrows. Then follow descriptions of the bows, one being, "The foule croked bowe hidous, that knotty was, and al roynous", and the other, "Without a blemish, graceful carved and painted". Five of the arrows are named as virtues, Beautee, Simplesse, Fraunchyse (nobility), Company and Fair Semblaunt. The re-mainder are "of other gyse", Pryde, Vilanye, Shame, Wanhope (despair) and New-Thought (inconstancy). Chaucer then promises a full and complete explanation of this interesting assortment, "as fer as I have remembrance: all shall be said, I undertake, er of this boke an ende I make." It is not unusual to find this sort of deep symbolic meaning applied to the bow or to find the components of archery used as similes to illustrate human emotions or relationships. "As unto the bow a cord is, so unto the man is woman", said Longfellow in *Hiawatha's Wooing*; "though she bends him, she obeys him, though she draws him, yet she follows; useless each without the other." The femininity of archery has intrigued many writers; "Archery is a woman and her mind is passionate," wrote Richard Carew;* and the twang of the bow-

*CAREW, RICHARD, *The Survey of Cornwall* (1602)

The bow and arrow were frequently used to illustrate special qualities and emotions in fable and romance. This illustration, from a medieval French *Romaunt*, shows such an allegorical use of archery.

string sounding in the warrior's ear was likened to a woman's endearments by the early Indians.

> *Close to his ear, as fain to speak, she presses,*
> *holding her well-loved friend in her embraces.*
> *Strained on the bow, she whispers like a woman –*
> *this bow-string that preserves us in combat.*

These meanderings through the often bizarre, sometimes incomprehensible, rarely completely understood and always intriguing world of superstition "when reason borrowed fancy's golden wings" have briefly illustrated the strange and variable ways in which man has accounted for the mystery of the bow and arrow. We have seen how, in a multitude of forms, he has held this most ancient weapon in respect and awe, and how, by carefully nurturing its supernatural powers, he has ensured its success in the chase and in battle. The history and folklore of many nations can provide endless examples similar to those which we have mentioned, but we must now consider several legends involving the use of bows and arrows, which have caught the fancy of story-tellers for many centuries. Their retelling, with possibly a few additional facts, completes our story of the bow and serves as a reminder of its supreme importance as a weapon and the respect it has claimed throughout the civilized world.

MARTYRED BY THE BOW

In all no less than twenty-two European saints are represented with arrows or bows as their particular emblems. The lives of three, who have tragic associations with the bow, claim our immediate attention—namely Sebastian, patron saint of archers; Ursula, who was martyred together with her maiden companions; and Edmund, king and martyr. Sebastian, who was to become one of the most renowned of the Roman martyrs, was a young nobleman of Narbonne in Gaul and a favourite of the Emperor Diocletian, under whom he commanded a company of the famed Praetorian Guard. His secret belief in Christ was revealed when he encouraged two of his fellow officers, who were being tortured for their belief, to die rather than renounce their faith. Diocletian ordered Sebastian to abandon his faith and return to the worship of the Roman gods. On his refusal the Emperor ordered that he be bound to a stake and shot to death with arrows. The order was carried out and he was left for dead. Irene, the mother of one of his martyred friends, discovered that he was still alive, however, and secretly nursed him to health, urging him to escape from Rome. The irrepressible Sebastian was still determined to declare his faith, and this he did on the steps of the Emperor's palace,

A medieval woodcut by the Meister des Amsterdamer Kabinets of the martyrdom of St Sebastian, one of the most renowned of the Roman martyrs, who died in A.D. 288. The coarseness with which his executioners have been drawn emphasises the horror of the event.

pleading for those who had been condemned and reproaching Diocletian for his intolerance. The consequence of this boldness was a reiterated death sentence and he was finally beaten to death with clubs in the arena. The date was A.D. 288. In order that his friends might not recover Sebastian's body, it was thrown into the great sewer of Rome; nevertheless it was found, recovered and buried in the catacombs at the feet of Saints Peter and Paul. In 367 Pope St Damascus built a basilica over Sebastian's tomb on the Appian Way, and this is now one of the seven principal churches of Rome. St Sebastian became the patron saint of Chiemsee, Mannheim, Oetting, Palma, Rome, Soissons, and of the makers of military lances, fencing foils and, of course, archers. In ancient times the plague was believed to be brought by the arrows of Apollo and accordingly Sebastian became one of the chief saints invoked against this dread visitation. As he survived his ordeal of being shot by arrows, he became one of the patron saints of all the victims of the plague. Many representations in drawings, paintings and sculpture can be found of St Sebastian, who is normally depicted as a young man tied to a stake or tree with his body transfixed by arrows.

Medieval legends greatly embellished the scanty facts of the story of St

Ursula and her virgin companions, who have been variously numbered from eleven to eleven thousand. The seventeenth centenary of their martyrdom was celebrated in 1937. Ursula was the only daughter of Nothus, an illustrious and wealthy British prince, and she was sought in marriage by Conan, the son of a "certain most ferocious tyrant". Ursula, however, had dedicated herself to celibacy, and her father was torn between fear of offending God by consenting to the union, and exasperating the king by refusing it. Ursula solved the problem by persuading her father to agree to the proposal of the tyrant, but only subject to the condition that she and a chosen number of young virgins should be allowed to cruise about for three years "in the sanctity of unsullied virginity". On their way home their travels took them to Cologne, where they became involved with the Huns who were, at the time, engaged in besieging the town. All were killed except Ursula, who was offered her life in exchange for her chastity. On her refusal the Hun leader drew his bow and drove three arrows through her body. Eight hundred years later, at the supposed site of the tragedy, bones and inscriptions belonging to men, and

An impressive interpretation of the martyrdom of St Sebastian which, by its very realistic treatment, serves as a particularly poignant reminder of the patron saint of archers. By Gerard van Honhorst, (1590–1666).

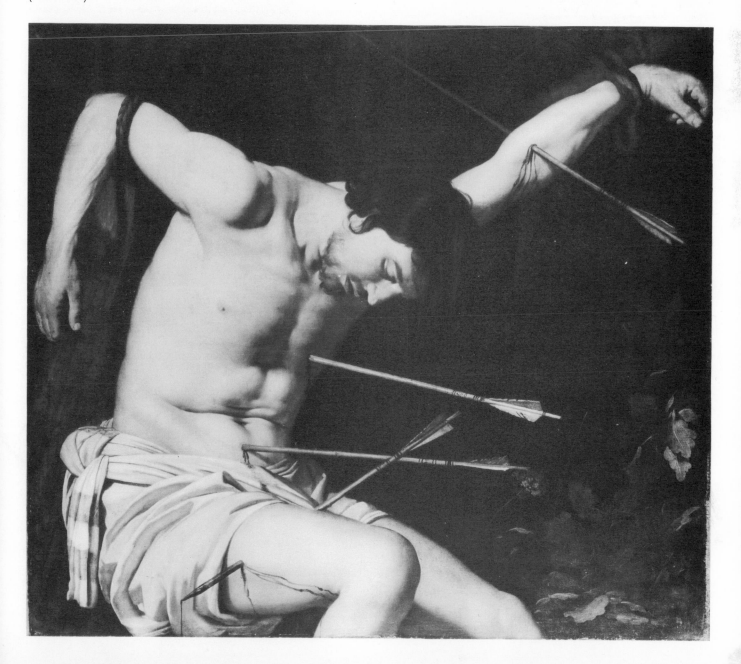

St Ursula, who with her maiden
companions suffered death at the
hands of the pagan Huns at
Cologne in the fourth century, is
shown holding the symbol of
her martyrdom in this painting
of the fifteenth century by Solario.

St Edmund, (849–870) King and
Martyr, done to death by raiding
Vikings at Hoxne, Suffolk, in 870.
His shrine gave its name to the
town of Bury St Edmunds. An
illuminated capital from John
Lydgate's *Life of St Edmund and
St Fremund*, late fourteenth
century.

later those of children, were exhumed. These startling and awkward discoveries, seriously compromising to the memory of Ursula and her companions, threw some suspicions on the official account, despite the explana-
tions offered by an ecstatic nun* who, whilst in a trance, accounted for the
presence of the unexpected male and infant relics. The feast of St Ursula was
subsequently suppressed in the calendar of the Benedictines. Whatever the
truth, the legend remains, bound up in the stories of terror created by the
early incursions of the pagan Huns into Europe, and the resistance offered by
the popular and pathetic figure of a young Christian virgin. To this day the
church of St Ursula at Cologne is visited by thousands who rely on the
intercession of this saint and still believe in the chastity and piety of Ursula
and her martyred companions.

The death, on November 20th, 870, of Edmund, king of the East Angles
from 855, has many strange aspects. The martyrdom of this saint, whose
shrine gave its name to the Benedictine abbey and town of Bury St Edmunds,
occurred on the occasion of a Danish raid into East Anglia during which the
young king was taken prisoner. As he would not renounce his faith, the Danes
tied him to a tree and shot him to death with arrows. His death, believed to
have been plotted by one Edricus, was said to have been carried out by means
of the *arc-qui-ne-faut*, a clever invention of a bow from which the arrow
never missed its mark. John Lydgate, who lived in the fourteenth century,
vividly recalled the event in his *Legend of St Edmund:*

> *The cursid danys [Danes] of new cruelte*
> *This martyr took, most gracious and benigne,*
> *Of hasty rancour bounde him to a tree.*
> *As for ther marke to sheete [shoot] at, and ther signe*
> *And in this wise, ageyne [against] hym thei maligne,*
> *Made with him arwis [arrows] of ther malis most wikke [evil]*
> *Rassemble an Yrchoun [hedgehog] fulfilled with spynys thikke.*

*Elizabeth of Shonau

After he had been killed his body was beheaded and thrown into a wood. His friends subsequently found his body and a legendary wolf is said to have found his head. The trunk and head were miraculously reunited and the last rites were paid to the martyred king. This was supposed to have taken place in Hoxne, in Suffolk, and an interesting local legend says that a small piece of iron, discovered embedded in the heart of the great St Edmund's Oak, was a surviving arrow-head from this incident. Doubt exists, however, as to its authenticity, and there is doubt also as to the actual location of this event. One of the arrows said to have been used to kill King Edmund was kept, as a sacred relic, in a church bearing his name in London. The rector of this church made arrangements to change benefices with another who resided in the country and one of the stipulations was that the arrow should also be transferred to the new parish. The rector made preparations to sail by London's river to his new living; but the boatman found he could not move the barge until the arrow was taken off, and the alternative route by road was mysteriously barred until the sacred relic was restored to its London home.

GHOSTS AND THE KNAVE OF CLUBS

Ghostly bowmen have their place among the legends connected with archery, and although such curious stories have developed into fictional entertainments, they are worthy of notice as their origins are undoubtedly rooted in folk-lore and legendary beliefs of considerable antiquity. Apart from some early tales of the more horrific type designed to scare the nervous on dark winter evenings, the archery ghost of more recent times seems to have been a sad and rather gloomy fellow, whose spectral visitations were of but brief duration. One such story concerned a Colonel Shepheard who, as a staff colonel in the 1914-18 War, travelled from Hazebrouck to Wimereux. During his journey he swears he saw the grey hooded archers of Crécy looming up in the mist, "Hooded, cloaked figures of silent, gazing men—rank beyond rank. There were thousands of them—all cloaked and hooded like monks. They rose slowly and every man stared fixedly at me. It was a queer, wistful, sad stare, like a dumb question or a dumb warning. Their cloaks were grey, almost luminous, with a fine, silvery bloom on them like moths' wings. I seemed to touch one and it came off on my fingers in a soft dust. Then slowly they sank back into the ground—rank after rank of hooded men sinking into the earth, their eyes fixed on me to the last!" Another modern ghost story concerning a vision of medieval archers during the same war was written by Arthur Machen, who was also responsible for the astounding legend of the Angels of Mons current in 1914.

The next of our archery legends concerns the Knave of Clubs. From a very early period the character depicted on this court card was shown holding

As early as the fifteenth century the Knave of Clubs was called Lancelot and looked upon as a patron of the chase and archery. From an early period he has swaggered with a great arrow. The Knave shown is taken from a Rouen court card of c. 1567, but the modern Jack of Clubs now only holds a staff with a faint suggestion of an arrow-head.

a glorified arrow as high as himself. He was considered to be the patron of sport, and particularly, it would appear, of archery, which was the pastime specially permitted and encouraged for the "fourth estate"–the peasantry and working classes. This Knave of Clubs was named Lancelot, familiar to us as the foremost knight of King Arthur's court. One story of Sir Lancelot concerns his visit to a hermit in Windsor Forest shortly before an important tournament at Westminster. A lady huntress dwelt nearby and "daily she used to hunt, and always she bore a bow with her, and no men went never with her, but always women, and they were shooters". This fair damsel, emulating the celestial Artemis, was hunting a hind which had taken refuge close to the spot chosen by Lancelot as a resting place. ". . . and she put a broad arrow in her bow and shot at the hind, and overshot the hind, and so by misfortune the arrow smote Sir Lancelot in the thick of the buttocks." The distraught lady was forgiven in true chivalric fashion, although the wound was "passing sore" and particularly embarrassing, for it was in such a place "that he might not sit in the saddle". However, Lancelot fulfilled his obligation at Westminster and smote down thirty knights, winning the prize of the tournament. He told King Arthur of the episode in the forest and how the wound was six inches deep "and in like long", which no doubt added to the glory of his exploits. On another occasion Lancelot was ambushed by archers but succeeded in extricating himself from yet another awkward situation. These stories would have endeared this knightly hero to the simple folk of medieval England, and especially to archers, who would particularly understand the extent of a wound created by an arrow; and this brave, but painful, episode would clearly account for his being shown as the Knave of Clubs with a king-size arrow.

WILLIAM TELL

Let us now consider the story of William Tell, in which James Joyce once discerned the theme of a father searching for his son, and the son searching for his father, and which, in or before the early seventeenth century, was accepted unreservedly in Switzerland as historical fact. This legend only achieved world-wide fame with the publication of Schiller's play* in 1804 and it was accepted, almost without question, until the early twentieth century when antiquarians began to recognise a resemblance in this story to legends of heroic archers from other lands. The legend of William Tell is almost too well known to need repetition. In the year 1307 Gessler, Vogt of the Emperor Albert of Hapsburg, set a hat on a pole as a symbol of imperial power, and ordered everyone who passed to do obeisance towards it. A mountaineer by the name of Tell boldly ignored this order, and by Gessler's command was

*SCHILLER, J. C. FRIEDRICH von, *William Tell*, translated by Major-General Patrick Maxwell (c. 1900)

The Swiss hero, William Tell, who played a great part in freeing his country from the Austrian yoke early in the fourteenth century. The extraordinary feat of marksmanship in shooting the apple off his son's head, shown here in an early woodcut, is regarded as legendary and has its origins in myth. From *Kronica von der Loblichen Eydtgnoschaft* (1507).

seized and brought before him. As Tell was known to be an expert archer, he was ordered, by way of punishment, to shoot an apple off the head of his own son. Despite his protestations he had to submit. The apple was placed on the child's head, Tell aimed his bow, the arrow sped and the apple fell to the ground. The Vogt, however, had noticed that Tell had stuck another arrow into his belt before shooting, and he inquired the reason. "It was for you," replied Tell; "had I shot my child, know that it would not have missed your heart." This event took place at the beginning of the fourteenth century, but

Saxo Grammaticus,* a Danish writer of the twelfth century, tells a story of a hero who lived in the tenth century in his own country, which is surprisingly similar to that of William Tell. This is how the incident is related: the hero of the story, Toko, who was in the king's service, had boasted that his skill at archery was such that, with the first shot of an arrow he could hit the smallest apple set on the top of a stick. The king upon hearing this, "transformed the confidence of the father to the jeopardy of the son", for he ordered Toko's boy to stand in place of the stick. As soon as the boy was led forth, Toko carefully instructed him to receive the whirr of the arrow as calmly as possible without moving his head, lest by a slight movement of his body the shot should prove fatal. He also made him stand with his back towards him in case he should be frightened at the sight of the arrow. Then he drew three arrows from his quiver and with the first struck the apple off the boy's head. The king queried the two remaining arrows and Toko replied, "That I might avenge on thee, the error of the first, by the point of the others, lest my innocence might happen to be afflicted, and thy injustice go unpunished." The same incident is told of Egil, brother of the mythical Velundr, in the Saga of Thidrik, and in Norwegian history the story appears, with variations, again and again. Geyto, the son of Aslak, was another archer hero who performed this feat, but this time the target becomes a nut on the boy's head.

> *On the string the shaft he laid,*
> *And God hath heard his prayer;*
> *He shot the little nut away,*
> *Nor hurt the lad a hair.*

In yet another version from the English ballads William of Cloudisley demonstrates his prowess:

> *And lay an apple on his head,*
> *And go six paces him fro*
> *And I myself with a broad arrow*
> *Shall cleave the apple in two.*

In 1584 Reginald Scot, in *The Discoverie of Witchcraft*, described the activities of a soldier named Pumher who was put on trial for witchcraft. He writes: "This was he that shot at a pennie on his sonnes head, and made ready another arrow, to have slain the duke Remgrave that commanded it." It is curious, to say the least, that these and other stories from Persia, Iceland, Denmark, Switzerland and England tell of the same incident with only minor variations, suggesting that the central theme emanated from one common

*SAXO GRAMMATICUS, *Gesta Danorum.*

source in the early folk history of a land not yet identified. Some day, possibly, new light will be thrown on this coincidence and a fresh understanding of early folk-lore will be revealed to us.

ROBIN HOOD

A work of this nature would be incomplete without reference to the most familiar character of archery legend, the prince of outlaws, Robin Hood. He has never been satisfactorily identified despite persistent efforts to trace his ancestry from the early fifteenth century to the present day by chroniclers, historians and antiquaries. Although an early writer on the subject declared that Robin Hood "existed no where but in the fertile brain of the poet", a great number of researchers have treated him as a real character and have endeavoured to discover his true pedigree. Among other data offered as "authoritative" evidence of Robin's true existence is a table of descent from Judith, a niece of the Conqueror, proving his claim to the earldom of Huntingdon. Another unlikely piece of evidence was the epitaph supposed to have been inscribed on his tombstone at Kirklees Abbey, the traditional scene of his death.

> Hear undernead dis laitl stean
> Laiz robert earl of Huntingtun
> Near arcir ver az hie sa geud
> An pipl kauld im robin heud
> Sick utlawz az hi an iz men
> Vil england nivr si agen
>
> obiit 24 Kal dekembris 1247

The literature on this subject is considerable, and there are many ingenious suggestions and theories to account for the life of this North Country outlaw who lived with his merry men in the greenwood and robbed the rich but spared the poor. Each successive writer on the matter has uncovered fresh information, rejected previous claims, or argued former theories, all of which has tended to confuse and complicate the issue rather than provide conclusive evidence of Robin Hood's historicity. His life has been assigned to the reigns of half-a-dozen kings between William I and Edward II, and obscure records have provided evidence of identification for several heroes any one of whom, if more were known, might turn out to be the original outlaw.

The people of England of the late twelfth and early thirteenth century, who were dragged down by poverty, lawlessness and extortion, found life utterly cheerless and without hope, and their outlook seemed very dark and miserable indeed. The utter lawlessness of the whole country led to misery and terror among all who were unprotected by wealth and estate, while the frightful conditions under which these lower classes existed, particularly in the country districts, bred nothing but apathy and disease. Beggars, outlaws, and wandering ruffians were left to roam unchecked, to the terror of all and sundry. It was from this maelstrom of injustice and oppression that the Robin Hood legend was born. Possibly the nearest we can get to the truth as to his existence is that the subsequent legends formed a composite hero, embodying all the affections of the peasants of the Middle Ages, who, through these tales, showed their indignation and desire for revenge against the oppression of those times. The lower classes were loyal to their king, but in the fight for a new justice their need was always for a leader, a lordly outlaw, who was not only of high birth but was also the poor man's friend. Here was hope for the future, a popular hero who caught the fancy of the people–Robin Hood fitted the part perfectly.

It is, of course, the stories with which we concern ourselves rather than the man himself, and something positive can be said of the legend, the earliest versions of which date from the fifteenth century. We know that stories of

An eighteenth-century engraving by the celebrated Thomas Bewick of the popular folk hero Robin Hood. From *Robin Hood* by Joseph Ritson (1795).

THE ENGLISH ARCHER, OR ROBIN HOOD's GARLAND.

I'll send this Arrow from my Bow,
And in a Wager will be bound,
To hit the Mark aright, although
It were for Fifteen Hundred Pounds:
Doubt not, I'll make the Wager good,
Or ne'er believe bold ROBIN HOOD.

LICHFIELD: Printed and Sold by M. MORGAN.

this outlaw were retailed before 1377–the date William Langland wrote *Piers Plowman*–for in that beautiful medieval poem in the alliterative metre, there is a reference to the "rymes of Robyn Hode". By the end of the fourteenth century Robin's fame was already universal and at this time his name was becoming proverbial. It is clear that Langland's reference was no accidental allusion to an obscure local figure, and other authors of this period mention the hero, such as the unknown writer of the *Reply of Friar Daw Topias to Jack Upland*, dated to about 1400, who said: "And many men speke of Robyn Hode, That shotte never in his bowe." Certain features recur in all the Robin Hood tales. In all of them the hero, a man denied justice and a dauntless champion of the poor and oppressed, asserts their rights and his through his wonderful skill with the long-bow. The end of the thirteenth century saw the long-bow rapidly take its place as the foremost weapon of the common people, notably among the yeomen of the Cheshire and Midland forests who had learnt its mastery from the Welsh hillmen during the wars of Edward I.

In all the ballads Robin is a marksman *sans pareil*, and the stories about him are full of incredible feats performed with the long-bow. He always succeeded in outshooting the other competitors at the various contests which he attended, often in disguise, and to this day an archery tournament is held each year in Nottingham as a reminder of his success at a contest for the sheriff's golden arrow, described in one of the ballads. "It was to Robin that the sheriff's men brought the gode arowe for the best archer that ever was." In all these activities Robin was symbolic of his race. English archers began to dominate the battles of this period, and skill at archery was becoming widespread in rustic England. By his prowess with the bow Robin set a fine example, for, in addition to being the personification of the common Englishman's resentment against oppression and injustice, he was also the model of the fighting virtues he admired.

THE BALLADS

There is a host of ballads of which Robin Hood is the hero. Most of them, at least in the form we have them, are compositions of the sixteenth and seventeenth centuries, when the traditional hero already belonged to the half-forgotten past, and as a result his story was sometimes changed out of recognition. Some of the ballads have changed little, however, and are still close enough, in all probability, to medieval versions. By far the most famous of all the ballads is the *Littel Geste of Robyn Hode and his Meiny*, and it is also one of the earliest, dating from the end of the fifteenth century. According to scholars the antique form of its language indicates that it has not been altered from a far older original, and it is possible that the poem as it stands could have been put together as early as 1400. There seem to have been at

The earliest collections of ballads of the celebrated outlaw, Robin Hood, were published in books like this *Garland*, in the possession of the Royal Toxophilite Society.

Early ballad sheets often used woodcuts such as this to illustrate the legends and stories which they contained.

least four stories which the writer of the *Geste* worked into his story; the ballad of *Robin Hood and the Knight;* the ballad of *Robin Hood, Little John and the Sheriff;* the ballad of *Robin Hood and the King;* and the ballad of *Robin Hood's Death.* Individual interpretations by later balladeers may have altered the details of these stories, but what matters is that the popularity of the story and its traditional quality remained. Robin Hood has been a popular hero for possibly eight hundred years and his stories are still eagerly sought, albeit by readers in the nursery. The subjects dealt with in these ballads were commonplace things which the ordinary folk could easily comprehend, and much of their charm is reflected in the opening lines of several of the tales, setting the rustic scene with a magic reminiscent of Chaucer. At least six of the ballads begin:

> *When shawes been sheene, and shraddes full fayre,*
> *And leves both large and longe,*
> *It is merye walking in the fair forest*
> *To heare the small birds' song.*

These ballads were invariably written by good scholars and contained matters of fact, but despite this there has been a tendency to place importance on the mythological, rather than on the historical origin of the Robin Hood legend. It is easy to confuse the imaginary folk-lore figure of these stories with heroes who really lived. In some of the ballads the leader of the outlaws is a real personage like Hereward the Wake, Fulk Fitzwarin—the baron who defied King John—or Adam of Gurdon, who held out against the future Edward I in the Hampshire forests after the fall of de Montfort. Even William

An Anglo-Saxon walrus ivory reliquary cross, dating from the eleventh century, with Ishmael, the archer son of Abraham and Hagar, carved on the lid. Representations of this biblical bowman are not uncommon in England from the eighth century.

In this detail of "The Crowning of Christ", the artist Hieronymus Bosch (1450–1515), has used a crossbow bolt as a symbol of impending death. A greater sense of tragedy and horror results when a commonplace object such as this is used in juxtaposition with the more evil components of such a scene.

Wallace of Scotland figures in one. Most of them, however, carry names that cannot be identified with any historical character, such as Adam Bell of the Clough, William Clowdisley and, of course, Robin Hood himself.

PAGAN ORIGINS

The name Robin Hood may have come down from pagan folk-lore. Robin is a spirit name; it is the commonest of all names given to familiars by witches, according to accounts of their trials, and it is the name of the most famous of all wood-spirits–Robin Goodfellow. It may also have been derived from Hudekin, the Saxon wood-sprite. Those who claim a mythological origin for our outlaw point out that the pranks of the spirits of the forest have a certain similarity with the deeds of Robin Hood; he too, misled wanderers in waste places, and he too rewarded the poor and deserving, performing their labours for them and leaving sixpences in their shoes or on their doorsteps. He has also been associated with rustic May Day rites and the Morris Dance. Robin Hood's "games" were condemned both by Bishop Latimer and by the Parliament of Scotland as "lewde sportes", their pagan, and no doubt lusty, nature understandably meeting with disapproval by the Church which was, at that time, struggling for power. The bowman-outlaw of legend has lent his name to many natural features which support the sup-

A rare fifteenth-century ceremonial arrow-head from Bohemia, probably the badge of office of the Captain of an Archers Guild or the Master of a Brotherhood of St Sebastian.

posed link with pagan myth. He has barrows at Whitby, Guisborough and Ludlow, and the English landscape is littered with his boulders, huge and queer-shaped stones, and various other topographical features all bearing his name.

Robin Hood, whose name has become a household word especially dear to archers both past and present, and who has captured the hearts of generations of ordinary folk, is undoubtedly rooted permanently in the Western world as a popular and familiar hero. The legends of this outlaw still command the attention of scholars who occasionally delve into the fascination of the history and myth of his existence and the consequence of his activities in the early Middle Ages. Every aspect of his character has been carefully deduced and analysed, and he usually emerges as a high-minded, selfless hero whose main purpose in life was to help those less fortunate than himself. He has his modern opponents though, one of whom described him as "a common thief" and the gang he assembled in Sherwood Forest as "a crew of cut-throat rogues". Another described him, with breath-taking pomposity, as "the active exponent of the fallacy that the end justifies the means". Whatever our regard for Robin Hood, whether childish fancy, adult affection or disbelief and contempt, and despite the enigma of his origin, the exciting and romantic legends that surround him are of compelling interest, and by their telling can still rouse in the heart of man some of the rumbustious feelings of the fight for freedom that our forefathers knew.

The foregoing miscellany of legends, myths, magic and superstition has by no means exhausted the vast store of tales and beliefs which have special associations with the bow and arrow. It would take several volumes to record all the wonderful and fascinating ways in which archery has featured in the folk-lore and traditional histories of most of the civilised world. The theme of all these stories is invariably a simple one, the contest between good and evil. We have seen how the arrow became an instrument of war and death, and a symbol of the plague, pain or pestilence. In its alternative rôle it represented pleasure and desire or personified masculinity in cult and tribal ritual. These "winged messengers of death" were often specially endowed with magical powers, and ceremonial arrows became important emblems of civic power and badges of rank, dignity and superiority. We have also seen how the bow became highly respected as a symbol of wordly power and how it was nobly employed as an insignia of kingship, and even how it was preserved as a sacred weapon. Archery has been enshrined in the English language by numerous proverbs and sayings which allude to various aspects of the use of the bow. "Straight as an arrow"; "a bolt from the blue"; "two strings to one's bow"; "wide of the mark"; "bolt upright"; "highly strung"; these and many other such commonplace toxophilitic references, all of ancient usage, indicate the familiarity with which the bow was once regarded. It is curious that these and many other expressions should still survive and be used by folk who have now little inkling as to their meaning or origin.

LAST WORD FROM THE BOW

Finally, from Richard Carew's *Survey of Cornwall* let the bow speak for itself: "My Deare Friends, I come to complaine upon you, but to yourselves: to blame you, but for your good; to espostulate with you, but in the way of reconciliation. Alas, that my desert can justify your abandoning my fellowship, and hanging me thus up, to be smoke-starved over your chimnies? I am no stranger unto you: but by birth, your Country woman; by dwelling, your neighbour; by education, your familiar: neither is my Company shameful; for I haunt the light and open fields: nor my Conversation dangerous; nay, it shields you from dangers, and those not the least, but of greatest Consequence, the dangers of Warre. And as in fight I give you Protection, so in Peace I supplie your Pastime; and both in Warre and Peace, to your lymmes I yeelde active Plyantnesse, and to your bodies healthful Exercise: yea, I provide

The bow and arrow was often used by medieval artists to symbolise death and destruction. This skeletal bowman, in a German woodcut of 1514, reminded the devout of the Middle Ages to reflect on the inevitability of man's mortality.

MICH·ANG·
BONAROTI·INV·

you food when you are hungrie, and helpe digestion when you are full.
Whence then proceedeth this unkinde and unusual strangenesse? Am I heavy
for burthen? Forsooth, a fewe light stickes of wood. Am I combrous for
Carriage? I couch a part of myself close under your girdle, and the other part
serveth for a walking-staff in your hand. Am I unhandsome in your sight?
Every Piece of mee is comely, and the whole keepeth an harmonical proportion.
Lastly, am I costly to bee provided? Or hard to be maintayned? No, Cheapness

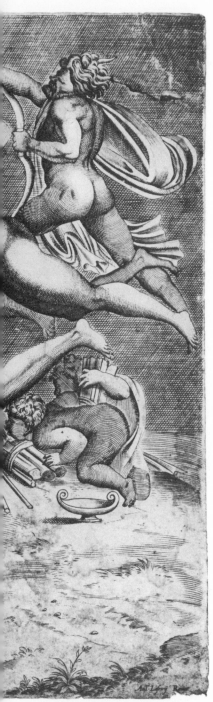

An engraving after Michelangelo (1475–1564), of a group of archers shooting at a *herma*. This representation of Hermes, of Greek myth, was usually found in doorways of private houses, at cross-roads or in the gymnasia. The reason why this image was used for target practice remains obscure.

is my Purveyour, Easiness my Preserver: Neither doe I make you blow away your Charges with my breath, or taynt your Nose with my scent, nor defile your face and fingers with my Colour, like that hell-borne Murderer, whome you accept before me. I appeale then to your valiant Princes, Edwards, and Henries, to the Battayles of Cresey, Poyters, Agincourt, and Flodden; to the Regions of Scotland, Fraunce, Spaine, Italy, Cyprus, yea and Jury; to be Umpires of this Controversie: all which (I doubt not) will with their evidence playnely prove, that when mine adverse party was yet scarcely borne, or lay in her swathling Clouts, through mee onely your Auncestours defended their Country, vanquished their enemies, succoured their friends, enlarged their Dominions, advaunced their Religion, and made their names fearefull to the present age, and their fame everlasting to those that ensue. Wherefore, my dear friends, seeing I have so substantially evicted the right of my cause, conforme your wils to reason, conforme your reason by practice, and convert your practice to the good of yourselves and your Country. If I be praise-worthy, esteeme mee: if necessary, admit mee: if profitable, employ mee: so shall you revoke my death to life, and shew yourselves no degenerate issue of such honourable Progenitours. And thus much for Archery, whose tale, if it be disordered, you must beare withall, for shee is a woman, and her minde is passionate."

SELECT BIBLIOGRAPHY

Benedictine Monks, The, (Compilers) *The Book of Saints* [1947]
Budge, Sir E. G. Wallis, *Amulets and Superstitions* [1930]
Carew, Richard, *Survey of Cornwall* [1602]
Chaucer, Geoffrey, *The Complete Works*, Edited by Rev. Walter Skeat [1894]
Coomaraswany, Ananda K., *The Symbolism of Archery*, [n.d.]
Crosland, Jessie, *Outlaws in Fact and Fiction* [1959]
Drake, Maurice and Wilfred, *Saints and their Emblems* [1916]
Edwards, C. B. & Heath, E. G., *In Pursuit of Archery* [1962]
Egan, Pierce, *Robin Hood and Little John* [1840]
Frazer, J. G., *The Golden Bough* [1957]
Funk & Wagnall, *Standard Dictionary of Folklore, Mythology and Legend*
Gutch, John Mathew, *A Lytell Geste of Robin Hode* [1842]
Harmatta, J., *The Golden Bow of the Huns*, Acta Archaeologia, Vol. I [1951]
Harris, P. Valentine, *The Truth about Robin Hood*, [n.d.]
Hervey, Lord Francis, *The History of King Eadmund the Martyr* [1929]
Homer, *The Odyssey*, trans. by E. V. Rieu [1945]
Keen, Maurice, *The Outlaws of Medieval Legend* [1961]
Longfellow, Henry, W., *The Collected Works* [1887]
Machen, Arthur, *The Bowmen and other Legends of the War* [1915]
Maude, Thomas, *Robin Hood's Garland* [1814]
Percy, Thomas, *Reliques of Ancient English Poetry* [1765]
Ritson, Joseph, *Robin Hood* [1832]
Roberts, John S., (Compiler) *The Legendary Ballads of England and Scotland*, [n.d.]
Scot, Reginald, *The Discoverie of Witchcraft* [1584]
Thurston, E., *Ethnographic Notes in Southern India* [1906]

Plain bows of wood only.

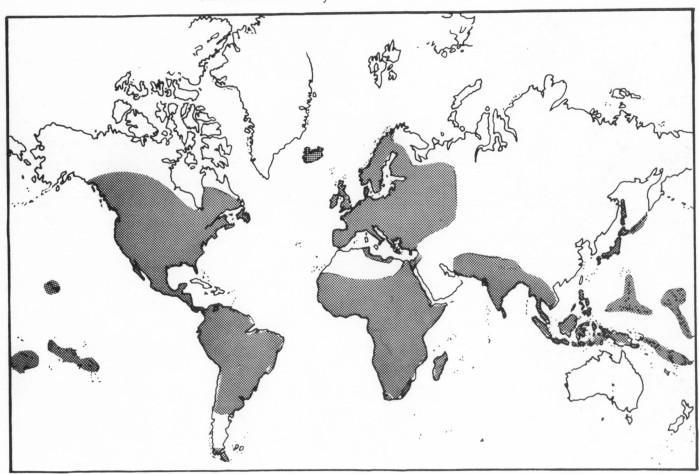

Plain bows allied to composite bows.

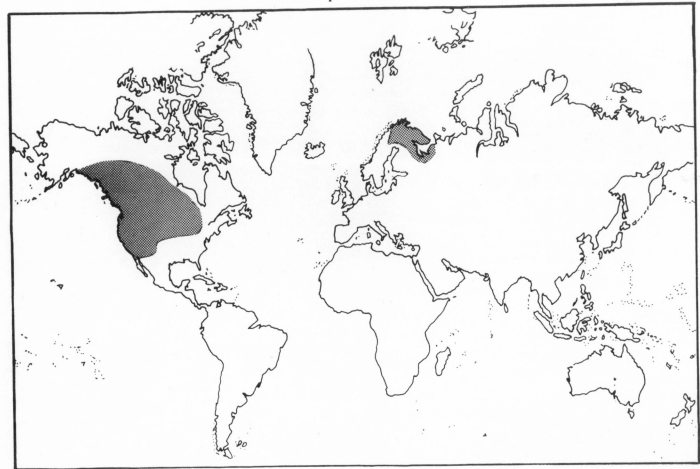

Composite bows with close backing.

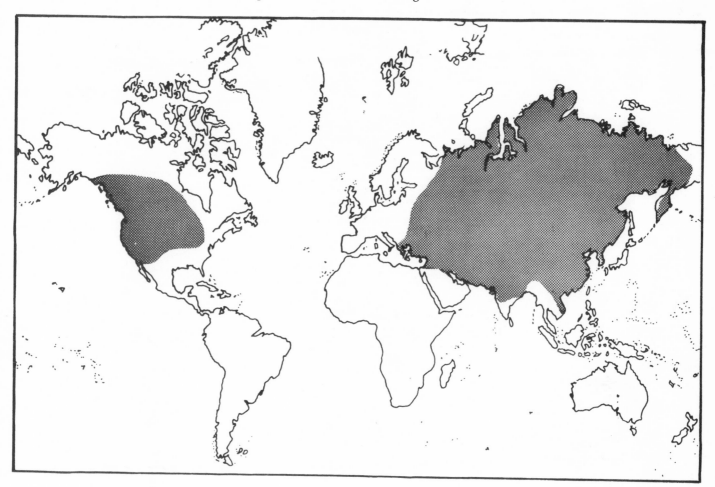

Composite bows with free backing.

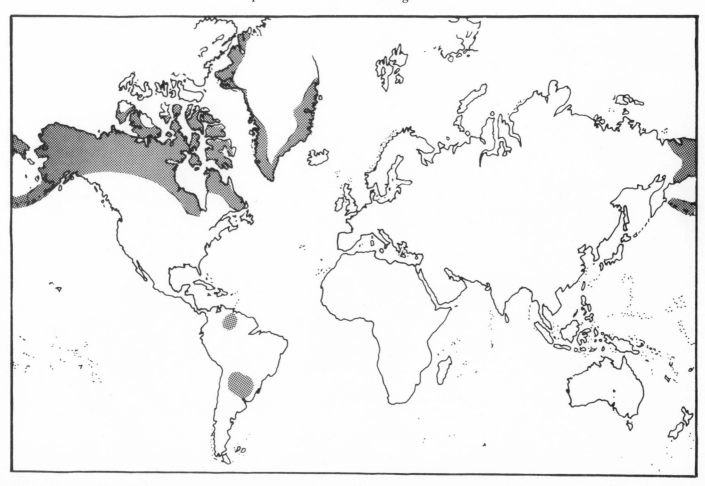

A General Bibliography of works consulted.

Archery

Adler, Bruno, *Der Nordasiatische Pfeil* [1901]

Barrington, The Hon. Daines, *Observations on the Practice of Archery in England*, Archaeologia, Vol. VII [1785]

Bill, J. H., *Sabre and Bayonet Wounds; Arrow Wounds*, The International Encyclopaedia
of Surgery, Vol. II [1882]

Bilson, Frank L. *English Archery*, [n.d.]

British Museum, *Handbook to the Ethnographical Collections* [1925]

Buchner, Max, *Das Bogenschiessen* [1906]

Burke, Edmund, *The History of Archery* [1958]

Canfield, J. W., *Handbook of Archery Terms, Publications and Records* [1936]

Clover, Patrick (Editor), *Bowman's Handbook* [1953]

Dreyer, Carl, *Med Bue og Pil* [1936]

Duff, James, *Bows and Arrows* [1927]

Elmer, Robert P., *Archery* [1926]

Elmer, Robert P., *Target Archery* [1946]

Gallice, H., *The Art of Archery* [1903]

Grimley, Gordon, *The Book of the Bow* [1958]

Hare, Kenneth, *The Archer's Chronicle and Greenwood Companion* [1929]

Heath, E. G., *Archery the Modern Approach* [1966]

Hill, Howard, *Wild Adventure* [1955]

Hodgkin, Adrian Eliot, *The Archer's Craft* [1951]

Hunt, W. Ben, *The Flat Bow* [1939]

Kroeber, A. L., *Arrow Release Distributions* [1927]

Lambert, Arthur W., *Modern Archery* [1929]

Leakey, L. S. B., *A New Classification of the Bow and Arrow in Africa*, The Journal of the
Royal Anthropological Institute, Vol. LVI [1926]

Longman, C. J., & Walrond, Col. H., *Archery* [1894]

Meyer, Hermann, *Bows and Arrows in Central Brazil*, Smithsonian Report [1896]

Morse, Edward S., *Additional Notes on Arrow Release* [1922]

Morse, Edward S., *Ancient and Modern Methods of Arrow Release* [1885]

Mylius, Dr. E., *The Theory of Archery* [1905]

Payne-Gallwey, Sir Ralph, *A Summary of the History, Construction and Effects in Warfare
of the Projectile-throwing Engines of the Ancients* [1907]

Pope, Saxton, *Hunting with Bow and Arrow* [1923]

Pope, Saxton, *The Adventurous Bowman* [1926]

Ratsel, Friedrich, *African Bows, Their Distribution and Inter-connection* [1891]

Rausing, Gad, *The Bow, Some Notes on its Origin and Development* [1967]

Smith-Turberville, H., *Archery* [1928]

Stein, Henri, *Archers d'Autrefois: Archers d'Aujourd'hui* [1925]

White, Stewart Edward, *Lions in the Path* [1926]

General

Boutell, Charles, *Arms and Armour* [1874]

Churchill, Winston S., *A History of the English-Speaking Peoples* [1956]

Clover, Patrick, (Editor), *The British Archer* [1949–]

Cranstone, B. A. L., *Melanesia, A Short Ethnography* [1960]

Demmin, Auguste, *Arms and Armour* [1877]

Francis, Rev. P. H., *A Study of Targets in Games* [1951]

Frobenius, Leo, *Morphology of the African Bow-Weapon*, translated by Blanche Lommel, [1932]

Hole, Christina, *English Custom and Usage* [1941]

Hole, Christina, *English Sports and Pastimes* [1948]

Kent Archaeological Society, *Archaeologia Cantiana*, various volumes

Maurois, André, *An Illustrated History of England* [1963]

Montgomery of Alamein, Lord, *A History of Warfare* [1968]

Oakeshott, R. Ewart, *The Archaeology of Weapons* [1960]

Parker, Clement C., *Compendium of Works on Archery* [1950]

Philips, Miss Chrystine, (Editor) *Archery News*, [1922–48]

Society of Archer-Antiquaries, *Journal*, various volumes

Stone, George Cameron, *A Glossary of the Construction, Decoration and Use of Arms and Armor* [1934]

Strutt, Joseph, *The Sports and Pastimes of the People of England* [1801]

Trevelyan, G. M., *English Social History* [1942]

Trevelyan, G. M., *History of England* [1926]

Wilton, The Right Hon. The Earl of, *On the Sports and Pursuits of the English* [1868]

Source of Illustrations

Those not acknowledged are from the Author's collection

Roger Viollet; p. 298 *upper* after Viollet le Duc, *lower* Musée de Cluny; pp. 299 and 300 after Viollet le Duc; p. 301 Society of Archer-Antiquaries; p. 303 Imperial War Museum; p. 304 The Metropolitan Museum of Art, New York: Gift of Mrs Ridgeley Hunt; p. 305 *lower* Roger Viollet; p. 306 Roger Viollet; p. 309 Azienda Autonoma di Soggiorno Turismo, Gubbio; p. 310 Powell-Cotton Museum; p. 311 Azienda Autonoma di Soggiorno Turismo, Gubbio; p. 316 Victoria and Albert Museum; p. 319 *lower* after Powell; p. 322 Roger Viollet; p. 324 The Mansell Collection; p. 325 National Gallery; p. 326 *upper* National Gallery, *lower* British Museum; p. 327 Society of Archer-Antiquaries; p. 332 *right* Royal Toxophilite Society; p. 335 *upper* Victoria and Albert Museum, *lower* National Gallery; p. 336 The Metropolitan Museum of Art, New York, Rogers Fund.

COLOUR PLATES

Frontispiece: Reproduced by gracious permission of Her Majesty the Queen. Facing page 32, British Museum; page 33, Giraudon; page 49 *lower left and right*, Dr Charles E. Grayson; page 96, Collection ville de Bayeux; page 112 *upper*, Royal Toxophilite Society, *lower*, R. Hungerford; page 113, British Museum; page 288, Royal Toxophilite Society.

Index

Figures in italics refer to captions.